Lecture Notes in Computer Science 2000

Edited by G. Goos, J. Hartmanis and J. van Leeuwen

Springer
*Berlin
Heidelberg
New York
Barcelona
Hong Kong
London
Milan
Paris
Singapore
Tokyo*

Reinhard Wilhelm (Ed.)

Informatics

10 Years Back,
10 Years Ahead

 Springer

Series Editors

Gerhard Goos, Karlsruhe University, Germany
Juris Hartmanis, Cornell University, NY, USA
Jan van Leeuwen, Utrecht University, The Netherlands

Volume Editor

Reinhard Wilhelm
Universität des Saarlandes, FR Informatik
Postfach 15 11 50, 66041 Saarbrücken, Germany
E-mail: wilhelm@cs.uni-sb.de

Cataloging-in-Publication Data applied for

Die Deutsche Bibliothek - CIP-Einheitsaufnahme

Informatics : 10 years back, 10 years ahead / Reinhard Wilhelm (ed.).
- Berlin ; Heidelberg ; New York ; Barcelona ; Hong Kong ; London ;
Milan ; Paris ; Singapore ; Tokyo : Springer, 2001
   (Lecture notes in computer science ; Vol. 2000)
   ISBN 3-540-41635-8

CR Subject Classification (1998): A.1, D, F, H, I, B, C

ISSN 0302-9743
ISBN 3-540-41635-8 Springer-Verlag Berlin Heidelberg New York

Springer-Verlag Berlin Heidelberg New York
a member of BertelsmannSpringer Science+Business Media GmbH
© Springer-Verlag Berlin Heidelberg 2001
Printed in Germany

Typesetting: Camera-ready by author, data conversion by Boller Mediendesign
Printed on acid-free paper   SPIN 10782222   06/3142   5 4 3 2 1 0

Preface

From August 27 to 31, 2000, the International Conference and Research Center for Computer Science in Schloss Dagstuhl, Dagstuhl for short, celebrated its 10th anniversary. Since its founding in 1990, the objective of the Center has been to promote world-class research in computer science, support leading-edge continuing education, and promote the exchange of knowledge and findings between academia and industry. It hosts research seminars at which promising young research scientists are afforded the opportunity of discussing their views and research findings with the international elite of their field in a specific cutting-edge field of computer science. The seminars enable new ideas to be showcased, topical problems to be discussed, and the course to be set for future development in this field. Roughly 15 000 scientists from all over the world and from all areas of computer science as well as from application areas have participated in about 500 meetings in Dagstuhl during these 10 years. They have all enjoyed the "Dagstuhl Magic", as several guests have called it, guaranteeing creative and productive meetings.

At the occasion of the 10th anniversary, a conference was held, under the name

Informatics - 10 Years Back, 10 Years Ahead.

It was meant to do *globally* what usually happens *locally* in one field or a few related fields of Informatics every week in Dagstuhl, namely that a group of scientists presents the state of the art, identifies relevant open problems, and develops visions for the future.

Internationally renowned researchers were asked to reflect upon what progress had been made in their field in the decade of Dagstuhl's existence and what will probably be waiting for us in the next decade. We shamelessly, but successfully exploited their feelings of gratitude towards Dagstuhl; only very little pressure was necessary to make them accept the invitation. The speakers invested considerable effort into preparing their talks, and their enthusiasm was contagious; the audience was overwhelmed by talks of high quality. It was particularly welcome that a broad range of topics was presented, covering many areas of Informatics. The talks provoked quite lively discussions.

The speakers agreed to contribute to this proceedings volume. The results of the discussions also found their way into the articles. Two authors, Fred Schneider and Robert Harper, even agreed to write a contribution jointly. Fred Schneider was originally grouped under Security, while Robert Harper had been asked to present Semantics. In Robert's opinion, Semantics is applied Type Theory, and currently one of the hottest applications of type theory is in the area of Security.

The speakers represented high competence across many areas of Informatics. It was therefore tempting to use their competence to discuss and identify Grand

Challenges in Informatics. This discussion process was started before and continued during the conference. A number of challenges were identified. However, it could not be claimed that they were **the** grand challenges of Informatics. The list of challenges is therefore not included in these proceedings, but presented on the Dagstuhl web site under http://www.dagstuhl.de/Challenges. It will be the starting point of an ongoing discussion process. Dagstuhl guests and scientists from outside are invited to contribute to this list.

We would like to acknowledge the kind support for the conference that was provided by a variety of sources. Saarland University, Saarbrücken, offered its premises. Compaq, SAP AG, Dresdner Bank, Microsoft Research, Siemens AG, SUN Microsystems, DaimlerChrysler AG, and sd&m provided financial support.

My very special thanks go to the speakers who invested time and energy into making the conference, and this volume, possible.

Information about the International Conference and Research Center for Computer Science in Schloss Dagstuhl, the concept, the organization, the application procedure for meetings, a description of the venue, photos, travel hints, the current program, and reports about past meetings, can be found under http://www.dagstuhl.de/

December 2000   Reinhard Wilhelm
                                                 Scientific Director
                               Intl. Conf. and Research Center
                                          for Computer Science,
                                      Schloss Dagstuhl, Germany

Table of Contents

A Political Issue: Open Source?

Architecture

Theory

... Why It Is Needed

... How It Becomes Practice

Artificial Intelligence

Graphics and Vision

Immersion into Other Disciplines

The Web in 2010: Challenges and Opportunities for Database Research

Gerhard Weikum

University of the Saarland, Saarbrücken, Germany
weikum@cs.uni-sb.de,
http://www-dbs.cs.uni-sb.de/

Abstract. The impressive advances in global networking and information technology provide great opportunities for all kinds of Web-based information services, ranging from digital libraries and information discovery to virtual-enterprise workflows and electronic commerce. However, many of these services still exhibit rather poor quality in terms of unacceptable performance during load peaks, frequent and long outages, and unsatisfactory search results. For the next decade, the overriding goal of database research should be to provide means for building zero-administration, self-tuning information services with predictable response time, virtually continuous availability, and, ultimately, "money-back" service-quality guarantees. A particularly challenging aspect of this theme is the quality of search results in digital libraries, scientific data repositories, and on the Web. To aim for more intelligent search that can truly find needles in haystacks, classical information retrieval methods should be integrated with querying capabilities for structurally richer Web data, most notably XML data, and automatic classification methods based on standardized ontologies and statistical machine learning. This paper gives an overview of promising research directions along these lines.

1 Introduction

1.1 Blessings and Curses of the World Wide Web

We are witnessing the proliferation of the global information society with a sheer explosion of information services on the World Wide Web. This opens up unprecedented opportunities for information discovery, virtual enterprises and cyberspace-based collaboration, and also more mundane things such as e-commerce. Using such services is, however, often a frustrating experience. Many information services, including Web search engines, deliver poor results - inconsistent, arbitrarily inaccurate, or completely irrelevant data - to their clients, break easily and exhibit long outages, or perform so poorly that unacceptable response times ultimately render the offered service useless. The bottom line is that the quality of services is highly unpredictable, and service quality *guarantees* are usually absent in today's fast-moving IT world.

R. Wilhelm (Ed.): Informatics. 10 Years Back. 10 Years Ahead, LNCS 2000, pp. 1–23, 2001.

Contrast this situation with the evolution of database systems. Over the last three decades, database systems have developed an outstanding reputation for keeping huge amounts of mission-critical data consistent, virtually never losing data, providing high availability, excellent performance for a very large number of concurrently active clients under a wide variety of workload patterns, and so on. Indeed most mature e-commerce servers use a database system as a backend server, behind a middle-tier Web application server, for critical processing such as purchases. The most important assets that database technology provides to such Web services are [43]:

1. declarative data access through high-level query languages based on predicate logic and exemplified in the SQL standard and
2. automatic preservation of data consistency through atomic transactions in the presence of concurrent accesses and transient system failures.

These two fundamental contributions have been recognized by the computer science community with the Turing Awards to Ted Codd and Jim Gray. Database systems have proven that they are among the most dependable, intensively stress-tested services within computer science and the IT business. On the flip side of the coin, however, we have to admit that full-fledged database systems are typically heavy-weight platforms, and many of their salient qualities can be achieved only in conjunction with a human support staff that takes care of system administration and performance tuning [2,44].

Information retrieval technology, the database area's neighboring field, is a cornerstone of digital libraries and text-oriented and, to some extent, even multimedia-enhanced search engines for the World Wide Web and in Intranets. Most notably, Gerard Salton's vector space model is prevalent, in some form or another, in virtually all search engines [3,5,23]. So information retrieval is among the most useful Web technologies for the masses. But a closer look reveals that it heavily draws on heuristics and its effectiveness in satisfying the information needs of advanced users quite often faces its limits.

1.2   Towards a Science of Service Quality Guarantees

Database technology has the potential for being a backbone of quality-conscious information services. However, the rapidly evolving, highly diverse world of global information services calls for a new blend of database technology [44,2]. Often only certain components of a database system are needed as building blocks that have to be integrated with other technologies such as workflow, multimedia, or security technologies; a prominent example for an application class with this characteristic is e-commerce. In addition, with a database system's cost of ownership being dominated by human feed and care for administration and tuning, a critical prerequisite for ubiquitous penetration of database technology is that it be completely self-tuning, with automatic adaptation to evolving workload characteristics and "zero administration" in general [9,49].

The elusive goal that we should strive for would be a generalized notion of *guaranteed service quality*. The notion of service quality (also known as quality of service or QoS for short) has come up in the context of multimedia communication (see, e.g., [22]), but has so far been limited to low-level issues like guaranteed packet delivery rates. What we need is a well-founded generalization of this notion to the application level, covering building blocks such as database access or middleware components like web application and workflow servers, Web or Intranet search engines, and also comprehensive, value-added information services on the Internet. These guarantees are given to the end-users of information services, but it must also be easy for service builders and providers to enforce the guarantees. More specifically, I envision the following three classes of guarantees:

- Response time of Web services must be predictable, and we must be able to guarantee that most service requests, say 99 percent, are served within user-acceptable time, say, 2 seconds, even during load peaks.
- As a result of globalization, services must be continuously available with downtimes limited to a few minutes per year. So services should be (more or less) always up.
- As a particularly important kind of Web service, search engines are becoming a key component for mastering the exploding volume and manifold of information in our modern society. Therefore, the quality of search results, in terms of completeness, accuracy, timeliness, and cost-effectiveness, needs to be drastically improved and should ideally be guaranteed (in a sense that will be discussed later).

Obviously, there are further aspects of service quality such as provably correct behavior or guaranteed security, but these will not be considered in this paper (as they are covered in other papers of this volume). Also note that quality guarantees are of fundamental importance in many areas of computer science (see, e.g., [19,50]), not just Web services, but I will focus on Web-related aspects in this paper.

1.3   Outline of the Paper

The rest of the paper is organized as follows. Section 2 discusses performance predictability and guarantees. Section 3 considers the goal of continuous availability. Section 4 discusses the quality of search results for Web search engines. All sections will first identify the state of the art, then outline the grand challenges, and finally point out promising research avenues.

2   Performance Guarantees

2.1   State of the Art

Today's lack of performance guarantees in Web services is often circumscribed by the nice term "best-effort performance", which essentially means that everything is unpredictable and nothing can be guaranteed. In general a number of components may cause delays: the client's connection to its Internet provider, the provider's proxy server, the wide-area network itself, the Web application server at the target site, or the content provider's backend data server. Usually, the network bandwidth is not the limiting bottleneck. Rather, the major reason for poor performance during peak hours is that requests suffer queueing delays at congested data servers or gateways. Mean response time may be acceptable when averaged over long time periods like a week or a month, and some application service providers even make contractual guarantees about such long-range metrics. However, these guarantees can be easily given yet do not tell much about the observed response time distribution during the most popular business hours, which is when performance matters most. The core of the problem lies in the Internet, application, or content providers' inability to predict the quantitative behavior of their servers at sufficient detail and to configure the server resources appropriately.

What we need is not just better response times in a general sense, but predictability and guarantees about the tail of the response time distribution. Ideally, we would wish to give an upper bound for the worst-case response time of client requests, but with the entire world being potential clients of a server, the workload can be characterized only statistically at best. Consequently the server resources needed for true worst-case guarantees would exceed all economically feasible limits. So response time guarantees should be stochastic, for example, specifying that the response time will be 2 seconds or less with probability 99 percent.

As an example for stochastic guarantees along these lines consider a media server that transfers video data streams to clients over an extended time period (i.e., the playback duration of a video). The server discretizes the continuous stream in a round-based manner, with round length T (e.g., one second), by periodically sending data fragments each of which holds enough data for say the next round of playback. For smooth playback at the client it is crucial that these fragments arrive just in time, to avoid glitches such as user-noticeable "hiccups". A complication is that video data is usually encoded with variable bit rate because of compression. So the size of fragments varies within a video (and also, of course, across video or audio objects). To ensure service quality for all simultaneously active streams the server employs an admission control. An additional data stream is admitted only if the fragment delivery deadlines can still be met for *all* subsequent fragments of *all* active streams including the new one.

For given server resources (e.g., number of disks, amount of memory) as well as data and workload profiles, the server needs to know the maximum number, N, of admissable concurrent streams. This limit can be derived in a conservative manner by assuming a maximum fragment size and worst-case disk access delays for all streams in all scheduling rounds (see, e.g., [22]). However, this crude assumption does not take into account the variability of the fragment size and the disks' performance behavior, and therefore tends to end up with a substantially underutilized server. A much better cost/performance ratio can be achieved by addressing this problem in a stochastic manner. What we need to compute is the maximum number of fragments, N, such that the total service time for fetching all N fragments from disk does not exceed the round length T with, specifiable, high probability (e.g., 99.99 percent). To this end, we decompose the service time into seek time, rotational delay, and transfer time - characterizing each in a stochastic manner, and then consider the convolution of these continuous random variables. Not surprisingly, this derivation is more tractable in terms of the Laplace transforms of the various distributions, and we can use results from large deviation theory, most notably, Chernoff bounds [35], to obtain an explicit result for the maximum sustainable number of streams [36]. The predictions and thus guarantees derived from this model are fairly accurate and can substantially improve the cost/performance of the server. In summary, such a stochastic model serves to configure the server, by choosing an appropriate limit for the admission control and determining the number of disks and the amount of memory such that the required service quality for the given workload can be guaranteed.

A similar methodology can be applied to predict the response time distribution of data requests to a conventional Web server that manages discrete data like text or image documents. An intriguing generalization that goes one step further is to consider mixed media servers that manage both continuous media and discrete data. For example, in teleteaching students should not simply watch tape-recorded lectures, but should also work with electronic textbooks, load demo programs, and so on. It is generally beneficial to hold both continuous and discrete data objects on a shared disk pool, so that load fluctuations can be smoothed to the best possible extent; otherwise, with two dedicated disk pools, we could end up with the discrete-data disks being overloaded at some point while at the same time the continuous-data disks could be underutilized. Such a load-sharing approach to a mixed media server requires special considerations on the disk scheduling of requests and a much more sophisticated stochastic model for predicting both the glitch rate of continuous data streams and the response time of discrete data acccesses. A solution for this problem has been developed in [37].

2.2 Grand Challenge

Performance guarantees along the lines outlined above should by no means be reserved to multimedia applications, but should rather be an integrated part of all information services on the Web. Like in our examples, it is crucial that such guarantees capture the tail of the response time distribution, as opposed to referring merely to mean values. ¿From a customer viewpoint, these should be money-back guarantees: unacceptable performance results in no payment or compensation by the service provider. In 2010 all services that do not provide such guarantees should be out of business within their first month of operation.

I envision the following to become common practice. Vendors or application service hosts will give free hardware and software to content providers for some trial period (e.g., a few weeks). During this period the system will capture a profile of the workload and will determine an appropriate system configuration. Then a contract is set up that includes money-back performance guarantees between the vendor and the content provider. An analogous contract will be in effect between the content provider and end-user customers. The stochastic guarantee would translate into a test on a concrete sample of actual information requests by a customer: if the response time is unacceptable in more than say 5 percent of all requests then the customer will get her money back. As the workload may evolve over time, the various self-tuning servers should monitor the criticality of their stochastic promises, automatically analyze potential bottleneck, and alert the content or application service provider about necessary resource upgrades. Note that this way we no longer rely on human administrators that often realize only after a week of poor performance that some action is overdue.

2.3   Research Avenues

A new research community has recently been emerging under the name Web Engineering. Obviously, providing better performance is a top item on their agenda, studying issues like hierarchical and distributed caching and prefetching as well as optimizations to network protocols. However, as pointed out above, this is not far-reaching enough. Performance *guarantees* are needed, and they require predictability of the function that relates workload and server as well as network configuration to the resulting performance metrics. This topic is, of course, not at all new: performance assessment based on stochastic modeling has been a very strong field in the seventies, but it has now disappeared from most computer science curricula. I claim that stochastic models are the key to predicting and thus controlling Web service performance. Without such rigorous underpinnings Web Engineering will fail.

It is, of course, well known that the mathematics of stochastic model becomes extremely difficult and sometimes intractable when the models reach a certain complexity, especially when certain standard assumptions such as Poisson arrivals are no longer justified (see, e.g., [24]). In such situations, there are two options:

- We can attempt to analyze a conservative approximation of the real system that serves as an upper bound for the actual performance. For example, for the mixed media server sketched in Subsection 2.1 we were faced with a mix of periodic and Poisson arrivals and a fairly sophisticated, dynamic (i.e., state-dependent) scheduling policy. The actual analyis considered a static scheduling policy for tractability, and we carefully reasoned that the dynamic policy does never perform worse. In a similar vein, when a comprehensive mathematical solution is out of reach, we may resort to simulation results, with proper statistical confidence, for submodels and derive higher-level metrics from such submodels using analytic methods.
- Sometimes the best remedy is to simplify the real system itself to make the analysis tractable. This would usually result in some performance losses, but the gain lies in predictability. With simpler building blocks absolute performance can often be boosted by simply scaling up hardware resources

(i.e., memory, disks, etc.), while still being able to give strong performance guarantees. For example, our mixed media server could be simplified by not exploiting any resource sharing between continuous and discrete data, essentially boiling down to separate servers for each of the two workload classes with disjoint resources. Then, of course, the analysis would become much simpler and even more accurate. This consideration can be viewed as an instance of the "pick the low hanging fruit" engineering rule of thumb. This is to say that often 90 percent of the solution (and the performance) can be achieved with 10 percent of the intellectual effort and resulting system complexity. Scientists should not be too proud to exploit this kind of pragmatic approach (notwithstanding the fact that long-term research towards the most general solution should be continued as well).

Unfortunately, too often neither of these options is pursued and rather the mathematical difficulty of the analysis is used as an excuse for merely providing "best-effort performance".

3 Continuous Availability

3.1 State of the Art

The availability of a server is the probability that a client request at an arbitrary timepoint will find the server listening and willing to process the request. The reason for temporarily being unavailable are transient failures and resulting downtimes. After a failure a server undergoes some recovery procedure, a "repair", and will then resume normal operation until the next failure occurs. In the long term (i.e., the stationary case with time approaching infinity) the availability of a server is given by the ratio $\frac{MTTF}{MTTF+MTTR}$ with $MTTF$ denoting the mean time to failure and $MTTR$ the mean time to repair.

To improve availability and approach the ideal value 1.0 the obvious approach seems to increase the MTTF. However, empirical observations tend to suggest that the MTTF cannot be advanced without limits. The main problem why servers occasionally crash are so-called Heisenbugs, virtually non-reproducible software errors that occur once in a while because of special race conditions or other synchronization bugs, exotic feature interactions, or inadequate configuration and administration settings in multi-threaded, heavily loaded servers under specific stress conditions [20]. Such bugs resemble Heisenberg's uncertainty relation: if we instrument the system for debugging then the bugs do not occur anymore. In many of the less mature Internet applications even Bohrbugs (the deterministic counterpart to Heisenbugs) are common because of poor debugging. Clearly, there is no real reason why it should not be possible to eliminate Heisenbugs (and Bohrbugs should definitely be eliminated by proper software engineering), but many existing information systems are so large and complex that even state-of-the-art verification and debugging methods will be inherently incomplete for quite a few years to come. In addition, Heisenbug problems are often aggravated by poor system administration, for example, inappropriate configuration or tuning settings. Note that periodic rebooting (e.g., once a week), which may be viewed as a prophylactic measure against Heisenbugs, leads to occasional downtime, too, and thus adversely affects availability.

The approaches that database systems have taken to cope with these problems are the following:

- Database servers should fail-stop upon the first indication of something going abnormal and provide fast and robust database recovery, based on transactional atomicity and persistence and highly optimized crash recovery algorithms [20,51].
- For mission-critical applications, data and server processes should be replicated on a backup site that can take over more or less immediately when the primary server fails. The backup may be within the same shared-disk cluster (i.e., in the same room or a neighboring building), or geographically remote (i.e., in a different city) if disaster recovery is an issue. In either case, the "failover" procedure by the backup involves rolling back active transactions and may thus be noticeable to application programs which then need special failure handling code.
- Whenever possible and affordable database systems should be administered by highly skilled and experienced (hence usually highly paid) humans who apply great care in system setup, monitoring, and occasional re-configuration.

These techniques have been developed to a fairly mature level in the database industry, and in conjunction with professional administration availability levels of 99.99 percent are the standard for mission-critical systems such as stock trading platforms or online banking. On first glance this figure seems impressive, but a closer look shows that it is still far from being satisfactory. 0.01 percent unavailability translates into approximately one hour downtime per year, and because of the Heisenbug phenomenon it is more likely that crashes hit during popular, heavy-load business hours. According to business analysts one minute downtime has a cost of up to a $ 100,000 because of its impact on the affected company's market position [39]. Furthermore and most importantly, the 99.99 percent availability figure solely refers to the data server, which is only the backend in modern Web applications. Because application programs need to be execute their failure handling logic for retrying aborted transactions the actual outages observed by end-users are significantly longer (e.g., when application programs need to open new ODBC sessions or perform long computations within the transaction). Often such code is incomplete or missing, and then failures are exposed to the user, for example, by showing a message like "status code -23495: no such transaction" in the user's Internet browser. For an e-commerce service such behavior is fairly embarrassing (and more than inconvenient to the user) when this happens upon the final checkout with a full shopping cart. On the other hand, the application program or the user must not blindly re-initiate a transaction even if no positive return code has been received, as the transaction may nevertheless have succeeded and its effects are not necessarily idempotent. Users that are not sufficiently careful may end up buying the same book twice. So, in summary, user-transparent recovery is not well understood for entire e-services that comprise Internet connections and middle-tier application servers that communicate with one or more backend database servers and possibly also other application servers in a federated manner (e.g., to implement company-wide business portals or value-added broker services such as electronic travel agencies).

3.2   Grand Challenge

Given that downtime, at the user-perceivable level, is so expensive, bold steps towards continuous availability should have very high priority on our research agenda. The grand challenge for 2010 is to achieve less than one minute expected downtime per year, which is equivalent to 99.9999 percent availability, a two orders of magnitude improvement of unavailability and a good approximation of truly non-stop services.

The most futuristic aspect of this challenge lies in the fact that availability should be measured from the end-user's perspective. It is not good enough that the database server is up (again) but the application itself is not responding to the user. To this end, a comprehensive notion of recovery is needed that integrates data, process, and message recovery in an efficient manner. Recovery procedures at the various levels should be coordinated so that *all* failures can be masked to the human users. With complex, multi-tier and federated, system architectures for modern Web services, this challenge amounts to some kind of world-wide failure masking.

Finally, because failures will still occur but should be masked by replication and fast failover, availability must really be assessed in combination with performance. During failover procedures and while some primary servers are down, the backup servers have to process a higher load and thus exhibit a certain response time degradation. Systems should be configured such that response time guarantees can still be satisfied in the presence of such degraded phases.

3.3   Research Avenues

In principle, world-wide failure masking is "merely" a matter of logging all data updates, messages and other events, and periodically saving the state of all involved processes. Such approaches have been pursued in the fault tolerance community for a long time [11,20], but practical solutions have been limited to dedicated server complexes for special applications (e.g., stock trading) and typically have high overhead. The difficulty in scaling up these approaches lies in the subtleties of the interplay of many, largely autonomous, components in a multi-tier federation and their recovery behavior. Orchestrating a large number of highly distributed logging and recovery managers in an efficient manner with all failures masked will probably require new principles. The reply logging method in [33] may be a promising starting point, but has to be generalized from client-server systems to general, multi-tier, Web applications. Also, as recovery code is really critical and the devil is in the details, rigorous correctness reasoning for this code is mandatory. This may call for a new comprehensive theory of recovery.

In addition to these fundamental advances that I envision for the next decade, the overriding goal of reaching 99.9999 percent availability requires significant progress on the engineering side as well. In particular, error-prone system administration tasks need to be automated to the largest possible extent (as already pointed out, from a different perspective, in Section 2). Furthermore, software maintenance must be possible without interrupting system operation. For example, it should be possible to upgrade to a new version of the operating system without having to bring down the database system on the same computer.

Finally, the key to satisfying performance goals even when some replicated components are down and have failed over to backup components is to configure the overall system appropriately. Most importantly, the degrees of replication, for data and processes, determine not only the absolute availability but also the effective performance. Note that in advanced services that involve many components the probability that some (replica of a) component will be temporarily down is non-negligible, so that we cannot simply carry over the optimal performance (with all replicas of all components simultaneously running) to the real state(s) of the overall system. The necessary conditioning of the relevant performance metrics with the probabilities of the various system states leads to the notion of "performability", a concept that has been around in the performance modeling community for quite a while [24] but is otherwise virtually unknown. So we need stochastic models along these lines and configuration tools for performability guarantees. An initial approach in this direction, although limited to a specific system context, can be found in [18].

4   Search Result Quality

4.1   State of the Art

All search engines for the Web, Intranets, or digital libraries mostly build on the vector space model that views text documents (including HTML documents) as vectors of term relevance scores. These terms, also known as features, represent word occurrences in documents after stemming and other normalizations. The relevance score of a term in a document is usually derived from the term frequency (tf) in the document and the overall number of documents with this term or the corresponding total term frequency, the so-called inverse document frequency (idf), giving rise to (several variants of) the somewhat pragmatic, but empirically well proven tf*idf formula. Queries are vectors, too, and we can then use a similarity metric between vectors, for example, the Euclidean distance or the cosine metric, to produce a ranked list of search results, in descending order of relevance scores (i.e., estimations of what the user who posed the query would rate as relevant). The quality of a search results is assessed a posteriori in terms of the empirical metrics precision and recall: precision is the fraction of truly relevant documents in the result or the top N matches in the result ranking (N typically being 10), and recall is the fraction of found documents out of the relevant documents that exist in the underlying corpus (or the entire Web). Experimentally studying precision and recall is itself a difficult issue.

A nice property of this classical approach is that it can be generalized to searching on multimedia objects such as images, videos, or music [14,22]. Once an appropriate feature space has been defined, for example, based on color distribution or contours in images, the principles of similarity ranking apply more or less directly. Of course, appropriate features heavily depend on the specific application. Current approaches on this issue still seem to be more of an art than scientific engineering. Notwithstanding this general assessment, there are some useful cases of multimedia similarity search in limited application contexts.

The above technology based on the vector space model is more than twenty years old and applicable to any kind of text document collection. But the Web is more than just a corpus of documents, given that its documents are extensively cross-related through hyperlinks, and also many Intranets are structured in such a fashion. A relatively recent trend has been to analyze the link structure between the documents, viewing the Web as a graph, and define the *authority* of Web sites or documents as an additional metric for search result ranking [5,28]. One way of doing this is to consider a random walk on (a large representative sample of) the Web where outgoing links are followed with uniform probabilities, adding up to $1 - \epsilon$, and a random jump is performed with probability ϵ. Then the stationary probabilities of hitting a URL can be computed from the underlying discrete-time Markov chain, and these probabilities are used as authority scores. There are alternative ways of defining and computing the notion of authority, but all lead to similar Eigenvalue problems. The point of this metric is that documents or sites with high authority should be preferred in search results, to achieve better precision (i.e., "to sort out the junk" in more colloquial terms).

It is important, however, to realize that authority is different from and complementary to the notion of relevance. In fact, search engines that make use of authority combine it with tf*idf-based relevance scores, for example, by computing a weighted sum of authority and relevance scores where the weights are chosen in a pragmatic, more or less ad hoc, manner. Further note that authority assessment is of help mostly for popular queries that would otherwise produce a huge result list (e.g., searching for famous pop stars, actors, or politicians). It does not help much for advanced, expert-style queries for which it is difficult to find any useful results at all (i.e., for which recall is the problem). As an example, searching for "Chernoff theorem" on Web search engines that take into account authority metrics leads to hardly any useful results. Typically, these search engines return frequently cited documents such as conference home pages that do have some relationship to stochastics and sometimes even large deviation theory, but the actual information that one is looking for (i.e., the theorem that explains what Chernoff bounds are) can at best be reached by manually traversing outgoing links (e.g., textbooks referenced in papers that appear in the conference whose home page was found). Of course, the relevance estimation problem shows up in this example as well, and this holds for both search engines with and without authority assessment. For example, one search engine returns a document about Fermat's theorem among the top ten (obviously collapsing all theorems into one topic, which is probably considered exotic enough for the masses of Web users), another engine points to a "model" Mikki Chernoff, and even the better engines tend to deliver scientific publications that cite Chernoff but are otherwise only remotely related to the query itself. The most useful result, a textbook on large deviation theory, was found (among the top ten) only by Yahoo, which uses a manually/intellectually produced directory and is thus actually incomparable to the fully automated search engines. One can easily think of many more advance examples with similarly poor search results (e.g., searching for infrequent allergies, people who share an exotic hobby, descriptions of specific hikes off the beaten path, etc.)

4.2   Grand Challenge

The Web can be viewed as a huge, global knowledge base that potentially bears the answers to almost all information needs for almost everybody: common people who are interested in sports, traveling, or other hobbies, business people who are interested in market data and financial news, scientists who are interested in background material from neighboring fields and results related to their own work, and so on. Our ability to exploit this great potential and find high quality results for advanced queries are still fairly immature. In particular, advanced queries that are, so to speak, looking for needles in haystacks are poorly handled by today's search engines. These are queries that would find few results even under ideal conditions; so recall rather than precision is the main problem here.

For 2010 I hope to see tremendous progress on the capabilities for intelligent information search. We are indeed forced to tackle this as a grand challenge in science in general, for otherwise we will inevitably be swamped with information without being able to retrieve any useful results. This follows from a simple extrapolation of the rapid growth of information in the world and the observation that advances in information retrieval have been fairly incremental in the last two decades. Currently there are still ways of compensating poor search engine results by manually navigating in the extended neighborhood of some reasonably promising URL or resorting to intellectually maintained directories of the Yahoo style. However, these methods are very time-consuming, and become less and less affordable with intellectual time being the most precious resource. Even worse, there is no way for these manual methods to scale up with the rapid growth of the Web.

Examples of the kind of advanced queries that intelligent search engines should be able to effectively (and efficiently) handle in a decade would be:

- A hiker seeking for information on a particular cross-country (i.e., trail-less) route that is not available in any guidebooks but likely to be discussed on personal homepages of a few adventurous hikers.

- A programmer searching for publicly available code for a specific algorithm (e.g., a B^+-tree with built-in concurrency control) in a specific language on a specific operating system.
- A mathematician (or computer scientist) who conjectures a certain result and searches for similar theorems that are already known (including more general theorems that cover the conjecture as a special case).
- A surgeon who prepares herself for a complicated brain surgery and searches for similar cases (including similar X-ray images or tomographies of tumors).

Ultimately, next-generation Web search engines should be able to find every piece of information that a human expert could retrieve if she had infinitely much time (and provided the requested information is somewhere on the Web at all). Needless to say that the search engine should be a lot faster, but speed alone is not an end by itself. For advanced queries of the kind mentioned above humans would surely tolerate a response time of up to a day if the results are useful and the search engine saves precious intellectual time.

The above emphasizes the effectiveness of searching in terms of finding good results. Equally important aspects are the completeness of the search in that all possible information sources are exhausted, and the efficiency of the search process. The Web as it is covered by the union of search engines today contains about 1 Billion (i.e., 10^9) documents with a total size of 20 Terabytes. In addition, however, there is a huge amount of interesting and relevant data behind Intranet gateways and other portals, typically but not necessarily in more schematic databases. This includes information sources such as CNN and other news providers, amazon.com which has descriptions and reviews of books, the US patent database, the library of congress, various climate data centers with lots of satellite images, and so on. This so-called "Deep Web" [4] is estimated to have 500 Billion documents with a total size of 8 Petabytes, and it is the fastest growing part of the entire web. So the "surface" Web that is in reach of today's search engines is less than 1 percent of all information sources. For 2010 I expect that a large fraction of the Deep Web will indeed be searchable in a unified manner, and that we will have found reasonable means to cope with the tremendous scalability problem that we are facing.

4.3   Research Avenues

4.3.1   The Great Synergy.   Progress in information retrieval has been incremental, and we cannot expect a breakthrough in the next decade given the extreme difficulty of the intelligent information search problem. However, there are a number of trends each of which will gradually improve the state of the art, and all of them together will hopefully lead to great synergy and major advances in the quality of search results:

- The *XML* standard has the potential to foster semantically richer annotations of text documents, and query languages for XML provide powerful pattern matching capabilities on these annotations.

- *Hierarchical ontologies* organize documents in topics and can contribute to much more precise query formulation as well as query refinement in a way that is largely transparent to the user.
- To automate the building and maintenance of large-scale ontologies, *automatic classification* algorithms, based on statistical learning, can be leveraged.

Note that these trends aim to automate the manual pre- and postprocessing that we have seen to be useful for better search results in the "Chernoff theorem" example of Subsection 4.1: XML pattern matching can replace the manual navigation in the environment of some promising URL, and ontologies with automatic classification should replace manually maintained, Yahoo-style, directories.

In the following subsections I will discuss the above research directions in more detail. I will also discuss implications on the architecture of a search engine under the perspectives of scalability and coverage of the "Deep Web".

4.3.2   XML.   XML is a W3C standard and widely considered as the main driving force in the ongoing endeavor for uniform data exchange and integration of heterogeneous data across the entire spectrum from largely unstructured to highly schematic data. In an abstract sense, all data is uniformly captured by a graph with nodes representing XML elements along with their attributes and with hyperlinks being elements of a special type [1]. A variety of query languages have been proposed for searching XML data (see, e.g., [8,12,29]). These languages combine SQL-style logical conditions over element names, contents, and attributes with regular-expression pattern matching along entire paths of elements. The result of a query is a set of paths or subgraphs from a given data graph that represents an XML document or document collection.

As an example consider the following three XML documents about vacation destinations and traveling. Note that the element names and the structure of the XML documents vary slightly; so there is no universal schema. We may think of the three documents as coming from two different information sources, one for the left-hand column and another one for the right-hand column.

```
<region> Europe                        <region> Overseas
<place> Sylt                           <sight> Townsville
  <location> Germany </location>         <country> Australia </country>
  <beach> sandy beach on the shore of    <attractions>
          the North Sea </beach>           <attraction> beach </attraction>
  <activities> dune hiking,               <attraction> coral reef
               surfing </activities>      </attraction>
  <season> summer </season>              <what-to-do>
</place> </region>                         <diving> scuba diving outside
                                                    the reef ? </diving>
                                           <snorkeling> snorkeling in the
<region> Europe                                        coral reef ?
<place> Bernese Oberland                   </snorkeling>
  <location> Switzerland </location>       </what-to-do>
  <activities> skiing, hiking,           </attractions>
               climbing </activities>    <time> all seasons </time>
  <season> winter, summer </season>    </sight> </region>
</place> </region>
```

It is important to note that the element names in the above example data are not chosen arbitrarily but rather comply, to a large extent, with certain standard terminology – or a domain-specific ontology as we may say. This is a key point of XML: although it merely provides a syntax, it is creating a big momentum in the industry and also the scientific community to organize data in a better way, for example, by using ontological frameworks. There are ongoing efforts to provide XML element names spaces and DTDs or even schemas for business-to-business e-commerce data (specifying the structure of purchase orders, invoices, etc.), publisher data (specifying book layouts), genome research and bioinformatics, mathematics (with element names such as <theorem> or <Abelian group>), and so on [17,38,41,52]

Element names that follow, to a large extent, certain terminological conventions, are semantically rich annotations that potentially capture the topic and content of a document in a clearer way than the document text alone and thus facilitate more precise queries. This is the opportunity for better search result quality that XML query languages aim to exploit. For example, a search for vacation destinations where you can swim in the summer can be expressed as follows (in the specific syntax of the language XXL [47], standing for "FleXible XML Search Language", but other XML query languages have very similar abstract syntax):

```
Select P
From http://my.holiday.edu/allsights.xml
Where region.(place | sight) As P
And P.# LIKE "%swimming%"
And P.#.season LIKE "%summer%"
```

Words put in boldface are keywords (e.g., Select), uppercase single letters are element variables (e.g., P), # is a wildcard for element paths of arbitrary length ≥ 0, and dots denote path concatenation. The Where clause of the query is a logical conjunction of *path expressions* which specify regular expressions (using constructors *, +, ? for ≥ 0, ≥ 1, ≤ 1 iterations, resp.) over elementary conditions on name or content of elements or attributes. Such elementary conditions include substring matching using the SQL-style LIKE operator and the wildcard symbol % for arbitrary strings within a single element's content. Element variables (e.g., P) are bound by the As clause to the end node of a path in the data graph that matches the corresponding path expression, and denote this node when used in other expressions.

Although the above query is a perfectly nice example that demonstrates the expressive power of XML query languages, it also shows the limitations of queries with a Boolean retrieval semantics, returning a set of qualifying results as it is usual in database query languages: the query result is the empty set, for none of the three given documents explicitly contains the word "swimming". This observation is not atypical for settings where the underlying data is partly or even largely unstructured such as the Web or comes from different, heterogeneous, information sources such as large Intranets.

To make XML querying truly Web-enabled, *ranked retrieval* must be supported where the result of a query is a list of element paths (or subgraphs in
general) in descending order of estimated relevance to the query. This kind of
similarity search, in the spirit of information retrieval technology, is being pursued in a few, very recent language proposals [10,16,47]. In XXL this capability is
provided by an additional elementary operator ~ that tests similarity of name or
content of elements or attributes, using an underlying ontology (i.e., thesaurus
in more mundane terms) that captures related terms and standard similarity
metrics like the tf*idf formula. The above information demand can be better
expressed by the following XXL query:

Select P
From http://my.holiday.edu/allsights.xml
Where region.~place **As** P
And P.#.(~swimming)? ~ "swimming"
And P.#.~season ~ "summer"

In this query the similarity operator ~ is used as both a unary operator
on element or attribute names and a binary operator on element or attribute
contents. For all kinds of elementary similarity conditions a similarity score is
computed, and the scores from different conditions are combined using simple
probabilistic arguments. The latter is based on postulating probabilistic independence between different conditions; better approaches that would capture
correlations among element names and terms in element contents are subject of
future research. The above query would return a ranked list with Townsville as
the best match (i.e., the XML element bound to variable P that has the highest
overall similarity score with regard to the query conditions) and Sylt as the second best match. This order is based on ontological similarity of element names
which would rate "swimming" as more closely related to "snorkeling" than to
"surfing".

More details on XXL can be found in [47], but note that this approach is
still in a fairly early state, especially with regard to efficient implementation
techniques. The key point that I wish to emphasize is that XXL and the few
related projects reconcile two different search paradigms: the logical condition
evaluation and pattern matching capabilities from database and XML querying,
on one hand, and the similarity search with ranked results from information
retrieval, on the other hand. It is this combination that bears a great potential
for better search result quality. In contrast, traditional information retrieval and
all current Web search engines completely miss the opportunity that arises from
the more explicit structure and semantically richer annotations (i.e., element
names) in XML documents.

4.3.3   Ontologies.   Ontologies have been around in the AI community for
more than a decade (see, e.g., [31,34,42]). The main goal has been to construct
a universal knowledge base as a backbone for all kinds of automated reasoning.
Consequently, the representation language was typically very rich, for example,

some form of description logic or higher-order logical assertions, but the scope and goal for *using* the ontology were not clearly defined. Today, we have a much clearer picture of what we would like to do with ontologies in the context of Web information retrieval. Furthermore, we should once again apply the engineering rule of "picking the low hanging fruit": relatively simple representations could already achieve most of the leverage within a reasonable timeframe, whereas perfect solutions often are elusive.

For example, the simplest kind of ontology would be a tree of topics (also known as categories or "concepts"): each topic could be characterized by a set of names (i.e., synonyms) for the topic, where the same name can appear under different topics (i.e., if it is a polysem) [15]. The edges of the tree would represent topic-subtopic (i.e., specialization) relationships. For example, a topic "science" would have subtopics "mathematics", "philosophy", "physics", etc.; "mathematics" would have subtopics "algebra", "stochastics", etc., and "stochastics" would in turn have finer-grained subtopics such as "statistical hypothesis testing" or "large deviation theory". Richer structures for ontologies are conceivable and not unlikely to be needed, for example, lattices of topics, but it is debatable whether a full-fledged logic-based knowledge representation language is worthwhile. Each topic in the ontology has its specific terminology, which could be captured in the form of "archetypical" sample documents or, more explicitly, as a set of specific terms with weights like tf and idf values or even correlation measures between terms; the latter can be computed from the sample documents. For example, we would expect terms such as "variability", "tail", or "bound" to have high weights within the subtopic "large deviation theory", and even "Chernoff bound" might be a term that is explicitly known in the ontology. In addition, with XML the description of a subtopic should also include typical element names or element paths along with statistical information about them.

Ontologies can, and often should, be domain-specific or even personalized in that they reflect the specific interests of an individual or community (see, e.g., [26,27,45]). Queries can be directed to a domain-specific ontology (just like we make use of domain-specific search engines already today) and would be enhanced by transforming them into a more precise form with richer annotations. For example, the search request for "Chernoff theorem" when issued to a mathematical ontology could be rewritten into the following query, specified in XXL because I ultimately expect all queries to be on XML data:

Select P
From http://my.math.ontology.edu/math.xml
Where #.math?.#.(~large deviation)?.#.theorem.~Chernoff **As** T

This obviously requires mapping the original query to the best fitting subtopic in the ontology and deriving the enhanced query from this subtopic's description. Likewise, queries that give some reasonable but not yet fully satisfactory results can be refined by having the user provide feedback and mapping the good results into the ontology to derive a refined query. All this can be done in a mostly implicit manner, with relatively little effort for the human user, through comfortable user interfaces. In fact, such relevance feedback is an old hat in information retrieval research, but has had amazingly little impact on Web searching so far. On the other hand, the combination with hierarchical ontologies and richer annotations in the form of XML elements does not seem to have been explored so far.

4.3.4 Automatic Classification.
Automating the building and maintenance of a hierarchical ontology requires automatic classification, typically using some form of supervised, statistics-based, learning. So we start out with a seed of training documents that have to be classified intellectually. Good training sets could be derived from users' bookmarks or other carefully chosen, archetypical documents (e.g., by extracting positive results from users' "surf trails" in a semi-automatic manner). This way each topic can now be characterized by its specific distribution of terms, element names, paths, etc., or *features* in general.

The key building block then is a statistical classifier which needs to estimate the conditional probability that a new, previously unseen, document belongs to some topic given its feature vector. Here we can exploit Bayes theorem or more powerful mathematical machinery to derive these probabilities from statistical parameter estimates that we obtain from the feature distributions of the training sample. Documents are assigned to the topic to which they belong with highest likelihood. The simplest and most popular classifier of this kind is known as the Naive Bayes method, which makes a number of strong, simplifying assumptions such as postulating independence of term frequencies. Naive Bayes often performs not much worse than many of the more sophisticated methods; after all, we only have to estimate the odds that a document belongs to a topic versus not belonging there [32]. Nevertheless, better classifiers, most notably, methods based on support vector machines, are absolutely worthwhile to explore for (XML or text) document classification (see, e.g., [13,25] and the references there).

The quality of automatic classification is measured empirically by intellectually inspecting the fraction of correctly classified documents. Unfortunately, exeriments in this field are fairly limited and would have to be viewed as toy experiments relative to the sheer size and diversity of the Web. For example, a typical benchmark looks at 10,000 short newswire articles from Reuters, which belong to about 100 different categories, takes 75 percent of these articles as training data, and then automatically classifies the remaining 25 percent. Note especially that all documents really come from one of the 100 categories, which would not be the case (or would not be known) for highly diverse Web data. And even in such a relatively simple setting, the best classifiers are typically correct only for about 80 percent of the documents.

So there is work to do along these lines, and we need to explore better statistical learning techniques and intensify our efforts on large-scale experimentation. A critical aspect is also the selection of which features of a document should be used for the classifier. The simplest approach would just look at tf and idf values of individual terms, but term pairs or triplets could be used as well and often it is better to use only a small subset of "meaningful" terms as features to eliminate "noise" and to achieve scalability. The latter approach incurs subtle but critical difficulties with hierarchical classification: a term that serves well as a discriminator at one level of the ontology may be an inflationary and thus meaningless term at the next lower level. For example, the (frequent occurrence of the) term "theorem" intuitively is a good indicator for a document to belong to the topic "mathematics" (say rather than "humanities"), but it does not provide any glues for identifying the proper subtopic within mathematics. There is some preliminary work on how to determine whether a feature is discriminative or not, based on information-theoretic considerations [6]. However, this is limited to simple terms (i.e., normalized word occurrences) in plain text documents; the same question is widely open for XML elements or element paths.

In general, our understanding of these issues still seems to be in its infancy, and I would very much wish to see a new "master theory" of information content and relevance. Obviously, such a theory should leverage information-theoretic principles, but needs to eliminate the fairly strong, and often unrealistic, assumptions (especially with regard to feature independence) that have typically been made in the prior literature on information retrieval (including the perhaps most ambitious work [40]). Such a theory would be useful for reasoning about the "optimality" of a search result, even if it cannot eliminate the inherent uncertainty in vague queries and even if it is not practical (e.g., for complexity reasons) but could still serve as a yardstick against which real search engines could be systematically compared.

4.3.5 Deep Search.

Current search engines do not reach the Deep Web because they rely almost exclusively on precomputed results: crawling the web and building up index structures, with query processing mostly boiling down to a few fast index lookups. For reaching data behind Intranet portals and for fully exploiting the capabilities of next-generation query languages such as XXL, more powerful "deep search" strategies are needed.

Index structures are still key for scalable query processing, but index lookups should only provide seeds for further automatic exploration in the neighborhood of promising URLs. Topic-specific crawlers [7] should be spawned from such URLs at the run-time of an individual query for "semantic" pattern matching according to the given XXL-style query. When coming across a portal behind which no direct crawling is allowed but which supports a search interface (e.g., sites such as CNN or amazon.com), a subquery should be dynamically generated and issued to the portal's local search engine. With XML and XML querying becoming ubiquitous standards, the most promising interface between the global search process and the local search engines would be in the form of a prevalent XML query language. To support the global search in generating the best possible subqueries, portals should describe their contents in terms of an XML schema or DTD and export also a local ontology along with statistical representations of the various subtopics.

The envisioned search method combines paradigms from today's (index-centric) Web search engines and prototypical approaches for query processing in database federations. Note that similar multi-tier search algorithms are already in use by some metasearch engines (or search brokers) that generate specific sub-queries for different underlying search engines (possibly including topic-specific engines) and (claim or aim to) take into account the thematic coverage and profile of the underlying information sources (see, e.g., [46]).

The biggest challenge in making this extremely flexible search process practically viable lies in the scalability aspect: coping with thousands of information sources and, ultimately, the entire "Deep Web". In this respect caching and prefetching are key technologies to achieve good performance on the Web. More specifically, speculative prefetching of data and asynchronous, speculative pre-execution of subqueries as well as query result caching would be intriguing approaches to hide latency and provide acceptable response times, but it is still a major step from existing techniques for data caching and prefetching (e.g, [30]) to the effective use of statistics-based speculation at all levels of a "deep search" engine.

5   Concluding Remarks

In this paper I have outlined three grand challenges for Web-based information systems: guaranteed performance, continuous availability, and intelligent search for information. None of these is truly new. The critical importance of predictable performance has been stressed also in the strategic report of the US President's Information Technology Advisory Board [48], zero-downtime Web services have been a high-priority goal for the last few years already, and the urgent need for self-tuning, "trouble-free" information servers has been recognized, for example, also in [2]. Finally the need for better search engines is something that everybody realizes almost every day. All three of my grand challenges are included, in some form or another, also in Jim Gray's list of important research goals presented in his Turing Award lecture [21].

The most elusive goal among the outlined challenges clearly is the intelligent search with guaranteed search result quality. This challenge has been around since Vannevar Bush's vision of a world knowledge device coined Memex (see, e.g., [21]) or may even be traced back to philosophers like Gottfried Leibniz. It may well take much longer than the next decade to build Web search engines that can truly find needles in haystacks with result quality as good as the best human experts could provide with infinite time resources. But ultimately it is the paramount importance of this problem that dictates tackling it as an absolutely top-priority grand challenge in computer science.

References

1. S. Abiteboul, P. Buneman, D. Suciu: Data on the Web – From Relations to Semistructured Data and XML, Morgan Kaufmann, 2000.
2. The Asilomar Report on Database Research, ACM SIGMOD Record Vol.27 No.4, 1998.

3. R. Baeza-Yates, B. Ribeiro-Neto: Modern Information Retrieval, Addison-Wesley, 1999.
4. BrightPlanet.com: The Deep Web: Surfacing Hidden Value, White Paper, http://www.completeplanet.com/Tutorials/DeepWeb/index.asp.
5. S. Brin, L. Page: The Anatomy of a Large Scale Hypertextual Web Search Engine, 7th WWW Conference, 1998.
6. S. Chakrabarti, B. Dom, R. Agrawal, P. Raghavan: Scalable Feature Selection, Classification and Signature Generation for Organizing Large Text Databases into Hierarchical Topic Taxonomies, The VLDB Journal Vol.7 No.3, 1998.
7. S. Chakrabarti, M. van den Berg, B. Dom: Focused Crawling: A New Approach to Topic-specific Web Resource Discovery, 8th WWW Conference, 1999.
8. D.D. Chamberlin, J. Robie, D. Florescu: Quilt: An XML Query Language for Heterogeneous Data Sources, 3rd Int. Workshop on the Web and Databases, 2000.
9. S. Chaudhuri (Editor): Special Issue on Self-Tuning Databases and Application Tuning, IEEE Data Engineering Bulletin Vol.22 No.2, 1999.
10. W.W. Cohen: Integration of Heterogeneous Databases Without Common Domains Using Queries Based on Textual Similarity, ACM SIGMOD Conference, 1998.
11. F. Cristian: Understanding Fault-Tolerant Distributed Systems, Communications of the ACM Vol.34 No.2, 1991.
12. A. Deutsch, M.F. Fernandez, D. Florescu, A.Y. Levy, D. Suciu: A Query Language for XML, 8th WWW Conference, 1999.
13. S. Dumais, H. Chen: Hierarchical Classification of Web Content, ACM SIGIR Conference, 2000.
14. C. Faloutsos: Searching Multimedia Databases By Content, Kluwer Academic Publishers, 1996.
15. C. Fellbaum (Editor): WordNet: An Electronic Lexical Database, MIT Press, 1998.
16. N. Fuhr, K. Großjohann: XIRQL: An Extension of XQL for Information Retrieval, ACM SIGIR Workshop on XML and Information Retrieval, 2000.
17. Gene Ontology Consortium, http://www.geneontology.org.
18. M. Gillmann, J. Weissenfels, G. Weikum, A. Kraiss: Performance and Availability Assessment for the Configuration of Distributed Workflow Management Systems, 7th Int. Conference on Extending Database Technology, 2000.
19. Graduate Studies Program on "Quality Guarantees for Computer Systems", Funded by the German Science Foundation (Deutsche Forschungsgemeinschaft), Department of Computer Science, University of the Saarland, Saarbruecken, Germany, http://www-dbs.cs.uni-sb.de/~weikum/gk.
20. J. Gray, A. Reuter: Transaction Processing: Concepts and Techniques, Morgan Kaufmann, 1993.
21. J. Gray: What Next? A Dozen Information-Technology Research Goals, Technical Report MS-TR-99-50, Microsoft Research, Redmond, 1999.
22. W.I. Grosky, R. Jain, R. Mehrotra: The Handbook of Multimedia Information Management, Prentice Hall, 1997.
23. V.N. Gudivada, V.V. Raghavan, W.I. Grosky, R. Kasanagottu: Information Retrieval on the World Wide Web, IEEE Internet Computing Vol.1 No.5, 1997.
24. G. Haring, C. Lindemann, M. Reiser (Eds.): Performance Evaluation: Origins and Directions, Springer, 2000.
25. M.A. Hearst (Ed.): Trends and Controversies: Support Vector Machines, IEEE Intelligent Systems, Vol.13 No.4, 1998.
26. J. Heflin, J. Hendler: Dynamic Ontologies on the Web, Proceedings of the Seventeenth National Conference on Artificial Intelligence (AAAI-2000), 2000.

27. M.N. Huhns, L.N. Stephens: Personal Ontologies, IEEE Internet Computing, Vol.3 No.5, 1999.
28. J.M. Kleinberg: Authoritative Sources in a Hyperlinked Environment, Journal of the ACM Vol.46 No.5, 1999.
29. D. Kossmann (Editor), Special Issue on XML, IEEE Data Engineering Bulletin Vol.22 No.3, 1999.
30. A. Kraiss and G. Weikum: Integrated Document Caching and Prefetching in Storage Hierarchies Based On Markov-Chain Predictions, The VLDB Journal Vol.7 No.3, 1998.
31. D. Lenat, R.V. Guha: Building Large Knowledge Based Systems, Addison-Wesley, 1990.
32. D.D. Lewis: Naive (Bayes) at Forty: The Independence Assumption in Information Retrieval, European Conference on Machine Learning, 1998.
33. D. Lomet, G. Weikum: Efficient and Transparent Application Recovery in Client-Server Information Systems, ACM SIGMOD Conference, 1998.
34. P. Mitra, G. Wiederhold, M.L. Kersten: Articulation of Ontology Interdependencies Using a Graph-Oriented Approach, 7th Int. Conference on Extending Database Technology, 2000.
35. R. Nelson: Probability, Stochastic Processes, and Queueing Theory: The Mathematics of Computer Performance Modeling, Springer, 1995.
36. G. Nerjes, P. Muth, and G. Weikum: Stochastic Service Guarantees for Continuous Data on Multi-Zone Disks, ACM Int. Symposium on Principles of Database Systems, 1997.
37. G. Nerjes, P. Muth, G. Weikum: A Performance Model of Mixed-Workload Multimedia Information Servers, 10th GI/NTG Conference on Performance Evaluation of Computer and Communication Systems, 1999.
38. OpenMath Content Dictionaries, http://www.openmath.org/cdfiles/html/extra.
39. Oracle8i with Oracle Fail Safe 3.0, White Paper, Oracle Corporation, 2000, http://www.oracle.com/tech/nt/failsafe/pdf/ofs30db.pdf.
40. C.H. Papadimitriou, P. Raghavan, H. Tamaki, S. Vempala: Latent Semantic Indexing: A Probabilistic Analysis, ACM Int. Symposium on Principles of Database Systems, 1998.
41. RosettaNet Partner Interface Processes, http://www.rosettanet.org.
42. S. Russell, P. Norvig: Artificial Intelligence – A Modern Approach, Prentice Hall, 1995.
43. A. Silberschatz, M. Stonebraker, J. Ullman (Editors): Database Research: Achievements and Opportunities Into the 21st Century, ACM SIGMOD Record Vol.25 No.1, 1996.
44. A. Silberschatz, S. Zdonik, et al.: Strategic Directions in Database Systems - Breaking Out of the Box, ACM Computing Surveys Vol.28 No.4, 1996.
45. S. Staab, J. Angele, S. Decker, M. Erdmann, A. Hotho, A. Mädche, H.-P. Schnurr, R. Studer: Semantic Community Web Portals, 9th WWW Conference, 2000.
46. A. Sugiura, O. Etzioni: Query Routing for Web Search Engines: Architecture and Experiments, 9th WWW Conference, 2000.
47. A. Theobald, G. Weikum: Adding Relevance to XML, 3rd Int. Workshop on the Web and Databases, 2000.
48. US President's Information Technology Advisory Committee Interim Report to the President, August 1998, http://www.ccic.gov/ac/interim/.
49. G. Weikum, C. Hasse, A. Moenkeberg, P. Zabback.: The COMFORT Automatic Tuning Project, Information Systems Vol.19 No.5, 1994.

50. G. Weikum: Towards Guaranteed Quality and Dependability of Information Ser-
    vices) (Invited Keynote), 8th German Conference on Databases in Office, Engi-
    neering, and Scientific Applications, 1999.
51. G. Weikum, G. Vossen: Fundamentals of Transactional Information Systems: The-
    ory, Algorithms, and Practice of Concurrency Control and Recovery, Morgan Kauf-
    mann, 2001.
52. The XML Cover Pages, http://www.oasis-open.org/cover/xml.html.

Challenges in Ubiquitous Data Management

Michael J. Franklin

EECS Computer Science Division
University of California,
Berkeley, CA 94720, USA
franklin@cs.berkeley.edu

Abstract. Ubiquitous computing is a compelling vision for the future that is moving closer to realization at an accelerating pace. The combination of global wireless and wired connectivity along with increasingly small and powerful devices enables a wide array of new applications that will change the nature of computing. Beyond new devices and communications mechanisms, however, the key technology that is required to make ubiquitous computing a reality is *data management*. In this short paper, I attempt to identify and organize the key aspects of ubiquitous computing applications and environments from a data management perspective and outline the data management challenges that they engender. Finally, I describe two on-going projects: *Data Recharging* and *Telegraph*, that are addressing some of these issues.

Introduction

The confluence of ever smaller and more powerful computing and communication devices, improved connectivity in both wired and wireless environments, and emerging and accepted standards for data transfer and presentation (e.g., HTML, XML, HTTP, WAP, etc.) are leading to a world in which computers are playing an ever increasing role in people's daily lives. It is reasonable to expect that ultimately, such devices will be so pervasive and so critical to our activities that they will be simply taken for granted – effectively disappearing into the background. This idea, known as "Ubiquitous Computing", has been a motivating vision underlying much Computer Science research in the past decade, going back to the seminal writings of Mark Wieser in which the term was coined [Wieser 91].

Of course, as anyone who depends upon computers or PDAs today realizes, there is still quite some progress to be made before this vision of ubiquitous computing is achieved. The necessary technology, however, is improving at an impressive rate and advances furthering the realization of ubiquitous computing are announced almost daily. Much of the research and development activity in this area is focused on improving the devices themselves and on the technologies they use to communicate. For devices, the emphasis has been on improving functionality, while reducing size, cost, and power requirements. For communications, the emphasis has been on improving bandwidth and coverage, and on developing protocols that are more tolerant of the error and connectivity characteristics of wireless and mobile devices.

R. Wilhelm (Ed.): Informatics. 10 Years Back. 10 Years Ahead, LNCS 2000, pp. 24-33, 2001.

Improved hardware and networking are clearly central to the development of ubiquitous computing, but an equally important and difficult set of challenges revolve around *Data Management* [AK93].   In order for computing to fade into the background while supporting more and more activities, the data required to support those activities must be reliably and efficiently stored, queried, and delivered. Traditional approaches to data management such as caching, concurrency control, query processing, etc. need to be adapted to the requirements and restrictions of ubiquitous computing environments. These include resource limitations, varying and intermittent connectivity, mobile users, and dynamic collaborations.

In this paper we first discuss the main characteristics of applications that ubiquitous computing aims to support and then focus on the requirements that such applications impose on data management technology. We then examine several different aspects of data management and how they are being adapted to these new requirements.

Applications and Data Management Requirements

While there is wide agreement on the great potential of ubiquitous computing, it is not yet clear what the "killer applications" (i.e., the uses that will result in widespread adoption) will be. Many researchers and product developers have created example scenarios to demonstrate the potential of the technology. Due to the integrated and universal nature of ubiquitous computing, these scenarios tend to include a large number of functions rather than any one single application. Thus, some in industry have begun to talk in terms of delivering a certain type of "user experience" rather than a particular application or suite of applications. These scenarios tend to involve users with several portable devices, moving between different environments (e.g., home, car, office, conference). The devices typically take an active (and often annoying) role in reminding the user of various appointments and tasks that are due, provide access to any and all information that may be relevant to these tasks, and facilitate communication among groups of individuals involved in the tasks.

Categories of Functionality

Rather than specify yet another such scenario, it is perhaps more useful to categorize the functionalities that such scenarios imply. This categorization can then be examined to determine the requirements that are imposed on data management. The functionalities can be classified into the following:

1) *Support for mobility* – the compactness of the devices combined with wireless communication means that the devices can be used in mobile situations. Thus, existing applications must be able to operate in varied and dynamic communication and computation environments, possibly

moving from one network or service provider to another. Furthermore, new applications that are location-centric will also be developed.

2) *Context awareness* – if devices become truly ubiquitous, then they will be used constantly in a wide range of continually changing situations. For the devices to be truly helpful, they must be aware of the environment as well as the tasks that the user is performing or will be performing in the near future. Context aware applications range from intelligent notification systems that inform the user of (hopefully) important events or data, to "smart spaces", that is, rooms or environments that adapt based on who is present and what they are doing.

3) *Support for collaboration* – another key theme of ubiquitous computing applications is the support of groups of people. This support consists of communications and conferencing as well as the storage, maintenance, delivery, and presentation of shared data. Collaborations may be performed in real-time, if all of the participants are available, or may be done asynchronously otherwise. In addition to supporting on-going collaboration, access to and analysis of traces of past activities is also required.

Adaptivity and User Interaaction

These functionalities provide a host of challenges for data management techniques, but one requirement is present across all of them, namely, the need for *adaptivity*. Mobile users and devices, changing contexts, and dynamic groups all impose requirements for flexibility and responsiveness that are simply not addressed by most traditional data management techniques. Thus, adaptivity is a common theme of the techniques that we discuss in the remainder of the paper.

It is also important to note that because ubiquitous computing is intended to augment human capabilities in the execution of various tasks, the nature of these applications is that the user is typically interacting in real-time with the computers. We are able to exploit this fact as part of the solution to adaptivity by, in some cases, depending on the users to make dynamic choices or to cope with some degree of ambiguity. A concrete example of such a design choice is the way that many groupware systems handle concurrent access and update to shared data. Rather than impose rules that restrict the types and degrees of interaction that users can have, as is done by concurrency control mechanisms in traditional database systems, a groupware data manager will typically impose less stringent rules. The relaxation of these rules limits the extent to which the system can autonomously handle conflicts. Thus, such systems typically handle whatever cases they can, and when they detect a conflict that cannot be handled automatically, they simply inform the user(s) that the conflict has occurred, and allow them to resolve it based on their knowledge of the situation. Thus, having users "in the loop" can be leveraged to provide more adaptive and flexible systems.

Requirements Due to Mobility

Other data management requirements are less universal across the three categories but yet must be addressed in order to support a comprehensive ubiquitous computing environment. For example, the issue of mobility raises a number of issues. First, the fact that the terminals (i.e. devices) are constantly moving, and often have limited storage capacity means that a ubiquitous computing system must be able to deliver data to and receive data from different and changing locations. This results in the need for various kinds of proxy solutions, where users are handed off from one proxy to another as they move. Protocols must be constructed in such a way as to be able to tolerate such handoffs without breaking. Mobility also raises the need for intelligent data staging and pre-staging, so that data can be placed close to where the users will be when they need it (particularly in slow or unreliable communications situations).

Secondly, mobility adds location as a new dimension to applications that does not typically play a role in stationary scenarios. For example, some of the most useful applications for mobile devices are *location-centric*. Consider a system that can answer questions such as "find the drugstores within 2 miles of my current location". Such a system must track the location of the current user and be able to access information based on relative locations and distances. On a broader scale, servers may have to track large numbers of moving objects (people, cars, devices, etc.) and be able to predict their future locations. For example, an automated traffic control system would have to track numerous cars, including their current positions, directions, and velocities. Location-centric computing requires special data structures in which location information can be encoded and efficiently stored, as well as ones in which the dynamic positions of objects can be maintained.

Requirements Due to Context-Awareness

Context-awareness imposes significant demands on the knowledge maintained by the system and the inferencing algorithms that use that knowledge. In order to be context aware, a system must maintain an internal representation of users' needs, roles, and preferences, etc. One example of such a system is a smart calendar that routes information to a user based on knowledge of the user's near-term schedule (as can be determined from the user's PIM calendar). If, for example, a user has a meeting with a particular client scheduled for the afternoon, such a system could send the user information that would be highly relevant to that meeting, such as data about the client's account, results of previous meetings with that client, news articles relevant to the topic of the meeting, etc.

More sophisticated systems might use various types of sensors to monitor the environment and track users' actions so as to be able to assist in the tasks the user is performing. Such sensor-based systems require the ability to process *data streams* in real-time and to analyze and interpret such streams. Thus, data-flow processing will play a key role in ubiquitous computing.

Whether the system obtains its context information from sensors, user input, PIM (personal information management) applications, or some combination of these, it must perform a good deal of processing over the data in order to be able to accurately assess the state of the environment and the intensions of the user. Thus, context-aware applications impose demanding requirements for *inferencing and machine learning* techniques. These processes will have to cope with incomplete and conflicting data, and will have to do so extremely efficiently in order to be able to interact with the user in a useful and unobtrusive manner.

Requirements Due to Collaboration

The final set of requirements we discuss here are those that result from the need to support collaborative work by dynamic and sometimes ad hoc groups of people. As stated above, a prime requirement that stems from such applications is adaptivity. In addition, however, there are several other types of support that are required beyond what has already been discussed. First, there is a need for synchronization and consistency support. At the center of any collaborative application is a set of shared data items that can be created, accessed, modified, and deleted by participants of the collaboration. This coordination function must be lightweight and flexible so that many different types of interactions can be supported, ranging from unmoderated chat facilities, to full ACID (Atomic, Consistent, Isolated, and Durable) transactions, as provided by traditional database systems.

A second requirement stemming from collaborative applications is the need for reliable and available storage of history. In particular, if the collaboration is to be performed in an asynchronous manner, users must be able to access a record of what has happened earlier in the collaboration. Likewise, if the participants in the collaboration can change over time (e.g., due to mobility, failures, or simply due to the nature of the collaboration), then a durable record of participants and their actions is essential to allow new members to join and come up to speed. Such durable storage is also useful for keeping a log of activity, that can be used later to trace through the causes of various outcomes of the collaboration, or as input into learning and data mining algorithms which may help optimize future collaborations.

Example Data Management Technologies – On-Going Projects

The preceding discussion addressed some of the *data management* challenges that must be addressed to support ubiquitous computing scenarios and outlined the application properties from which they arise. In this section, we briefly describe two on going projects that are addressing some of these aspects. The first project, called Data Recharging, exploits user interest and preference information to deliver data updates and other relevant items to users on their portable devices. The second project, called Telegraph, is building an adaptive data-flow processing architecture to process long-running queries over variable streams of data, as would arise in sensor-based and other highly dynamic data environments.

Data Recharging: Profile-Based Data Dissemination and Synchronization

Mobile devices require two key resources to function: power and data. The mobile nature of such devices combined with limitations of size and cost makes it impractical to keep them continually connected to the fixed power and data (i.e., the Internet) grids. Mobile devices cope with disconnection from these grids by "caching". Devices use rechargeable batteries for caching power, while local storage is used for caching data. Periodically, the device-local local resources must be ``recharged" by connecting with the fixed power and data grids. With existing technology, however, the process of recharging the device resident data is much more cumbersome and error-prone than recharging the power. Power recharging can be done virtually anywhere in the world, requires little user involvement, and works progressively – the longer the device is recharged, the better the device-stored power becomes. In contrast, data ``recharging" has none of these attributes.

The Data Recharging project is developing a service and corresponding infrastructure that permits a mobile device of any kind to plug into the Internet at any location for any amount of time and as a result, end up with more useful data than it had before [CFZ00]. As with power recharging, the initiation of a *data charge* simply requires "plugging in" a device to the network. The longer the device is left plugged in, the more effective the charge. Although similar to battery recharging, data recharging is more complex; the type and amount of data delivered during a data charge must be tailored to the needs of the user, the capabilities of the recharged device, and the tasks that the recharged data is needed to support.

Different mobile users will have different data needs. A business traveler may want updates of contact information, restaurant reviews and hotel pricing guides specific to a travel destination. Students may require access to recent course notes, required readings for the next lecture and notification about lab space as it becomes available. Data recharging represents specifications of user needs as *profiles*. Profiles can be thought of as long-running queries that continually sift through the available data to find relevant items and determine their value to the user.

Profiles for data recharging contain three types of information: First, the profile describes the types of data that are of interest to the user. This description must be *declarative* in nature, so that it can encompass newly created data in addition to existing data. The description must also be flexible enough to express predicates over different types of data and media. Second, because of limitations on bandwidth, device-local storage, and recharging time, only a bounded amount of information can be sent to a device during data recharging. Thus, the profile must also express the user's preferences in terms of priorities among data items, desired resolutions of multi-resolution items, consistency requirements, and other properties. Finally, user context can be dynamically incorporated into the recharging process by parameterizing the user profile with information obtained from the device-resident Personal Information Management (PIM) applications such as the calendar, contact list, and To Do list.

Our previous work on user profiles has focused on 1) efficiently processing profiles over streams of XML documents (i.e., the "XFilter" system) [AF00], 2) learning and maintaining user profiles based on explicit user feedback [CFG00], and 3) development of a large-scale, reliable system for mobile device synchronization

[DF00].   Data recharging can build upon this work, but requires the further development of a suitable language and processing strategy for highly expressive user profiles (i.e., that include user preference and contextual information), and the development of a scalable, wide-area architecture that is capable of providing a data recharging service on a global basis to potentially millions of users.

Adaptive Dataflow Query Processing

A second important aspect of ubiquitous computing environments is the variable nature of data availability and the challenges of managing and processing dynamic data flows. In mobile applications for example, data can move throughout the system in order to follow the users who need it.   Conversely, in mobile applications where the data is being created at the endpoints (say, for example, a remote sensing application) data streams into the system in an erratic fashion to be processed, stored, and possibly acted upon by agents residing in the network. Information flows also arise in other applications, such as data dissemination systems in which streams of newly created and modified data must be routed to users and shared caches.

Traditional database query processing systems break down in such environments for a number of reasons: First, they are based on *static* approaches to query optimization and planning.   Database systems produce query plans using simple cost models and statistics about the data to estimate the cost of running particular plans. In a dynamic dataflow environment, this approach simply does not work because there are typically no reliable statistics about the data and because the arrival rates, order, and behavior of the data streams are too unpredictable [UFA98].

Second, the exisiting approaches cannot adequately cope with failures that arise during the processing of a query. In current database systems, if the failure of a data source goes undetected, the query processor simply blocks, waiting for the data to arrive. If a failure is detected, then a query is simply aborted and restarted. Neither of these situations is appropriate in a ubiquitous computing environment in which sources and streams behave unpredictably, and queries can be extremely long-running (perhaps even "continuous").

Third, existing approaches are optimized for a *batch* style of processing in which the goal is to deliver an entire answer (i.e., they are optimized for the delivery of the *last* result). In a ubiquitous computing environment, where users will be interacting with the system in a fine-grained fashion, such approaches are unacceptable. Processed data (e.g., query results, event notifications, etc.) must be passed on to the user as soon as they are available. Furthermore, because the system is interactive, a user may choose to modify the query on the basis of previously returned information or other factors. Thus, the system must be able to gracefully adjust to changes in the needs of the users [HACO+99].

The *Telegraph* project at UC Berkeley [HFCD+00] is investigating these issues through the development of an adaptive dataflow processing engine. Telegraph uses a novel approach to query execution based on "eddies", which are dataflow control structures that route data to query operators on an item-by-item basis [AH00]. Telegraph does not rely upon a traditional query plan, but rather, allows the "plan" to develop and adapt during the execution. For queries over continuous streams of data, the system can continually adapt to changes in the data arrival rates, data characteristics, and the availability of processing, storage, and communication resources.

In addition to novel control structures, Telegraph also employs non-blocking, symmetric query processing operators, such as XJoins [UF00] and Ripple Joins [HH99], which can cope with changing and unpredictable arrival of their input data. The challenges being addressed in the Telegraph project include the development of cluster-based and wide-area implementations of the processing engine, the design of fault-tolerance mechanisms (particularly for long-running queries), support for continuous queries over sensor data and for profile-based information dissemination, and user interface issues.

Conclusions

Ubiquitous computing is a compelling vision for the future that is moving closer to realization at an accelerating pace. The combination of global wireless and wired connectivity along with increasingly small and powerful devices enables a wide array of new applications that will change the nature of computing. Beyond new devices and communications mechanisms, however, the key technology that is required to make ubiquitous computing a reality is *data management*. Data lies at the heart of all ubiquitous computing applications, but these applications and environments impose new and challenging requirements for data management technology.

In this short paper, I have tried to outline the key aspects of ubiquitous computing from a data management perspective. These aspects were organized into three categories: 1) support for *mobility*, 2) *context-awareness*, and 3) support for *collaboration*. I then examined each of these to determine a set of requirements that they impose on data management. The over-riding issue that stems from all of these is the need for *adaptivity*. Thus, traditional data management techniques, which tend to be static and fairly rigid, must be rethought in light of this emerging computing environment.

I also described two on-going projects that are re-examining key aspects of data management techniques: the *DataRecharging* project, which aims to provide data synchronization and dissemination of highly relevant data for mobile users based on the processing of sophisticated user profiles; and the *Telegraph* project, which is developing a dynamic dataflow processing engine to efficiently and adaptively process streams of data from a host of sources ranging from web sources to networks of sensors.

Of course, there are a number of very important data management issues that have not been touched upon in this short paper. First of all, the ability to interoperate among multiple applications and types of data will depend on standards for data-interchange, resource discovery, and inter-object communication. Great strides are being made in these areas, and the research issues are only a small part of the effort involved in the standardization process. Another important area, in which on-going research plays a central role, is the development of global-scale, secure and archival information storage utilities. An example of such a system is the OceanStore utility, currently under development at UC Berkeley [KBCC+00].

In summary, ubiquitous computing raises a tremendous number of opportunities and challenges for data management research and will continue to do so for the foreseeable future. It is crucial to recognize that although it is tempting to focus on the latest "gadget" or communications protocol, data management plays a central role in the development of ubiquitous computing solutions and that advances in this area will ultimately depend on our ability to solve these new and difficult data management problems.

Acknowledgements

The ideas and opinions expressed in this article are the result of many discussions over a number of years with colleagues in both academic and industrial settings. The two projects discussed in this paper are on-going collaborations with several people: The Data Recharging project is a three-university collaboration with Mitch Cherniack of Brandeis University and Stan Zdonik of Brown University. Matt Denny and Danny Tom of UC Berkeley have made important contributions to the project. The Telegraph project is being done at UC Berkeley with Joe Hellerstein. Students currently working on the project include: Sirish Chandrasekaran, Amol Deshpande, Kris Hildrum, Nick Lanham, Sam Madden, Vijayshankar Raman, and Mehul Shah.

The work described in this paper is partially funded by DARPA as part of the "Endeavour Expedition" under Contract Number N66001-99-2-8913, by the National Science Foundation under the "Data Centers" project of the Information Technology Research program, and by research funds from IBM, Siemens, Microsoft, and the Okawa Foundation.

Thanks also to the organizers of the Dagstuhl 10th Anniversary Conference and in particular, to Reinhard Wilhelm for his hard work and patience in putting together an extremely successful symposium.

References

[AF00] Mehmet Altinel, Michael J. Franklin. Efficient Filtering of XML Documents for Selective Dissemination of Information, *Proceedings of the International Conference on Very Large Data Bases*, Cairo, September 2000.

[AK93] Rafael Alonso, Henry F. Korth. Database System Issues in Nomadic Computing. *Proceedings of the ACM SIGMOD Conference*, Washington, D.C., June 1993, pp388-392.

[AH00] Ron Avnur, Joseph M. Hellerstein. Eddies: Continuously Adaptive Query Processing, *Procedings of the ACM SIGMOD Conference,* Philadelphia, PA, June 2000,

[CFG00] Ugur Cetintemel, Michael J. Franklin, and C. Lee Giles. Self-Adaptive User Profiles for Large-Scale Data Delivery, *Proceedings of the International Conference on Data Engineering*, San Diego, CA, February, 2000, pp 622-633

[CFZ00] Mitch Cherniack, Michael J. Franklin, Stan Zdonik. Expressing User Profiles for Data Recharging, *submitted for publication,* October, 2000.

[DF00] Matthew Denny, Michael J. Franklin. Edison: Database-Supported Synchronization for PDAs, *submitted for publication,* November, 2000.

[HFCD+00] Joseph M. Hellerstein, Michael J. Franklin, Sirish Chandrasekaran, Amol Deshpande, Kris Hildrum, Sam Madden, Vijayshankar Raman, Mehul Shah. Adaptive Query Processing: Technology in Evolution, *IEEE Data Engineering Bulletin,* June 2000, pp 7-18.

[HACO+99] Joseph M. Hellerstein Ron Avnur, Andy Chou, Chris Olston, Vijayshankar Raman, Tali Roth, Christian Hidber, Peter J.Haas. Interactive Data Analysis with CONTROL, *IEEE Computer 32(8),* August, 1999, pp. 51-59.

[HH99] Peter J. Haas, Joseph M. Hellerstein. Ripple Joins for Online Aggregation, *Procedings of the ACM SIGMOD Conference,* Philadelphia, PA, June, 1999, pp. 287-298.

[KBCC+00] John Kubiatowicz, David Bindel, Yan Chen, Steven Czerwinski,   Patrick Eaton, Dennis Geels, Ramakrishna Gummadi, Sean Rhea, Hakim Weatherspoon, Westley Weimer, Chris Wells, and Ben Zhao. OceanStore: An Architecture for Global-Scale Persistent Storage, *Proceeedings of the Ninth Iinternational Conference on Architectural Support for Programming Languages and*
Operating Systems (ASPLOS 2000), November 2000.

[UFA98] Tolga Urhan, Michael J. Franklin, Laurent Amsaleg. Cost Based Query Scrambling for Initial Delays,*Procedings of the ACM SIGMOD Conference,* Seattle, WA, June 1998, pp. 130-141.

[UF 00] Tolga Urhan, Michael J. Franklin. XJoin: A Reactively-Scheduled Pipelined Join Operator. *IEEE Data Engineering Bulletin,* 23(2), June, 2000, pp. 27-33.

[Weiser 91] Weiser, Mark. The Computer for the Twenty-First Century. *Scientific American.* September 1991. pp. 94-104.

Programmable Networks

Andrew T. Campbell[1], Michael E. Kounavis[1] and John B. Vicente[2]

[1]Center for Telecommunications Research,
Columbia University
[2] Intel Corporation
genesis@comet.columbia.edu

Abstract. A number of important innovations are creating a paradigm shift in networking leading to higher levels of network programmability. These innovations include the separation between transmission hardware and control software, availability of open programmable network interfaces and the accelerated virtualization of networking infrastructure. The ability to rapidly create, deploy and manage new network services in response to user demands is a key factor driving the programmable networking research community. The goal of programmable networking is to simplify the deployment of network services, leading to networks that explicitly support the process of service creation and deployment. This chapter examines the state-of-the-art in programmable networks.

1. Introduction

The Internet is currently being transformed from simple network architecture to a more sophisticated information delivery system. New technologies such optical networking, software radios and pervasive computing are expected to impact the way people communicate. In the near future, competition between Internet Service Providers (ISPs) could solely hinge on the speed at which one service provider can respond to new market demands over another. The introduction of new services is, however, a challenging task and calls for major advances in methodologies and toolkits for service creation. A vast amount of service-specific computation, processing and switching must be handled and new network programming environments have to be engineered to enable future networking infrastructures to be open, extensible and programmable.

Before we can meet this challenge, we need to better understand the limitations of existing networks and the fundamentals for making networks more programmable. There is growing consensus that network fundamentals are strongly associated with the deployment of new network programming environments, which explicitly recognize service creation, deployment and management in the network infrastructure. For example programmable networks could be based on active network execution environments [42] operating on node operating systems [40] or open signaling network kernels [30] supporting the coexistence of multiple control architectures [33]. Both of these proposals squarely address the same problem: how to 'open' the network up and accelerate its programmability in a controlled and secure manner for the deployment of new architectures, services and protocols.

R. Wilhelm (Ed.): Informatics. 10 Years Back. 10 Years Ahead, LNCS 2000, pp. 34-49, 2001.

The separation of communications hardware (i.e., switching fabrics, routing engines) from control software is fundamental to making the network more programmable. Such a separation is difficult to realize today. The reason for this is that switches and routers are vertically integrated - akin to mainframes of the 70s. Typically, service providers do not have access to switch/router control environments (e.g. Cisco's IOS operating system), algorithms (e.g. routing protocols) or states (e.g., routing tables, flow states). This makes the deployment of new network services, which may be many orders of magnitude more flexible than proprietary control systems, impossible due to the closed nature of network nodes. The question is, how do we go about 'opening up' the switches and routers for deployment of third party control software and services?

A programmable network is distinguished from other networking environments by the fact that it can be programmed from a minimal set of APIs to provide a wide array of higher level services. A number of research groups are actively designing and developing programmable network prototypes. Each group tends to use its own terminology. However, on examination one can observe a common set of characteristics that govern the construction of programmable networks. We use these characteristics to better understand the field:

- *networking technology*, which implicitly limits the programmability that can be delivered to higher levels. For example, some technologies are more QOS programmable (e.g., ATM), scalable (e.g., Internet) or limited in bandwidth availability (e.g., mobile networks);

- *level of programmability*, which indicates the method, granularity and time scale over which new services can be introduced into the network infrastructure. This in turn is strongly related to language support, programming methodology or middleware adopted. For example, distributed object technology can be based on RPC [46] or mobile code [45] methodologies resulting in quasi-static or dynamically composed network programming interfaces;

- *programmable communications abstractions*, which indicate the level of virtualization and programmability of networking infrastructure requiring different middleware and potentially network node support (e.g., switch/router, base station). For example, programmable communications abstractions include virtual switches [30], switchlets [33], active nodes [40], universal mobile channels [32] and virtual active networks [21]; and

- *architectural domain*, which indicates the targeted architectural or application domain (e.g., signaling, management, transport). This potentially dictates certain design choices and impacts the construction of architectures, and services offered, calling for a wide range of middleware support. Examples include, composing application services [4], programmable QOS control [30] and network management [41]).

This chapter examines the state of the art in programmable networks. We present a number of research projects and characterize them in terms of the characteristics discussed above. Section 2 examines how networking technology impacts programmable networking. Following this, Section 3, discusses the level of programmability that these prototype networks can offer, and Section 4, discusses programmable communication abstractions ranging from node abstractions to programmable virtual networks. Section 5 examines a number of architectural domains where programmable networks can be used. Finally, Section 6 makes a number of observations about the direction of the field. We believe that a number of important innovations are creating a paradigm shift in networking leading to higher levels of network programmability.

2. Networking Technology

A number of programmable network prototypes have been targeted to specific networking technologies. The motivation behind these projects is to make the targeted networking technology more programmable in an attempt to overcome particular deficiencies associated with supporting communication services.

2.1 IP Networks: Smart Packets

The University of Kansas has developed smart packets, a code-based packet concept implemented in a programmable IP environment [29]. Smart packets represent elements of in-band or out-of-band mobile code based on Java classes. Smart packets propagate state information in the form of serialized objects and carry identifiers for authentication purposes. An active node architecture supports smart packets by exposing a set of resource abstractions and primitives made accessible to smart packets. Active nodes incorporate:

- resource controllers, which provide interfaces to node resources;

- node managers, which impose static limits on resource usage; and

- state managers, which control the amount of information smart packets may leave behind at an active node.

The active node supports a feedback-scheduling algorithm to allow partitioning of CPU cycles among competing tasks and a credit-based flow-control mechanism to regulate bandwidth usage. Each smart packet is allocated a single thread of CPU and some amount of node resources. Active nodes also include router managers that support both default routing schemes and alternative routing methods carried by smart packets. The smart packets testbed has been used to program enhanced HTTP and SMTP services that show some performance benefits over conventional HTTP and SMTP by reducing excessive ACK/NAK responses in the protocols. A beacon routing scheme supports the use of multiple routing algorithms within a common physical IP network based on smart packets.

2.2 ATM Networks: xbind

ATM technology provides connection-oriented communications and has been tailored towards QOS provisioning of multimedia networks. Although essential features of

QOS provisioning, such as admission control and resource reservation, are inherently supported by the ATM technology, its signaling component is unsuitable for practical usage due to its significant complexity. xbind [15] overcomes these service creation limitations by separating control algorithms from the telecommunications hardware. Emphasis is placed on the development of interfaces to provide open access to node resources and functions, using virtual switch and virtual link abstractions. The interfaces are designed to support the programmability of the management and control planes in ATM networks.

The xbind broadband kernel [47], which is based on the XRM model [15], incorporates three network models abstracting a broadband network, multimedia network and service network. The multimedia network supports programmable network management, network control, state management, connection management and media stream control. The xbind testbed incorporates multivendor ATM switches using open signaling and service creation to support a variety of broadband services, transport and signaling systems with QOS guarantees.

2.3 Mobile Networks: Mobiware

Mobiware [6] is a software-intensive open programmable mobile architecture extending the xbind model of programmability to packet based mobile networks for the delivery of adaptive mobile services over time-varying wireless links. Mobiware incorporates object-based, CORBA programmability for the control plane but also allows active transport objects (i.e., code plug-ins) based on Java byte code to be loaded into the data path. At the transport layer, an active transport environment injects algorithms into base stations providing value-added service support at strategic points inside the network. At the network layer, a set of distributed objects that run on mobile devices, access points and mobile-capable switches, interact with each other to support programmable handoff control and different styles of QOS adaptation. The MAC layer has also been made programmable.

The following mobile services have been programmed using the mobiware toolkit [37]:

- QOS-controlled handoff, which supports automatic media scaling and error control based on an adaptive-QOS API and wireless channel conditions;

- mobile soft-state, which provides mobile devices with the capability to respond to time varying QOS through a periodic reservation and renegotiation process; and

- flow bundling, which supports fast handoff in cellular access networks.

The mobiware testbed supports a variety of scalable audio and video services to mobile devices in addition to traditional web based data services.

3. Level of Programmability

The level of programmability expresses the granularity at which new services can be introduced into the network infrastructure. One can consider a spectrum of possible choices from highly dynamic to more conservative levels of programmability. At one end of this spectrum, capsules [42] carry code and data enabling the uncoordinated deployment of protocols. Capsules represent the most dynamic means of code and service deployment into the network. At the other end of the spectrum there are more conservative approaches to network programmability based on quasi-static network programming interfaces using RPCs between distributed controllers [46] to deploy new services. Between the two extremes lie a number of other methodologies combining dynamic plug-ins, active messaging and RPC. Different approaches have a direct bearing on the speed, flexibility, safety, security and performance at which new services can be introduced into the infrastructure.

3.1 Capsules: ANTS

ANTS [45], developed at MIT, enables the uncoordinated deployment of multiple communication protocols in active networks providing a set of core services including support for the transportation of mobile code, loading of code on demand and caching techniques. These core services allow network architects to introduce or extend existing network protocols. ANTS provides a network programming environment for building new capsule-based programmable network architectures. Examples of such programmed network services include enhanced multicast services, mobile IP routing and application-level filtering. The ANTS capsule-driven execution model provides a foundation for maximum network programmability in comparison to other API approaches. Capsules serve as atomic units of network programmability supporting processing and forwarding interfaces. Incorporated features include node access, capsule manipulation, control operations and soft-state storage services on IP routers. Active nodes execute capsules and forwarding routines, maintain local state and support code distribution services for automating the deployment of new services. The ANTS toolkit also supports capsule processing quanta as a metric for node resource management.

3.2 Active Extensions: Switchware

Switchware [3], being developed at University of Pennsylvania, attempts to balance the flexibility of a programmable network against the safety and security requirements needed in a shared infrastructure such as the Internet. The Switchware toolkit allows the network architects to trade-off flexibility, safety, security, performance and usability when programming secure network architectures. At the operating system level, an active IP-router component is responsible for providing a secure foundation that guarantees system integrity. Active extensions can be dynamically loaded into secure active routers through a set of security mechanisms that include encryption, authentication and program verification. The correct behavior of active extensions can be verified off-line by applying 'heavyweight' methods, since the deployment of such extensions is done over slow time scales.

Active extensions provide interfaces for more dynamic network programming using active packets. Active packets can roam and customize the network in a similar way as capsules do. Active packets are written in functional languages (e.g., Caml and PLAN [28]) and carry lightweight programs that invoke node-resident service routines supported by active extensions. There is much less requirement for testing and verification in the case of active packets than for active extensions, given the confidence that lower level security checks have already been applied to active extensions. Active packets cannot explicitly leave state behind at nodes and they can access state only through clearly defined interfaces furnished by active extension software. Switchware applies heavyweight security checks on active extensions, which may represent major releases of switch code, and more lightweight security checks on active packets. This approach allows the network architect to balance security concerns against performance requirements. The security model of Switchware considers public, authenticated and verified facilities.

3.3 Composition Languages: CANEs

Capsules, active messages and active extensions promote the creation of new services through the composition of new building blocks or by adding components to existing services. The CANEs project led by researchers at University of Kentucky and Georgia Tech. aim to define and apply service composition rules as a general model for network programmability [14]. A composition method is used to construct composite network services from components. A composition method is specified as a programming language with enhanced language capabilities that operates on components to construct programmable network services. Attributes of a good composition method include high performance, scalability, security and ease of management. Features of well-structured composition methods combine:

- control on the sequence in which components are executed;

- control on shared data among components;

- binding times, which comprise composite creation and execution times;

- invocation methods, which are defined as events that cause a composite to be executed; and

- division of functionality among multiple components, which may either reside at an active node or be carried by packets.

PLAN, ANTS and Netscript [21] (described in Section 4.4.2) are examples of composition methods. LIANE is proposed within the CANEs project as a composition method that incorporates all the aforementioned features. The key idea of LIANE is that services are composed from basic underlying programs that contain processing slots. Users insert programs for customization in these slots. The CANEs definition of service composition encompasses the Opensig approach to network programmability indicating how different approaches to programmable networking complement each other by addressing the same goal from different perspectives.

3.4 Network APIs: xbind

The xbind broadband kernel is based on a binding architecture and a collection of node interfaces referred to as Binding Interface Base (BIB) [2]. The BIB provides abstractions to the node state and network resources. Binding algorithms run on top of the BIB and bind QOS requirements to network resources via abstractions. The BIB is designed to support service creation through high-level programming languages. The interfaces are static while supporting universal programmability. The quasi-static nature of the BIB interfaces, allow for complete testing and verification of the correctness of new functions, on emulation platforms, before any service is deployed. The concept of active packets or capsules containing both programs and user data is not considered in the xbind approach to programmability. Rather, communication is performed using RPCs between distributed objects and controllers based on OMG's CORBA. The approach taken by xbind promotes interoperability between multi-vendor switch market supporting resource sharing and partitioning in a controlled manner.

4. Programmable Communications Abstractions

Abstractions and partitioning of resources are essential concepts in programmable networking. Programmable communications abstractions may range from node resources to complete programmable virtual networks. Other programmable communications abstractions include programmable virtual routers, virtual links and mobile channels. Abstracting the network infrastructure through virtualization and making it programmable is a major contribution of the field that encompasses a number of different projects.

4.1 Active Node Abstractions: NodeOS

Members of the DARPA active network program [20] are developing an architectural framework for active networking [11]. A node operating system called NodeOS [40] represents the lowest level of the framework. NodeOS provides node interfaces at routers utilized by multiple execution environments, which support communication abstractions such as threads, channels and flows. Development of an execution environment is a nontrivial task and it is anticipated [12] that the total number of execution environments will not be large. Encapsulation techniques based on an active network encapsulation protocol (ANEP) [5] support the deployment of multiple execution environments within a single active node. ANEP defines an encapsulation format allowing packets to be routed through multiple execution environments coexisting on the same physical nodes. Portability of execution environments across different types of physical nodes is accomplished by the NodeOS, by exposing a common, standard interface. This interface defines four programmable node abstractions: threads, memory, channels and flows. Threads, memory and channels abstract computation, storage, and communication capacity used by execution environments, whereas flows abstract user data-paths with security, authentication and admission control facilities. An execution environment uses the NodeOS interface to create threads and associate channels with flows. The NodeOS supports QOS using scheduling mechanisms that regulate the access to node computation and communication resources. The architectural framework for active networking is being implemented in the ABONE testbed [1] allowing researchers to prototype new active architectures.

4.2 Virtual Active Networks: Netscript

The Netscript project [49] at Columbia University takes a functional language-based approach to capture network programmability using universal language abstractions. Netscript is a strongly typed language that creates universal abstractions for programming network node functions. Unlike other active network projects that take a language-based approach Netscript is being developed to support Virtual Active Networks as a programmable abstraction. Virtual Active Network [21] abstractions can be systematically composed, provisioned and managed. In addition, Netscript automates management through language extensions that generate MIBs. Netscript leverages earlier work on decentralized management and agent technologies that automatically correlate and analyze the behavior monitored by active MIB elements. A distinguishing feature of Netscript is that it seeks to provide a universal language for active networks in a manner that is analogous to postscript. Just as postscript captures the programmability of printer engines, Netscript captures the programmability of network node functions. Netscript communication abstractions include collections of nodes and virtual links that constitute virtual active networks.

4.3 Virtual ATM Networks: Tempest

The Tempest project at the University of Cambridge [34] has investigated the deployment of multiple coexisting control architectures in broadband ATM environments. Novel technological approaches include the usage of software mobile agents to customize network control and the consideration of control architectures dedicated to a single service. Tempest supports two levels of programmability and abstraction. First, switchlets, which are logical network elements that result from the partition of ATM switch resources, allow the introduction of alternative control architectures into an operational network. Second, services can be refined by dynamically loading programs that customize existing control architectures. Resources in an ATM network can be divided by using two software components: a switch control interface called ariel and a resource divider called prospero. Prospero communicates with an ariel server on an ATM switch, partitions the resources and exports a separate control interface for each switchlet created. A network builder creates, modifies and maintains control architectures.

5. Architectural Domains

Most programmable network projects are related to the introduction of services into networks. However, most projects are targeted to a particular architectural domain (e.g., QOS control, signaling, management, transport and applications). In what follows we discuss three projects that address the application, resource management and network management domains.

5.1 Application-Level: Active Services

In contrast to the main body of research in active networking, Amir et al. [4] call for the preservation of all routing and forwarding semantics of the Internet architecture by restricting the computation model to the application layer. The Active Services version 1 (AS1) programmable service architecture enables clients to download and run service agents at strategic locations inside the network. Service agents called "servents" are restricted from manipulating routing tables and forwarding functions that would contravene the IP-layer integrity. The AS1 architecture contains a number of architectural components:

- a service environment, which defines a programming model and a set of interfaces available to servents;

- a service-location facility, which allows clients to 'rendezvous' with the AS1 environment by obtaining bootstrapping and configuration mechanisms to instantiate servents[1];

- a service management system, which allocates clusters of resources to servents using admission control and load balancing of servents under high-load conditions;

- a service control system, which provides dynamic client control of servents once instantiated within an AS1 architecture;

- a service attachment facility, which provides mechanisms for clients that can not interact directly with the AS1 environment through soft-state gateways; and

- a service composition mechanism, which allows clients to contact multiple service clusters and interconnect servents running within and across clusters.

The AS1 architecture is programmable at the application layer supporting a range of application domains. In [4], the MeGa architecture is programmed using AS1 to support an active media gateway service. In this case, servents provide support for application-level rate control and transcoding techniques.

---

[1] Servents are launched into the network by an active service control protocol (ASCP), which includes an announce-listen protocol for servers to manage session state consistency, soft-state to manage expiration due to timeouts and multicast damping to avoid flooding the environment with excessive servents.

5.2   Resource Management: Darwin

The Darwin Project [17] at Carnegie Mellon University is developing a middleware environment for the next generation IP networks with the goal of offering Internet users a platform for value-added and customizable services. The Darwin project is focused toward customizable resource management that supports QOS. Architecturally, the Darwin framework includes Xena, a service broker that maps user requirements to a set of local resources, resource managers that communicate with Xena using the Beagle signaling protocol, and hierarchical scheduling disciplines based on service profiles. The Xena architecture takes the view that the IP forwarding and routing functions should be left in tact and only allows restricted use of active packet technology in the system. Alongside the IP stack, Darwin introduces a control plane that builds on similar concepts such as those leveraged by broadband kernels [30] and active services [4]. The Xena architecture is made programmable and incorporates active technologies in a restricted fashion. A set of service delegates provides support for active packets. Delegates can be dynamically injected into IP routers or servers to support application specific processing (e.g., sophisticated semantic dropping) and value-added services (e.g., transcoders). A distinguishing feature of the Darwin architectural approach is that mechanisms can be customized according to user specific service needs defined by space, organization and time constraints.

5.3   Network Management: Smart Packets

The Smart Packets Project [41] (not to be confused with University of Kansas smart packets) at BBN aims to improve the performance of large and complex networks by leveraging active networking technology. Smart Packets are used to move management decision making points closer to the nodes being managed, target specific aspects of the node for management and abstract management concepts to language constructs. Management centers can send programs to managed nodes. Thus the management process can be tailored to the specific interests of the management center reducing the amount of back traffic and data requiring examination. A smart packet consists of a header and payload encapsulated using ANEP [5]. Smart packets may carry programs to be executed, results from execution, informational messages or reports on error conditions. Smart Packets are written in two programming languages:

- sprocket, which is a high-level C-like, language with security threatening constructs, and

- spanner, which is a low-level assembly-like language, that can result in tighter, optimized code.

Sprocket programs are compiled into spanner code, which in turn is assembled into a machine-independent binary encoding placed into smart packets. Meaningful programs perform networking functions and MIB information retrieval.

6. Discussion

6.1 Open Programmable Interfaces

The use of open programmable network interfaces is evident in many programmable network projects discussed in this chapter. Open interfaces provide a foundation for service programming and the introduction of new network architectures.

The xbind broadband kernel supports a comprehensive Binding Interface Base using CORBA/IDL to abstract network ATM devices, state and control. A number of other projects focussed on programming IP networks (e.g., ANTS, Switchware, CANEs) promote the use of open APIs that abstract node primitives, enabling network programmability and the composition of new services. Many network programming environments take fundamentally different approaches to providing open interfaces for service composition. The programming methodology adopted (e.g., distributed object technology based on RPC, mobile code or hybrid approaches) has a significant impact on an architecture's level of programmability; that is, the granularity, time scales and complexity incurred when introducing new APIs and algorithms into the network.

Two counter proposals include the xbind and ANTS APIs. While the ANTS approach to the deployment of new APIs in extremely flexible presenting a highly dynamic programming methodology it represents a complex programming model in comparison to the simple RPC model. In contrast, the xbind binding interfaces and programming paradigm is based on a set of CORBA IDL and RPC mechanisms. In comparison to capsule-based programmability the xbind approach is rather static in nature and the programming model less complex. These approaches represent two extremes of network programmability.

One could argue that quasi-static APIs based on RPC is a limited and restrictive approach. A counter argument is that the process of introducing and managing APIs is less complex than the capsule-based programming paradigm, representing a more manageable mechanism for service composition and service control. Similarly one could argue that active message and capsule-based technologies are more 'open' because of the inherent flexibility of their network programming models given that capsules can graft new APIs onto routers at runtime. The xbind approach lacks this dynamic nature at the cost of a simplified programming environment. Other projects adopt hybrid approaches. For example the mobiware toolkit combines the static APIs with the dynamic introduction of Java service plug-ins when needed [7]. A clear movement of the field is to open up the networks and present APIs for programming new architectures, services and protocols. As we discuss in the next section the field is arguing that the switches, routers and base stations should open up ultimately calling for open APIs everywhere.

6.2 Virtualization and Resource Partitioning

Many projects use virtualization techniques to support the programmability of different types of communication abstractions. The Tempest framework [33] presents a good example of the use of virtualization of the network infrastructure. Low-level physical switch interfaces are abstracted creating sets of interfaces to switch partitions called switchlets. Switchlets allow multiple control architectures to coexist and share the same physical switch resources (e.g., capacity, switching tables, name space, etc.). Typically, abstractions found in programmable networks are paired with safe resource partitioning strategies that enable multiple services, protocols and different programmable networking architectures to coexist. Virtualization of the network in this manner presents new levels of innovation in programmable networks that have not been considered before. All types of network components can be virtualized and made programmable from switches and links [15] to switchlets [33], active nodes [40], routelets [13] and virtual networks [21], [34], [13].

The NodeOS interface [40] provides a similar abstraction to node resources. The use of open interfaces allows multiple network programming environments (or execution environments using active networking terminology) to coexist within a common physical node architecture. In this case, the ANEP [5] protocol provides encapsulation as a mechanism for delivering packets to distinct execution environments.

Using encapsulation in this manner allows for different overlay execution environments (e.g., ANTS, Switchware, or Netscript) to execute on the same router using a single, common node kernel. The notion of virtualization is not a new concept, however. Similar motivation in the Internet community has led to the advent of the Mbone. New directions in the virtualization of the Internet have prompted the proposal for X-bone [44], which will provide a network programming environment capable of dynamically deploying overlay networks. Other projects such as Supranet [23] advocate tunneling and encapsulation techniques for the separation and privacy among coexisting, collaborative environments.

6.3 Programmable Virtual Networking

The dynamic composition and deployment of new services can be extended to include the composition of complete network architectures as virtual networks. The Netscript project [49] supports the notion of Virtual Active Networks [21] over IP networks. Virtual network engines interconnect sets of virtual nodes and virtual links to form virtual active networks. The Tempest framework [34] supports the notion of virtual networks using safe partitioning over ATM hardware. Tempest offers two levels of programmability. First, network control architectures can be introduced over long time scales through a 'heavyweight' deployment process. Second, 'lightweight' application-specific customization of established control architectures take place over faster time scales. The abstraction of physical switch partitions within the Tempest framework has led to the implementation of multiple coexisting control architectures. The Tempest strategy aims to address QOS through connection-oriented ATM technology and investigates physical resource sharing techniques between alternative control architectures. Both Darwin [17] and Netscript [49] projects support the notion of sharing the underlying physical infrastructure in a customized way as well. As discussed in the previous section, the NodeOS [40] project also provides facilities for coexisting execution environments.

6.4 Spawning Networks

In [13] we describe spawning networks, a new class of programmable networks that automate the creation, deployment and management of distinct network architectures "on-the-fly". The term "spawning" finds a parallel with an operating system spawning a child process, typically operating over the same hardware. We envision programmable networks as having the capability to spawn not processes but complex network architectures [31]. The enabling technology behind spawning is the Genesis Kernel [13], a virtual network operating system that represents a next-generation approach to the development of network programming environments.

A key capability of Genesis is its ability to support a virtual network life cycle process for the creation and deployment of virtual networks through:

- profiling, which captures the "blueprint" of a virtual network architecture in terms of a comprehensive profiling script;

- spawning, which executes the profiling script to set-up network topology, and address space and bind transport control and management objects into the physical infrastructure; and

- management, which supports virtual network architecting and resource management.

Virtual networks, spawned by the Genesis Kernel operate in isolation with their traffic being carried securely and independently from other networks. Furthermore, "child" networks, created through spawning by "parent" networks inherit architectural components from their parent networks, including life cycle support. Thus a child virtual network can be a parent (i.e., provider) to its own child networks, creating a notion of "nested virtual networks" within a virtual network.

7. Conclusion

In this chapter, we have discussed the state-of-the-art in programmable networks. We have presented a set of characteristics for programmable networks, which has allowed us to better understand the relationship between the existing body of work. We believe that a number of important innovations are creating a paradigm shift in networking leading to higher levels of network programmability. These are the separation of hardware from software, availability of open programmable interfaces, virtualization of the networking infrastructure, rapid creation and deployment of new network services and safe resource partitioning and coexistence of distinct network architectures over the same physical networking hardware. Programmable networks provide a foundation for architecting, composing and deploying virtual network architectures through the availability of open programmable interfaces, resource partitioning and the virtualization of the networking infrastructure. We believe that a key challenge is the development of programmable virtual networking environments based on these foundations.

8. References

[1]   ABONE, Active network Backbone, http://www.csl.sri.com/ancors/abone/

[2]   Adam, C.M., Lazar, A.A., Lim, K.-S., and Marconcini, F., "The Binding Interface Base Specification Revision 2.0", *OPENSIG Workshop on Open Signalling for ATM, Internet and Mobile Networks*, Cambridge, UK, April 1997.

[3]   Alexander, D.S., Arbaugh, W.A., Hicks, M.A., Kakkar P., Keromytis A., Moore J.T., Nettles S.M., and Smith J.M., "The SwitchWare Active Network Architecture", *IEEE Network Special Issue on Active and Controllable Networks*, vol. 12 no. 3, 1998.

[4]   Amir E., McCanne S., and Katz R., "An Active Service Framework and its Application to real-time Multimedia Transcoding", *Proceedings ACM SIGCOMM' 98*, Vancouver, Canada

[5]   Alexander D.S., Braden B., Gunter C.A., Jackson W.A., Keromytis A.D., Milden G.A., and Wetherall D.A., "Active Network Encapsulation Protocol (ANEP)", *Active Networks Group Draft*, July 1997

[6]   Angin, O., Campbell, A.T., Kounavis, M.E., and Liao, R.R.-F., "The Mobiware Toolkit: Programmable Support for Adaptive Mobile Networking", *IEEE Personal Communications Magazine, Special Issue on Adaptive Mobile Systems*, August 1998.

[7]   Balachandran, A., Campbell, A.T., and Kounavis, M.E, "Active Filters: Delivering Scalable Media to Mobile Devices", *Proc. Seventh International Workshop on Network and Operating System Support for Digital Audio and Video*, St Louis, May, 1997.

[8]   Bershad,B.N., et al., "Extensibility, Safety and Performance in the SPIN Operating System", *Fifth ACM Symposium on Operating Systems* Principles, Copper Mountain, December 1995.

[9]   Biswas, J., et al., " The IEEE P1520 Standards Initiative for Programmable Network Interfaces" *IEEE Communications Magazine, Special Issue on Programmable Networks*, October, 1998.

[10]   Braden,B., "Active Signaling Protocols", *Active Networks Workshop*, Tucson AZ, March 1998.

[11]   Calvert, K. et al, "Architectural Framework for Active Networks", *Active Networks Working Group Draft*, July 1998.

[12]   Calvert, K. et. al, "Directions in Active networks", *IEEE Communications Magazine, Special Issue on Programmable Networks*, October 1998.

[13]   Campbell A.T., De Meer H.G., Kounavis M.E., Miki K., Vicente J.B., and Villela D., "The Genesis Kernel: A Virtual Network Operating System for Spawning Network Architectures", *Second International Conference on Open Architectures and Network Programming (OPENARCH)*, New York, 1999.

[14]   "CANEs: Composable Active Network Elements", http://www.cc.gatech.edu/ projects/canes/

[15]   Chan, M.-C., Huard, J.-F., Lazar, A.A., and Lim, K.-S., "On Realizing a Broadband Kernel for Multimedia Networks", *3rd COST 237 Workshop on Multimedia Telecommunications and Applications*, Barcelona, Spain, November 25-27, 1996.

[16]   Chen and Jackson, Editorial, IEEE Network Magazine, *Special Issue on Programmable and Active Networks*, May 1998

[17] Chandra, P. et al., "Darwin: Customizable Resource Management for Value-added Network Services", *Sixth IEEE International Conference on Network Protocols (ICNP'98)*, Austin, October 1998.

[18] Coulson, G., et al., "The Design of a QOS-Controlled ATM-Based Communications System in Chorus", *IEEE Journal of Selected Areas in Communications*, vol.13, no.4, May 1995.

[19] Cplane Inc., www.cplane.com

[20] DARPA Active Network Program, http://www.darpa.mil/ito/research/anets/projects. html, 1996.

[21] Da Silva, S., Florissi, D. and Yemini, Y., "NetScript: A Language-Based Approach to Active Networks", *Technical Report, Computer Science Dept., Columbia University* January 27, 1998.

[22] Decasper, D., Parulkar, G., Plattner, B., "A Scalable, High Performance Active Network Node", *IEEE Network*, January 1999.

[23] Delgrossi, L. and Ferrari D., "A Virtual Network Service for Integrated-Services Internetworks", *7th International Workshop on Network and Operating System Support for Digital Audio and Video*, St. Louis, May 1997.

[24] Engler, D.R., Kaashoek, M.F. and O'Toole ,J., "Exokernel: An Operating System Architecture for Application-Level Resource Management", *Fifth ACM Symposium on Operating Systems* Principles, Copper Mountain, December 1995.

[25] Feldmeier, D.C., at al. "Protocol Boosters", *IEEE Journal on Selected Areas in Communications, Special Issue on Protocol Architectures for the 21st Century*, 1998.

[26] Ferguson, P. and Huston, G., "What is a VPN?", *OPENSIG'98 Workshop on Open Signalling for ATM, Internet and Mobile Networks*, Toronto, October 1998.

[27] Hartman, J., et al., "Liquid Software: A New Paradigm for Networked Systems", *Technical Report 96-11, Dept. of Computer Science, Univ. of Arizona*, 1996.

[28] Hicks, M., et al., "PLAN: A Programming Language for Active Networks", *Proc ICFP'98*, 1998.

[29] Kulkarni, A.B. Minden G.J., Hill, R., Wijata, Y., Gopinath, A., Sheth, S., Wahhab, F., Pindi, H., and Nagarajan, A., "Implementation of a Prototype Active Network", *First International Conference on Open Architectures and Network Programming (OPENARCH)*, San Francisco, 1998.

[30] Lazar, A.A.,"Programming Telecommunication Networks", *IEEE Network,* vol.11, no.5, September/October 1997.

[31] Lazar, A.A., and A.T Campbell, "Spawning Network Architectures", *Technical Report, Center for Telecommunications Research*, Columbia University, 1997.

[32] Liao, R.-F. and Campbell, A.T., "On Programmable Universal Mobile Channels in a Cellular Internet", *4th ACM/IEEE International Conference on Mobile Computing and Networking (MOBICOM'98)* , Dallas, October, 1998

[33] Van der Merwe, J.E., and Leslie, I.M., "Switchlets and Dynamic Virtual ATM Networks", *Proc Integrated Network Management V*, May 1997.

[34] Van der Merwe, J.E., Rooney, S., Leslie, I.M. and Crosby, S.A., "The Tempest - A Practical Framework for Network Programmability", *IEEE Network*, November 1997.

[35] DARPA Active Network Mail List Archives, 1996. http://www.ittc.ukans.edu/Projects/ Activenets

[36] Montz, A.B., et al., "Scout: A Communications-Oriented Operating System", *Technical Report 94-20, University of Arizona, Dept. of Computer Science*, June 1994.

[37] Mobiware Toolkit v1.0 source code distribution http://www.comet.columbia.edu/ mobiware

[38] Multiservice Switching Forum (MSF) , www.msforum.org

[39] Open Signaling Working Group comet.columbia.edu/opensig/

[40] Peterson L., "NodeOS Interface Specification", *Technical Report, Active Networks NodeOS Working Group*, February 2, 1999

[41] Schwartz, B., Jackson, W.A., Strayer W.T., Zhou, W., Rockwell, R.D., and Partridge, C., "Smart Packets for Active Networks", *Second International Conference on Open Architectures and Network Programming (OPENARCH)*, New York, 1999.

[42] Tennenhouse, D., and Wetherall, D., "Towards an Active Network Architecture", *Proceedings, Multimedia Computing and Networking*, San Jose, CA, 1996.

[43] Tennenhouse, D., et al., "A Survey of Active Network Research", *IEEE Communications Magazine*, January 1997.

[44] Touch, J. and Hotz, S., "The X-Bone", Third *Global Internet Mini-Conference in conjunction with Globecom '98* Sydney, Australia, November 1998.

[45] Wetherall, D., Guttag, J. and Tennenhouse, D., "ANTS: A Toolkit for Building and Dynamically Deploying Network Protocols", *Proc. IEEE OPENARCH'98*, San Francisco, CA, April 1998.

[46] Vinoski, S.,"CORBA: Integrating Diverse Applications Within Distributed Heterogeneous Environments", *IEEE Communications Magazine*, Vol. 14, No. 2, February, 1997.

[47] xbind code http://comet.columbia.edu/xbind

[48] Xbind Inc., www.xbind.com

[49] Yemini, Y., and Da Silva, S, "Towards Programmable Networks", *IFIP/IEEE International Workshop on Distributed Systems: Operations and Management*, L'Aquila, Italy, October, 1996.

Multilateral Security: Enabling Technologies and Their Evaluation*

Andreas Pfitzmann

TU Dresden, Department of Computer Science, 01062 Dresden, Germany
pfitza@inf.tu-dresden.de

Abstract. First, multilateral security and its potential are introduced. Then protection goals as well as their synergies and interferences are described. After pointing out some basic facts about security technology in general, a structured overview of technologies for multilateral security is given. An evaluation of the maturity and effectiveness of these technologies shows that some should be applied immediately, while others need quite a bit of further research and development. Finally, a vision for the future is given.

1 Introduction and Overview

Multilateral Security means providing security for all parties concerned, requiring each party to only minimally trust in the honesty of others:

- Each party has its particular *protection goals*.
- Each party can *formulate* its protection goals.
- Security conflicts are recognized and compromises *negotiated*.
- Each party can *enforce* its protection goals within the agreed compromise.

In the same way as enlightenment freed human beings from the suppression imposed by superstitious mental models and authoritarian political systems, technology for multilateral security has the potential to free users of IT systems from a lack of self-determination concerning their (in)security.

To set the tone, I begin with a rather comprehensive ensemble of protection goals, their synergies and interferences.

Thereafter, I state some basic facts about the constraints on security technology in general, and on multilateral security in particular. This helps to identify which technologies are particularly helpful, or even essential, for the construction, use, and maintenance of secure IT systems.

Some of these technologies can unilaterally be employed by various parties. To use others, at least bilateral cooperation is needed, e.g. the cooperation of both communication partners. For some, at least trilateral cooperation is required. An example are legally binding digital signatures which need not only cooperation of the at least two communicants, but additionally at least one somewhat

---

* Part of this work has been published in G. Müller, K. Rannenberg (Eds.): Multilateral Security in Communications, Addison-Wesley 1999.

R. Wilhelm (Ed.): Informatics. 10 Years Back. 10 Years Ahead, LNCS 2000, pp. 50–62, 2001.

Protection of / Threats	Content	Circumstances
unauthorized access to information	Confidentiality Hiding	Anonymity Unobservability
unauthorized modification of information	Integrity	Accountability
unauthorized impairment of functionality	Availability	Reachability Legal Enforceability

Table 1. An ordered ensemble of protection goals

trusted third party for the certification of public keys. For other technologies, even the multilateral cooperation of a large number of independent parties is necessary. I use this distinction to structure a short overview of what is known about technology for (multilateral) security, providing pointers to the relevant literature.

In conclusion, I give an evaluation of the maturity and effectiveness of the different described technologies for (multilateral) security. This emphasizes which technologies should be introduced immediately in order to enhance existing IT systems or as a basis for new ones. Furthermore I give my opinion which technologies need quite a lot of further research and/or development.

Finally, I give my vision for the future of the field.

2   Protection Goals, Their Synergies and Interferences

Twenty years ago, security was nearly equated with *confidentiality*, e.g. in the Orange Book [13]. 15 years ago, *integrity* of information and *availability* of functionality have been added, e.g. by Voydock and Kent [22] and in the European Security Evaluation Criteria [16]. Ten years ago, *accountability* has been added as a fourth protection goal, e.g. in the Canadian Criteria [12].

Outside the mainstream of government dominated security research, *anonymity* and *unobservability* became a big issue 15 years ago [7,18], when the technical advance of storage technology made it possible to store all person-related information forever nearly for free. In recent years, attempts of governments to control the use of cryptography and the pressure of the music and film industries to develop digital copy protection technology, gave a big boost to steganography, i.e. the art of *hiding* information within other, unsuspicious data. Mobile networks, which technically allow people to be reached irrespective

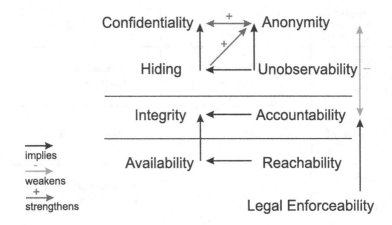

Fig. 1. Synergies and interferences between protection goals

of where they are and what they do, gave rise to the protection goal *reachability*, i.e. to control who is able to reach whom under what circumstances by which media. Electronic-commerce caused attention to be given to *legal enforceability*, i.e. users have to fulfill their legal responsibilities within a reasonable period of time.

To impose some order on this ensemble of protection goals in the context of communication over networks, it proves fruitful to discern between the content and the circumstances of communication [23], cf. Table 1.

Of course, there are quite a few synergies and interferences between these protection goals, which are explained in detail in [23] and depicted in Fig. 1.

In addition, it has to be expected that additional protection goals will be defined and will become important in the future.

3   Basic Facts

If the parties concerned, e.g. users, service providers and network operators, are unwilling or, perhaps even unable, to express the security properties they expect, it is unlikely that they will get what they require.

→ Users, service providers and network operators must be willing and able to formulate all the security properties they expect.

The security properties expected by different parties tend to be quite diverse in respect of applications and even transactions with different partners using the same application. Moreover, the security properties expected may change dramatically over time, e.g. as a result of negative personal experiences, or reports by the media.

→ Security properties have to be dynamically adaptable.

The security of a human user can only be as good as the security of the device he or she is directly interacting with.[1] (Whether the device is secure for other parties concerned, is only of secondary interest.)

→ Devices which are secure for their user(s) are needed.

If a user device is built to integrate more than one application, its security has to be adequate for its most demanding application. If a general purpose user device is built, its security has to be adequate for the most demanding application perceivable during its lifetime. If this is not achieved, the user device is clearly not general purpose – which applies to all Windows 98 based PCs.

→ The security target of user devices is set by the most demanding application the device is intended to be used for.

If the designers are cautious, the security target will even be set by the most demanding application the device will ever be used for – and this application may not yet be known at the time the device is being designed.

→ User devices have to provide a very, very secure basis to bootstrap further security properties during their lifetime.

The erasure of data ever available in a globally networked IT system is by no reasonable means really to assure. In addition, the technical progress makes transfer, storage and usage of huge amounts of data very cheap. Therefore, wherever possible, the parties concerned have to be able to hinder even the ability to gather their data.

→ Data avoidance techniques for anonymity, unobservability, and unlinkability are needed. If accountability is required, a suitable form of pseudonymity should be used.[2]

4   Overview of Technologies for Security

Security technologies are mentioned and briefly explained in this section. It is structured according whether security technologies are uni-, bi-, tri-, or even multilateral.

---

[1] This is certainly true within the IT system. Outside the IT system, there may be compensation for security breaches. But this can work at best for those security properties where compensation is possible at all. Compensation is not possible for confidentiality properties – information which got public cannot be de-publicized –, but compensation is possible with regard to integrity and availability properties, e.g. accountability and legal enforceability, cf. [4].

[2] A structured explanation, definitions of and interrelationships between anonymity, unobservability, unlinkability, accountability, and pseudonymity can be found in [23].

4.1   Unilateral Technologies

Unilateral technologies can be decided on by each party for itself. Therefore, neither coordination nor negotiation is needed concerning their usage. Important unilateral technologies for multilateral security are:

Tools to help even inexperienced users to formulate all their protection goals, if necessary for each and every application or even each and every single action, cf. [20,23]. Fig. 2 gives some examples.

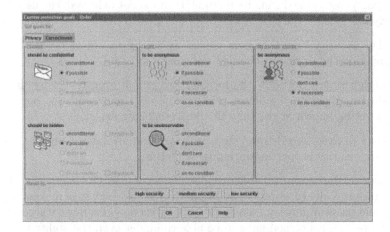

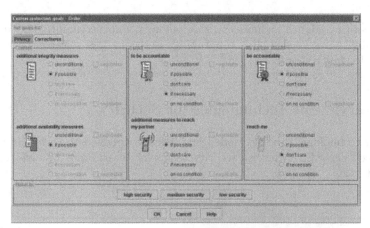

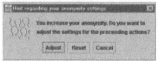

Fig. 2. User interface screen shots

(Portable) devices which are secure for their users in order to bootstrap security. The devices need at least minimal *physical protection* comprising direct input/output with their users [19] and, if they are multi-purpose, an *operating system* providing fine-grained access control and administration of rights for applications, adhering to the principle of least privilege, cf. Fig. 3. This is essential to limit the spread of Trojan horses, and can prevent computer viruses completely.

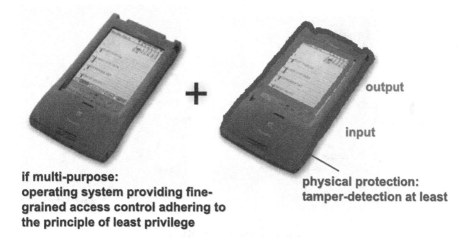

Fig. 3. Portable devices secure for their users

Encryption of local storage media to conceal and/or authenticate its contents.

Hiding of secret data in local multimedia contents or in the local file system [2] using steganographic techniques, not only to conceal the contents of the secret data, but also its very existence.

Watermarking or *fingerprinting* digital data using steganographic techniques to help prove authorship or copyright infringements.

Using only *software* whose *source code is published and well checked* or the *security of which is certified* by a trustworthy third party[3] having access to the complete source code and all tools used for code generation. The best technique is to combine both approaches with regard to as much of the software as possible. It is only by using at least one of these two approaches that you can be reasonably certain that the software you use does not contain Trojan horses. More or less the same applies to hardware where all sources and tools used for design and production are needed as well to check for the absence of Trojan horses.

---

[3] Here, other parties are counted than in uni-, bi-, and trilateral technologies, where only the parties actively involved at the runtime of the IT system are counted.

4.2   Bilateral Technologies

Bilateral technologies can only be used if at least two parties cooperate, e.g. both communication partners. This means that some coordination and negotiation is needed concerning their usage. Important bilateral technologies for multilateral security are:

Tools to negotiate bilateral protection goals and security mechanisms, cf. [20] and Fig. 4.

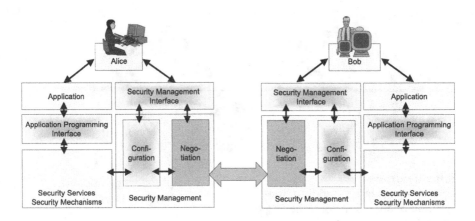

Fig. 4. Tools to negotiate

Cryptographic mechanisms and *steganographic mechanisms* to secure the communication content, cf. Figs. 5 and 6.

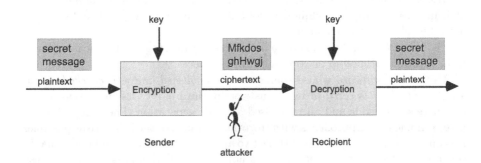

Fig. 5. Cryptography to achieve confidentiality and integrity of the communication contents

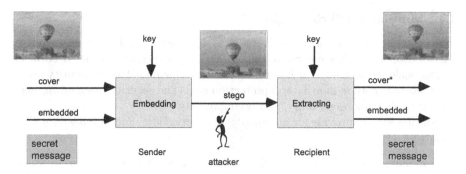

Fig. 6. Steganography to achieve hiding, i.e. secrecy of the confidentiality of the communication contents

4.3   Trilateral Technologies

Trilateral technologies can only be used if at least three parties cooperate. This means that even more coordination and negotiation is needed concerning their usage. Important trilateral technologies for multilateral security are:

Tools to negotiate trilateral security mechanisms, e.g. for accountability.

A *public-key infrastructure* (PKI) to provide users with certified public keys of other users to test their digital signatures and to give users the ability to revoke their own public key if the corresponding private key has been compromised.

Fig. 7. Security gateways

Security gateways to bridge incompatibilities with regard to security mechanisms or their details, cf. Fig. 7. Security gateways work well concerning integrity and accountability mechanisms, but are of questionable value concerning confidentiality and anonymity mechanisms. Of course, security gateways cannot bridge incompatibilities concerning protection goals.

4.4   Multilateral Technologies

Multilateral technologies can only be used if a large number of independent parties cooperate. This means that coordination and negotiation are needed on a large scale. Important multilateral technologies for multilateral security are:

Tools to negotiate multilateral protection goals and security mechanisms, e.g. for anonymity, unobservability, and pseudonymity.

Mechanisms to provide for *anonymity, unobservability,* and *unlinkability* with regard to

– communications, i.e. protect who communicates when to whom from where to where [6,7,18,11,14,17,21,15], cf. Fig. 8,
– payments, i.e. protect who pays what amount to whom and when [8,1], and
– value exchange, i.e. protect electronic shopping from observation [5,3], cf. Fig. 9,

without compromising integrity, availability, or accountability.

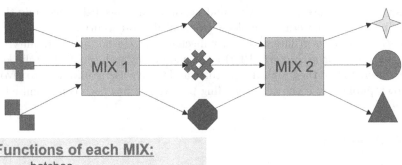

Functions of each MIX:
 – batches
 – discards repeats
 – changes encoding (decryption)
 – changes order
–> **hides relation between in-
    and outgoing messages**

MIXes can be used to protect
• e-mail and Web-access,
  e.g. Onion Routing, and
• mobile communications

Fig. 8. Anonymity, unobservability, and unlinkability for communication

Mechanisms to provide for *digital pseudonyms*[4], i.e. a suitable combination of anonymity and accountability [6]. In particular, there are mechanisms to securely transfer signatures (expressing authorizations, called credentials) between different pseudonyms of the same party [7,9,10]. This is called *transferring signatures between pseudonyms.*

---

[4] If we only consider the accountability aspect, digital pseudonyms are a trilateral technology. But taking into account anonymity as well, digital pseudonyms are clearly a multilateral technology.

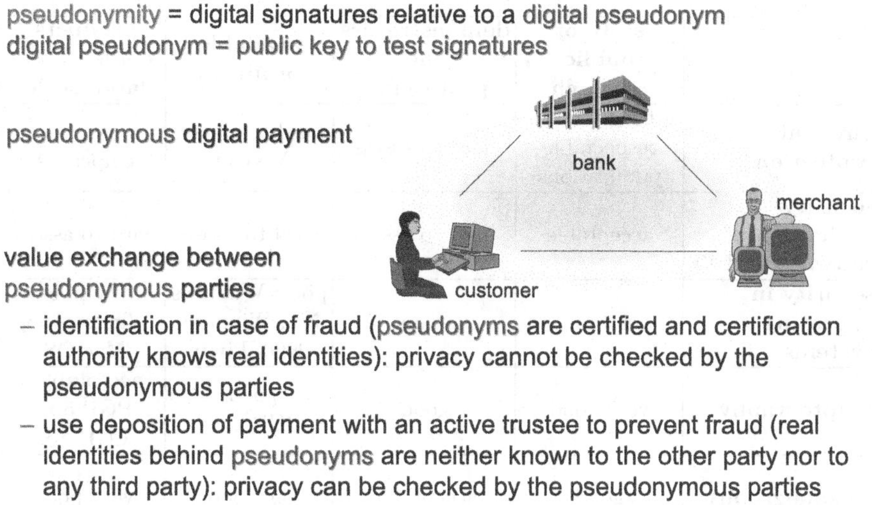

pseudonymity = digital signatures relative to a digital pseudonym
digital pseudonym = public key to test signatures

pseudonymous digital payment

bank

merchant

value exchange between
pseudonymous parties

customer

- identification in case of fraud (pseudonyms are certified and certification
  authority knows real identities): privacy cannot be checked by the
  pseudonymous parties
- use deposition of payment with an active trustee to prevent fraud (real
  identities behind pseudonyms are neither known to the other party nor to
  any third party): privacy can be checked by the pseudonymous parties

Fig. 9. Pseudonymous digital payment and value exchange between pseudonymous parties

5 Evaluation of Maturity and Effectiveness

Table 2 gives my evaluation of the maturity and effectiveness of the technologies
for security mentioned in the last sections. Their sequence in the table is mainly
bottom-up, i.e. a technology for security placed in a particular row is required
before a technology listed below can be effective. In some places, examples are
given following a semicolon.

As can be seen, the weakest link of the security chain today is the user device,
in particular its physical protection and operating system. Much has to be done
to improve both.

Obviously, security evaluation of software as well as IT and integration of
security technologies are those challenges for research that have the most impact
on IT security.

6 A Vision

Without multilateral security, e-commerce will be severely hindered and there
will be definitely no e-democracy. Therefore, I expect that portable devices secure
for their users will finally be developed and find their way into the mass market.
The diverse projects to introduce secure and legally binding digital signatures
are important first steps. Building on devices secure for their users, cryptography
will prove as a very powerful enabling technology for all kinds of security services.

	state of public research	demonstrators and prototypes	available products	products fielded on a large scale
physical protection	hardly any respectable publications	hard to assess	hard to assess; Me-chip	very poor; chipcards
security evaluation of software and IT	acceptable	hard to assess	hard to assess	hard to assess
security in operating systems	very good	good	poor; Windows NT, Windows 2000, Linux	very poor; Windows 98, Mac OS
cryptography	very good	good	good; PGP 2.6.x	acceptable; PGP 5.x, PGP 6.x
steganography	good	acceptable	very poor	very poor
public-key infrastructure	very good	good	hard to assess	-
security gateways	good	acceptable	-	-
mechanisms for anonymity, unobservability, and unlinkability	very good	good	acceptable; Onion Routing, Freedom	poor; proxies
digital pseudonyms	very good	good	good; PGP 2.6.x	acceptable; PGP 5.x, PGP 6.x
transferring signatures between pseudonyms	good	-	-	-
tools to help even inexperienced users to formulate and negotiate	good	acceptable	-	-
integration of these technologies	acceptable	poor	poor	very poor

Table 2. Maturity and effectiveness of security technologies

Of course, we will experience broad discussions (and at least some attempts of various secret services to achieve facts without any public discussion at all) what the balance between electronic surveillance and digital privacy should be. It is well known and agreed for at least three decades that nearly complete surveillance is possible by IT systems. I am happy that public research has shown in the last two decades that strong digital privacy is possible as well. So society is free to decide how we shall live in cyberspace – and beyond.

I am sure that multilateral security and privacy enhancing technologies are prerequisites for the long term acceptance of IT systems in general and for ubiquitous computing in particular in a democratic society as we know it.

References

1. N. Asokan, Phillipe A. Janson, Michael Steiner, Michael Waidner: The State of the Art in Electronic Payment Systems; Computer 30/9 (1997) 28–35.
2. Ross Anderson, Roger Needham, Adi Shamir: The Steganographic File System; Information Hiding, 2nd Workshop, Portland, Oregon, LNCS 1525, Springer, Heidelberg 1998, 73–82.
3. N. Asokan, Matthias Schunter, Michael Waidner: Optimistic Protocols for Fair Exchange; 4th ACM Conference on Computer and Communications Security, Zürich, April 1997, 6-17.
4. Birgit Baum-Waidner: Ein Service zur Haftungsverteilung für kompromittierte digitale Signaturen; Verläßliche IT-Systeme, GI-Fachtagung VIS '99, DuD Fachbeiträge, Vieweg, Braunschweig 1999, 203–223.
5. Holger Bürk, Andreas Pfitzmann: Value Exchange Systems Enabling Security and Unobservability; Computers & Security 9/8 (1990) 715–721.
6. David Chaum: Untraceable Electronic Mail, Return Addresses, and Digital Pseudonyms; Communications of the ACM 24/2 (1981) 84–88.
7. David Chaum: Security without Identification: Transaction Systems to make Big Brother Obsolete; Communications of the ACM 28/10 (1985) 1030–1044.
8. David Chaum: Privacy Protected Payments - Unconditional Payer and/or Payee Untraceability; SMART CARD 2000: The Future of IC Cards, Proc. of the IFIP WG 11.6 Intern. Conference; Laxenburg (Austria), 1987, North-Holland, Amsterdam 1989, 69–93.
9. David Chaum: Showing credentials without identification: Transferring signatures between unconditionally unlinkable pseudonyms; Auscrypt '90, LNCS 453, Springer, Berlin 1990, 246–264.
10. David Chaum: Achieving Electronic Privacy; Scientific American (August 1992) 96–101.
11. David A. Cooper, Kenneth P. Birman: Preserving Privacy in a Network of Mobile Computers; 1995 IEEE Symposium on Research in Security and Privacy, IEEE Computer Society Press, Los Alamitos 1995, 26–38.
12. Canadian System Security Centre; Communications Security Establishment; Government of Canada: The Canadian Trusted Computer Product Evaluation Criteria; April 1992, Version 3.0e.
13. Department of Defense Standard: Department of Defense Trusted Computer System Evaluation Criteria; December 1985, DOD 5200.28-STD, Supersedes CSC-STD-001-83, dtd 15 Aug 83, Library No. S225,711.

14. Hannes Federrath, Anja Jerichow, Andreas Pfitzmann: Mixes in mobile communication systems: Location management with privacy; Information Hiding, 1st Workshop, Cambridge, UK, LNCS 1174, Springer, Heidelberg 1996, 121–135.
15. David Goldschlag, Michael Reed, Paul Syverson: Onion Routing for Anonymous and Private Internet Connections; Communications of the ACM 42/2 (1999) 39–41.
16. European Communities - Commission: ITSEC: Information Technology Security Evaluation Criteria; (Provisional Harmonised Criteria, Version 1.2, 28 June 1991) Office for Official Publications of the European Communities, Luxembourg 1991 (ISBN 92-826-3004-8).
17. Anja Jerichow, Jan Müller, Andreas Pfitzmann, Birgit Pfitzmann, Michael Waidner: Real-Time Mixes: A Bandwidth-Efficient Anonymity Protocol; IEEE Journal on Selected Areas in Communications 16/4 (May 1998) 495–509.
18. Andreas Pfitzmann, Michael Waidner: Networks without user observability; Computers & Security 6/2 (1987) 158–166.
19. Andreas Pfitzmann, Birgit Pfitzmann, Matthias Schunter, Michael Waidner: Trustworthy User Devices; in: G. Müller, K. Rannenberg (Eds.): Multilateral Security in Communications, Addison-Wesley 1999, 137–156.
20. Andreas Pfitzmann, Alexander Schill, Andreas Westfeld, Guntram Wicke, Gritta Wolf, Jan Zöllner: A Java-based distributed platform for multilateral security; IFIP/GI Working Conference "Trends in Electronic Commerce", Hamburg, LNCS 1402, Springer, Heidelberg 1998, 52–64.
21. Michael K. Reiter, Aviel D. Rubin: Anonymous Web Transactions with Crowds; Communications of the ACM 42/2 (1999) 32–38.
22. Victor L. Voydock, Stephen T. Kent: Security Mechanisms in High-Level Network Protocols; ACM Computing Surveys 15/2 (1983) 135–171.
23. Gritta Wolf, Andreas Pfitzmann: Properties of protection goals and their integration into a user interface; Computer Networks 32 (2000) 685–699.

Cryptography 2000±10

Ueli Maurer

Department of Computer Science
Swiss Federal Institute of Technology (ETH), Zurich
CH-8092 Zurich, Switzerland,
maurer@inf.ethz.ch

Abstract. Cryptography is both a fascinating mathematical science and a key technology for the emerging information society, with theory and applications being closely related. This article reviews some highlights of the past ten years of research in cryptography and its applications and discusses some of the main challenges for future research.
A major future research theme is to weaken the assumptions on which security proofs are based, in particular computational intractability assumptions, trust assumptions, and physical assumptions. These assumptions must be made explicit. Computation and communication are physical processes rather than mathematically idealized objects, involving for example quantum phenomena. This fact could have a profound impact on cryptographic research and implementations.

1 Introduction

1.1 Scope of This Article

The task set to the authors of articles in this volume was to review the past ten years of research in their respective fields, and to speculate about possible developments in the next ten years. Due to space limitations and the mathematical nature of cryptography, it is impossible to include sufficient material for the paper to be a self-contained tutorial, nor a comprehensive overview of all important results of the past decade; the selection of topics is bound to be incomplete. The treatment is informal rather than technical, and the main focus is on identifying important issues and trends. We refer the newcomer to the books [65,75,85] and to Rivest's 1990 tutorial [73], which can also serve as a good point of reference for this article to address new developments in the decade since then.

1.2 Information Security

The emerging global information infrastructure has a dramatic impact on the economy and the society at large. One of the main paradigm shifts is that information is becoming a crucial if not the most important resource. Information differs radically from other resources; for instance, it can be copied without cost, it can be erased without leaving traces, and its value can change very rapidly depending on time and context. Protecting the new resource information is a major

R. Wilhelm (Ed.): Informatics. 10 Years Back. 10 Years Ahead, LNCS 2000, pp. 63–85, 2001.

issue in the information economy, in particular when considering the increasing exposure of information to all sorts of risks and attacks, including illegitimate access to information (e.g. network sniffing), modification or insertion of information (e.g. IP spoofing), denial of service attacks, traffic analysis, replay attacks, malicious software (e.g. viruses and Trojan horses), and even "social engineering".

Three basic security requirements are (1) hiding information, e.g. the content of a message (confidentiality), the identity of a user (anonymity), or the existence of information (steganography); (2) authentication of information; and (3) controlling access to information. More complex security requirements include the ability to prove facts related to information, for instance knowledge of a piece of information without revealing it (e.g. a password), or agreement to a piece of information (e.g. a digital contract). New applications like voting over the Internet, digital payment systems, the protection of personal privacy, the software piracy problem, distributed databases, or the protection of digital intellectual property lead to new and more complex security requirements. Many of them still remain to be identified.

One of the fundamental problems in information security is the distinction between "good" and "bad" information, for instance between good or malicious software or e-mail attachments, or between good or bad network traffic (e.g. through a firewall). This distinction problem (e.g. deciding whether a piece of software meets a given specification) is undecidable and therefore can generally not have a clean solution.

In contrast, cryptography[1] is generally used to solve well-defined problems with a clean solution (except for the fact that the security can usually not yet be rigorously proven). The power of cryptography is generally unleashed only when a problem is well-defined. Therefore, formalizing information security problems and determining whether a cryptographic solution exists is an important part of cryptographic research. In fact, some of the most important, and perhaps the most fascinating contributions in cryptographic research are intriguing and sometimes paradoxical solutions to certain information security problems for which, at first sight, no solution seems to exist. These outstanding contributions deserve mentioning in the first place of such an article (see Section 2).

1.3   History: From an Old Art to a Young Science

Cryptography, and even more so cryptanalysis, has played an important role in history, for instance in both world wars. We refer to [47,84] for very good accounts of the history of cryptography. Until after the second world war, cryptography can be seen as an art more than a science, mainly used for military applications, and concerned almost exclusively with encryption. The encryption

---

[1] The term cryptography is often used in a narrower sense, namely for the design of cryptographic systems, in contrast to cryptanalysis, the term used for breaking systems; cryptology is often used as the term that covers cryptography and cryptanalysis.

schemes were quite ad-hoc with essentially no theory supporting their security. In sharp contrast, modern cryptography is a science with a large variety of applications other than encryption, often implemented by sophisticated cryptographic protocols designed by mathematicians and computer scientists, and used primarily in commercial applications and critical components of the information infrastructure.

There are perhaps two single most important papers which triggered the transition of cryptography from an art to a science. First is Shannon's 1949 paper "Communication theory of secrecy systems" [80], a companion paper of [79] where the foundations of information theory are laid. Second, and even more influential, is Diffie and Hellman's 1976 paper "New directions in cryptography" [27], in which they describe their discovery of public-key cryptography.[2]

1.4   The Role of Assumptions and Trust

The security of every cryptographic system depends on certain assumptions. An obvious assumption, which is usually not stated explicitly, is that randomness exists, i.e. that the world is not deterministic. Note that quantum theory was the first major physical theory in which randomness is an inherent feature. Moreover, one implicitly assumes that random values can be independent. This implies, for instance, that telepathy does not exist, at least that it cannot be applied in a cryptographic context.

There are cryptographic systems[3] that no amount of computation can break. Such a system is called *information-theoretically secure*. However, most systems could theoretically be broken by a sufficient amount of computation, for instance by an exhaustive key search. The security of these systems relies on the computational infeasibility of breaking it, and such a system is referred to as *computationally secure*. Since no general and useful proofs of the computational difficulty of any problem (let alone a cryptographically significant one) are known (see Section 3), computational cryptography relies entirely on computational intractability assumptions.

Some security proofs are based on physical assumptions, for instance that quantum theory is correct, that certain devices are tamper-resistant, or that a communication channel is subject to a minimal noise level (see Section 9).

Other crucial assumptions made explicitly in cryptography are about the trustworthiness of certain entities and/or system components.

---

[2] Ralph Merkle had previously proposed ideas that cover the general concept of public-key cryptography, but his ideas, less cleanly formulated and hardly practical, went unnoticed for a while [67]. In the late 90's, the British government announced that public-key cryptography was originally invented at the Government Communications Headquarters (GCHQ) in Cheltenham in the early 70's (see [84]) by James Ellis and Clifford Cocks, including what became known later as the Diffie-Hellman protocol and the RSA system.

[3] e.g. the one-time pad that encrypts the binary plaintext sequence by adding (bitwise modulo 2) a completely random binary key sequence.

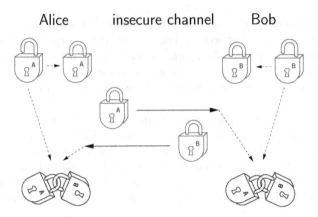

Fig. 1. Mechanical analog of the Diffie–Hellman key agreement protocol. The padlock stands for a one-way function, i.e. a function that is easy to compute but computationally infeasible to invert; it is easy to close the padlock, but infeasible to open it. Alice and Bob each choose a padlock in the open state (i.e. x_A and x_B, respectively) and produce the closed version (i.e. compute y_A and y_B, respectively). The closed locks are exchanged over an insecure channel. Thus both Alice and Bob can produce an identical configuration, namely the two padlocks interlocked, which the adversary cannot generate without breaking one of the locks.

The goal of cautious cryptographic design is to make these assumptions both explicit and as weak as possible. Reducing the necessary assumptions and trust requirements for achieving a certain security objective is a major theme of current and future research in cryptography.

2 Cryptography – Science of Paradoxes

Many cryptographic inventions are quite paradoxical. The first and best example of a paradox, mentioned in Section 1.2, is the discovery of public-key cryptography by Diffie and Hellman [27] who showed that two entities Alice and Bob, not sharing a secret key initially, can generate such a key by communicating solely over an authenticated but otherwise insecure channel.[4]

The protocol works as follows. Let G be a finite cyclic group with order $|G|$ generated by the element g, such that computing discrete logarithms in G to the base g (i.e., for a given $b \in G$, to compute $a \in \mathbf{Z}$ such that $g^a = b$) is computationally infeasible.[5] Alice and Bob secretly choose integers x_A and

---

[4] In fact, the most important feature of public-key cryptography is that it allows to exploit channels that are only authenticated but not confidential. Such channels were useless before public-key cryptography was invented.

[5] The discrete logarithms problem is today the most important cryptographic problem (e.g., see [76]). Whether it is feasible or infeasible depends on the group. The group

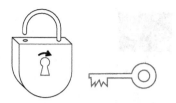

Fig. 2. Mechanical analog of a public-key cryptosystem. Encryption corresponds to closing the padlock, an operation anyone can perform, and decryption corresponds to opening the lock, which requires a secret key.

x_B, respectively, at random from the interval $[0, |G| - 1]$. Then they compute $y_A = g^{x_A}$ and $y_B = g^{x_B}$, respectively, and exchange these group elements over the insecure public channel. Finally, Alice and Bob compute $s_{AB} = y_B^{x_A} = g^{x_A x_B}$ and $s_{BA} = y_A^{x_B} = g^{x_B x_A}$, respectively. Since $s_{AB} = s_{BA}$, this quantity can be used as a secret key shared by Alice and Bob. A mechanical analog of the Diffie-Hellman key agreement protocol is shown in Figure 1.

Some other examples of paradoxical concepts in cryptography are described below. Diffie and Hellman in [27] also proposed the concepts of a *public-key cryptosystem* and of a *digital signature scheme*, but the first realization for both concepts was proposed by Rivest, Shamir, and Adleman [74] in 1978. Public-key cryptosystems (see the mechanical analog in Figure 2) are closely related to public-key key-agreement. A digital signature scheme allows a signer to generate a signature for a digital document such that everybody (including a judge) can verify such signatures but nobody can forge them.

The basic idea of the RSA system [74] is as follows. To set up the system one publishes a group (with its group operation) but keeps the order t of the group secret. Computing e-th powers (for some publicly known e) is easy, but computing e-th roots without knowledge of t is infeasible. Encryption (signature verification) hence corresponds to raising an element x of the group to a fixed known power e, $y = x^e$, whereas decryption (signature generation) corresponds to computing the e-th root of an element y, which can be achieved by computing $x = y^d$, where d is the multiplicative inverse of e modulo the order of the group: $de \equiv 1 \pmod{t}$. The group proposed in [74] is $\mathbf{Z}_n^*$, where $n = pq$ is the product of two large primes, with p and q being the secret key. The order of the group is $(p-1)(q-1)$ and can be computed if and only if p and q are known.

Blind digital signatures, proposed by Chaum [18] in 1983, allow a signer to digitally sign a message without even knowing (or being able to know) the message that he signs (see Figure 3.) Two applications are anonymous digital cash and certain types of voting schemes. RSA signatures can be issued blindly by multiplying the message m to be signed by r^e, where r is a random blinding factor, and letting the signer sign $\tilde{m} = r^e m$. The signature on $\tilde{m}$ is $\tilde{m}^d = $

---

operation proposed in [27] is multiplication modulo a large prime p; the corresponding group $\mathbf{Z}_p^*$ has $p - 1$ elements.

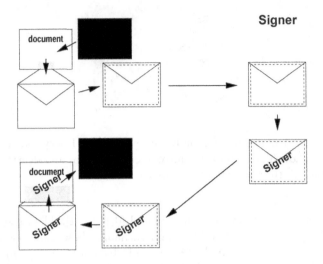

Fig. 3. Mechanical analog of a blind signature scheme. The recipient of the signature (left) puts the document to be signed into an envelope, together with a sheet of carbon paper. The signer (right) signs on the envelope, thus implicitly also signing the document inside.

$(r^e m)^d = r m^d$. The receiver of this signature can now divide by r to obtain the signature m^d on m.

Zero-knowledge interactive proofs, proposed by Goldwasser, Micali, and Rackoff [37] allow a prover, roughly speaking, to prove a statement (e.g. a mathematical theorem) to a verifier in such a way that the verifier learns nothing he did not know before (except that the statement is true) even if he misbehaves in the protocol. More formally, an interactive proof for a given statement (e.g. a mathematical conjecture) is a protocol between a prover and verifier, at the end of which the verifier makes a binary decision to either accept or reject the proof. If the statement is true, then the verifier accepts with overwhelming probability, and if the statement is false, no prover can make the verifier accept. That the verifier learns nothing means that he can simulate the entire transcript of the protocol, indistinguishable from a real execution of the protocol, without actually talking to the prover. A fundamental result states that every statement which has a conventional proof can also be proved interactively in zero-knowledge [34] (see also [15]).

Secure multi-party computation, another fascinating and paradoxical topic, will be discussed in Section 8.

3   Computational Complexity Theory

One of the main goals of complexity theory (see also Hartmanis' article in the this volume) is to prove lower bounds on the resources (e.g. time and/or space) needed to solve a certain computational problem. Cryptography can therefore be seen as its main "customer". While complexity theory has flourished and generated some beautiful and deep results, the needs of the very demanding customer have not even closely been met. The fundamental problems are still wide open.

To begin with, in order to be independent of the details of the computational model, the complexity is not defined for a specific function, but only for an infinite class of functions parameterized with a parameter k (e.g. the input size). The complexity is a function of k. In contrast to such asymptotic definitions, concrete cryptosystems (e.g. DES) are fixed and an asymptotic extension is usually not defined. Moreover, often one distinguishes only between polynomial and super-polynomial complexity, but a finer distinction is of course possible and desirable for concrete security statements and reductions.

Second, for the most part, classical complexity theory deals with worst-case complexity, a concept useless in cryptography where breaking a system must be hard for almost all instances, not just for some of them. Ajtai's celebrated worst-case average-case hardness result [1] was a break-through in the right direction. In cryptography even average-case complexity results are not sufficient: hardness almost everywhere is required.

Third, instead of proving the hardness of finding an exact solution to a computational problem, one would like to prove that even approximating the correct solution is hard. There has been substantial progress in complexity theory in this direction, initiated by Feige et al. [30], based on the theory of probabilistically checkable proofs (e.g., see [45]).

Fourth, the state of the art in lower bound proofs for the computational complexity of any NP-problem is devastating, even only for worst-case complexity. The best lower bounds are linear in the input size, which corresponds basically to the time needed to read the input. For example, in the circuit model of computation, a simple counting argument shows that almost all functions from n bits to 1 bit (i.e. $\{0,1\}^n \rightarrow \{0,1\}$) have circuit complexity $\Theta(2^n/n)$, but the best lower bound for any concrete function is only $3n$ gates [11]. Proving a lower bound of $4n$, let alone $n \log n$ or n^2, would be a major breakthrough.

Fifth, in 1994 the discussion about the right model of computation as the basis for complexity lower bounds was reopened when Peter Shor [81] showed that certain problems[6] can be solved in polynomial time on a quantum computer. While a quantum computer is still a theoretical model which may perhaps never be implemented at sufficiently large scale to be of practical interest, computer scientist need to rethink the concept of computation. Basically, any process consistent with the laws of physics should be considered a computation, not just steps on an idealized computational model like a Turing machine.

---

[6] in fact the two most relevant cryptographic problems, namely factoring integers and computing discrete logarithms.

From a cryptographic viewpoint, the most pressing research problem in complexity theory is to prove non-trivial lower bounds, perhaps polynomial[7], perhaps super-polynomial, on the complexity of breaking concrete cryptographic systems, for instance a one-way function.

4   Security Definitions

One of the major research achievements of the past decade or two is the precise definition of the security of many types of cryptographic schemes. Moreover, security proofs of a number of proposed schemes have been given, relative to some well-defined computational intractability assumptions. Some of these results will be mentioned in the corresponding sections below.

For example, an intuitive security definition for an encryption scheme could be that it is infeasible to compute the plaintext when given the ciphertext, without knowledge of the secret key. However, such a security definition is unsatisfactory for two reasons. First, it should be infeasible to compute any information about the plaintext, even to guess a single bit or Boolean predicate of the plaintext with success probability significantly greater than 50%. Second, this should be true even if the adversary can mount various attacks on the cryptosystem, for instance adaptively choose plaintext and receive the corresponding ciphertext, as well as choose ciphertext and receive the corresponding plaintext.

A security definition must specify two things: (1) the adversary's capabilities, i.e. the types of allowed queries to the system under attack and the computational resources, and (2) the task the adversary is required to solve in order to be successful. Strong security definitions are obtained when the adversary is assumed to be as powerful as possible and his task is as easy as possible.

A general methodology for defining the adversary's task is as follows: A purely theoretical *perfect system* is defined which (trivially) satisfies the desired security goals of the type of system under investigation. The adversary's task is defined as the simplest conceivable task, namely only to be able to distinguish between two possible settings: whether it interacts with the real cryptographic system or whether it interacts with the perfect system. If such a distinction is infeasible then, obviously, the real system has all the properties of the perfect system, at least for a computationally bounded observer.[8]

Let us discuss a few examples. The first definition of this kind, proposed by Blum and Micali [10] was for a *pseudo-random bit generator*. Such a generator generates an arbitrarily long sequence of bits, depending on a secret key (often

---

[7] Even if P=NP were proved, which would rule out the existence of secure cryptosystems in a classical complexity-theoretic framework, secure cryptography might still be possible within the realm of polynomial computation.

[8] To make this more formal, assume that each of the two systems is selected with probability 1/2. Then they are indistinguishable if for any efficient algorithm the probability of guessing correctly which one is used is only negligibly greater than 1/2. Negligible is usually defined as asymptotically decreasing (as a function of the security parameter) faster the inverse of any polynomial.

called the seed). It is defined to be secure if no algorithm not knowing the seed can efficiently distinguish the generated sequence from a truly random sequence.

For a block cipher one assumes that the attacker can, using an adaptive strategy, obtain the ciphertexts for chosen plaintexts, and vice versa. The perfect system for a block cipher is a random permutation on the input space, which would trivially be secure. Proving security of a block cipher would mean to prove that it cannot efficiently be distinguished from a random permutation, i.e. that it is a pseudo-random permutation [56].

The security of a *message authentication code (MAC)*[9] can be defined similarly, where the perfect system is a random function from the bit strings of finite length to the range of the MAC (e.g., the 64-bit strings).

A cryptographic scheme (say A) is often constructed from another, typically simpler cryptographic scheme (say B). Denote the combined system by $A(B)$. For instance, the CBC-MAC (e.g. see [4]) is based on a block cipher used in a special feedback mode. Let $\tilde{A}$ and $\tilde{B}$ be the perfect systems corresponding to A and B, respectively. Then the security proof for system $A(B)$, based on the assumption that system B is secure, often consists of the following two steps (although this is often not made explicit in the literature):

1. The proof that $\tilde{A}$ and $A(\tilde{B})$ are indistinguishable, even with infinite computing power, but with at most a polynomial number of queries. This proof is purely probability-theoretic or information-theoretic.
2. The trivial step that $A(\tilde{B})$ and $A(B)$ are computationally indistinguishable. (This follows from that fact that A would be a legitimate distinguisher for $\tilde{B}$ and B, and such a distinguisher cannot exist by assumption.)

The standard notion of security of a signature scheme, introduced in [38], is that after performing an adaptive chosen-message attack the adversary is not able to forge a signature for any message whatsoever not used during the attack.

The strongest security definition for a public-key cryptosystem, proposed by Rackoff and Simon, is semantic security against an adaptive chosen ciphertext attack [72]. The adversary is allowed to adaptively choose ciphertexts and obtain the corresponding plaintexts. His task is to specify two plaintexts m_0 and m_1 such that when he is given encryptions of m_0 and m_1 in random order, they are indistinguishable. Note that this security notion makes sense only for a probabilistic public-key encryption scheme; for a deterministic one (like RSA), the adversary can himself compute the (unique) ciphertext.

A more intricate security notion, introduced by Dolev, Dwork and Naor [29], is *non-malleability*, which captures the notion that it should be infeasible to modify a ciphertext even without knowing the plaintext, in any way that would have a predictable effect on the corresponding plaintext. For example, when given the ciphertext of a bid in an auction, it should be infeasible to come up with the encryption of a smaller bid, with success probability any greater

---

[9] A MAC scheme takes a secret key and a message and generates an authenticator value, often called the MAC. Without knowledge of the secret key it should be infeasible to compute the MAC for any message.

than without being given the ciphertext, even if it is not required to know the plaintext corresponding to the generated ciphertext. This definition shows that secrecy and independence are two separate issues in cryptography. However, it turns out that in the context of an adaptive chosen ciphertext attack, semantic security and non-malleability are equivalent [29].

5   Keyless Cryptographic Functions

Not all cryptographic schemes have a secret key. A *one-way function f* from a domain D to a range R is a fixed function that, roughly speaking, is easy to compute on all inputs but for which it is infeasible, for a y chosen at random from R, to compute an x such that $f(x) = y$. (It may be easy to compute many bits of such an x, but not the entire x.) One-way functions are probably the most fundamental primitive in complexity-based cryptography. Nothing is known about whether one-way functions exist, but intuitively it seems quite easy to design a one-way function. The best known provable result is by Hiltgen [40] who describes a function with linear circuit complexity and with a factor 2 between the complexity of computing the function and its inverse.

A very important class of one-way functions are *cryptographic hash functions*, where $D = \{0,1\}^*$ is the set of all finite-length binary strings and $R = \{0,1\}^k$ for some suitable k, e.g. $k = 128$. Cryptographic hash functions are used for many different purposes, including hashing of messages before signing them, pseudo-random bit generation (e.g, key derivation from master keys), message authentication codes, the conversion of a public-key based challenge-response identification protocol into a signature scheme, by replacing the challenge by a hash value, etc.

The usual definition of cryptographic security of a hash function h is *collision-resistance*, meaning that it should be infeasible to find two distinct inputs $x, x' \in \{0,1\}^*$ such that $h(x) = h(x')$.[10] Most hash functions were designed with collision-resistance as the design goal in mind. But note that each application places a different security requirement on the hash function, and the diversity of applications is enormous. It is an important research topic to determine which security properties are needed in which applications, and which properties can be achieved by a good implementation of a hash function. To avoid such application-dependent investigations, the *random oracle model* was proposed informally in [31] and more formally in [5]. A random oracle is a random function from $D = \{0,1\}^*$ to $R = \{0,1\}^k$, an idealized concept that does not exist in reality. Many system have been proved secure in the random oracle

---

[10] Note that this definition makes sense only when stated for a large class of functions, indexed by a randomly chosen but public parameter (which is given as input to the collision finder algorithm). For a single hash function there always exists a trivial collision finder, namely the algorithm that outputs a particular collision (x, x'). This is the general problem that one cannot define the difficulty of an instance of a problem (e.g., factoring a particular large integer), but only of a problem class (e.g. factoring integers).

model, but in [16] it was shown that this methodology is inherently problematic: a signature scheme was demonstrated which is secure in the random oracle model but insecure for every implementation of the random oracle by a class of hash functions.

There have been some impressive successes in the cryptanalysis of hash functions (e.g., see [28]).

6 Symmetric Cryptography

6.1 Cipher Design: Towards the Eternally Secure Cipher

A symmetric cryptosystem, called a *cipher*, is an invertible transformation, depending on a secret key, from the plaintext space to the ciphertext space. The first cryptographic algorithm designed to be published was the Data Encryption Standard (DES) standardized for U.S. government use in 1974. Although the design criteria for the S-boxes were never published, it has become clear that this is a master piece of cryptographic design, except for its very small key size of only 56 bits, which today, at best, is only marginally secure.

The second widely used cipher is IDEA, with a 128-bit key, designed by Lai and Massey [52]. One of its remarkable features is that it contains no tables like the S-boxes in DES, and hence the design of tables need not be justified. Instead, IDEA is based purely on the algebraic incompatibility of three group operations on the set of 16-bit strings: bitwise exclusive OR, addition modulo 2^{16}, and multiplication modulo $2^{16} + 1$, with 0 interpreted as 2^{16}. Since $2^{16} + 1$ is a prime number, this corresponds to the multiplicative group of the finite field $GF(2^{16} + 1)$.

Undoubtedly, the third single most important algorithm will become Rijndael [26], designed by Daemen and Rijmen and recently selected among 15 submitted proposals as the proposed new U.S. encryption standard, after a extensive evaluation by the international cryptographic community. The whole submission and evaluation process was one of the most remarkable cryptographic endeavors in the past decade.

The main research goal in symmetric cryptography, as mentioned earlier, would be to devise an encryption algorithm for which the security can be rigorously proven in a reasonable model of computation. This goal seems very far away. However, if one is satisfied without a complete security proof, the state of the art in cipher design is very good: It appears possible today to design a cipher that remains secure for eternity, even assuming that the entire energy and matter of the known universe is thrown at breaking the cipher, provided our present understanding of computation (including quantum computation) remains valid, that $P \neq NP$, and that the algorithm is implemented in a secure environment. Such a cipher would need to have a block size and a key size of a few thousand bits, and it could for instance be based on a combination of many known cipher design principles. In other words, in symmetric cryptography an ultimate victory of the codemakers over the codebreakers is possible.

6.2 Cryptanalysis

Looking back ten years, perhaps more remarkable than the mentioned new cipher proposals are the contributions to cryptanalysis of symmetric ciphers, which of course can also be interpreted as contributions to the design of secure ciphers. Some impressive generic cryptanalytic techniques are differential cryptanalysis of block ciphers invented by Biham and Shamir [8], linear cryptanalysis proposed by Matsui [58], correlation attacks on stream ciphers proposed by Siegenthaler, generalized by Meier and Staffelbach [63], and subsequently refined by many other authors, and Kocher's timing attacks [50] and differential power analysis [51] of cryptographic implementations (see Section 9). The first two have substantially improved our understanding of what constitutes a secure block cipher and have had a profound impact on all the proposals submitted to the AES competition.

6.3 Security Proofs

In this section we describe some of the results on various types of security proofs for symmetric cryptosystems.

One of the most important result on pseudo-random bit generators[11], due to Impagliazzo, Levin, and Luby [46,55], is that they can be constructed from any one-way function. This result is remarkable because a scheme satisfying a very strong notion of indistinguishability is constructed from a scheme for which the security notion is merely the infeasibility of computing a value satisfying a certain predicate.

One can prove that the cascade of several ciphers with independent keys is at least as secure as the first cipher, but not necessarily as secure as every cipher in the cascade [57].[12] While this result is less powerful for general cascades than one might hope, it implies that a cascade of commuting ciphers is as secure as the strongest component cipher. Fortunately, additive stream ciphers do commute, a potential advantage over block ciphers.

Luby and Rackoff [56] proved that one can construct pseudo-random permutations from pseudo-random functions [33], which is a function family indistinguishable from a random function. This paper, though much more complicated than necessary in retrospective, has initiated a substantial body of research, including the proof that the CBC-MAC is secure if the underlying block cipher is a pseudo-random function [4].

---

[11] Their main application is as the key stream generator in a so-called additive stream cipher, in which the pseudo-random bit sequence is added bitwise modulo 2 to the binary plaintext sequence. Stream ciphers are still widely used in military and government applications.

[12] In fact, one can give examples of ciphers [57] which are secure but become insecure when pre-cascaded with another cipher.

7   Public Key Cryptography and Digital Signatures

Public-key cryptography is more fascinating than symmetric-key cryptography because the paradoxical asymmetric functionality of a public-key scheme is much harder to achieve and requires substantial mathematical structure, for instance an algebraic group with special properties. Because there is no general design principle for finding such structure, only a limited number of public-key systems have been proposed, in contrast to the large number of proposed symmetric cryptosystems. We mention some of those proposed recently, without having space to describe them.

In addition to new public-key schemes, a number of new concepts were also proposed, for instance fail-stop signatures [71], undeniable signatures [20], and group signature schemes [21].

7.1   New Systems

At present, the discrete logarithm problem in a finite group is the most useful mathematical problem to base public-key cryptography on. A large number of schemes and protocols depend on it. Of particular interest are elliptic curves over finite fields (e.g., see [64]) because for general elliptic curves the fastest known discrete logarithm algorithm are the generic ones that work for any group (see Section 7.3), independently of the representation of the group elements.

In the quest for new public-key systems, several new mathematical principles were proposed as the basis of public-key schemes. The first was McEliece's 1978 proposal [62], based on the hardness of decoding general linear error-correcting codes.

Another important line of research is on multivariate cryptography. The basic idea is that each ciphertext digit is given as a low-degree multi-variate polynomial of the plaintext digits. The public key, consisting of these polynomials, contains a special hidden structure (the secret key) which can be used to decrypt, i.e. solve the system of equations. Several schemes were proposed and some were broken. For instance, Shamir's scheme [78] was broken in [23], and Patarin's hidden fields equations (HFE) scheme [70] was cryptanalysed in [48]. We refer to [49] for a discussion of some such algebraic cryptosystems.

Lattices[13] are playing an important role in cryptanalysis: many cryptosystems have been broken using lattice reduction techniques. Recently, a number of public-key cryptosystems were proposed based on hard problems on lattices, for instance finding the lattice point closest to a given point $P \in \mathbf{R}^n$. Among these are the Ajtai-Dwork scheme [2], the Goldreich-Goldwasser-Halevi scheme [32], and the NTRU scheme [44].

---

[13] An n-dimensional lattice is given by a set of n basis vectors in $\mathbf{R}^n$, and consists of all integer linear combinations of the basis vectors.

7.2   Cryptanalysis

Only three years after Lenstra's 1987 publication of the elliptic curve factoring algorithm [54], the last decade began with another big bang in factoring: the 1990 discovery of the number field sieve factoring algorithm [53] which drove the asymptotic running time for factoring a k-bit integer from $O(e^{(c+o(1))\sqrt{k \ln k}})$ for some c (for the quadratic sieve) down to $O(e^{(c+o(1))k^{1/3}(\ln k)^{2/3}})$ for some c. This algorithm was used to establish the impressive factoring record to date [17], RSA Inc.'s 512-bit factoring challenge. It can also be adapted to compute discrete logarithms modulo a prime number. In the past decade substantial progress in computational number theory was made, not only in factoring.

Some remarkable results in the cryptanalysis of public-key schemes were the sub-exponential discrete logarithm algorithm for super-singular elliptic curves due to Menezes et al. [66], the breaking by Vaudenay [86] of the Chor-Rivest cryptosystem, the various attacks against multivariate cryptosystems mentioned above, Bleichenbacher's attack on the RSA encryption standard PKCS #1 [9], and the Phong-Stern [69] attack against the Ajtai-Dwork scheme. This list is not complete.

7.3   Security Proofs

As mentioned earlier, Dolev et al. introduced non-malleability as a concept and also proposed a provably non-malleable but not practical public-key cryptosystem (based on an intractability assumption).

Shoup [82] proved that every generic discrete logarithm algorithm (i.e. one that works in any group) has complexity $O(\sqrt{q})$, where q is the largest prime factor of the group order. In [60] it is proved that one can construct groups for which breaking the Diffie-Hellman protocol is provably as hard as computing discrete logarithms, and this equivalence holds for any group if a plausible number-theoretic conjecture holds.

The Cramer-Shoup cryptosystem [25] was the first practical public-key scheme provably secure against adaptive chosen ciphertext attacks, based on the Decision-Diffie-Hellman assumption. This assumption states that it is infeasible in certain groups of large prime order to distinguish a Diffie-Hellman triple (g^a, g^b, g^{ab}) from a random triple (say (g^a, g^b, g^c)) of group elements.

In the past years, researchers have devised practical schemes provably secure against more powerful adversaries, but often the price was a stronger intractability assumption. Another such assumption is the so-called strong RSA assumption, namely that it is infeasible, for a given integer n with unknown factorization and a given random y, to find x and e such that $x^e \equiv y \pmod{n}$. Note that the regular RSA assumption is a weaker assumption because e is also fixed and hence there is less freedom in finding a solution. In the future we will have to prove the security of practical schemes for much weaker assumptions.

For several public-key schemes it was proved that computing certain bits of the secret (the plaintext or the shared key in case of the Diffie-Hellman protocol) is as hard as computing the entire value [3,13,39].

8 Cryptographic Protocols

Cryptographic protocols, often based on public-key functionality, are among the most delicate and fascinating topics in cryptography. In the past decade there has been an extensive research activity on various types of protocols, in particular on interactive proofs and zero-knowledge protocols (see Section 2), as well as on secure multi-party computation. For lack of space, we only discuss the latter.

Secure multi-party computation, introduced by Yao [87], enables a set of n players to compute an arbitrary agreed function of their private inputs. The correctness of the outputs and the secrecy of the players' inputs is guaranteed, even if any t of the players are corrupted by an adversary and misbehave maliciously. Surprisingly, this task is possible if $t < n/2$ [35], based on cryptographic intractability assumptions, and without such assumptions if $t < n/3$ [7,19], assuming the players are connected by pairwise secure channels.

After these fundamental results were published in the late eighties, multi-party computation has seen a revival in the late nineties. Some results are mentioned briefly. Efficient protocols for concrete problems were developed, for instance for voting [24,43], shared RSA key generation [12], and threshold public-key cryptosystems and signature schemes (e.g. see [83] and the references therein). Threshold adversaries were generalized to general adversary structures [41], and the efficiency of protocols that work for any function were improved from n^6 to n^3 per multiplication in the function specification [42].

9 The Role of Physics

Algorithms, both for using and breaking cryptographic systems, are traditionally modeled as mathematical objects, and therefore cryptography and cryptanalysis are traditionally seen as mathematical disciplines. However, all processes in the real world, including computation and communication, are physical processes involving noise, quantum effects, and other uncertainty factors. This fact can be used both for the benefit and detriment of cryptography.

On the negative side, two developments should be mentioned. The first is quantum computing, leading potentially to efficient methods for factoring large numbers and computing discrete logarithms [81] (see also Vitanyi's article in this volume). The second is the exploitation (by the cryptanalyst) of different types of side information channels which are available because a cryptosystem is implemented and embedded in a physical environment (e.g. a smart-card). Examples of such channels are the time required for a certain computation [50], the power consumption as a function of what is computed [51], electro-magnetic radiation, or the behavior of a device when faults are provoked, e.g. by setting the power level outside of the specifications, by physical stress, or by applying electro-magnetic fields.

Designing tamper-resistant devices with only low-capacity side channels is a core issue in security engineering. Cryptographic research must propose adequate models of side channels and resistant implementation techniques, for instance by masking key values or reordering the sequence of instructions. In addition, one should try to devise algorithms whose implementations can be inherently less vulnerable to side-channel attacks.

On the positive side, one can exploit the fact that an adversary does not know the exact state of a physical system. A first possible source of uncertainty for the adversary is the inherent impossibility of measuring quantum states exactly. For instance, one can measure at most one bit of information about the polarization of a photon, which is a continuous quantity. Quantum cryptography (e.g., see [6]) is the discipline that exploits this fact.

A second source of uncertainty for the adversary is the noise in communication channels. Cryptography is usually used in a context where error-free communication channels (e.g. a TCP connection) is available. In such a model, Shannon's theorem [80] applies which states that information-theoretic secrecy is possible only if, roughly speaking, the key is as long as the message. It was shown in [59] that by combining cryptographic coding and error-control coding, perfect information-theoretic secrecy can be achieved by public discussion between two parties not sharing a secret key initially, by exploiting information available to them as well as (even more reliably) to the adversary.

10   Applications and Politics

The potential of public-key cryptography for large scale applications, where classical key management is infeasible, was recognized immediately after its discovery. But neither the technology for implementing it efficiently, nor the market was there. Only around 1990, and in particular due to the success of the Internet after the mid-nineties, the commercial market for cryptography began to develop. But the market is still far from where it should be given the very strong current interest and need for cryptography in Internet-based applications.

Why is cryptography not yet built into every software product where this would be appropriate? The single most important reason is probably the U.S. export control regulation which, until very recently, did not allow U.S. companies to export cryptographic systems with keys longer than 40 bits, which is quite insecure.[14] One may ask why it makes sense to forbid the export of the source code of DES, as an example, when implementing DES is trivial. But the effect of the U.S. export restrictions was substantial: they prevented standardization from happening because U.S. companies had little interest in defining standards to allow the rest of the world to penetrate the growing global security market. Hence the National Security Agency's export control campaign can be seen as quite successful in reaching its goal, namely keeping secure systems away from

---

[14] This policy had some quite strange consequences. For example, Pretty Good Privacy (PGP) [88], a product of Network Associates, Inc., was exported from the U.S. in full compliance with the law, by publishing the source code as a book, legally exporting the book, and scanning it in Switzerland to reproduce a fully compatible version of PGP.

those the United States wants to be able to eavesdrop on. Cryptography will continue to be a political topic.

The first global success story of a cryptographic implementation was Phil Zimmermann's Pretty Good Privacy (PGP) e-mail encryption program [88], which since its release on the Internet in the early nineties was used by millions of users. The most remarkable feature of PGP is its key management concept, which allowed the Internet community to build a rudimentary public-key infrastructure (called by Zimmermann the "grass-roots approach") long before the term PKI became a buzz word in the commercial world.

Another success story is the Secure Socket Layer (SSL) protocol, designed by Netscape, which is now used in a large number of e-business applications. One of the most useful applications, solutions for which are studied theoretically but are still not surfacing in the marketplace, is a global secure payment system. The spectrum of technical possibilities is wide, ranging from secure privacy-enhanced funds-transfer systems to fully anonymous on-line or off-line digital cash (e.g., see [14]). Which types of system will prevail will depend more on the market forces than on technical issues. In fact, perhaps the greatest commercial failure of cryptographic solutions can be found in the payment arena: Digicash went bankrupt despite its technically innovative products. It is difficult to speculate about how long it will take until normal cash has more or less disappeared in the modern world, but I expect this to happen within the next 20 years.

The main requirement for cryptographic application to become universal is a global inter-operable public-key infrastructure (PKI). There exist many initiatives to build a PKI in certain application contexts, but it may take a number of years before a global PKI is available.

11   The Future of Cryptography

The crucial components of the emerging global information infrastructure will have to be systems that operate reliably and securely in a potentially highly adversarial environment. The dependence on information systems will increase strongly. Security breaches and system failures will not only be a nuisance and a cost factor, but will be intolerable, possibly major disasters.

Information security engineering involves many different disciplines, including most prominently cryptography. There is no doubt that cryptography will be a crucial discipline for the emerging information society. While security was in the past often seen as an expensive obstacle for IT projects, thanks to cryptography it is more and more perceived as an enabling technology, laying the basis for electronic commerce.

There is also a backside. The information society will depend strongly on the security of cryptographic schemes, in particular digital signature schemes. Cryptanalysis is therefore a potential source of major disasters. For instance, the discovery (and publication) of a fast factoring algorithm would be a catastrophe today, but in ten years it might be not much short of a collapse of the world economy, unless utmost care is taken in the design of future security systems, in the choice of cryptographic algorithms, and in legislation. Very cautious crypto-graphic design (for instance the parallel use of several signature schemes) is of paramount importance, especially because not only future transactions, but the validity of all existing signatures is in danger. Moreover, fall-back scenarios for the case that a cryptosystem is broken must be part of cryptographic design.

A major future research theme is to weaken the assumptions on which security proofs are based, and to make these assumptions explicit:

- *Computational intractability assumptions.* Given the lack of full-fledged complexity-theoretic security proofs we need to continue the nice research of the past decade on weakening these assumptions.
- *Trust assumptions.* As the important paradigm of secure multi-party computation shows, trust in one particular entity, person, software or hardware component can be reduced by distributed protocols involving several parties, only some of which need to be trusted.
- *Physical assumptions.* Computation and communication are physical processes involving noise, quantum effects, and other uncertainty factors. This fact can be used both for the benefit and detriment of cryptographic applications.

Acknowledgments

I would like to thank Cynthia Dwork, Ron Rivest, and Jacques Stern for interesting discussions on the past and the future of cryptography.

References

1. M. Ajtai, Generating hard instances of lattice problems, *Proc. 28th ACM Symposium on the Theory of Computing (STOC)*, pp. 99–108, 1996.
2. M. Ajtai and C. Dwork, A public-key cryptosystem with worst-case/average-case equivalence, *Proc. 29th ACM Symposium on the Theory of Computing (STOC)*, pp. 284–293, 1997.
3. W. Alexi, B. Chor, O. Goldreich, and C. Schnorr, RSA and Rabin functions: certain parts are as hard as the whole, *SIAM Journal on Computing*, vol. 17, no. 2, pp. 194–209, 1988.
4. M. Bellare, J. Kilian, and P. Rogaway, The security of the cipher block chaining message authentication code, *Advances in Cryptology - CRYPTO '94*, Lecture Notes in Computer Science, vol. 839, pp. 455–469, Springer-Verlag, 1995.
5. M. Bellare and P. Rogaway, Random oracles are practical: A paradigm for designing efficient protocols, *Proc. First ACM Conference on Computer and Communication Security*, pp. 62–73. Association for Computing Machinery, 1993.
6. C. H. Bennett, F. Bessette, G. Brassard, L. Salvail, and J. Smolin, "Experimental quantum cryptography," *Journal of Cryptology*, vol. 5, no. 1, pp. 3–28, Springer-Verlag, 1992.
7. M. Ben-Or, S. Goldwasser, and A. Wigderson, Completeness theorems for non-cryptographic fault-tolerant distributed computation, *Proc. 20th ACM Symposium on the Theory of Computing (STOC)*, pp. 1–10, 1988.

8. E. Biham and A. Shamir, Differential cryptanalysis of the Data Encryption Standard, New York: Springer-Verlag, 1993.

9. D. Bleichenbacher, Chosen ciphertext attacks against protocols based on the RSA encryption standard PKCS #1, *Advances in Cryptology — CRYPTO '98*, Lecture Notes in Computer Science, vol. 1462, pp. 1–12, Springer-Verlag, 1998.

10. M. Blum and S. Micali, How to generate cryptographically strong sequences of pseudo-random bits, *SIAM Journal on Computing*, vol. 13, no. 4, pp. 850–864, 1984.

11. N. Blum, A boolean function requiring $3n$ network size, *Theoretical Computer Science*, vol. 28, pp. 337–345, 1984.

12. D. Boneh and M. Franklin, Efficient generation of shared RSA keys, *Advances in Cryptology - CRYPTO '97*, Lecture Notes in Computer Science, vol. 1294, pp. 425–439, Springer-Verlag, 1997.

13. D. Boneh and R. Venkatesan, Hardness of computing the most significant bits of secret keys in Diffie-Hellman and related schemes, *Advances in Cryptology - CRYPTO '96*, Lecture Notes in Computer Science, vol. 1109, pp. 129–142, Springer-Verlag, 1996.

14. S. Brands, Electronic cash systems based on the representation problem in groups of prime order, *Advances in Cryptology - CRYPTO '93*, Lecture Notes in Computer Science, vol. 773, pp. 302–318, Springer-Verlag, 1994.

15. G. Brassard, D. Chaum, and C. Crépeau, Minimum disclosure proofs of knowledge, *Journal of Computer and System Sciences*, vol. 37, no. 2, pp. 156–189, 1988.

16. R. Canetti, O. Goldreich, and S. Halevi, The random oracle methodology, revisited, *Proc. 30th ACM Symposium on the Theory of Computing (STOC)*, pp. 209–218, 1998.

17. S. Cavallar et al., Factorization of a 512-bit RSA modulus, *Advances in Cryptology - EUROCRYPT 2000*, Lecture Notes in Computer Science, vol. 1807, pp. 1–18, Springer-Verlag, 2000.

18. D. Chaum, Blind signature systems, *Advances in Cryptology — CRYPTO '83*, p. 153, Plenum Press, 1984.

19. D. Chaum, C. Crépeau, and I. Damgård, Multiparty unconditionally secure protocols, *Proc. 20th ACM Symposium on the Theory of Computing (STOC)*, pp. 11–19, 1988.

20. D. Chaum and H. van Antwerpen, Undeniable signatures, *Advances in Cryptology - CRYPTO '89*, Lecture Notes in Computer Science, vol. 435, pp. 212–216, Springer-Verlag, 1990.

21. D. Chaum and E. van Heyst, Group signatures, *Advances in Cryptology — EUROCRYPT '91*, Lecture Notes in Computer Science, vol. 547, pp. 257–265, Springer-Verlag, 1991.

22. D. Coppersmith, M. Franklin, J. Patarin, and M. Reiter, Low-exponent RSA with related messages, *Advances in Cryptology - EUROCRYPT '96*, Lecture Notes in Computer Science, vol. 1070, pp. 1–9, Springer-Verlag, 1996.

23. D. Coppersmith, J. Stern, and S. Vaudenay, The security of the birational permutation signature schemes, *Journal of Cryptology*, vol. 10, no. 3, pp. 207–221, 1997.

24. R. Cramer, R. Gennaro, and B. Schoenmakers, A secure and optimally efficient multi-authority election scheme, *European Transactions on Telecommunications*, vol. 8, pp. 481–489, Sept. 1997.

25. R. Cramer and V. Shoup, A practical public-key cryptosystem provably secure against adaptive chosen ciphertext attack, *Advances in Cryptology — CRYPTO '98*, Lecture Notes in Computer Sc., vol. 1462, pp. 13–25, Springer-Verlag, 1998.

26. J. Daemen and V. Rijmen, The Rijndael block cipher – AES Proposal, see http:/csrc.nist.gov/encryption/aes/rijndael/.

27. W. Diffie and M. E. Hellman, New directions in cryptography, *IEEE Transactions on Information Theory*, vol. 22, no. 6, pp. 644–654, 1976.

28. H. Dobbertin, Cryptanalysis of MD4, *Journal of Cryptology*, vol. 11, no. 4, pp. 253–271, 1998.

29. D. Dolev, C. Dwork, and M. Naor, Non-malleable cryptography, *Proc. 23rd ACM Symposium on the Theory of Computing (STOC)*, pp. 542–552, 1991. (Also to appear in *SIAM Journal on Computing*.)

30. U. Feige, S. Goldwasser, L. Lovász, S. Safra, and M. Szegedy, Approximating clique is almost NP-complete, *Proc. 32nd Annual Symposium on Foundations of Computer Science (FOCS)*, pp. 2–12, IEEE Press, 1991.

31. A. Fiat and A. Shamir, How to prove yourself: practical solution to identification and signature problems, *Advances in Cryptology - CRYPTO '86*, Lecture Notes in Computer Science, vol. 263, pp. 186–194, Springer-Verlag, 1987.

32. O. Goldreich, S. Goldwasser, and S. Halevi, Public-key cryptosystems from lattice reduction problems, *Advances in Cryptology - CRYPTO '97*, Lecture Notes in Computer Science, vol. 1294, pp. 112–131, Springer-Verlag, 1997.

33. O. Goldreich, S. Goldwasser, and S. Micali, How to construct random functions, *Journal of the ACM*, vol. 33, no. 4, pp. 210–217, 1986.

34. O. Goldreich, S. Micali, and A. Wigderson, How to prove all NP statements in zero-knowledge, and a methodology of cryptographic protocol design, *Advances in Cryptology - CRYPTO '86*, Lecture Notes in Computer Science, vol. 263, pp. 171–185, Springer-Verlag, 1987.

35. O. Goldreich, S. Micali, and A. Wigderson, How to play any mental game – a completeness theorem for protocols with honest majority, *Proc. 19th ACM Symposium on the Theory of Computing (STOC)*, pp. 218–229, 1987.

36. S. Goldwasser and S. Micali, Probabilistic encryption, *Journal of Computer and System Sciences*, vol. 28, pp. 270–299, 1984.

37. S. Goldwasser, S. Micali, and C. Rackoff, The knowledge complexity of interactive proof systems, *SIAM Journal on Computing*, vol. 18, pp. 186–208, 1989.

38. S. Goldwasser, S. Micali, and R. Rivest, A digital signature scheme secure against adaptive chosen-message attacks, *SIAM Journal on Computing*, vol. 17, no. 2, pp. 281–308, 1988.

39. J. Håstad and M. Näslund, The security of individual RSA bits, *Proc. 39th IEEE Symposium on the Foundations of Computer Science (FOCS)*, pp. 510–519, IEEE Press, 1998.

40. A. Hiltgen, Constructions of feebly-one-way families of permutations, *Advances in Cryptology – Auscrypt '92*, Lecture Notes in Computer Science, pp. 422–434, Springer-Verlag, 1993.

41. M. Hirt and U. Maurer, Player simulation and general adversary structures in perfect multi-party computation, *Journal of Cryptology*, vol. 13, no. 1, pp. 31–60, 2000.

42. M. Hirt, U. Maurer, and B. Przydatek, Efficient secure multi-party computation, to appear in *Advances in Cryptology - Asiacrypt 2000*, Lecture Notes in Computer Science, Springer-Verlag, 2000.

43. M. Hirt and K. Sako, Efficient receipt-free voting based on homomorphic encryption, *Advances in Cryptology - EUROCRYPT 2000*, Lecture Notes in Computer Science, vol. 1807, pp. 539–556, Springer-Verlag, 2000.

44. J. Hoffstein, J. Pipher, and J. Silverman, NTRU: A ring based public key cryptosystem, *Algorithmic Number Theory (ANTS III)*, Lecture Notes in Computer Science, vol. 1423, pp. 267–288, Springer-Verlag, 1998.

45. S. Hougardy, H. J. Prömel, and A. Steger, Probabilistically checkable proofs and their consequences for approximation algorithms, *Discrete Mathematics*, vol. 9, pp. 175–223, North Holland, 1995.

46. R. Impagliazzo, L. Levin, and M. Luby, Pseudo-random generation from one-way functions, *Proc. 21st ACM Symposium on the Theory of Computing (STOC)*, pp. 12–24, 1989.

47. D. Kahn, *The code breakers, the story of secret writing*, MacMillan, New York, 1967.

48. A. Kipnis and A. Shamir, Cryptanalysis of the HFE public key cryptosystem by relinearization, *Advances in Cryptology - CRYPTO '99*, Lecture Notes in Computer Science, vol. 1666, pp. 19–30, Springer-Verlag, 1999.

49. N. Koblitz, *Algebraic Aspects of Cryptography*, Berlin: Springer-Verlag, 1998.

50. P. Kocher, Timing attacks on implementations of Diffie-Hellman, RSA, DSS, and other systems, *Advances in Cryptology - CRYPTO '96*, Lecture Notes in Computer Science, vol. 1109, pp. 104–113, Springer-Verlag, 1996.

51. P. Kocher, J. Jaffe, and B. Jun, Differential power analysis, *Advances in Cryptology - CRYPTO '99*, Lecture Notes in Computer Science, vol. 1666, pp. 388–397, Springer-Verlag, 1999.

52. X. Lai and J. L. Massey, A proposal for a new block encryption standard, *Advances in Cryptology – EUROCRYPT '90*, Lecture Notes in Computer Science, vol. 473, pp. 389–404, Springer-Verlag, 1991.

53. A. K. Lenstra, H.W. Lenstra, M.S. Manasse, and J.M. Pollard, The number field sieve, *Proc. 22nd ACM Symposium on Theory of Computing*, pp. 564–572, 1990.

54. H. W. Lenstra, Jr., Factoring integers with elliptic curves, *Annals of Mathematics*, vol. 126, pp. 649–673, 1987.

55. M. Luby, *Pseudorandomness and Cryptographic Applications*, Princeton University Press, 1996.

56. M. Luby and C. Rackoff, How to construct pseudorandom permutations from pseudorandom functions, *SIAM Journal on Computing*, vol. 17, no. 2, pp. 373–386, 1988.

57. J. L. Massey and U. Maurer, Cascade ciphers: the importance of being first, *Journal of Cryptology*, vol. 6, no. 1, pp. 55–61, 1993.

58. M. Matsui, Linear Cryptanalysis Method for DES Cipher, *Advances in Cryptology – EUROCRYPT '93*, Lecture Notes in Computer Science, vol. 765, pp. 386–397, Springer-Verlag, 1994.

59. U. Maurer, Secret key agreement by public discussion from common information, *IEEE Transactions on Information Theory*, vol. 39, no. 3, pp. 733–742, 1993.

60. U. Maurer and S. Wolf, On the complexity of breaking the Diffie-Hellman protocol, *SIAM Journal on Computing*, vol. 28, pp. 1689–1721, 1999.

61. K. S. McCurley, The discrete logarithm problem, in *Cryptology and computational number theory*, C. Pomerance (Ed.), Proc. of Symp. in Applied Math., vol. 42, pp. 49–74, American Mathematical Society, 1990.

62. R. J. McEliece, A public-key cryptosystem based on algebraic coding theory, DSN progress report 42–44, Jet Propulsion Laboratory, Pasadena, 1978.

63. W. Meier and O. Staffelbach, Fast correlation attacks on stream ciphers, *Journal of Cryptology*, vol. 1, no. 3, pp. 159–176, 1989.

64. A. J. Menezes, *Elliptic curve public key cryptosystems*, Kluwer Academic Publishers, 1993.

65. A. J. Menezes, P.C. van Oorschot, and S.A. Vanstone, Handbook of Applied Cryptography, Boca Raton: CRC Press, 1997.
66. A. J. Menezes, T. Okamoto, and S.A. Vanstone, Reducing elliptic curve logarithms to logarithms in a finite field, *Proc. 23rd ACM Symposium on the Theory of Computing (STOC)*, pp. 80–89, 1991.
67. R. Merkle, Secure communication over insecure channels, *Communications of the ACM*, vol. 21, no. 4, pp. 294–299, 1978.
68. R. Merkle, A certified digital signature, *Advances in Cryptology – CRYPTO '89*, Lecture Notes in Computer Science, vol. 435, pp. 218–238, Springer-Verlag, 1990.
69. P. Nguyen and J. Stern, Cryptanalysis of the Ajtai-Dwork cryptosystem, *Advances in Cryptology — CRYPTO '98*, Lecture Notes in Computer Science, vol. 1462, pp. 243–256, Springer-Verlag, 1998.
70. J. Patarin, Hidden fields equations (HFE) and isomorphisms of polynomials (IP): two new families of asymmetric algorithms, *Advances in Cryptology — EUROCRYPT '96*, Lecture Notes in Computer Science, vol. 1070, pp. 33–48, Springer-Verlag, 1996.
71. B. Pfitzmann and M. Waidner, Fail-stop signatures and their application, *Proc. SECURICOM '91*, pp. 145–160, 1991.
72. C. Rackoff and D. Simon, Noninteractive zero-knowledge proof of knowledge and chosen ciphertext attack, *Advances in Cryptology — CRYPTO '91*, Lecture Notes in Computer Science, vol. 576, pp. 377–391, Springer-Verlag, 1991.
73. R. L. Rivest, Cryptography, Chapter 13 in *Handbook of Theoretical Computer Science*, (J. van Leeuwen, ed.), MIT Press, 1990.
74. R. L. Rivest, A. Shamir, and L. Adleman, "A method for obtaining digital signatures and public-key cryptosystems," *Communications of the ACM*, vol. 21, no. 2, pp. 120–126, 1978.
75. B. Schneier, *Applied Cryptography*, Wiley, 2nd edition, 1996.
76. C. P. Schnorr, Efficient signature generation for smart cards, *Journal of Cryptology*, vol. 4, no. 3, pp. 239–252, 1991.
77. A. Shamir, IP = PSPACE, *Proc. 31st Annual Symposium on Foundations of Computer Science (FOCS)*, vol. I, pp. 11–15, IEEE Press, 1990.
78. A. Shamir, Efficient signature schemes based on birational permutations, *Advances in Cryptology – CRYPTO '93*, Lecture Notes in Computer Science, vol. 773, pp. 1–12, Springer-Verlag, 1994.
79. C. E. Shannon, "A mathematical theory of communication," *Bell System Technical Journal*, vol. 27, pp. 379–423, 623–656, 1948.
80. C. E. Shannon, "Communication theory of secrecy systems," *Bell System Technical Journal*, vol. 28, pp. 656–715, 1949.
81. P. W. Shor, Algorithms for quantum computation: discrete log and factoring, *Proc. 35th IEEE Symposium on the Foundations of Computer Science (FOCS)*, pp. 124–134, IEEE Press, 1994.
82. V. Shoup, Lower bounds for discrete logarithms and related problems, *Advances in Cryptology - EUROCRYPT '97*, Lecture Notes in Computer Science, vol. 1233, pp. 256–266, Springer-Verlag, 1997.
83. V. Shoup, Practical threshold signatures, *Advances in Cryptology - EUROCRYPT 2000*, Lecture Notes in Computer Science, vol. 1807, pp. 207–220, Springer-Verlag, 2000.
84. S. Singh, *The Code Book*, Fourth Estate, London, 1999.
85. D.R. Stinson, *Cryptography – Theory and Practice*, CRC Press, 1995.

86. S. Vaudenay, Cryptanalysis of the Chor-Rivest cryptosystem, *Advances in Cryptology — CRYPTO '98*, Lecture Notes in Computer Science, vol. 1462, pp. 243–256, Springer-Verlag, 1998.

87. A. C. Yao, Protocols for secure computations, *Proc. 23rd IEEE Symposium on the Foundations of Computer Science (FOCS)*, pp. 160–164, IEEE Press, 1982.

88. P. R. Zimmermann, *The Official PGP User's Guide*, MIT Press, 1995.

A Language-Based Approach to Security

Fred B. Schneider[1], Greg Morrisett[1], and Robert Harper[2]

[1] Cornell University, Ithaca, NY
[2] Carnegie Mellon University, Pittsburgh, PA

Abstract. Language-based security leverages program analysis and program rewriting to enforce security policies. The approach promises efficient enforcement of fine-grained access control policies and depends on a trusted computing base of only modest size. This paper surveys progress and prospects for the area, giving overviews of in-lined reference monitors, certifying compilers, and advances in type theory.

1 Introduction

The increasing dependence by industry, government, and society on networked information systems means that successful attacks could soon have widespread and devastating consequences. Integrity and availability now join secrecy as crucial security policies, not just for the military but also for the ever-growing numbers of businesses and individuals that use the Internet. But current systems lack the technology base needed to address these new computer-security needs [16].

For the past few years, we and others have been exploring the extent to which techniques from programming languages—compilers, automated program analysis, type checking, and program rewriting—can help enforce security policies in networked computing systems. This paper explains why this *language-based security* approach is considered so promising, some things that already have been accomplished, and what might be expected. But the paper also can be seen as a testament to research successes in programming languages, giving evidence that the area is poised to have an impact far beyond its traditional scope.

Section 2 discusses two computer security principles that suggest the focus on language-based security is sensible. Then, section 3 discusses the implementation of reference monitors for policy enforcement. Three language-based security paradigms—in-lined reference monitors, type systems, and certifying compilers—are the subject of section 4. Some concluding remarks appear in section 5.

2 Some Classic Principles

Work in language-based security is best understood in terms of two classic computer security principles [15]:

R. Wilhelm (Ed.): Informatics. 10 Years Back. 10 Years Ahead, LNCS 2000, pp. 86–101, 2001.

Principle of Least Privilege. Throughout execution, each principal should be accorded the minimum access necessary to accomplish its task.

Minimal Trusted Computing Base. Assurance that an enforcement mechanism behaves as intended is greatest when the mechanism is small and simple.

These principles were first articulated over twenty-five years ago, at a time when economics dictated that computer hardware be shared and, therefore, user computations had to be protected from each other. Since it was kernel-implemented abstractions that were being shared, security policies for isolating user computations were formulated in terms of operating system objects. Moreover, in those days, the operating system kernel itself was small and simple. The kernel thus constituted a minimal trusted computing base that instantiated the Principle of Least Privilege.

Computing systems have changed radically in twenty-five years. Operating system kernels are no longer simple or small. The source code for Windows 2000, for example, comprises millions of lines of code. One reason today's operating systems are so large is to support basic services (*e.g.*, windowing, graphics, distributed file systems) needed for the varied tasks they now perform. But another reason is performance—subsystems are no longer isolated from each other to avoid expensive context switches during execution. For example, the graphics subsystem of Windows is largely contained within the kernel's address space(!) to reduce the cost of invoking common drawing routines. So operating system kernels today constitute an unmanageably large and complicated computing base—a far cry from the minimal trusted computing base we seek.

Moreover, today's operating system kernels enforce only coarse-grained policies.

- Almost all code for a given machine is run on behalf of a single user, and principals are equated with users. Consequently, virtually all code runs as a single principal under a single policy (*i.e.*, a single set of access permissions).

- Many resources are not implemented by the operating systems kernel. Thus, the kernel is unable to enforce the policies needed for protecting most of the system's resources.

This *status quo* allows viruses, such as Melissa and the Love Bug, to propagate by hiding within an email message a script that is transparently invoked by the mail-viewer application (without an opportunity for the kernel to intercede) when the message is opened.[1] In short, today's operating systems do not and cannot enforce policies concerning application-implemented resources, and individual subsystems lack the clear boundaries that would enable policies concerning the resources they manage to be enforced.

---

[1] Because the script runs with all the privileges of the user that received the message, the virus is able to read the user's address book and forward copies of itself, masquerading as personal mail from a trusted friend.

Though ignored today, Principle of Least Privilege and Minimal Trusted Computing Base, remain sound and sensible principles, as they are independent of system architecture, computer speed, and the other dimensions of computer systems that have undergone radical change. Traditional operating system instantiations of these principles might no longer be feasible, but that does not preclude using other approaches to policy enforcement. Language-based security is one such approach.

3   The Case for Language-Based Security

A *reference monitor* observes execution of a target system and halts that system whenever it is about to violate some security policy of concern. Security mechanisms found in hardware and system software typically either implement reference monitors directly or are intended to facilitate the implementation of reference monitors. For example, an operating system might mediate access to files and other abstractions it supports, thereby implementing a reference monitor for policies concerning those objects. As another example, the context switch (trap) caused whenever a system call instruction is executed forces a transfer of control, thereby facilitating invocation of a reference monitor whenever a system call is executed.

To do its job, a reference monitor must be protected from subversion by the target systems it monitors. Memory protection hardware, which ensures that execution by one program cannot corrupt the instructions or data of another, is commonly used for this purpose. But placing the reference monitor and target systems in separate address spaces has a performance cost and restricts what policies can be enforced.

- The performance cost results from the overhead due to context switches associated with transferring control to the reference monitor from within the target systems. The reference monitor must receive control whenever a target system participates in an event relevant to the security policy being enforced. In addition, data must be copied between address spaces.

- The restrictions on what policies can be enforced arise from the means by which target system events cause the reference monitor to be invoked, since this restricts the vocabulary of events that can be involved in security policies. Security policies that govern operating system calls, for example, are feasible because traps accompany systems calls.

The power of the Principle of Least Privilege depends on having flexible and general notions of principal and minimum access. Any interface—not just the user/kernel interface—might define the objects governed by a security policy. And an expressive notion of principal is needed if enforcement decisions might depend on, among other things, the current state of the machine, past execution history, who authored the code, on who's behalf is the code executing, and so on.

Language-based security, being based on program analysis and program rewriting, supports the flexible and general notions of principal and minimum access needed in order the instantiate the Principle of Least Privilege. In particular, software, being universal, can always provide the same functionality (if not performance) as a reference monitor. An interpreter, for instance, could include not only the same checks as found in hardware or kernel-based protection mechanisms but also could implement additional checks involving the application's current and past states.

The only question, then, is one of performance. If the overhead of unadulterated interpretation is too great, then compilation technology, such as just-in-time compilers, partial evaluation, run-time code generation, and profile-driven feedback optimization, can be brought to bear. Moreover, program analysis, including type-checking, dataflow analysis, abstract interpretation, and proof-checking, can be used to reason statically about the run-time behavior of code and eliminate unnecessary run-time policy enforcement checks.

Beyond supporting functionality equivalent to hardware and kernel-supported reference monitoring, the language-based approach to security offers other benefits. First, language-based security yields policy enforcement solutions that can be easily extended or changed to meet new, application-specific demands. Second, if a high-level language (such as Java or ML) is the starting point, then linguistic structures, such as modules, abstract data types, and classes, allow programmers to specify and encapsulate application-specific abstractions. These same structures can then provide a vocabulary for formulating fine-grained security policies. Language-based security is not, however, restricted to systems that have been programmed in high-level languages. In fact, much work is directed at enforcing policies on object code because (i) the trusted computing base is smaller without a compiler and (ii) policies can then be enforced on programs for which no source code is available.

EM Security Policies

A program analyzer operating on program text (source or object code) has more information available about how that program could behave than does a reference monitor observing a single execution.[2] This is because the program text is a terse representation of all possible behaviors and, therefore, contains information—about alternatives and the future—not available in any single execution. It would thus seem that, ignoring questions of decidability, program analysis can enforce policies that reference monitors cannot. To make the relationship precise, the class of security policies that reference monitors can enforce was characterized in [17], as follows.

A *security policy* defines execution that, for one reason or another, has been deemed unacceptable. Let EM (for Execution Monitoring) be the class of security policies that can be enforced by monitoring execution of a target system and

---

[2] We are assuming that a reference monitor sees only security-relevant actions and values. Once the entire state of the system becomes available, then the reference monitor would have access to the program text.

terminating execution that is about to violate the security policy being enforced. Clearly, EM includes those policies that can be enforced by security kernels, reference monitors, firewalls, and most other operating system and hardware-based enforcement mechanisms that have appeared in the literature. Target systems may be objects, modules, processes, subsystems, or entire systems; the execution steps monitored may range from fine-grained actions (such as memory accesses) to higher-level operations (such as method calls) to operations that change the security-configuration and thus restrict subsequent execution.

Mechanisms that use more information than would be available only from monitoring a target system's execution are, by definition, excluded from EM. Information provided to an EM mechanism is thus insufficient for predicting future steps the target system might take, alternative possible executions, or all possible target system executions. Therefore, compilers and theorem-provers, which analyze a static representation of a target system to deduce information about all of its possible executions, are not considered EM mechanisms. Also excluded from EM are mechanisms that modify a target system before executing it. The modified target system would have to be "equivalent" to the original (except for aborting executions that would violate the security policy of interest), so a definition for "equivalent" is thus required to analyze this class of mechanisms.

We represent target system executions by finite and infinite sequences, where Ψ denotes a universe of all possible finite and infinite sequences. The manner in which executions are represented is irrelevant here. Finite and infinite sequences of atomic actions, of higher-level system steps, of program states, or of state/action pairs are all plausible alternatives. A target system S defines a subset Σ_S of Ψ corresponding to the executions of S.

A characterization of EM-enforceable security policies is interesting only if the definition being used for "security policy" is broad enough so that it does not exclude things usually considered security policies.[3] Also, the definition must be independent of how EM is defined, for otherwise the characterization of EM-enforceable security policies would be a tautology, hence uninteresting. We therefore adopt the following.

Definition of Security Policy: A *security policy* is specified by giving a predicate on sets of executions. A target system S *satisfies* security policy $\mathcal{P}$ if and only if $\mathcal{P}(\Sigma_S)$ equals *true*.

By definition, enforcement mechanisms in EM work by monitoring execution of the target. Thus, any security policy $\mathcal{P}$ that can be enforced using a mechanism from EM must be specified by a predicate of the form

$$\mathcal{P}(\Pi) : \ (\forall \sigma \in \Pi : \ \widehat{\mathcal{P}}(\sigma)) \tag{1}$$

where $\widehat{\mathcal{P}}$ is a predicate on (individual) executions. $\widehat{\mathcal{P}}$ formalizes the criteria used by the enforcement mechanism for deciding to terminate an execution that would otherwise violate the policy being enforced. In [1] and the literature on linear-time concurrent program verification, a set of executions is called a *property* if

---

[3] However, there is no harm in being liberal about what is considered a security policy.

set membership is determined by each element alone and not by other members of the set. Using that terminology, we conclude from (1) that a security policy must be a property in order for that policy to have an enforcement mechanism in EM.

Not every security policy is a property. Some security policies cannot be defined using criteria that individual executions must each satisfy in isolation. For example, information flow policies often characterize sets that are not properties (as proved in [10]). Whether information flows from variable x to y in a given execution depends, in part, on what values y takes in other possible executions (and whether those values are correlated with the value of x). A predicate to specify such sets of executions cannot be constructed only using predicates defined on single executions in isolation.

Not every property is EM-enforceable. Enforcement mechanisms in EM cannot base decisions on possible future execution, since that information is, by definition, not available to such a mechanism. Consider security policy $\mathcal{P}$ of (1), and suppose σ' is the prefix of some finite or infinite execution σ where $\widehat{\mathcal{P}}(\sigma) = true$ and $\widehat{\mathcal{P}}(\sigma') = false$ hold. Because execution of a target system might terminate before σ' is extended into σ, an enforcement mechanism for $\mathcal{P}$ must prohibit σ' (even though supersequence σ satisfies $\widehat{\mathcal{P}}$).

We can formalize this requirement as follows. For σ a finite or infinite execution having i or more steps, and τ' a finite execution, let

$\sigma[..i]$ denote the prefix of σ involving its first i steps
$\tau' \sigma$ denote execution τ' followed by execution σ

and define Π^- to be the set of all finite prefixes of elements in set Π of finite and/or infinite sequences. Then, the above requirement for $\mathcal{P}$—that $\mathcal{P}$ is *prefix closed*—is:

$$(\forall \tau' \in \Psi^-: \neg\widehat{\mathcal{P}}(\tau') \Rightarrow (\forall \sigma \in \Psi: \neg\widehat{\mathcal{P}}(\tau'\sigma))) \qquad (2)$$

Finally, note that any execution rejected by an enforcement mechanism must be rejected after a finite period. This is formalized by:

$$(\forall \sigma \in \Psi : \neg\widehat{\mathcal{P}}(\sigma) \Rightarrow (\exists i : \neg\widehat{\mathcal{P}}(\sigma[..i]))) \qquad (3)$$

Security policies satisfying (1), (2), and (3) are *safety properties* [8], properties stipulating that no "bad thing" happens during any execution. Formally, a property Γ is defined in [9] to be a safety property if and only if, for any finite or infinite execution σ,

$$\sigma \notin \Gamma \Rightarrow (\exists i: (\forall \tau \in \Psi: \sigma[..i]\, \tau \notin \Gamma)) \qquad (4)$$

holds. This means that Γ is a safety property if and only if Γ can be characterized using a set of finite executions that are prefixes of all executions excluded from Γ. Clearly, a security policy $\mathcal{P}$ satisfying (1), (2), and (3) has such a set of finite prefixes—the set of prefixes $\tau' \in \Psi^-$ such that $\neg\widehat{\mathcal{P}}(\tau')$ holds—so $\mathcal{P}$ is satisfied by sets that are safety properties according to (4).

The above analysis of enforcement mechanisms in EM has established:

Non EM-Enforceable Security Policies: If the set of executions for a security policy $\mathcal{P}$ is not a safety property, then an enforcement mechanism from EM does not exist for $\mathcal{P}$.

One consequence is that ruling-out additional executions never causes an EM-enforceable policy to be violated, since ruling-out executions never invalidates a safety property. Thus, an EM enforcement mechanism for any security policy $\mathcal{P}'$ satisfying $\mathcal{P}' \Rightarrow \mathcal{P}$ also enforces security policy $\mathcal{P}$. However, a stronger policy $\mathcal{P}'$ might proscribe executions that do not violate $\mathcal{P}$, so using $\mathcal{P}'$ is not without potentially significant adverse consequences. The limit case, where $\mathcal{P}'$ is satisfied only by the empty set, illustrates this problem.

Second, Non EM-Enforceable Security Policies implies that EM mechanisms compose in a natural way. When multiple EM mechanisms are used in tandem, the policy enforced by the aggregate is the conjunction of the policies that are enforced by each mechanism in isolation. This is attractive, because it enables complex policies to be decomposed into conjuncts, with a separate mechanism used to enforce each of the component policies.

We can use the Non EM-Enforceable Security Policies result to see whether or not a given security policy might be enforced using a reference monitor (or some other form of execution monitoring). For example, access control policies, which restrict what operations principals can perform on objects, define safety properties. (The set of proscribed partial executions contains those partial executions ending with an unacceptable operation being attempted.) Information flow policies do not define sets that are properties (as discussed above). And, availability policies, if taken to mean that no principal is forever denied use of some given resource, is not a safety property—any partial execution can be extended in a way that allows a principal to access the resource, so the defining set of proscribed partial executions that every safety property must have is absent. Thus we conclude that access control policies can be enforced by reference monitors but neither information flow nor availability policies (as we formulated them) can be.

4   Enforcing Security Policies

The building blocks of language-based security are program rewriting and program analysis. By rewriting a program, we can ensure that the result is incapable of exhibiting behavior disallowed by some security policy at hand. And by analyzing a program, we ensure only those programs that cannot violate the policy are ever given an opportunity to be executed.

That is the theory. Actual embodiments of the language-based security vision invariably combine program rewriting and program analysis. Today's research efforts can be grouped into two schools. One—in-lined reference monitors—takes program rewriting as a starting point; the other—type-safe programming languages—takes program analysis, as a starting point. In what follows, we discuss the strengths and weaknesses of each of these schools. We then discuss an emerging approach—certifying compilation—and how the combination of all three techniques (rewriting, analysis, and certification) yield a comprehensive security framework.

4.1   In-Lined Reference Monitors

An alternative to placing the reference monitor and the target system in separate address spaces is to modify the target system code, effectively merging the reference monitor in-line. This is, in effect, what is done by software-fault isolation (SFI), which enforces the security policy that prevents reads, writes, or branches to memory locations outside of certain predefined memory regions associated with a target system [20]. But a reference monitor for any EM security policy could be merged into a target application, provided the target can be prevented from circumventing the merged code.

Specifying such an *in-lined reference monitor* (IRM) involves defining [6]

- *security events*, the policy-relevant operations that must be mediated by the reference monitor;

- *security state*, information stored about earlier security events that is used to determine which security events can be allowed to proceed; and

- *security updates*, program fragments that are executed in response to security events and that update the security state, signal security violations, and/or take other remedial action (*e.g.*, block execution).

A load-time, trusted *IRM rewriter* merges checking code into the application itself, using program analysis and program rewriting to protect the integrity of those checks. The IRM rewriter thus produces a *secured application*, which is guaranteed not to take steps violating the security policy being enforced. Notice, with the IRM approach, the conjunction of two policies can be enforced by passing the target application through the IRM rewriter twice in succession—once for each policy. And also, by keeping policy separate from program, the approach makes it easier to reason about and evolve the security of a system.

Experiments with two generations of IRM enforcement suggest that the approach is quite promising. SASI (Security Automata SFI Implementation), the first generation, comprised two realizations [5]. One transformed Intel x86 assembly language; the other transformed Java Virtual Machine Language (JVML). Second generation IRM enforcement tools PoET/PSLang, (Policy Enforcement Toolkit/Policy Specification Language) transformed JVML [6].

The x86 SASI prototype works with assembly language output of the GNU gcc C compiler. Object code produced by gcc observes certain register-usage conventions, is not self-modifying, and is guaranteed to satisfy two assumptions:

- Program behavior is insensitive to adding stutter-steps (*e.g.*, nop's).

- Variables and branch-targets are restricted to the set of labels identified by gcc during compilation.

These restrictions considerably simplify the task of preventing code for checking and for security updates from being corrupted by the target system. In particular, it suffices to apply x86 SASI with the simple memory-protection policy enforced by SFI in order to obtain target-system object code that cannot subvert merged-in security state or security updates.

The JVML SASI prototype exploits the type safety of JVML programs to prevent merged-in variables and state from being corrupted by the target system in which it resides. In particular, variables that JVML SASI adds to a JVML object program are inaccessible to that program by virtue of their names and types; and code that JVML SASI adds cannot be circumvented because JVML type-safety prevents jumps to unlabeled instructions—these code fragments are constructed so they do not contain labels.[4]

The type-safety of JVML also empowers the JVML SASI user who is formulating a security policy that concerns application abstractions. JVML instructions contain information about classes, objects, methods, threads, and types. This information is made available (though platform-specific functions) to the author of a security policy. Security policies for JVML SASI thus can define permissible computations in terms of these application abstractions. In contrast, x86 code will contain virtually no information about a C program it represents, so the author of a security policy for x86 SASI may be forced to synthesize application events from sequences of assembly language instructions.

Experience with the SASI prototypes has proved quite instructive. A reference monitor that checks every machine language instruction initially seemed like a powerful basis for defining application-specific security policies. But we learned from SASI that, in practice, this power is difficult to harness. Most x86 object code, for example, does not make explicit the application abstractions that are being manipulated by that code. There is no explicit notion of a "function" in x86 assembly language, and "function calls" are found by searching for code sequences resembling the target system's calling convention. The author of a security policy thus finds it necessary to embed a disassembler (or event synthesizer) within a security policy description. This is awkward and error-prone.

One solution would be to obtain IRM enforcement by rewriting high-level language programs rather than object code. Security updates could be merged into the high-level language program (say) for the target system rather than being merged into the object code produced by a compiler. But this is unattractive because an IRM rewriter that modifies high-level language programs adds a compiler to the trusted computing base. The approach taken in JVML SASI seemed the more promising, and it (along with a desire for a friendlier language

---

[4] JVML SASI security policies must also rule out indirect ways of compromising the variables or circumventing the code added for policy enforcement. For example, JVML's dynamic class loading and program reflection must be disallowed.

for policy specification) was the motivation for PoET/PSLang. The lesson is to rely on annotations of the object code that are easily checked and that expose application abstractions. And that approach is not limited to JVML code or even to type-safe high-level languages. Object code for x86 could include the necessary annotations by using TAL [11] (discussed below).

4.2 Type Systems

Type-safe programming languages, such as ML, Modula, Scheme, or Java, ensure that operations are only applied to appropriate values. They do so by guaranteeing a number of inter-related safety properties, including *memory safety* (programs can only access appropriate memory locations) and *control safety* (programs can only transfer control to appropriate program points).

Type systems that support type abstraction then allow programmers to specify new, abstract types along with signatures for operations that prevent unauthorized code from applying the wrong operations to the wrong values. For example, even if we represent file descriptors as integers, we can use type abstraction to ensure that only integers created by our implementation are passed to file-descriptor routines. In this respect, type systems, like IRMs, can be used to enforce a wider class of fine-grained, application-specific access policies than operating systems. In addition, abstract type signatures provide the means to enrich the vocabulary of an enforcement mechanism in an application-specific way.

The key idea underlying the use of type systems to enforce security policies is to shift the burden of proving that a program complies with a policy from the code recipient (the end user) to the code producer (the programmer). Not only are familiar run-time mechanisms (*e.g.*, address space isolation) insufficiently expressive for enforcing fine-grained security policies but, to the extent that they work at all, these mechanisms impose the burden of enforcement on the end user through the imposition of dynamic checks. In contrast, type-based methods impose on the programmer the burden of demonstrating compliance with a given security policy. The programmer must write the program in conformance with the type system; the end user need only type check the code to ensure that it is safe to execute.

The only run-time checks required in a type-based framework are those necessary for ensuring soundness of the type system itself. For example, the type systems of most commonly-used programming languages do not attempt to enforce value-range restrictions, such as the requirement that the index into an array is within bounds. Instead, any integer-valued index is deemed acceptable but a run-time check is imposed to ensure that memory safety is preserved.

However, it is important to note that the need to dynamically check values, such as array indices, is not inherent to type systems. Rather, the logics underlying today's type systems are too weak, so programmers are unable to express the conditions necessary to ensure soundness statically. This is largely a matter of convenience, though. It is possible to construct arbitrarily expressive type systems with the power of any logic. Such type systems generally require sophisticated theorem provers and programmer guidance in the construction of a proof of type soundness. For example, recent work on dependent type systems [3,21] extends type checking to include the expression of value-range restrictions sufficient to ensure that array bounds checks may (in many cases) be eliminated, but programmers must add additional typing annotations (*e.g.*, loop invariants) to aid the type checker.

Fundamentally, the only limitation on the expressiveness of a type system is the effort one is willing to expend demonstrating type correctness. Keep in mind that this is a matter of proof—the programmer must demonstrate to the checker that the program complies with the safety requirements of the type system. In practice, it is common to restrict attention to type systems for which checking is computable with a reasonable complexity bound, but more advanced programming systems such as NuPRL [3] impose no such restrictions and admit arbitrary theorem proving for demonstrating type safety.

In summary, advances in the design of type systems now make it possible to express useful security properties and to enforce them in a lightweight fashion, all the while minimizing the burden on the end user to enforce memory and control safety.

4.3 Certifying Compilers

Until recently, the primary weakness of type-based approaches to ensuring safety has been that they relied on

High-Level Language Assumption. The program must be written in a programming language having a well-defined type system and operational semantics.

In particular, the programmer is obliged to write code in the high-level language, and the end user is obliged to correctly implement both its type system (so that programs can be type checked) and its operational semantics (so that it can be executed). These consequences would have questionable utility if they substantially increased the size of the trusted computing base or they reduced the flexibility with which systems could be implemented. But they don't have to. Recent developments in compiler technology are rapidly obviating the High-Level Language Assumption without sacrificing the advantages of type-based approaches. We now turn to that work.

A *certifying compiler* is a compiler that, when given source code satisfying a particular security policy, not only produces object code but also produces a *certificate*—machine-checkable evidence that the object code respects the policy. For example, Sun's `javac` compiler takes Java source code that satisfies a type-safety policy, and it produces JVML code that respects type-safety. In this case, the "certificate" is the type information embedded within the JVML bytecodes.

Certifying compilers are an important tool for policy enforcement because they do their job from outside the trusted computing base. To verify that the output object code of a certifying compiler respects some policy, an automated *certificate checker* (that is part of the trusted computing base) is employed. The certificate checker analyzes the output of the certifying compiler and verifies that this object code is consistent with the characterization given in a certificate. For example, a JVML bytecode verifier can ensure that bytecodes are type-safe independent of the Java compiler that produced them.

Replacing a trusted compiler with an untrusted certifying compiler plus a trusted certificate checker is advantageous because a certificate checker, including type-checkers or proof-checkers, is typically much smaller and simpler than a program that performs the analysis and transformations needed to generate certified code. Thus, the resulting architecture has a smaller trusted computing base than would an architecture that employed a trusted compiler or analysis.

Java is perhaps the most widely disseminated example of this certifying compiler architecture. But the policy supported by the Java architecture is restricted to a relatively primitive form of type-safety, and the bytecode language is still high-level, requiring either an interpreter or just-in-time compiler for execution.

The general approach of certifying compilation is really quite versatile. For instance, building on the earlier work of the TIL compiler [19], Morrisett *et al.* showed that it is possible to systematically build type-based, certifying compilers for high-level languages that produce Typed Assembly Language (TAL) for concrete machines (as opposed to virtual machines) [12]. Furthermore, the type system of TAL supports some of the refinements, such as value ranges, needed to avoid the overhead of dynamic checks. Nonetheless, as it stands today, the set of security policies that TAL can enforce are essentially those that can be realized through traditional notions of type-safety.

Perhaps the most aggressive instance of certifying compilers was developed by Necula and Lee, who were the first to move beyond implicit typing annotations and develop an architecture in which certificates were explicit. The result, called Proof-Carrying Code (PCC) [13,14], enjoys a number of advantages over previous work. In particular, the axioms, inference rules, and proofs of PCC are represented as terms in a meta-logical programming language called LF [7], and certificate checking corresponds to LF type-checking. The advantages of using a meta-logical language are twofold:

- It is relatively simple to customize the logic by adding new axioms or inference rules.

- Meta-logical type checkers can be quite small, so in principle a PCC-based system can have an extremely small trusted computing base. For example, Necula implemented an LF type checker that is about 6 pages of C code [13].

Finally, unlike the JVML or TAL, PCC is not limited to enforcing traditional notions of type safety. It is also not limited to EM policies. Rather, as long as the logic is expressive enough to state the desired policy, and as long as the certifying compiler can construct a proof in that logic that the code will respect the policy, then a PCC-based system can check conformance.

4.4   Putting the Technologies Together

Combine in-lined reference monitors, type systems, and certifying compilers—the key approaches to language-based security—and the sum will be greater than the parts. In what follows, we discuss the remarkable synergies among these approaches.

Integrating IRM enforcement with Type Systems. Static type systems are particularly well-suited for enforcing security policies that have been negotiated in advance. Furthermore, enforcement through static checking usually involves less overhead than a more dynamic approach. And finally, static type systems hold the promise of enforcing liveness properties (*e.g.*, termination) and polices that are not properties (*e.g.*, absence of information flow)—things that reference monitors cannot enforce. However, static type systems are ill-suited for the enforcement of policies that depend upon things that can be detected at runtime but cannot be ascertained during program development. Also, it may be simpler to insert a dynamic check than to have a programmer develop an explicit proof that the check is not needed. Consequently, by combining IRMs with advanced type systems, we have both the opportunity to enforce a wider class of policies and more flexibility in choosing an appropriate enforcement mechanism.

Extending IRM enforcement with Certifying Compilers. Program rewriting without subsequent optimization generally leads to systems exhibiting poor performance. However, an IRM rewriter could reduce the performance impact of added checking code by inserting checks only where there is some chance that a security update actually needs to be performed. For example, in enforcing a policy that stipulates messages are never sent after certain files have been read, an IRM rewriter needn't insert code before and after every instruction. A small amount of simple analysis would allow insertions to be limited to those instructions involving file reads and message sends; and a global analysis might allow more aggressive optimizations. Optimization technology, then, can recover performance for the IRM approach.

But an IRM rewriter that contains a global optimizer is larger and more complicated than one that does not. Any optimizations had better always be done correctly, too, since bugs might make it possible for the security policy at hand to be violated. So, optimization routines—just like the rest of the IRM rewriter—are part of the trusted computing base. In the interest of keeping the trusted computing base small, we should hesitate to employ a complicated IRM rewriter.

Must an IRM architecture sacrifice performance on the alter of minimizing the trusted computing base? Not if the analysis and optimization are done with the lesson of certifying compilers in mind. An IRM rewriter can add checking code and security updates and then do analysis and optimization to remove unnecessary checking code, provided the IRM rewriter produces a certificate along with the modified object code. That certificate should describe what code was added everywhere and the analysis that allowed code to be deleted, thereby enabling a certificate checker (in the trusted computing base) to establish independently that the output of the IRM rewriter will indeed never violate the security policy of interest. Thus, the IRM rewriter is extended if ideas from certifying compilers are adopted.

Extending Certifying Compilers with IRM enforcement. Certifying compilers are limited to analysis that can be done automatically. And, unfortunately, there are deep mathematical reasons why certain program analysis cannot be automated—analysis that would be necessary for policies much simpler than found in class EM. Must a certifying compiler architecture sacrifice expressiveness on the alter of automation?

In theory, it would seem so. But in practice, much analysis becomes possible when program rewriting is first allowed. This is an instance of the familiar tradeoff between static and dynamic checks during type checking. For instance, rather than verifying at compile time that a given array index never goes out of bounds, it is a simple matter to have the compiler emit a run-time check. Static analysis of the modified program is guaranteed to establish that the array access is never out of bounds (because the added check prevents it from being so).

The power of a certifying compilers is thus amplified by the capacity to do program rewriting. In the limit, what is needed is the means to modify a program and obtain one in which a given security policy is not violated—exactly what an IRM rewriter does. Thus, the power of certifying compilers is extended if deployed in concert with an IRM rewriter.

5   Concluding Remarks

In-lined reference monitors, certifying compilers, and advanced type systems are promising approaches to system security. Each allows rich instantiations of the Principle of Least Privilege; each depends on only a minimal trusted computing base, despite the ever-growing sizes for today's operating systems, compilers, and programming environments.

The idea of using languages and compilers to help enforce security policies is not new. The Burroughs B-5000 system required applications to be written in a high-level language (Algol), and the Berkeley SDS-940 system employed object-code rewriting as part of its system profiler. More recently, the SPIN [2], Vino [22,18], and Exokernel [4] extensible operating systems have relied on language technology to protect a base system from a limited set of attacks by extensions.

What is new in so-called language-based security enforcement is the degree to which language semantics provides the leverage. The goal is to obtain integrated mechanisms that work for both high-level and low-level languages; that are applicable to an extremely broad class of fine-grained security policies; and that allow flexible allocation of work and trust among the elements responsible for enforcement.

Acknowledgments

The views and conclusions contained herein are those of the authors and should not be interpreted as necessarily representing the official policies or endorsements, either expressed or implied, of these organizations or the U.S. Government.

Schneider is supported in part by ARPA/RADC grant F30602-96-1-0317, AFOSR grant F49620-00-1-0198, Defense Advanced Research Projects Agency (DARPA) and Air Force Research Laboratory Air Force Material Command USAF under agreement number F30602-99-1-0533, National Science Foundation Grant 9703470, and a grant from Intel Corporation.

Morrisett is supported in part by AFOSR grant F49620-00-1-0198, and the National Science Foundation under Grant No. EIA 97-03470.

Harper is sponsored by the Advanced Research Projects Agency CSTO under the title "The Fox Project: Advanced Languages for Systems Software", ARPA Order No. C533, issued by ESC/ENS under Contract No. F19628-95-C-0050.

References

1. B. Alpern and F.B. Schneider. Defining liveness. *Information Processing Letters* 21(4):181–185, Oct. 1985.
2. B. Bershad, S. Savage, P. Pardyak, E. Sirer, M. Fiuczynski, D. Becker, C. Chambers, and S. Eggers. Extensibility, safety and performance in the SPIN operating system. In *Proc. 15th ACM Symp. on Operating System Principles (SOSP)*, pages 267–284, Copper Mountain, Dec. 1995.
3. R. L. Constable *et al. Implementing Mathematics with the NuPRL Proof Development System.* Prentice-Hall, 1986.
4. D. Engler, M. Kaashoek, and J. O'Toole. Exokernel: An operating system architecture for application-level resource management. In *Proc. 15th ACM Symp. on Operating System Principles (SOSP)*, Copper Mountain, 1995.
5. U. Erlingsson and F. B. Schneider. SASI enforcement of security policies: A retrospective. In *Proceedings of the New Security Paradigms Workshop*, Ontario, Canada, Sept. 1999.
6. U. Erlingsson and F. B. Schneider. IRM enforcement of java stack inspection. In *IEEE Symposium on Security and Privacy*, Oakland, California, May 2000.
7. R. Harper, F. Honsell, and G. Plotkin. A framework for defining logics. *Journal of the ACM*, 40(1):143–184, Jan. 1993.
8. L. Lamport. Proving the correctness of multiprocess programs. *IEEE Transactions on Software Engineering*, SE-3(2):125–143, March 1977.
9. L. Lamport. Logical Foundation. In *Distributed Systems-Methods and Tools for Specification*, pages 119-130, Lecture Notes in Computer Science, Vol 190. M. Paul and H.J. Siegert, editors. Springer-Verlag, 1985, New York.
10. J. McLean. A general theory of composition for trace sets closed under selective interleaving functions. In *Proc. 1994 IEEE Computer Society Symposium on Research in Security and Privacy*, pages 79–93, Oakland, Calif., May 1994.
11. G. Morrisett, D. Walker, K. Crary, and N. Glew. From System F to typed assembly language. In *Proc. 25th ACM Symp. on Principles of Programming Languages (POPL)*, pages 85–97, San Diego California, USA, January 1998.
12. G. Morrisett, D. Walker, K. Crary, and N. Glew. From System F to typed assembly language. *ACM Transactions on Programming Languages and Systems*, 21(3):528–569, May 1999.

13. G. C. Necula and P. Lee. Safe kernel extensions without run-time checking. In *Proceedings of Operating System Design and Implementation*, pages 229–243, Seattle, Oct. 1996.

14. G. C. Necula. Proof-carrying code. In *Proc. 24th ACM Symp. on Principles of Programming Languages (POPL)*, pages 106–119, Jan. 1997.

15. J. Saltzer and M. Schroeder. The protection of information in computer systems. *Proceedings of the IEEE*, 9(63), Sept. 1975.

16. F. B. Schneider, editor. *Trust in Cyberspace*. National Academy Press, Washington, D.C., 1999.

17. F. B. Schneider. Enforceable security policies. *ACM Transactions on Information and System Security*, 2(4), Mar. 2000.

18. M. Seltzer, Y. Endo, C. Small, and K. Smith. Dealing with disaster: Surviving misbehaved kernel extensions. In *Proc. USENIX Symp. on Operating Systems Design and Implementation (OSDI)*, pages 213–227, Seattle, Washington, Oct. 1996.

19. D. Tarditi, G. Morrisett, P. Cheng, C. Stone, R. Harper, and P. Lee. TIL: A type-directed optimizing compiler for ML. In *ACM Conf. on Programming Language Design and Implementation*, pages 181–192, Philadelphia, May 1996.

20. R. Wahbe, S. Lucco, T. Anderson, and S. Graham. Efficient software-based fault isolation. In *Proc. 14th ACM Symp. on Operating System Principles (SOSP)*, pages 203–216, Asheville, Dec. 1993.

21. H. Xi and F. Pfenning. Eliminating array bound checking through dependent types. In *Proc. ACM SIGPLAN Conference on Programming Language Design and Implementation (PLDI)*, pages 249–257, Montreal Canada, June 1998.

22. E. Yasuhiro, J. Gwertzman, M. Seltzer, C. Small, K. A. Smith, and D. Tang. VINO: The 1994 fall harvest. Technical Report TR-34-94, Harvard Computer Center for Research in Computing Technology, 1994.

Software Engineering
in the Years 2000 Minus and Plus Ten

Jochen Ludewig

Stuttgart University, Germany
Breitwiesenstr. 20-22, D 70565 Stuttgart
http://www.informatik.uni-stuttgart.de/ifi/se/people/ludewig.html

Abstract. Software engineering is what is being done everywhere in the world where people ("software engineers") develop, or modify, software. Good software engineering is not too common.

Researchers in the field of software engineering often fail to address the problems software engineers actually have. They have lost contact to the practitioners, while many practitioners never expected to benefit from research, and never tried to. Therefore, many well-known problems are still waiting for solutions, as the results of a Dagstuhl-Seminar in 1999 indicate.

The situation of software engineers has not changed significantly since 1990, except for their equipment, and there is no reason to believe that there will be far more changes in the next decade. In order to improve the general level of software engineering, more emphasis should be put on education, and on close co-operation of software engineers and researchers.

1 What Is Software Engineering?

The term "software engineering" was introduced by F.L. Bauer in 1968; in a conference at Garmisch, Bavaria, he made his now famous comment (see Bauer, 1993):

> *The whole trouble comes from the fact that there is so much tinkering with software. It is not made in a clean fabrication process, which it should be. What we need, is **software engineering**.*

As several pioneers of the field pointed out in a Dagstuhl-Seminar in 1996 (Aspray, Keil-Slawik, Parnas, 1996), the real history of software engineering did not start before the seventies, when Bauer, Boehm and others published papers on that subject. Several authors and committees tried to define "software engineering". Here is the definition offered by the IEEE-Computer Society (Standard Glossary of Software Engineering Terminology, IEEE Std. 610.12, 1990)

---

software engineering
(1) The application of a systematic, disciplined, quantifiable approach to the development, operation, and maintenance of software; that is, the application of engineering to software.
(2) The study of approaches as in (1).

R. Wilhelm (Ed.): Informatics. 10 Years Back. 10 Years Ahead, LNCS 2000, pp. 102-111, 2001.

Quite obviously, this is *not* a definition, but a goal. Otherwise, we should confess that very little software engineering is being practised, because only very few people in the world meet all the criteria listed in the "definition". It is like defining a marriage as a contract between two people of different sex, which guarantees happiness at any time as long as both are alive: The definition is beautiful, except that you will not find too many married people then.

Definitions should not be confused with judgements or commandments. Therefore, I prefer the following one:

> **software engineering**
> Any activity related to the production or modification of software pursuing some goal(s) beyond the software itself.

This definition allows for good and bad software engineering, it includes successful projects as well as failures, and it is very appropriate for all the work that is actually being done. In short: software engineering is taking place **everywhere in the world**.

Software engineering as done in **universities** and **research centres** is included, but only as an extremely small fraction.

2   The Current State of Software Engineering

2.1   The State of Practice

Broad investigations on the actual state of software engineering are rarely done; collecting the information is a huge effort, while few people appreciate the results. Zelkowitz et al. (1984) showed that there was a large gap of ca. 15 years between the state of the art, as known to the experts, and the actual practice. Beck and Perkins (1983) did a similar survey about the local industry[1] in Texas. Though those papers were written almost twenty years ago, their content is still consistent with the author's recent observations in many contacts with industry; maybe the gap is larger now. New techniques are widely accepted, though after a considerable delay, if and only if they are wrapped in tools and programming environments. Object oriented programming is a good example. People will reluctantly switch to a new programming language provided it looks like the old one. But even when new ideas are adopted, it is not at all clear that the concepts are really well understood.

Changing the process is much harder, because it needs a change of behaviour. Many well-established techniques that have been around for 20 years or more are still not applied in a majority of sites where software is being developed. Software requirements engineering and software quality assurance are examples. We do know that the requirements specifications are extremely important, and we know how they can be done. Still, decent specs are everything but normal. The same is true about

---

[1] "industry" and "software industry", as I use the words, include all companies where software is developed or modified, e.g. banks and insurance companies and possibly even the administration.

software reviews. We know they work, and we know that a high return on investment is guaranteed. But far from all people use them, and many of those who do do it badly.

It seems that the software industry is in a situation where many can survive even though they ignore most of the wisdom that has been collected in the field of software engineering.

Proposition 1: Large parts of the software industry are far behind the state of the art. They feel quite comfortable that way, and do not try hard to recover their backlog.

2.2   The State of Research

When it all began in the seventies, software engineering research was a new and exciting area. Starting from the software life cycle as published by Royce (1970), deficiencies were identified and attacked. Since the central part of the life cycle, i.e. coding and compilation, was well understood already, research concentrated on the early phases (requirements specifications and design, cost estimation) and on the late phases (test and integration). B.W. Boehm contributed very important empirical data. Many of the papers written in those days are still worth reading, and if they would be studied as often as they are quoted, they would still be very useful and influential.

But those early results were more or less ignored in practice. Information hiding (Parnas, 1972) was a great idea, well known to the academics, and soon supported by new programming languages like MODULA-2 (1978) and ADA (1980). But in industry, few people knew about information hiding, and if they did, they had no chance to use it because they had to use archaic programming languages like COBOL or FORTRAN or PL/I. The achievements were published, but not adopted in practice.

For the researchers, this posed a difficult problem. When your results are ignored, what can you do?

(a)   You can try to convince the practitioners that your achievements are indeed very useful for them. In particular, you can participate in real projects, and help them by coaching and consulting.

(b)   You can ignore the practitioners by continuing your research despite the fact that any results are definitely useless for them because they have not even made the first steps towards improvement yet.

(a) is highly desirable, but not very promising for the researchers. If the practitioners do not care for any advantages they might reap, they will not care for coaching and consulting either. Furthermore, transferring know how and coaching people in industry is not considered scientific work, and it does not contribute to a traditional academic career.

Therefore, most researchers chose (b). Since funding was never based on actual success outside academia, but on scientific value, as it is recognised by other scientists, this decision was safe. Software engineering research became a theatre performance without an audience, but on stage every night. Since the absent audience did not miss anything, nobody would complain.

> **Proposition 2**: Most of current software engineering research
> - is not related to the problems practical software engineers suffer from
> - is aiming at solving problems nobody has encountered yet
> - produces results that cannot be applied by average software people

When researchers use the word "software engineering", they often have their research topics in mind rather than the situation in industry. Many people in academia do not even know the situation in industry, because they have never left their castles.

In short: **software engineering** has a meaning for those who actually do it, but a very different meaning for those who teach it, and do research.

2.3   Who Is to Blame?

Both sides are, or nobody is. Growth and profit are, at least for the time being, more important than soundness and stability. One of the reasons that Bill Gates could make such a fortune within a couple of years is that he never endangered himself by granting priority to good quality. His decision was unpleasant for those who believe in traditional values, but it was highly successful from an economical point of view.

On the other hand, researchers cannot be expected to hibernate until their previous results have been sucked up by the industry. They have to proceed, whether or not the crowd is following.

> **Proposition 3**: Much effort is wasted both in research and in industry because they do not co-operate as they should, and could.
> In order to increase the mutual benefits, researchers should check their solutions for applicability. Practitioners should make sure that they collect all the data necessary for process assessment and process improvements.

2.4   Results of the Dagstuhl-Seminar "Software Engineering Research and Education: Seeking a New Agenda"

Those who regard themselves as ferry men between research and practice cannot be satisfied by the current state. Some of them met at Dagstuhl (Dagstuhl-Seminar 99071, February 14-19, 1999) in order to *"take stock of software engineering research and education"*, and to answer the questions *"What do we know? What should we know?"* (quotations from the call for participation).

The workshop was organised by Dan Hoffman and David L. Parnas in Canada, Ernst Denert and Jochen Ludewig in Germany. The other participants were Joanne Atlee, Motoei Azuma, Wolfram Bartussek, Jan Bredereke, Karol Frühauf, Martin Glinz, Heinrich Hußmann, Pankaj Jalote, Ridha Khedri, Peter Knoke, Stefan Krauß, Lutz Prechelt, Johannes Siedersleben, Paul Strooper, Walter Tichy, David Weiss, and Andreas Zeller.

As part of the announcement and invitation, a list of eleven suggested tasks was distributed, ranging from "Analyse intended application, write requirements documents." to "Revise and enhance software systems." Those who intended to participate were asked to submit a position paper on at least one of the subjects, and to judge the current state of all the subjects.

At the beginning of the workshop, participants reduced and modified the topics for various reasons, until nine topics were selected for discussion and elaboration. The topics and the most fundamental questions related to these topics are listed bel ow.

For each topic, one of the participants was selected as the "secretary". Most attendees participated in two of the subgroups. Plenary meetings were held once or twice the day, allowing for critical discussions and feedback.

All results were (almost) uniformly cast into tables, using criteria and attributes that had been agreed in the plenary meetings. These schematic judgements were often complemented by remarks.

2.5   The Topics

Below, all topics are listed, together with some findings. The names in the headers designate the secretaries. See the workshop report (Denert et al., 1999) for a complete documentation.

(1) Requirements (Joanne Atlee)
How can we analyse the intended application to determine the requirements that must be satisfied? How should we record those requirements in a precise, well organised and easily used document?

In practice, this goal is rarely achieved. In most projects, a significant number of software development errors can be traced back to incomplete or misunderstood requirements.

We need to improve the state of requirements engineering by improving our application of existing practices and techniques, evaluating the strengths and weaknesses of the existing practices and techniques, and developing new practices and techniques where the existing ones do not suffice.

(2) Software Design (Johannes Siedersleben)
How can we design the basic structures of the software, evaluate competing design alternatives, and reuse existing designs whenever possible?

Participants felt that the design task is solved at the level of individual modules, but not solved at the level of system architecture. Designing system architectures, the known techniques are not sufficient. Another important question is how to relate different levels of abstraction in a large system.

We need a collection of architectural patterns, i.e. proven architectural building blocks aimed at particular problems, possibly domain-specific.

(3) Implementation (Peter Knoke)
The problem is that the quality of the software implementation (i.e. the code) is generally not as good as it could be, and should be. How can this situation be improved by various means, including teaching, research, or other means?

The participants agreed in the importance of this field that is often neglected in higher education. Good programming is not that easy; it should be taught, and it should be generally recognised.

There is little need for research in this area, but education should be greatly improved, emphasising good craftsmanship.

(4) COTS (Commercial-Off-the-Shelf) (Paul Strooper)

In many software projects, we can save time and/or effort by using standard software (COTS) instead of implementing new software from scratch. But using COTS has significant implications on the development process.

There are serious problems with the integration of COTS software, and there is a lack of documented solutions and experience reports dealing with these problems. It was therefore concluded that the problem of integrating COTS products into software products is mainly unsolved, except for small-scale COTS products, such as GUI and component libraries.

(5) Test (Dan Hoffman)

How can we perform systematic or statistical testing of the software and the integrated computer system?

Many companies do no systematic testing. Some companies do perform systematic testing; it is often reasonably effective but very expensive in effort and calendar time. Unit testing is usually ad hoc, if performed at all. Test automation is primitive. Test education, especially in universities, is poor.

Given the importance of testing to industry, there is relatively little research done.

(6) Families (David Weiss)

As Parnas stated (1976), program families are defined as sets of programs whose common properties are so extensive that it is advantageous to study the common properties of the programs before analysing individual members.

In general, few techniques exist for defining families, i.e. for performing the analysis needed to identify a defined family. There are a few techniques that have become commercially available in the last two to three years, but they are just starting to be tried by the early adopters in industry. As a result, the problem was rated as partially solved.

(7) Maintenance (Andreas Zeller)

How can we maintain a product's integrity during its evolution?

This problem is partially solved. There is a number of well-understood solutions that help in software maintenance. However, there is a need and a potential for better solutions, especially in the areas of reverse engineering and re-engineering.

(8) Measurement (Motei Azuma)

Specifically, when dealing with software using metrics, we can assess metrics with the following basic questions: Are we able to describe and forecast process and product characteristics by metrics? Are we able to control process and product using metrics, possibly continuously?

Some metrics are widely known and sometimes used in practice. Yet there are many metrics to be developed, validated and taught for practical use. Therefore the general problem is only partially solved.

The leading role of some standards organisations was pointed out (ISO/IEC JTC1/SC7, JTC1/SC7/WG6).

(9) Software Configuration Management (Walter Tichy)
How can we manage and control the evolution of a product?

This problem is solved for standard situations. Software configuration management is a well-understood discipline that offers a number of solutions for managing software evolution.

Distributed software configuration management still requires more attention. Also, composition of complex systems from versioned components brings problems with configuration consistency.

2.6   Summary of the Dagstuhl-Seminar

- Most of the problems that were discussed are **"partially solved"**.
- In many areas, the **available results are not applied for practical work**.
- **Research** has **not addressed** most of these highly important problems recently.
- Topics which are not very attractive for research tend to be neglected in teaching too (e.g. high quality coding, configuration management, use of checklists).

Proposition 4: What we teach in most of the universities about software engineering does not provide the equipment our graduates need when they try to introduce better concepts and techniques in industry.

3   Software Engineering – 10 Years Back and 10 Years Ahead

When we try to foresee the future, we have to extrapolate our experiences from the past. Things that did not change for a long time are likely to be stable in the future. Trends that became visible only recently may become very powerful, or go as fast as they came.

Big changes we have seen in the past were either triggered from within our field (like information hiding, abstract data types, and object oriented programming), or from outside (like personal computers, and the World Wide Web). Both the PC and the WWW have changed our working environment fundamentally. If there are more innovations of that size in the pipeline, all forecasts are obsolete.

3.1   The Past: What Was Different?

Not too much. Most differences are related to our environment:

- *Computers* were less powerful; there was a clear distinction between PCs and workstations.

- *Networking* was still in the beginning (from the software point of view).
- We did have *e-mail*, but no *WWW*
- Software was hardly both useful and public domain, i.e. LINUX, GNU etc. were missing.

The way software was produced and maintained was *basically the same it is today*.

When F.P. Brooks wrote his paper "No silver bullet" in 1987, he tackled the same problem we tackle today: He would analyse the past in order to foresee the future.

Brooks found that miracles ("silver bullets" in his story) would probably not happen. The same old problems remain, and the solutions at hand are basically the same all the time.

3.2   The Trend: What Is Currently Changing?

Some trends, which have been visible for some time, will most probably continue, and will strongly affect the world of software engineering.

3.2.1   Software from Components versus High Quality?
The most important principle to teach a software engineer is,
"Don't build software (if you can help it)." Brooks (1987)

Object oriented programming, or at least coding in object oriented programming languages, became very popular after 1990. As stated above, not all the programs written in C++ or Java can legitimately be called "object oriented".

But one side effect was very important: Ten years ago, people would not use program libraries except in certain limited areas. Meanwhile, using class libraries became quite common. As a result, people nowadays build programs by combining and adapting existing components rather than by handcrafting individual statements.

Software engineers no longer implement user interfaces, just as they no longer implement database systems or compilers. But using a compiler did not require any adaptation, one compiler would fit all. Using GUI builders is only possible using object-oriented technology. Now we can reuse and adapt an existing class without changing its implementation; we create a new class as a subclass of the given one, and modify that subclass. This technique provides a highly attractive combination of two properties (stability and adaptability) which used to be incompatible until inheritance was invented.

But this technique also creates new problems. Some time ago, software engineers would implement their systems more or less from scratch. Except for a few bugs smuggled in by the compilers, they knew that *they* were to blame when anything went wrong.

This is no longer true in systems, which are built on top of a large and complex class library. The optimistic approach most developers take in object oriented programming ("let us code and see!") will lead them quickly to a running system, but not to a correct one. When they use classes whose deficiencies are not visible, they cannot reliably deliver good software, even though they try as hard as possible.

For certain classes of software, these effects will be tolerated. Some of the word processing software we use today are terrible in terms of quality, but highly successful. It seems that the majority of users do not care.

For other classes of software, reliability is not just "nice to have", but essential. Software engineers in those fields will demand class libraries, which are extremely well done, even to the degree that their producers will be required to guarantee correctness. The world of software will split into one continent where functionality and gimmicks determine the champions, while users in other areas cannot do without a provably high level of correctness and reliability.

3.2.2 Domain Specific Software Engineering

Until recently, software engineering was taught in a similar way like mathematics: We, the teachers, believe that our message is applicable in any field, so we do not care where you will apply it.

Maybe this idea was useful long time ago, maybe not, but it is certainly no longer true. Engineers who design clockworks for wristwatches have very little in common with those who construct large ships, though both do mechanical engineering. Software engineering will inevitably fan out into many different fields, with different requirements for correctness and reliability, with different notations and programming languages, with different development processes, and with results of extremely different size. This separation started long time ago already, first in the area of commercial systems ("data processing systems") and in the field of telecommunications.

In such a domain specific software engineering, there is no place for "super software engineers"; their knowledge (about requirements engineering, metrics, and testing, e.g.) will be spread over all the developers involved. While software engineering, as a body of knowledge, will remain highly important for the foreseeable future, there will no longer be the "high priests" who are far more competent than the laymen who actually do the work. In electrical engineering, everybody is an electrical engineer. We should be glad when software engineering has achieved a similar maturity.

3.3   What Else Will Change? What Could Be Changed?

So far, Brooks' conclusion seems to remain valid: No wonders, no sudden changes in our world! If we would like to see changes (and who would not like to see *some* changes?), we have to make them happen.

3.3.1 Research and Transfer

Research could be much more useful if it were directed towards the *problems people actually suffer from*. Empirical work should be emphasised in order to replace "common sense" (which is not common at all) by sound data.

The question *why people do not apply the results* that are available (and have been available for some time) ought to be treated as a *research problem*. Then, we will inevitably learn that most of our results are *not mature enough* for being actually used.

Funding should emphasise *application of existing know-how* rather than production of new know-how whose value is questionable. The same ideas apply for software engineering education.

3.3.2 Education

As stated above, software engineering takes place *in the minds of millions of people*. In order to change the state of software engineering, we must

* either hire different people (and get rid of those who are currently doing the job)
* or change their minds.

Both processes are *extremely slow*, and the first one is everything but desirable.

Software engineering is not a dynamic area, it will not change a lot by 2010. In order to move at least a little bit forward, we have to put *far more effort into the education*

* of those who are *currently doing the job* (including managers), and
* of those who will *soon do the job*

At the University of Stuttgart, Germany, we have launched a new software engineering curriculum in 1996 (Ludewig, Reißing, 1998). It differs from existing courses in its emphasis on important, but often neglected topics like software project management, software quality assurance, requirements engineering. Students have to participate in a first project (6 months) and in two advanced projects (10 months each), which cover the whole life cycle from requirements analysis to delivery, and often include the modification of existing components.

References

Aspray, W., R. Keil-Slawik, D. Parnas (eds.) (1996): The History of Software Engineering. Dagstuhl-Report 153 on the Dagstuhl-Seminar 9635, August 1996.

Bauer, F.L. (1993): Software Engineering – wie es begann. Informatik-Spektrum 16, 259f.

Beck, L.L., T.E. Perkins (1983): A Survey of Software Engineering Practice: tools, methods, and results. IEEE Transactions on Software Engineering, SE-9, 5, 541-561.

Brooks, F.P., Jr. (1987): No silver bullet - essence and accidents of software engineering. IEEE COMPUTER 20, 4, 10-19.

Denert, E., D. Hoffman, J. Ludewig, D. Parnas (1999): SE Research and Education: Seeking a new Agenda. Seminar-Report 230, Dagstuhl, February 1999. The report is available from http://www.dagstuhl.de/DATA/Seminars/99/#99071

Ludewig, J., R. Reißing (1998): Teaching what they need instead of teaching what we like – the new software engineering curriculum at the University of Stuttgart. Information and Software Technology 40 (4), 239 - 244. The paper (and more recent ones in German) is available from http://www.informatik.uni-stuttgart.de/ifi/se/publications

Parnas, D.L. (1972): On the criteria to be used in decomposing systems into modules. Communications of the ACM, 15, 1053-1058.

Parnas, D.L. (1976): On the design and development of program families. IEEE Transactions on Software Engineering, SE-2 (1), 1-9.

Royce, W.W. (1970): Managing the development of large software systems. IEEE WESCON, August 1970, pp.1-9. reprinted in Proc. of the 9th ICSE (IEEE), pp.328-338.

Zelkowitz, M.V., R.T. Yeh, R.G. Hamlet, J.D. Gannon, V.R. Basili (1984): Software Engineering Practices in the US and Japan. IEEE COMPUTER, 1984, June, 57-66.

Thinking Tools for the Future of Computing Science

Cliff B. Jones

Department of Computing Science,
University of Newcastle
NE1 7RU, UK
cliff.jones@ncl.ac.uk

Abstract. This paper argues that "formal methods" can (continue to) provide the thinking tools for the future of computing science. Every significant engineering or scientific discipline has advanced only with systematic and formally based notations. To see just how ubiquitous the need for notation is, one can look beyond the sciences and observe the importance of written notation in the development of music. Map making is another area where the importance of notation and the understanding of the need for (levels of) abstraction is recognised. Formal methods provide notations to navigate the future of computing science.

1 Background

All engineering disciplines make progress by employing mathematically based notations and methods. Research on "formal methods" follows this model and attempts to identify and develop mathematical approaches that can contribute to the task of creating computer systems (both their hardware and software components). Clearly, mathematical calculation will not solve all of the problems faced in the creation of large systems: neither design skills, nor the problems inherent in organising large groups of people, seem obvious candidates for formalisation. Equally clearly, to believe that hugely complex computer systems can be designed without any formalism other than the running code is to emulate Icarus and court disaster after a hugely successful first half century of computing.

The development of ever faster and cheaper micro-electronic devices has made computing widely available but it is software which has brought about the IT revolution. There is much to be proud of in the systems that are deployed today and would have been unthinkable even twenty years ago. Progress in software has come from increased functionality in operating and windowing systems, from better interfaces and improved models of linking such as objects and components, from procedures for review and testing, and (as will be suggested below) by the selective adoption of some formal methods ideas. It would be stupid to under value the contribution of Moore's law, but it is one sided to contribute today's widespread use of computing to the exponential improvement in performance: but for software, hardware circuits could switch arbitrarily quickly and make no impact on society.

R. Wilhelm (Ed.): Informatics. 10 Years Back. 10 Years Ahead, LNCS 2000, pp. 112–130, 2001.

Much then has already been achieved; is there a need for research on formal methods? It is not really the place of the current paper to argue this case in detail; it seems reasonable to accept that the design of any huge artifact needs all the help it can get whether from better management or from notations which make it possible to calculate –rather than postulate– an outcome. If the use of formally based methods can help –as in other engineering disciplines– it is surely unacceptable to ignore them when society's wealth, smooth running and even existence are increasingly reliant of software products.[1]

There is another key argument and that is that the amount of reinvention in software is huge and unsustainable. There are estimates of between one and two million people in the US being involved in some form of programming. It is unlikely that even the majority of these people are well-trained software engineers; furthermore the growth in the percentage of the population involved in this activity cannot be sustained. Carefully documented specifications and reliable implementations (possibly including their justification) are a prerequisite for widespread reuse. In addition, it is necessary that any components of reuse have a carefully designed interface and fit into architectures which facilitate composition. The role of notation in design and architecture is now accepted but the level of formality in widely used notations such as UML is low. This is both regrettable and avoidable. A key (Popper-like) test for any notation is the extent to which inconsistent texts in the notation can be detected: completely automatic checks –as with type checking– are invaluable; checks which can be the subject of calculation or proof are almost as good; but the value of any "notation" whose texts can only be the subject of debate is limited.

In general, this section sets out the current situation, comments on a few pieces of past research and their state of adoption and draws some lessons from the past. Subsequent sections of this paper turn to future challenges.

1.1   Current Use of Formal Methods

Various approaches which are recognised as formal methods are used in the design of safety critical systems. Indeed, for such systems where malfunction can result in loss of life, there have been moves to require the use of formalism. It is the genesis of one of the challenges for the future that many safety critical systems are concurrent programs. Apart from such easily identified use of model checking or verification ideas, there is much wider use of ideas that derive from research into formal approaches. An obvious example is the use of loop invariants even in informal discussions of programs. As is made clear below, it is often the case that ideas which originate as part of formal methods research are no longer seen as formal when they are adopted into wider use. Furthermore, avoiding emphasis on formality can often be a key to adoption. Good examples are Michael

---

[1] One of the interesting discussions at the Dagstuhl anniversary conference was on the potential for liability lawsuits against software producers; Fred Schneider made the important point that in many arenas the producer is deemed negligent if "best practice" has not been employed.

Jackson's influential writings (e.g. [Jac83, Jac00]) and the wider use of model checking tools than verification technology. Personally, I have moved from a position where formal methods were presented as an all-or-nothing technology to a position branded as "formal methods light" in [Jon96b].

So, there is some direct –although not necessarily acknowledged– use of formal methods in general computing practice as well as in the narrower safety-critical arena. But it has to be conceded that the vast majority of software available today has not been designed using formal methods. Regrettably, one can go much further than this and state with some confidence that most software is not developed using anything like "best practice". An issue which is tackled in Section 5 is how the better developers might come to create a larger percentage of software and how formalism might influence the programming paradigm employed.

The most important long-term contribution of studying theoretical underpinnings of computing has been the insight gained into fundamental concepts. Examples like the distinction between non-determinacy and under-determined characterisations in specifications, the role of unbounded non-determinacy and the fundamental distinction between synchronous and asynchronous communication would all justify lengthy discussions of their own.[2] The purpose here is to look at new challenges which will be done after a brief review of what can be learned from some examples of earlier research into formal methods.

1.2   Historical Comment on Syntax Description

The choice of topics here is made to illustrate key points and is in no way a measure of the intrinsic importance of the material. Many other selections could have been made and the choice of say concurrency theory or theorem proving would have made a more compelling justification of past research; here the purpose is to see what can be learned for the future.

The first illustrative historical note relates to the description of the syntax of programming languages. The original work of John Backus and Peter Naur goes back over forty years and the description of the (context-free) syntax of languages is now standard practice. Several observations can however be made. The use of a precise notation makes the question of syntactic validity unambiguous: there is no argument as to whether a program is syntactically correct; it is only necessary to see if it can be generated from the grammar for the language. Formally based notations avoid contradictions.

The understanding of context-free grammars facilitated the automatic creation of parsers. Precise notations are also essential for the creation of meaningful tools. This observation becomes important when discussing the relative advantages of informal (often graphical) notations below.

---

[2] The fundamental understanding on the complexity of classes of algorithmic tasks is a major intellectual achievement but its discussion can safely be left to experts who were well represented at the Dagstuhl anniversary.

The adoption of BNF was not without difficulties. Although it is hard to believe today, some language designers saw even this level of formality as unnecessary. Furthermore there were genuine questions about what constituted "syntax": were the (context-sensitive) constraints which govern declaration and use of variables to be regarded as syntactic in nature because they were concerned with structure or were they to be considered "static semantics" because they were beyond Chomsky Type 2 grammars?

But the most important realisation is that, with the adoption of syntactic formalisms into everyday practice, they are no longer viewed as a part of formal methods. This is a pattern which has been repeated many times. Bob Harper's comments on type theory, the widespread use of the once exotic idea of (especially on-the-fly) "garbage collection" and many others were alluded to during the Dagstuhl anniversary.

1.3   Historical Comment on Semantic Description

Beyond syntax, comes semantics. Early work on formally describing the semantics of programming languages dates back to the 1960s. The main purpose of commenting on this history[3] here is to sound a warning note because it must be recognised that this research has had little practical impact in spite of its huge potential.

McCarthy's work in the early 1960s established the approach of writing "abstract interpreters" for programming languages. He and other key researchers met at the 1964 Baden-bei-Wien conference on "Formal Language Description Languages" (see [Ste66] for excellent proceedings which record many fascinating discussions). The initiator of this conference –Professor Heinz Zemanek– was director of the IBM Laboratory in Vienna. Researchers there applied and extended the basic "operational semantics" idea in an attempt to tame the programming language which came to be called PL/I. Apart from including most things which could have been claimed to be comprehended at that time, PL/I embraced the ill-understood topics of exception handling and concurrent tasks. The huge formal definition was a *tour de force* and with hindsight its most important contribution might have been to clean up a language whose ancestors included both FORTRAN and COBOL.

Unfortunately, many aspects of the "Vienna Definition Language" (VDL) operational semantics descriptions made them difficult to use in reasoning about the design of compilers and this fact, more than the desire for more mathematical base, led the Vienna group to embrace –in the 1970s– the research on Denotational Semantics which had been led by Strachey, Landin, Scott and others. The so-called "Vienna Development Method" had its genesis in the denotational description of the ECMA/ANSI version of PL/I. Fortunately for the authors, the standards bodies had rejected the tasking proposals in PL/I and the language to be described was non-deterministic rather than truly parallel. Attempts to

---

[3] A proper scientific history of this field of research would be useful.

provide denotational models for parallelism led to Power Domains which were not for the faint-hearted.

Plotkin's 1981 paper [Plo81] is widely seen as the first to show that those aspects of operational semantics which had made them difficult to understand could be avoided without the need to provide denotational descriptions. It was particularly gratifying that concurrent languages could be described without heavy mathematics. "Structured Operational Semantics" is now an eminently teachable subject which ought to be part of the training of any computer scientist.

That there is a clear need for formal semantic descriptions of significant systems should be clear. I have moved several times between industry and academia: during a recent spell in a software house, a project was built on top of CORBA. Impressive in scope, CORBA's imprecise semantics and poor implementations are squandering the huge potential for object brokers to free information from being locked into propriety interfaces.

In spite of the recognised need for moving beyond the description of syntactic details of interfaces to describing their semantics, it must be conceded that formal semantics is used only in narrow fields. Some of the difficulty is due to the history of the subject and the infatuation of some researchers with mathematical depth without measuring the value of new concepts to practitioners. The lack of well chosen example descriptions must be seen as another tactical mistake. Almost certainly, an opportunity was missed in not providing better tools for experimentation with semantic descriptions. Above all, the desperate need for thinking tools which would help designers come up with clearer and easier-to-use architectures has only been met to a limited extent by the literature on formal semantic description techniques.

1.4   Historical Comment on Reasoning about Programs

Although the history of work on reasoning about programs in some respects mirrors –and indeed is dependent upon– the work on the semantics of languages, it has had a significantly larger impact on practice. The research on reasoning about programs has provided key "thinking tools" which are in wide use.

Here again there is a rich history to be written and [Jon92] can only be regarded as useful source material.[4] But the essence of the argument is that the idea of reasoning about whether a program could be said to satisfy its specification was present from the early days of programming with both Alan Turing and John von Neumann discussing the idea in papers in the 1940s. The thesis is that what has followed has been a "search for tractability". Seen thus, Floyd, Naur, van Wijngaarden and Hoare were all seeking ways to present formal arguments in an acceptable way. In particular, Hoare's paper [Hoa69] offers a much more telling presentation of Floyd's earlier idea [Flo67]. Hoare generously concedes his debt to Floyd and van Wijngaarden (see historical notes [HJ89, pp45–46]). In

---

[4] The report [Jon92] was commissioned for a scientific encyclopedia which has not appeared; it is now being revised for publication in the IEEE Annals of Computing.

mathematics, it is often a key step to propose a tractable notation. Furthermore, it is central to the thesis of the current paper that issues of presentation are often the deciding factor in creating thinking tools.

The history of reasoning about programs does not stop with Hoare's 1968 paper and one could trace the development of Dijkstra's Predicate Transformers [Dij76, DS90] and subsequent program calculi from Back and Morgan but the main points of the historical note in this section can be understood by anyone who has met Hoare's axiom for the while statement:

$$\frac{\{p \wedge b\}\ S\ \{p\}}{\{p\}\ while\ b\ do\ S\ od\ \{p\ \wedge\ \neg b\}}$$

This rule is both elegant and memorable.

Moreover, the invariant p provides a fundamental thinking tool. If one trained programmer wants to convince another that a loop construct serves its intended purpose, the invariant is a key part of the argument. This is true whether the challenge to justify the loop comes in an informal walkthrough or in an attempt to get a formal proof checked by a computer verification system.

Interestingly, another aspect of the correctness of loop constructs is not covered by the rule as shown. Hoare's 1968 paper left the subject of termination to separate argumentation. Here, Dijkstra's *variant function* [Dij76] is most often used and offers another thinking tool for reasoning that programs satisfy their specifications.

It is instructive to investigate further aspects that are not covered in the above rule. For example, issues of "clean termination" (cf. [Sit74]) are not addressed. The advantages of using post-conditions which are relations (and the search for tractable rules) are discussed in [Jon99]. It might be argued that part of the success of Hoare's axiomatic programme was that it avoided trying to do too much.

There is however an absolutely crucial point about Hoare's rules which has made them essential thinking tools for the progress of computing science and that is that they are *compositional*: the rules can be used to divide a problem into smaller problems whose solutions can be judged solely with respect to their individual specifications.[5] The topic of compositional development is the source of a challenge in Section 3.1 but its practical importance should already be clear: for a large task, one needs ways of creating correct designs; it is not enough to have methods or tools for checking the finished product. Such tools are valuable in their own way but do not help the design process.

One further key contribution in the area of thinking tools for the design process is the story of *data reification* (or refinement). A note on this is included in [Jon99] with further references to earlier papers and a comprehensive review is contained in [dRE99]. Suffice it to say here that brief and perspicuous specification of a system is likely to owe more to well chosen data abstractions than to cute post-conditions.

---

[5] Technically, this depends on the programming combinators being monotonic over the specification ordering.

A word of reservation about the success of the thinking tools for reasoning about programs is in order. It was long my claim that every designer and programmer should be able to read and write formal specifications. To some extent, many researchers felt that the difficulty of teaching VDM or Z might lie in the notation itself. Reluctantly, I at least have accepted that many people find the *process* of abstraction difficult and that it is not learning to write "upside down ∀s" which is the obstacle.

Perhaps the most important observation is that assertions are an orthogonal check on the code of a program. It has often been observed that the attempt to show that a program satisfies a specification uncovers errors in the latter as well as the former. It is however a constructive diversity to have both assertions and algorithm.

In closing this review of a relatively successful deployment of a formal methods idea, it is again encouraging to look at the provision of tools. From complete systems to aid the verification of programs, to the much more approachable *extended static checkers* described in this conference by Rustan Leino, it is clear the presence of underlying formal understanding is essential for meaningful (mechanical) tools.

1.5   Lessons

If the formal methods community is to maximise its future impact on practical computing applications, there are a number of lessons which are worth spelling out from the past. It is, for example, difficult to conduct controlled experiments of any useful scale. Small programs are not difficult to get right and a university experiment on 50 line programs is never likely to show the pay off for using careful specification and stepwise design. Unfortunately, huge programs are incredibly expensive to build and no organisation will attempt to build the same product two ways. But it has not been the practice in other engineering disciplines to conduct –for example– controlled experiments of bridge designs with and without stress analysis. The proposal for a new engineering method might require learning some new mathematical tools. Where an engineering culture exists, the burden is readily accepted. Two things work against such acceptance by software engineers: many are untrained in any engineering mathematics; and the consequences of software bugs are either not recognised by liability or they are perceived as easy to correct.

There are however messages for the formalists as well. The educational load of a new proposal must not be ignored: if the main gain from learning a new branch of mathematics is to cite erudite papers, users will not be persuaded. There has to be a direct value of a new field to make it worth its adoption. Nor is it the case that all computing problems will succumb to an *existing* body of mathematical knowledge. To take one example that I have written about in several places, the assumption that classical logic is appropriate for reasoning about specifications and programs where partial functions abound might be unfortunate.[6] Kline wrote that "More than anything, mathematics is a method" which we could take as a claim that formal methods should offer mathematically sound approaches but not necessarily ones which are parts of recognised mathematics. It is particularly important that the mathematics should fit the real problem rather than the problem be bent to fit the mathematics.

There have, with hindsight, been many missed opportunities in the realm of formal methods. There have been premature attempts to develop new specification languages where old ones were not understood; there have been unnecessary differences between basically similar approaches; and there have been extended developments of closed research schools. There is probably nothing unusual in these aspects of a scientific field. Perhaps more frustrating is the perpetual growth of informal notations which are often diagrammatic and which achieve widespread use in spite of their lack of precise semantics. There is nothing inherently wrong with diagrams; but it is the repeated experience of *post hoc* formalisation that many things are clarified and simplified.

The strongest message from the experience with formal methods is that they have had an impact on practical development although the adoption of formal ideas is often coupled with a denial of their origin. Concepts like data type invariants, compositional development methods, reasoning about termination etc. have become thinking tools of the better educated programmer and designer. Some specification languages such as VDM, Z or B are used in practical projects and commercially available tools support such use. More advanced tools like theorem provers and model checkers[7] are used on critical projects. The wider acceptance of the latter class of tools has interesting lessons and warnings. Although model checking tools are certainly not for the untrained, it is true that they can be deployed both on finished code and without design history. That is attractive especially if the need is to find errors in a product. The thinking tools thesis of this paper would of course argue for ideas which tend to create correct designs rather than for tools –however good– to detect problems at the end of the development phase. It is my experience that trying to prove an extant program satisfies some specification almost invariably results in discarding the program and conducting a new design activity using formal arguments at each stage of design.

2 Some Incremental Challenges

There are a number of obvious steps which could be taken both in the development and deployment of formal methods. This section mentions a few incremental items so that the more significant challenges in later sections can be seen in context.

There is clearly a need for work on standards for formal methods. There has been for some years an ISO standard for the VDM Specification Language and

---

[6] The case for a Logic of Partial Functions is set out in [CJ91] where further references can be found.

[7] See Ed Clarke's chapter of these proceedings.

the Z specification language is nearing that status. More challenging is to look at connections between approaches and [BBD+00] reports on work to link VDM and B. It is of course tempting to say that it might be less work to devise a new language with the best features of both — but the danger here is of an unending proliferation as has been seen in the programming language arena. Standards work might not be exciting to all researchers but it has an effect both on user preparedness to adopt new methods and to the provision of tool support. Both the VDM and Z standardisation activities uncovered significant issues that needed resolution.

The provision of tools is seen by many as necessary for the adoption of formal methods. In many cases, this is actually an excuse since tools do not replace the need for quite fundamental shifts in approach and training. Where tools do become important is in the inevitable maintenance of older formal texts. Links between tools like the IFAD VDM Toolset [WWW00c] and theorem proving systems [WWW00a] are also the subject of ongoing work. Tools for theorem proving will require more research before they are widely used.

A more fundamental missing synergy is between the "correct by construction" camp and the *post hoc* model checking approaches.[8] Saying that the approaches can be viewed as complimentary is a first step but it will require research to devise languages which can carry information about abstractions from the design phase into the state exploration of the final code; linked tool support is a considerable engineering challenge.

Recent recognition of software architecture (cf. [SG96]) as a topic of research is encouraging because it offers the prospect of re-use of intellectual effort (Software Patterns and Components are other approaches). This could be a key area for the use of formal methods. It is not difficult to argue that the most damaging contribution to the "Total Cost of Ownership" of computer systems is their poor architecture. In all but the most critical applications, the cost of bugs fades into insignificance compared with the time that users waste in not having a model (cf. [Nor88]) of the system (which they had been sold on the basis that it would help them).[9] Formal methods have –since their role in the evolution of PL/I– been thinking tools for cleaning up messy architectures.

3   Conceptual Gaps

This section indicates some areas where research is required which is not simply incremental. Any author would list their own set of conceptual gaps and two lists would rarely coincide: the attempt is to indicate the sort of challenge rather than to provide a complete catalogue. Clearly the choice is influenced by my own research and thus largely relates to concurrency.

---

[8] This was addressed by both Amir Pneuli and John Rushby at the FM'99 conference.
[9] A particularly insidious example of the hidden cost of ownership came up at the conference where two speakers pointed out the difficulty they had experienced in accessing their own 1990 texts which had been created on software which has since been "upgraded".

3.1   Compositional Development of Concurrent Systems

Section 1.4 claims that compositionality is key for the development of sequential programs: one step of design can be justified before effort is put into development of the sub-components. The essence of concurrency is *interference*. With shared variable programs, interference manifests itself by several processes changing the same portion of the state of a computation. Much early research on concurrency was concerned with ways of controlling when processes could access and update the state. Some researchers saw the idea of shared state as the root of the problem and shifted attention to communication based concurrency.[10] But, since one can precisely simulate the notion of a shared-variable as a process, what happens is that the problem shifts to communication interference. The fundamental problem of more than one process generating activity (which can influence other processes) is inherent to concurrency. One can argue that one or another approach facilitates reasoning about interference but does not make it go away.

The sobering realization is that interference makes it difficult to conceive compositional development methods for concurrent systems. Early attempts to present ways of reasoning about concurrent programs barely noticed this problem since the state-of-the-art even for sequential programs was to construct *post-facto* proofs. It was true that those techniques which proposed looking at the cross-product of control points between processes would not scale but this initial objection missed the point that one needed to undertake some proof long before the final code (and its control points) were available.

A widely cited technique for the development of concurrent programs is that in Susan Owicki's thesis [Owi75] and often called the "Owicki/Gries" method. This makes some progress in that part of the proof obligation associated with decomposing a task into sub-tasks is discharged before the sub-tasks are developed but there is still a final stage in which one must check whether the steps of one process can interfere with the proof of others. So one could still decompose a task into sub-tasks; develop them to satisfy their separate specifications and then be forced to discard them and start again when the developed code is shown to interfere with something in the other process. This is clearly non-compositional.

With hindsight the step to specifying interference might seem obvious. The point of this section is to argue that in spite of many theses and other papers, there is still not a completely satisfactory way of reasoning about interference.

The idea of adding rely- and guarantee-conditions to pre- and post-conditions is proposed in [Jon81] and developed in [Stø90, Xu92, Col94, Din00]. Essentially, a rely-condition documents the interference that the (developer must make sure the) program can tolerate and the guarantee-condition records the interference that other processes will have to put up with if they run in parallel with the developed code. These extra predicates are one way of recording interference expectations and they (together with the associated proof rules — see [Jon96a]) regain the key property of compositionality. As with post-conditions in VDM,

---

[10] See CSP [Hoa85], CCS [Mil89] and the π-calculus [MPW92].

both rely and guarantee-conditions are relations (predicates over two states). The proof rules are more complicated than the rules for sequential programming constructs but that is almost certainly inevitable. It is worth pointing out that complexity in formal proofs often comes from the design: the effect of formalisation is to expose rather than cause difficulty. A poor interface will make justification difficult whether formal or informal. Ignoring a difficulty at one step of development can result in major costs in subsequent correction; worst of all is repeated patching of code to work around an early design flaw.

Although the eventual form of the proof rule for parallel composition with rely/guarantee-conditions is reasonably memorable, it is complex enough that it is worth avoiding its use where possible. (Indeed, juggling clauses between pre/rely and post/guarantee conditions is non-trivial as shown in [CJ00].) For this reason, it is useful to look at ways of localising areas of potential interference. This of course echoes early concurrency research from semaphores to modules. A series of papers (see [Jon96a] for references) show the role of a parallel object-based language in fixing such limitations.

Rely/guarantee-conditions are one form of assumption-commitment specification and there are several others. One that is less well-known than it deserves is Kees Middelburg's use of Temporal Logic to capture interference [Mid93]. An excellent survey of existing compositional approaches to concurrency is being published by de Roever and colleagues.

There is then work required in evaluating different approaches; but there are also gaps that need addressing in all approaches. In known approaches there is –for some applications– a need to include some form of "ghost variable" which keeps track of the point in control flow where assertions hold. A particularly trivial and annoying case is where two parallel processes are each tasked with incrementing a variable, say x, by 1. This class of limitations prompts the idea that there ought to be a totally different way of discussing the combined effects of operations which are in the same algebraic group: where such operators commute, their combined effect on x is the same independent of their order. So one shortcoming of the current rely/guarantee reasoning about interference is that it tries too hard to do everything with predicates.[11] There is here an indication of a much deeper question. In some sense, a development method is made valuable by what it avoids making explicit. So the Hoare rule for assignment expresses neatly what does change without making explicit what stays constant. The trade off between ghost variables and the power of proof rules is an intriguing subject which deserves more explicit research. Other ways in which interference arguments need to be extended are in the handling of real-time and probabilistic specifications.

---

[11] There are other difficulties but these are being covered in a longer and more detailed paper on compositionality for a volume of contributions by members of IFIP's Working Group 2.3; the editors are McIver and Morgan.

3.2 Design by Atomicity Refinement

It is clear from both the work on specification by post-conditions (say "what", rather than "how") and the use of abstract objects in specifications that abstraction is the main tool to tackle complexity. If a specification is to be at least one order of magnitude shorter than an eventual implementation, knowing what to omit is essential. One powerful abstraction is that of pretending atomicity. I first encountered the idea in reasoning about concurrent object-oriented programs. Essentially, it was easy to show that an abstract program achieved a desired effect by assuming that certain operations –although executed in a non-deterministic order– were atomic. A subsequent stage of development showed that although the allegedly atomic operations were composed of smaller steps, these steps could not influence other processes and that steps of separate processes could overlap. What is more exciting is that the idea of refining atomic operations occurs in many areas. The basic correctness notion for database transactions is that any implementation should give a result that could have been obtained from some order of executing transactions atomically. Any reasonable implementation will actually overlap transactions and operate a variety of clash avoidance or detection algorithms to simulate the atomicity abstraction. Similar comments can be made about distributed caches and the same issue comes up again in the design of asynchronous circuits such as AMULET.

Several researchers have considered aspects of this problem but I am not aware of any general treatment of design by atomicity refinement. Such ubiquitous problems are usually challenging and their solutions powerful.

3.3 Unification of State and Communication

The discussion of compositional development methods for concurrency alluded to the distinction between state-based and communication-based concurrency. At some level, this distinction appears to be spurious in that either can be simulated in the other. Indeed, looking down from the abstraction of a programming language to the physics of the hardware devices, one appears to switch to and fro between these views. It would appear therefore to be unfortunate that the (generally predicate-based) methods for reasoning about states and the (generally trace-based) ways of documenting communication are separate. One specific example is the view taken of specifying the circumstances under which something should terminate. State-based specification languages like VDM and B[12] separate out a pre-condition over which the specified operation must terminate. In contrast, trace-based assertions adopt divergences and refusals that are linked to the evolving computation. There is a suspicion that there are two notions here which could each be applied in the other domain. There are earlier authors who sensed this challenge: Hewitt's Actors being the earliest example.

Another related point came up when attempting to verify some equivalences of the parallel object-based language referred to in Section 3.1. The proofs

---

[12] Many users of Z also distinguish the pre-condition from the post-condition but the language itself merges them.

in [Jon94] were based on a translation into the π-calculus. As Robin Milner had prophesied, this turned out to be a rather low-level language and coding everything as communication clouded the reasoning. This prompted the suspicion that some halfway house of what might be called "stateful processes" would be more tractable. Both David Walker and Davide Sangiorgi have published papers on the required equivalence results and particularly the notion of "uniformly receptive processes" in [San99] would appear to be a step in this direction. The challenge is to find a useful notion of stateful process that has a nice algebra and clearly links state and communication.

4 A Grand Challenge: Dependability

Contributors to the Dagstuhl conference were encouraged to identify grand challenges in their research areas: I am now the Project Director of a six-year research project on *Dependability of Computer-Based Systems* (DIRC) [WWW00b], so it is natural to view this as a grand challenge. The term dependability is preferred to reliability because of the wish to encompass topics such as availability, security etc. The phrase "computer-based" systems is chosen to indicate that the collaboration will consider broad user and society issues as well as technical computer questions. This section points to material on the overall project and pinpoints one example of a topic for future research.

Researchers in the consortium have worked for many years on aspects of the dependability of computer systems themselves. Earlier research on computer fault-tolerance and avoidance has led to concepts like recovery blocks and Coordinated Atomic Actions (see [Ran00] for references). There is no sense in which the computer scientists in the new collaboration regard all of the computer research issues as resolved and –for example– researchers at Newcastle are involved in two significant European projects on "Dependable Systems of Systems" and tolerating malicious attacks. But there is a clear realisation that, as computers enter ever more into everyday life, many system failures occur at the link between humans and computers. Nor is this problem confined to HCI questions, important though they are. The DIRC collaboration includes researchers from psychology, sociology and management science as well as computer scientists. An example of an application to which they would like their research to contribute is the proposed introduction of a Electronic Health Record in the UK. Obvious dependability issues include availability, security and reliability. Without an understanding of the notions of trust and responsibility that are current in the medical profession, a computer system could be devised which is a complete disaster (even were it to completely satisfy its formal specification!).

The general area then is *Dependability of Computer-Based Systems*; specific research themes cover risk, diversity, timeliness, trust and structure. As an example of an idea which I wish to study under the "structure" research theme, the topic of *faults as interference* is described. In order to discuss fault-tolerance, one needs to document the sort of faults that are to be tolerated. This observation was made when consulting on what was known as the Inherently Safe Automatic [Reactor] Trip; ISAT is described in [SW89]. In that project it was shown that rely-conditions (see Section 3.1 above) could be used to specify faults as though they were interference and then to show that the system developed could tolerate that level of interference.[13] There are many aspects of this idea which need study even as they relate to computer systems alone. In particular, it was clear from the ISAT work that the understanding of "faults" is often recorded at a much lower level of abstraction than one wants to reason about with a top-level specification. (One might then have to construct fault-containment abstraction levels.) Replication for fault-tolerance and data fragmentation for security are other interesting aspects to be investigated as is the idea of proof carrying guarantee-conditions for code which is imported. There are many examples in the literature such as the Karlsruhe Production cell and the Gas burner system (this originated in a Dagstuhl seminar and is described in [GNRR93]). Michael Jackson's new book [Jac00] also shows how to address a system wider than the machine and provides the traffic light example which was used as an illustration at the conference. Examples with timing assumptions and constraints become particularly interesting. But linking back to the broader view of Computer-Based systems, it is intriguing to study the extent to which the idea of faults as interference could cope with human errors. It is inevitable that humans make mistakes. One of the many contributions that psychologists bring to our understanding of computer-based systems is their attempts to characterise human mistakes — see for example [Rea90]. Such a categorisation could be linked with the idea of faults as interference and make it possible to record which sorts of human errors a system is claimed to tolerate.

As indicated in [Nor88], many so-called operator errors result from a false model of what is going on within a system. The interesting approach of John Rushby in [Rus99] is to attempt to record both an actual system model and a model of how a user perceives that system. Rushby shows how his approach can explain –and even mechanically find– some errors which are made at a pilot/control interface but concedes that it is difficult to extract the model of the user's view of a system. It might be easier to express assertions about the user's view (than elicit a finite state model) and "faults as interference" reasoning could be employed. There is anyway much research in this specific area and even more in broader issues of the dependability of computer-based systems.

5   A Grand Challenge: Programming Paradigms

The procedural programming paradigm has had a remarkably long innings. Many different languages have come and gone; a few genuinely new concepts like objects have been adopted; somehow, natural selection seems to favour the Baroque over the simple and elegant. But most programming is still done in an imperative style. Improvements in both machine performance and compiler technology have

---

[13] At the Dagstuhl meeting, Fred Schneider pointed out that he had written about a related idea in [SS83].

given new impetus to functional programming; logic programming has its adherents; it could even be argued that people using spreadsheets are programming non-declaratively. But the need in so many applications to access and change something like a database gives imperative programs a head start. Unfortunately, it is all too clear that constructing such programs is expensive and creates error-laden implementations which are extremely fragile when modifications become necessary. What can be done? Is a complete change of paradigm thinkable? I have no instant proposal but I believe that something different will arise. In lieu of a concrete proposal, I'd like to make some observations that might suggest that programming could be different.

Careful programmers do write assertions and I am aware of large systems where such assertions are compiled into running code.[14] The argument for doing this is that failing an assertion often detects a bug before other data is corrupted and the origin of the error obscured. Assertions then can be a form of redundancy not just in the design process but in the executing system. Human systems rely on redundancy and often detect errors and even correct them by using redundant information. There are also claims that the overall "mean time between failure" of telephone switch software has been dramatically extended by evaluating assertions and selectively dropping suspect calls. Obviously one can now dive into technical questions: how rich is the assertion language? are the predicates over one state or can they refer to older states (the recovery block idea permitted a limited form of relational check)? what action is prescribed when an assertion is false? could one find an efficient way of periodically "retrieving" the abstractions used in the abstract design? But for now, all that is important is the idea of redundancy and some coherence check. Suppose the assertions were given priority over the algorithm. Furthermore, suppose they were not just validity assertions but they described "desirable states" which actions perturbed. As an example, a desirable state for a hospital is that it has no sick patients; the arrival of a sick person is a perturbation; a better state than one where someone has undiagnosed symptoms is that they have been diagnosed and are undergoing treatment.[15] Would it be easy to write routines which moved from less to more desirable states? could they be redundant? would such systems be easier to maintain?[16]

I might of course be on totally the wrong tack. Perhaps the real villain is the assignment statement and we should revisit Wadge's Lucid or McCarthy's Elephant languages. Estimates were given at the Dagstuhl anniversary of millions of people who are employed in something approximating to programming. It is clear that this growth cannot go on (anymore than the early extrapolations of the number of people required to operate manual telephone exchanges were

---

[14] This idea is at least as old as [Sat75].

[15] Notice that this contrasts with *process modelling* in which the patient approximates to an instruction counter in a more-or-less fixed procedure.

[16] There were discussions at the Dagstuhl meeting about how to deploy parallel processes in novel ways: some approach like that above appears to have more inherent parallelism than could ever be detected in FORTAN code!

sustainable). Moreover, it is fairly clear from the quality of current software, that a reduction not an increase is highly desirable. Either (good) programmers have to start producing ubiquitous artifacts which avoid the wasteful recreation of close approximations to other systems and/or the task of programming has to be made more resilient.

6   A Grand Challenge: Information Access

This final offering has little to do with formal methods except in so far as they might be used –as always– to clarify thinking. Computing as a way of providing computation power has been the most dramatic success of the century just finished; but for providing information, we haven't even started. The WWW is certainly not a counter argument: even if the information one wants is available, it is almost impossible to find it in what is becoming the "World Wide Wastebasket". Not only is it difficult to locate information structured and stored by others, one can get locked out of one's own information by "upgrades" to software. This moved John Gurd and I to decline to prophesy the future of our own research specialties in an earlier crystal ball activity and to write instead [GJ96]. The "Global yet Personal Information System" was a dream whose availability was not offered at the Dagstuhl conference. Others at this conference are more versed than us in the current state of the art but the challenge of providing (controlled) access to both free-form and structured information has to be one of the key tests for computing science in the new century.

7   Conclusions

The thesis of this paper must be clear: formal methods can and must offer the thinking tools which will both ensure progress in computing and elucidate fundamental concepts. To achieve this, one cannot ignore the real problems which exist. One can decry the rush to get systems to market; one can warn that we are "headed for a spill"; but we must at least see in which direction the main line is moving.

The need for thinking tools cannot be clearer than in the early stages of system development. Tools to help simplify and generalise designs are necessary. Ways of getting the design right from the beginning are a means to make a dramatic improvement in productivity.

The adoption of formal methods will be gradual and be influenced more by good engineering training than any single idea.

Acknowledgements

I am grateful to Reinhard Wilhelm and his colleagues both for the invitation to take part in the Dagstuhl event and for their generous hospitality. To the other participants, I should like to express my thanks for many stimulating discussions. I gratefully acknowledge the financial support of the UK EPSRC for the Interdisciplinary Research Collaboration "Dependability of Computer-Based Systems". Most of my research is influenced by, and has been discussed with, members of IFIP's Working Group 2.3.

References

[BBD+00] J. Biccaregui, Matthew Bishop, Theo Dimitakos, Kevin Lano, Brian Matthews, and Brian Ritchie. Supporting co-use of VDM and B by translation. In J. S. Fitzgerald, editor, *VDM in 2000*, 2000.

[CJ91] J. H. Cheng and C. B. Jones. On the usability of logics which handle partial functions. In C. Morgan and J. C. P. Woodcock, editors, *3rd Refinement Workshop*, pages 51–69. Springer-Verlag, 1991.

[CJ00] Pierre Collette and Cliff B. Jones. Enhancing the tractability of rely/guarantee specifications in the development of interfering operations. In Gordon Plotkin, Colin Stirling, and Mads Tofte, editors, *Proof, Language and Interaction*, chapter 10, pages 275–305. MIT Press, 2000.

[Col94] Pierre Collette. *Design of Compositional Proof Systems Based on Assumption-Commitment Specifications – Application to UNITY*. PhD thesis, Louvain-la-Neuve, June 1994.

[Dij76] E. W. Dijkstra. *A Discipline of Programming*. Prentice-Hall, 1976.

[Din00] Jürgen Dingel. *Systematic Parallel Programming*. PhD thesis, Carnegie Mellon University, 2000. CMU-CS-99-172.

[dRE99] W. P. de Roever and K. Engelhardt. *Data Refinement: Model-Oriented Proof Methods and Their Comparison*. Cambridge University Press, 1999.

[DS90] Edsger W Dijkstra and Carel S Scholten. *Predicate Calculus and Program Semantics*. Springer-Verlag, 1990. ISBN 0-387-96957-8, 3-540-96957-8.

[Flo67] R. W. Floyd. Assigning meanings to programs. In *Proc. Symp. in Applied Mathematics, Vol.19: Mathematical Aspects of Computer Science*, pages 19–32. American Mathematical Society, 1967.

[GJ96] J. R. Gurd and C. B. Jones. The global-yet-personal information system. In Ian Wand and Robin Milner, editors, *Computing Tomorrow*, pages 127–157. Cambridge University Press, 1996.

[GNRR93] R. L. Grossman, A. Nerode, A. P. Ravn, and H. Rischel, editors. *Hybrid Systems VIII*, volume 736 of *Lecture Notes in Computer Science*. Springer-Verlag, 1993.

[HJ89] C. A. R. Hoare and C. B. Jones. *Essays in Computing Science*. Prentice Hall International, 1989.

[Hoa69] C. A. R. Hoare. An axiomatic basis for computer programming. *Communications of the ACM*, 12(10):576–580, 583, October 1969.

[Hoa85] C. A. R. Hoare. *Communicating Sequential Processes*. Prentice-Hall, 1985.

[Jac83] Michael Jackson. *System Design*. Prentice-Hall International, 1983.

[Jac00] Michael Jackson. *Problem Frames: Structring and Analysing Software Development Problems*. Addison-Wesley, 2000.

[Jon81] C. B. Jones. *Development Methods for Computer Programs including a Notion of Interference*. PhD thesis, Oxford University, June 1981. Printed as: Programming Research Group, Technical Monograph 25.

[Jon92]   C. B. Jones. The search for tractable ways of reasoning about programs. Technical Report UMCS-92-4-4, Manchester University, 1992.

[Jon94]   C. B. Jones. Process algebra arguments about an object-based design notation. In A. W. Roscoe, editor, *A Classical Mind*, chapter 14, pages 231–246. Prentice-Hall, 1994.

[Jon96a]   C. B. Jones. Accommodating interference in the formal design of concurrent object-based programs. *Formal Methods in System Design*, 8(2):105–122, March 1996.

[Jon96b]   C. B. Jones. A rigorous approach to formal methods. *IEEE, Computer*, 29(4):20–21, 1996.

[Jon99]   C. B. Jones. Scientific decisions which characterize VDM. In *FM'99 – Formal Methods*, volume 1708 of *Lecture Notes in Computer Science*, pages 28–47. Springer-Verlag, 1999.

[Mid93]   Cornelius A. Middelburg. *Logic and Specification: Extending VDM-SL for advanced formal specification*. Chapman and Hall, 1993.

[Mil89]   R. Milner. *Communication and Concurrency*. Prentice Hall, 1989.

[MPW92]   R. Milner, J. Parrow, and D. Walker. A calculus of mobile processes. *Information and Computation*, 100:1–77, 1992.

[Nor88]   Donald A Norman. *The Psychology of Everyday Things*. Basic Books, 1988.

[Owi75]   S. Owicki. *Axiomatic Proof Techniques for Parallel Programs*. PhD thesis, Department of Computer Science, Cornell University, 1975. 75-251.

[Plo81]   G. D. Plotkin. A structural approach to operational semantics. Technical report, Aarhus University, 1981.

[Ran00]   B. Randell. Facing up to faults. *The Computer Jopurnal*, 43(2):95–106, 2000.

[Rea90]   James Reason. *Human Error*. Cambridge University Press, 1990.

[Rus99]   John Rushby. Using model checking to help discover mode confusions and other automation surprises. In *Proceedings of 3rd Workshop on Human Error*, pages 1–18. HESSD'99, 1999.

[San99]   Davide Sangiorgi. Typed π-calculus at work: a correctness proof of Jones's parallelisation transformation on concurrent objects. *Theory and Practice of Object Systems*, 5(1):25–34, 1999.

[Sat75]   Edwin H. Satterthwaite. *Source Language Debugging Tools*. PhD thesis, Stanford University, 1975.

[SG96]   Mary Shaw and David Garlan. *Software Architecture: Perspectives on an Emerging Discipline*. Prentice Hall, 1996.

[Sit74]   R.L. Sites. Some thoughts on proving clean termination of programs. Technical Report STAN-CS-74-417, Computer Science Department, Stanford University, May 1974.

[SS83]   F. B. Schneider and R. D. Schlichting. Fail-stop processors: an approach to designing fault-tolerant computing systems. *TOCS*, 1(3):222–238, 1983.

[Ste66]   T. B. Steel. *Formal Language Description Languages for Computer Programming*. North-Holland, 1966.

[Stø90]   K. Stølen. *Development of Parallel Programs on Shared Data-Structures*. PhD thesis, Manchester University, 1990. available as UMCS-91-1-1.

[SW89]   I. C. Smith and D. N. Wall. Programmamable electronic systems for reactor safety. *Atom*, (395), 1989.

[WWW00a]   WWW. www.dcs.gla.ac.uk/prosper/, 2000.
[WWW00b]   WWW. www.dirc.org.uk, 2000.
[WWW00c]   WWW. www.ifad.dk/products/vdmtools.htm, 2000.
[Xu92]   Qiwen Xu. *A Theory of State-based Parallel Programming*. PhD thesis, Oxford University, 1992.

Orientations in Verification Engineering of Avionics Software

Famantanantsoa Randimbivololona

EADS Airbus SA
Systems and Services – BP M8621
316 route de Bayonne
31060 Toulouse cedex 03 – France
famanta.randim@airbus.aeromatra.com

Abstract. The avionics domain and its environment are changing rapidly. Current engineering can hardly address the new verification problems. Orientations for the development of adequate enabling verification techniques are presented.

1 Introduction

The purpose of this paper is the presentation of orientations that should be taken for developing new verification techniques. This would lead to improvements of verification engineering in accordance with trends observed in the avionics domain.

The choice of these orientations is based on experience gained by the Systems and Services Division of EADS Airbus SA in avionics software developments encompassing the A300 to A340 aircrafts. These software systems are: Electrical Flight Control System, Flight Warning System, Central Maintenance Computer and the air/ground communication Air Traffic Service Unit.

The structure of the paper is as follows: Section 2 is a presentation of avionics elements and the relationships between system equipment, computer and software. Section 3 is an overview of present avionics software engineering where a focus is given to the verification processes. Section 4 describes the change factors and then presents some foreseen orientations in the future.

2 Avionics Elements

Dependability is a central notion in avionics. Safety requirements are totally integrated within each system definition and architecture. The kind and level of architectural redundancy, functional dissymetry and technological dissemblance depend on the failure condition category of the system. From the most critical to the less critical, there are five failure condition categories: catastrophic, hazardous, major, minor, no effect.

R. Wilhelm (Ed.): Informatics. 10 Years Back. 10 Years Ahead, LNCS 2000, pp. 131-137, 2001.
© Springer-Verlag Berlin Heidelberg 2001

A system is made up of one or several equipments among which the functions and the safety requirements of the system are allocated. On modern aircrafts, equipments are more and more digital embedded computers that are usually interconnected by use of ARINC 429 serial buses.

Within a computer, typical functions performed by software are:

□ numerical and Boolean computations,
□ hardware handling and monitoring,
□ communication protocols,
□ fault-tolerance mechanisms.

While executing, the software must exhibit the expected dynamic properties that may be categorised into:

□ functional properties,
□ real-time properties,
□ run-time properties.

Functional properties are directly related to the functions that are performed. Real-time properties come from constraints imposed by the environment that is controlled by the computer. Guaranteeing real-time behaviour depends both on the computer hardware characteristics as well as on the complexity of the software computations. Run-time properties are correctness properties of elementary operations.

3 Today's Engineering

3.1 Certification

Aeronautical certification is the most influential factor in avionics software engineering. Its software considerations are taken into account within the framework of the DO-178B standards. These standards are world-wide-agreed guidance materials -based on appropriate industry-accepted engineering- for satisfying airworthiness requirements. These guidance materials are safety-directed. They define processes and process data so that the level of assurance and the completion criteria are coherent with the level of the software. The level assignment is set according to the software contribution to potential failure conditions of the system it is part of. There are five levels related to failure condition categories: A, B, C, D, E where level A is the most critical. Efforts along the life cycle are directly related to the level criticality: The highest level requires the highest efforts.

3.2 Life Cycle Processes

The software life cycle is made up of three group of engineering processes: planning process, development processes and integral processes.

Planning Process
The planning process deals with the co-ordination of all the activities within the life cycle.

Development Processes

The development processes are intended to ultimately produce the binary executable that is put onto the embedded computer. The dependability-related purpose of the development processes is error avoidance.

These processes are the specification process, the design process, the coding process and the integration process. During these processes, high level requirements are refined into modular low level detailed requirements that are implemented into source code components: a large program is made up of a great number of components.

Integral Processes

Integral processes ensure the correctness, control, and confidence of the software life cycle processes and their outputs. Dependability-related purpose of integral processes is error detection.

These processes are the verification process, the configuration management process, the quality assurance process and the certification liaison process. Integral processes run throughout the software cycle concurrently with the development processes.

Among all these processes, a specific attention has to be paid to verification. Most of the costs, most of the resources, most of the tools and also most of the difficulties are due to verification. As a common figure, verification costs represent 50 % of the overall costs and depending on the software level, this can be significantly exceeded.

3.3 Verification Process

The purpose of verification is to detect and report errors that may have been introduced during the development processes. Verification is achieved through a combination of review, analysis and testing.

Review and Analysis

Review is a qualitative assessment. Analysis is an exhaustive verification or investigation of a piece of software. Both are "manual" techniques and they are not appropriate for verifying large volume of data. This lack of computer-supported tools is a severe limitation of these techniques.

Testing

Testing is the state-of-the-practice, privileged technique for verification. Tests are run on target hardware compatible with the final computer. Dedicated hardware and software test harnesses are required to control the execution of the code and to observe state changes: testing is hardware-intrusive and software-intrusive.

Also it has to be noted that these harnesses are closely related to the test objectives: testing a real-time property involves harnesses that are not useful for testing a functional property. Commonly, for one line of code, there are at least two lines of test harness. For some pathological cases, up to 10 lines of test harness may be required for one line of code.

Testing uses requirements-based methods and proceeds - generally - in a progressive manner from components to the complete program configuration throughout unit testing, integration testing and validation testing.

Unit Testing
Unit testing is performed on a per-component basis, the objective is to ensure that a component satisfies its low-level requirements. Typical errors that can be revealed include erroneous algorithm, incorrect logic decision, incorrect loop operation, and inadequate algorithm precision.

Integration Testing

Software/software integration
This testing is performed for a group of components, the objective is to ensure that the interactions of components are correct. Typical errors that can be revealed include incorrect initialisation of variables, incorrect sequencing of operations, parameter passing errors.

Hardware/software integration
This testing is performed for components running on the final target hardware, the objective is to ensure that interactions with the hardware are correct. Typical errors that can be revealed include stack overflow, incorrect handling of interrupt, worst-case execution time violation, execution period violation.

Validation Testing
Validation testing is a conformance-oriented verification. It is based on the final complete software operating on the target computer. The objective is to ensure that the high-level requirements are satisfied. Typical errors that can be revealed are identical to those revealed during hardware/software integration stage.

4 The Future

4.1 Change Factors

The Avionics Domain
The introduction of new functionalities, function sophistication, more complex architectures, and transfer of implementation from hardware to software are the observed trends. Avionics is becoming more and more software-intensive, and the hardware evolves towards a role of a -more or less generic- platform supplying computing power to the software functions. In so doing, the software volume is increasing quickly (roughly exponential). As a side effect safety-related requirements -and hence safety-dedicated functions- are moving from hardware into software.

Technology Domain
These trends in software are closely related to a change in basic technologies, mainly microprocessor and memory components. The most influential aspect is the tremendous increase in computing power delivered by modern microprocessors. Its high level of performance and its large memory meet the needs of the foreseen evolution of avionics software. However, this increased performance is achieved by the means of architectural features -pipelining, multilevel caches, parallel units- that induce a non-deterministic, unpredictable real-time behaviour. Thus current techniques used for the verification of real-time properties -typically the worst case execution time, periodic task guarantee, jitters bounds- are totally inadequate: new approaches and new techniques have to be investigated.

The Standard Domain
The DO-178B guidance materials are subject to revisions in order to take into account evolutions in the state-of-the-art. Revisions lead to more precise guidance and they reinforce the requirements.

The Computer Science Domain
Scientific results obtained in verification techniques such as abstract interpretation, model checking and theorem proving have led to the development of prototypes or even early versions of commercial tools.

4.2 Orientations

New Approach in Verification Engineering
The software engineering challenges raised by these coming changes are mainly verification challenges. Current techniques can hardly scale-up and for some of the new problems, they have no satisfactory answer. The first limit will be verification costs: review and analysis are "manual" techniques that can handle efficiently small quantities of software. Testing will be faced with combinatory explosion. Developing new approaches in verification engineering seems to be one of the best ways in improving the capabilities of the verification process.

Computer-Supported Static Analysis Technology
Based on available scientific results, the choice should be the development of computer-supported static analysis tools. Each tool should be specialised in the verification of a well-defined class of properties. The corresponding verification methodologies have to be developed, too. Development of these new technology (tools and methodologies) have to be understood as technology transfer involving both academics and industry.

Practical Objectives
Th ultimate goal is the improvement of the practice. The development of a new technology should target an introduction on the operational development within a short-term time limit (no more than 3 years).

Priorities

The introduction of this new technology should:

□ Target safety-critical software verification

□ Address verification problems related to: microprocessor architecture evolutions (execution time properties), computation evolutions (numerical computation, run-time properties), safety-related software properties

□ Provide tools able to process directly either source code written in widely used programming languages such as C, C++ or JAVA or executable binary code (for execution time properties).

Feasibility Conditions

Non intrusive
Programs submitted to the analyses must be kept totally unchanged.

Scale-up to real size program
Tools must be able to process real size programs in reasonable time. Real size means the size of the entity that has to be verified: If the scope of a tool is low-level requirements verification, real size is the size of a software component.

Ease of learn and use
"Normal" avionics software developers must be able to use the tools. Initial training must not exceed a few days. Interactions with tools must be compatible with the industrial development context.

Early payback
The new verification processes must have better characteristics in terms of productivity and quality-effectiveness. Benefits of the new technology must be effective since the first operational use.

Smooth integration
The use of a new technology should not break down the current verification process and environment. Integration within the development cycle must pass through controlled, progressive, accepted changes of the current process. In such an approach, the preparation of this integration is a very important task.

5 Concluding Remarks

The viewpoint and the orientations presented in this paper have been thought as a realisable way in developing verification engineering. The hope is that this verification technology based on computer-supported static analysis will become a part of the state-of-the-practice within the coming decade. Remarks and comments are welcome.

References

1. RTCA-EUROCAE: DO-178B/ED-12B, Software considerations in airborne systems and equipment certification (1992)
2. C.A.R. Hoare: An axiomatic basis for computer programming, Comm ACM 12(10), pp. 567-580 (1969)
3. Patrick Cousot, Radhia Cousot, Abstract interpretation: a unified lattice model for static analysis of programs by construction or approximation of fixpoints, in: Proc. 4th ACM Symp. On Principles of Programming languages, pp. 238-252 (1977)
4. Patrick Cousot: Progress on Abstract Interpretation Based Formal Methods and Future Challenges in Reinhard Wilhelm (Ed.): Informatics: 10 Years Back - 10 Years Ahead, Springer Verlag, LNCS 2000
5. Rustan M. Leino: Extended Static Checking: a Ten-Year Perspective in Reinhard Wilhelm (Ed.): Informatics: 10 Years Back - 10 Years Ahead, Springer Verlag, LNCS 2000
6. Edmund Clarke, Orna Grumberg, Somesh Jha, Yuan Lu, Helmut Veith: Progress on the State Explosion Problem in Model Checking in Reinhard Wilhelm (Ed.): Informatics: 10 Years Back - 10 Years Ahead, Springer Verlag, LNCS 2000

Abstract Interpretation Based Formal Methods and Future Challenges

Patrick Cousot

École normale supérieure, Département d'informatique,
45 rue d'Ulm, 75230 Paris cedex 05, France
Patrick.Cousot@ens.fr
http://www.di.ens.fr/~cousot/

Abstract. In order to contribute to the solution of the software reliability problem, tools have been designed to analyze statically the run-time behavior of programs. Because the correctness problem is undecidable, some form of approximation is needed. The purpose of *abstract interpretation* is to formalize this idea of *approximation*. We illustrate informally the application of abstraction to the *semantics* of programming languages as well as to *static program analysis*. The main point is that in order to reason or compute about a complex system, some information must be lost, that is the observation of executions must be either partial or at a high level of abstraction.

A few challenges for static program analysis by abstract interpretation are finally briefly discussed.

The electronic version of this paper includes a comparison with other formal methods: *typing*, *model-checking* and *deductive methods*.

1 Introductory Motivations

The evolution of hardware by a factor of 10^6 over the past 25 years has lead to the explosion of the size of programs in similar proportions. The scope of application of very large programs (from 1 to 40 millions of lines) is likely to widen rapidly in the next decade. Such big programs will have to be designed at a reasonable cost and then modified and maintained during their lifetime (which is often over 20 years). The size and efficiency of the programming and maintenance teams in charge of their design and follow-up cannot grow in similar proportions. At a not so uncommon (and often optimistic) rate of one bug per thousand lines such huge programs might rapidly become hardly manageable in particular for safety critical systems. Therefore in the next 10 years, the *software reliability problem* is likely to become a major concern and challenge to modern highly computer-dependent societies.

In the past decade a lot of progress has been made both on *thinking/methodological tools* (to enhance the human intellectual ability) to cope with complex software systems and *mechanical tools* (using the computer) to help the programmer to reason about programs.

R. Wilhelm (Ed.): Informatics. 10 Years Back. 10 Years Ahead, LNCS 2000, pp. 138–156, 2001.

Mechanical tools for computer aided program verification started by executing or simulating the program in as much as possible environments. However debugging of compiled code or simulation of a model of the source program hardly scale up and often offer a low coverage of dynamic program behavior.

Formal program verification methods attempt to mechanically prove that program execution is correct in all specified environments. This includes *deductive methods, model checking, program typing* and *static program analysis.*

Since program verification is undecidable, computer aided program verification methods are all partial or incomplete. The undecidability or complexity is always solved by using some form of *approximation.* This means that the mechanical tool will sometimes suffer from practical time and space complexity limitations, rely on finiteness hypotheses or provide only semi-algorithms, require user interaction or be able to consider restricted forms of specifications or programs only. The mechanical program verification tools are all quite similar and essentially differ in their choices regarding the approximations which have to be done in order to cope with undecidability or complexity. The purpose of *abstract interpretation* is to formalize this notion of approximation in a unified framework [10,17].

2   Abstract Interpretation

Since program verification deals with properties, that is sets (of objects with these properties), abstract interpretation can be formulated in an application independent setting, as a theory for approximating sets and set operations as considered in set (or category) theory, including inductive definitions [24]. A more restricted understanding of abstract interpretation is to view it as a theory of approximation of the behavior of dynamic discrete systems (e.g. the formal semantics of programs or a communication protocol specification). Since such behaviors can be characterized by fixpoints (e.g. corresponding to iteration), an essential part of the theory provides constructive and effective methods for fixpoint approximation and checking by abstraction [19,23].

2.1   Fixpoint Semantics

The *semantics of a programming language* defines the semantics of any program written in this language. The *semantics of a program* provides a formal mathematical model of all possible behaviors of a computer system executing this program in interaction with any possible environment. In the following we will try to explain informally why the semantics of a program can be defined as the solution of a fixpoint equation. Then, in order to compare semantics, we will show that all the semantics of a program can be organized in a hierarchy by abstraction. By observing computations at different levels of abstraction, one can approximate fixpoints hence organize the semantics of a program in a lattice [15].

2.2   Trace Semantics

Our finer grain of observation of program execution, that is the most precise of
the semantics that we will con-
sider, is that of a *trace semantics*
[15,19]. An execution of a program for a given specific interaction with its environment is a
sequence of states, observed at
discrete intervals of time, starting from an initial state, then
moving from one state to the
next state by executing an atomic
program step or transition and

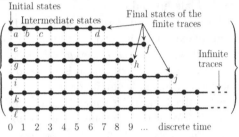

Fig. 1. Examples of Computation Traces

either ending in a final regular or erroneous state or non terminating, in which
case the trace is infinite (see Fig. 1).

2.3   Least Fixpoint Trace Semantics

Introducing the *computational partial ordering* [15], we define the trace semantics
in fixpoint form [15], as the least solution of an equation of the form $X = \mathcal{F}(X)$
where X ranges over sets of finite and infinite traces.

More precisely, let **Behaviors** be the set of execution traces of a program,
possibly starting in any state. We denote by **Behaviors**$^+$ the subset of finite
traces and by **Behaviors**$^\infty$ the subset of infinite traces.

A finite trace $\overset{a}{\bullet}\!\!-\!\!\cdots\!\!-\!\!\overset{z}{\bullet}$ in **Behaviors**$^+$ is either reduced to a final state
(in which case there is no possible transition from state $\overset{a}{\bullet} = \overset{z}{\bullet}$) or the initial state
$\overset{a}{\bullet}$ is not final and the trace consists of a first computation step $\overset{a}{\bullet}\!-\!\overset{b}{\bullet}$ after which,
from the intermediate state $\overset{b}{\bullet}$, the execution goes on with the shorter finite trace
$\overset{b}{\bullet}\!\!-\!\!\cdots\!\!-\!\!\overset{z}{\bullet}$ ending in the final state $\overset{z}{\bullet}$. The finite traces are therefore all well
defined by induction on their length.

An infinite trace $\overset{a}{\bullet}\!\!-\!\!\cdots\!\!-\!\!\cdots$ in **Behaviors**$^\infty$ starts with a first computation step $\overset{a}{\bullet}\!-\!\overset{b}{\bullet}$ after which, from the intermediate state $\overset{b}{\bullet}$, the execution goes
on with an infinite trace $\overset{b}{\bullet}\!\!-\!\!\cdots\!\!-\!\!\cdots$ starting from the intermediate state
$\overset{b}{\bullet}$. These remarks and **Behaviors** = **Behaviors**$^+$ $\cup$ **Behaviors**$^\infty$ lead to the
following fixpoint equation:

$$\textbf{Behaviors} = \{\overset{a}{\bullet} \mid \overset{a}{\bullet} \text{ is a final state}\}$$
$$\cup \{\overset{a}{\bullet}\!-\!\overset{b}{\bullet}\!\!-\!\!\cdots\!\!-\!\!\overset{z}{\bullet} \mid \overset{a}{\bullet}\!-\!\overset{b}{\bullet} \text{ is an elementary step \&}$$
$$\overset{b}{\bullet}\!\!-\!\!\cdots\!\!-\!\!\overset{z}{\bullet} \in \textbf{Behaviors}^+\}$$
$$\cup \{\overset{a}{\bullet}\!-\!\overset{b}{\bullet}\!\!-\!\!\cdots\!\!-\!\!\cdots \mid \overset{a}{\bullet}\!-\!\overset{b}{\bullet} \text{ is an elementary step \&}$$
$$\overset{b}{\bullet}\!\!-\!\!\cdots\!\!-\!\!\cdots \in \textbf{Behaviors}^\infty\}$$

In general, the equation has multiple solutions. For example if there is only one non-final state $\overset{a}{\bullet}$ and only possible elementary step $\overset{a}{\bullet}\!\!-\!\!\overset{a}{\bullet}$ then the equation is **Behaviors** = $\{\overset{a}{\bullet}\!\!-\!\!\overset{a}{\bullet}\!\!-\ldots-\ldots \mid \overset{a}{\bullet}\!\!-\ldots-\ldots \in$ **Behaviors**$\}$. One solution is $\{\overset{a}{\bullet}\!\!-\!\!\overset{a}{\bullet}\!\!-\!\!\overset{a}{\bullet}\!\!-\!\!\overset{a}{\bullet}\!\!-\ldots-\ldots\}$ but another one is the empty set $\emptyset$. Therefore, we choose the least solution for the *computational partial ordering* [15]:

$$\ll \textit{More finite traces \& less infinite traces} \gg.$$

2.4 Abstractions & Abstract Domains

A programming language semantics is more or less precise according to the considered observation level of program execution. This intuitive idea can be formalized by *Abstract interpretation* [15] and applied to different languages, including for proof methods.

The *theory of abstract interpretation* formalizes this notion of approximation and abstraction in a mathematical setting which is independent of particular applications. In particular, abstractions must be provided for all mathematical constructions used in semantic definitions of programming and specification languages [19,23].

An *abstract domain* is an abstraction of the concrete semantics in the form of *abstract properties* (approximating the concrete properties **Behaviors**) and *abstract operations* (including abstractions of the concrete approximation and computational partial orderings, an approximation of the concrete fixpoint transformer $\mathcal{F}$, etc.). Abstract domains for complex approximations of designed by composing abstract domains for simpler components [19], see Sec. 2.10.

If the approximation is coarse enough, the abstraction of a concrete semantics can lead to an abstract semantics which is less precise, but is *effectively computable* by a computer. By effective computation of the abstract semantics, the computer is able to analyze the behavior of programs and of software before and without executing them [16]. *Abstract interpretation algorithms* provide approximate methods for computing this abstract semantics. The most important algorithms in abstract interpretation are those providing effective methods for the exact or approximate iterative resolution of fixpoint equations [17].

We will first illustrate formal and effective abstractions for sets. Then we will show that such abstractions can be lifted to functions and finally to fixpoints.

The abstraction idea and its formalization are equally applicable in other areas of computer science such as artificial intelligence e.g. for intelligent planning, proof checking, automated deduction, theorem proving, etc.

2.5 Hierarchy of Abstractions

As shown in Fig. 2 (from [15], where **Behaviors**, denoted τ^{∞} for short, is the lattice infimum), all abstractions of a semantics can be organized in a lattice (which is part of the lattice of abstract interpretations introduced in [19]). The

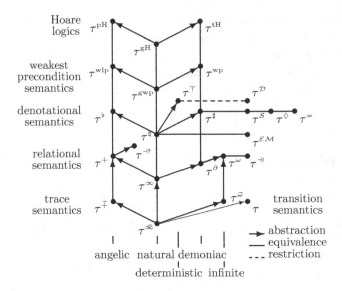

Fig. 2. The Hierarchy of Semantics

approximation partial ordering of this lattice formally corresponds to logical implication, intuitively to the idea that one semantics is more precise than another one.

Fig. 3 illustrates the derivation of a *relational semantics* (denoted τ^∞ in Fig. 2) from a trace semantics (denoted τ^{∞} in Fig. 2). The abstraction α_r from trace

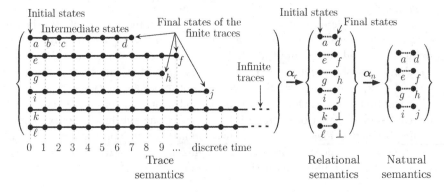

Fig. 3. Abstraction from Trace to Relational and Natural Semantics

to relational semantics consists in replacing the finite traces $\overset{a}{\bullet}\!\!-\!\!-\cdots\overset{z}{\bullet}$ by the pair $\langle a, z \rangle$ of the initial and final states. The infinite traces $\overset{a}{\bullet}\!\!-\!\!-\!\!\overset{b}{\bullet}\!\!-\cdots\!\!-\cdots$

are replaced by the pair $\langle a, \perp \rangle$ where the symbol $\perp$ denotes non-termination. Therefore the abstraction is:

$$\alpha_r(X) = \{\langle a, z \rangle \mid \overset{a}{\bullet}\!\!-\!\!-\ldots\!-\!\!\overset{z}{\bullet} \in X\} \ \cup \ \{\langle a, \perp \rangle \mid \overset{a}{\bullet}\!\!-\!\!\overset{b}{\bullet}\!-\ldots\!-\ldots \in X\}.$$

The *denotational semantics* (denoted $\tau^{\natural}$ in Fig. 2) is the isomorphic representation of a relation by its right-image:

$$\alpha_d(R) = \boldsymbol{\lambda}\, a \cdot \{x \mid \langle a, x \rangle \in R\}.$$

The abstraction from relational to *big-step operational or natural semantics* (denoted τ^+ in Fig. 2) simply consists in forgetting everything about non-termination, so $\alpha_n(R) = \{\langle a, x \rangle \in R \mid x \neq \perp\}$, as illustrated in Fig. 3.

A non comparable abstraction consists in collecting the set of initial and final states as well as all transitions $\langle x, y \rangle$ appearing along some finite or infinite trace $\overset{a}{\bullet}\!-\!\!-\ldots\overset{x}{\bullet}\!-\!\!\overset{y}{\bullet}\ldots$ of the trace semantics. One gets the *small-step operational or transition semantics* (denoted τ in Fig. 2 and also called Kripke structure in modal logic) as illustrated in Fig. 4.

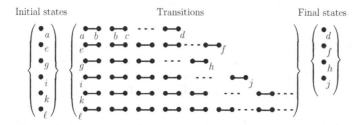

Initial states   Transitions   Final states

Fig. 4. Transition Semantics

A further abstraction consists in collecting all states appearing along some finite or infinite trace as illustrated in Fig. 5. This is the *partial correctness semantics* or the *static/collecting semantics* for proving invariance properties of programs.

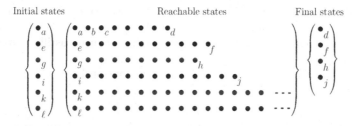

Initial states   Reachable states   Final states

Fig. 5. Static / Collecting / Partial Correctness Semantics

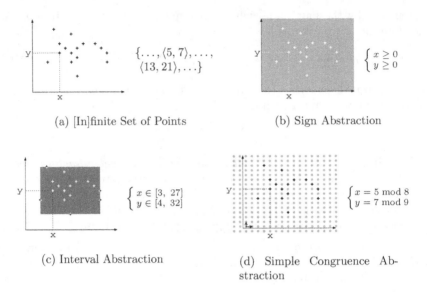

(a) [In]finite Set of Points

(b) Sign Abstraction

(c) Interval Abstraction

(d) Simple Congruence Abstraction

Fig. 6. Non-relational Abstractions

All abstractions considered in this paper are "from above" so that the abstract semantics describes a superset or logical consequence of the concrete semantics. Abstractions "from below" are dual and consider a subset of the concrete semantics. An example of approximation "from below" is provided by debugging techniques which consider a subset of the possible program executions or by existential checking where one wants to prove the existence of an execution trace prefix fulfilling some given specification. In order to avoid repeating two times dual concepts and as we do usually, we only consider approximations "from above", knowing that approximations "from below" can be easily derived by applying the duality principle (as found e.g. in lattice theory).

2.6   Effective Abstractions

Numerical Abstractions Assume that a program has two integer variables X and Y. The trace semantics of the program (Fig. 1) can be abstracted in the static/collecting semantics (Fig. 5). A further abstraction consists in forgetting in a state all but the values x and y of variables X and Y. In this way the trace semantics is abstracted to a set of points (pairs of values), as illustrated in the plane by Fig. 6(a).

We now illustrate informally a number of effective abstractions of an [in]finite set of points.

Non-relational Abstractions The non-relational, attribute independent or cartesian abstractions [19, example 6.2.0.2] consists in ignoring the possible re-

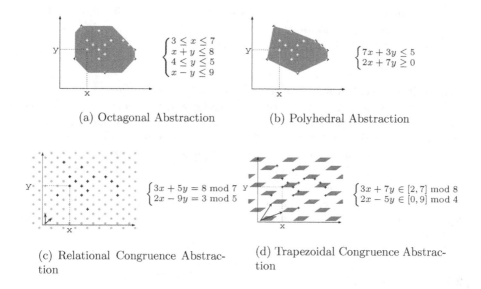

(a) Octagonal Abstraction   (b) Polyhedral Abstraction

(c) Relational Congruence Abstraction

(d) Trapezoidal Congruence Abstraction

Fig. 7. Relational Abstractions

lationships between the values of the X and Y variables. So a set of pairs is approximated through projection by a pair of sets. Each such set may still be infinite and in general not exactly computer representable. Further abstractions are therefore needed.

The *sign abstraction* [19] illustrated in Fig. 6(b) consists in replacing integers by their sign thus ignoring their absolute value. The *interval abstraction* [16] illustrated in Fig. 6(c) is more precise since it approximates a set of integers by it minimal and maximal values (including $-\infty$ and $+\infty$ as well as the empty set if necessary).

The *congruence abstraction* [37] (generalizing the parity abstraction [19]) is not comparable, as illustrated in Fig. 6(d).

Relational Abstractions Relational abstractions are more precise than non relational ones in that some of the relationships between values of the program states are preserved by the abstraction.

For example the *polyhedral abstraction* [29] illustrated in Fig. 7(b) approximates a set of integers by its convex hull. Only non-linear relationships between the values of the program variables are forgotten.

The use of an *octagonal abstraction* illustrated in Fig. 7(a) is less precise since only some shapes of polyhedra are retained or equivalently only linear relations between any two variables are considered with coefficients +1 or -1 (of the form $\pm x \pm y \leq c$ where c is an integer constant).

A non comparable relational abstraction is the *linear congruence abstraction* [38] illustrated in Fig. 7(c).

A combination of non-relational dense approximations (like intervals) and relational sparse approximations (like congruences) is the *trapezoidal linear congruence abstraction* [47] as illustrated in Fig. 7(d).

Symbolic Abstractions Most structures manipulated by programs are *symbolic structures* such as control structures (call graphs), data structures (search trees, pointers [32,33,53,58]), communication structures (distributed & mobile programs [35,40,57]), etc. It is very difficult to find compact and expressive abstractions of such sets of objects (sets of languages, sets of automata, sets of trees or graphs, etc.). For example Büchi automata or automata on trees are very expressive but algorithmically expensive.

A compromise between semantic expressivity and algorithmic efficiency was recently introduced by [48] using *Binary Decision Graphs* and *Tree Schemata* to abstract infinite sets of infinite trees.

2.7 Information Loss

Any abstraction introduces some loss of information. For example the abstraction of the trace semantics into relational or denotational semantics loses all information on the computation cost since all intermediate steps in the execution are removed.

All answers given by the abstract semantics are always correct with respect to the concrete semantics. For example, if termination is proved using the relational semantics then there is no execution abstracted to $\langle a, \perp \rangle$, so there is no infinite trace $\overset{a}{\bullet}\!\!\!-\!\!\!\overset{b}{\bullet}\!\!\!-\!\!\!-\ldots-\ldots$ in the trace semantics, whence non termination is impossible when starting execution in initial state a.

However, because of the information loss, not all questions can be definitely answered with the abstract semantics. For example, the natural semantics cannot answer questions about termination as can be done with the relational or denotational semantics. These semantics cannot answer questions about concrete computation costs.

The more concrete is the semantics, the more questions it can answer. The more abstract semantics are simpler. Non comparable abstract semantics (such as intervals and congruences) answer non comparable sets of questions.

To illustrate the loss of information, let us consider the problem of deciding whether the operation 1/(X+1-Y) appearing in a program is always well defined at run-time. The answer can certainly be given by the concrete semantics since it has no point on the line $x + 1 - y = 0$, as shown in Fig. 8(a).

In practice the concrete abstraction is not computable so it is hardly usable in a useful effective tool. The dense abstractions that we have considered are too approximate as is illustrated in Fig. 8(b).

However the answer is positive when using the relational congruence abstraction, as shown in Fig. 8(c).

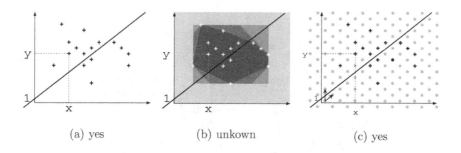

(a) yes   (b) unkown   (c) yes

Fig. 8. Is `1/(X+1-Y)` well-defined?

2.8   Function Abstraction

We now show how the abstraction of complex mathematical objects used in the semantics of programming or specification languages can be defined by composing abstractions of simpler mathematical structures.

For example knowing abstractions of the parameter and result of a monotonic function on sets, a function F can be abstracted into an abstract function $F^\sharp$ as illustrated in Fig. 9 [19]. Mathematically, $F^\sharp$ takes its parameter x in the abstract domain. Let $\gamma(x)$ be the corresponding concrete set (γ is the adjoined, intuitively the inverse of the abstraction function α). The function F can be applied to get the concrete result $\circ F \circ \gamma(x)$. The abstraction function α can then be applied to approximate the result $F^\sharp(x) = \alpha \circ F \circ \gamma(x)$.

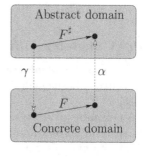

$$F^\sharp = \alpha \circ F \circ \gamma$$

Fig. 9. Function Abstraction

In general, neither F, α nor γ are computable even though the abstraction α may be effective. So we have got a formal specification of the abstract function $F^\sharp$ and an algorithm has to be found for an effective implementation.

2.9   Fixpoint Abstraction

A fixpoint of a function F can often be obtained as the limit of the iterations of F from a given initial value $\perp$. In this case the abstraction of the fixpoint can often be obtained as the abstract limit of the iteration of the abstraction $F^\sharp$ of F starting from the abstraction $\alpha(\perp)$ of the initial value $\perp$. The basic result is that the concretization of the abstract fixpoint is related to the concrete fixpoint by the approximation relation expressing the soundness of the abstraction [19]. This is illustrated in Fig. 10.

Often states have some finite component (e.g. a program counter) which can be used to partition into fixpoint system of equations by projection along that

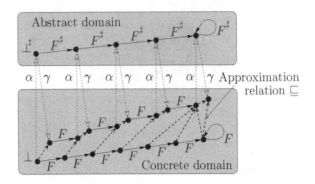

Fig. 10. Fixpoint Abstraction lfp $F \sqsubseteq \gamma(\text{lfp } F^\sharp)$

component. Then *chaotic* [18] and *asynchronous iteration strategies* [10] can be used to solve the equations iteratively. Various efficient iteration strategies have been studied, including ones taking particular properties of abstractions into account and others to speed up the convergence of the iterates [26].

2.10   Composing Abstractions

Abstractions hence abstract interpreters for static program analysis can be designed compositionally by stepwise abstraction, combination or refinement [36,13].

An example of stepwise abstraction is the functional abstraction of Sec. 2.8. The abstraction of a function is parameterized by abstractions for the function parameters and the function result which can be chosen later in the modular design of the abstract interpreter.

An example of abstraction combination is the *reduced product* of two abstractions [19] which is the most abstract abstraction more precise than these two abstractions or the *reduce cardinal power* [19] generalizing case analysis. Such combination of abstract domains can be implemented as parameterized modules in static analyzer generators (e.g. [45]) so as to partially automate the design of expressive analyses from simpler ones.

An example of refinement is the *disjunctive completion* [19] which completes an abstract domain by adding concrete disjunctions missing in the abstract domain. Another example of abstract domain refinement is the *complementation* [8] adding concrete negations missing in the abstract domain.

2.11   Sound and Complete Abstractions

Abstract interpretation theory has mainly been concerned with the *soundness* of the abstract semantics/interpreter, relative to which questions can be answered correctly despite the loss of information [17]. Soundness is essential in practice and leads to a formal design method [19].

However *completeness*, relative to the formalization of the loss of information in a controlled way so as to answer a given set of questions, has also been intensively studied [19,36], including in the context of model checking [14].

In practice complete abstractions, including a most abstract one, always exist to check that a given program semantics satisfies a given specification. Moreover any given abstraction can be refined to a complete one. Nevertheless this approach has severe practical limitations since, in general, the design of such complete abstractions or the refinement of a given one is logically equivalent to the design of an inductive argument for the formal proof that the given program satisfies the given specification, while the soundness proof of this abstraction logically amounts to checking the inductive verification conditions or proof obligations of this formal proof [14]. Such proofs can hardly be fully automated hence human interaction is unavoidable. Moreover the whole process has to be repeated each time the program or specification is modified.

Instead of considering such strong specifications for a given specific program, the objective of static program analysis is to consider (often predefined) specifications and all possible programs. The practical problem in static program analysis is therefore to design useful abstractions which are computable for all programs and expressive enough to yield interesting information for most programs.

3   Static Program Analysis

Static program analysis is the automatic static determination of dynamic runtime properties of programs.

3.1   Foundational Ideas of Static Program Analysis

Given a program and a specification, a program analyzer will check if the program semantics satisfies the specification (Fig. 11). In case of failure, the analyzer will provide hints to understand the origin of errors (e.g. by a backward analysis providing necessary conditions to be satisfied by counter-examples).

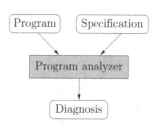

The principle of the analysis is to compute an approximate semantics of the program in order to check a given specification. Abstract in-

Fig. 11. Program Analysis

terpretation is used to derive, from a standard semantics, the approximate and computable abstract semantics. The derivation can often be done by composing standard abstractions to fit a particular kind of information which has to be discovered about program execution. This derivation is itself not (fully) mechanizable but *static analyzer generators* such as PAG [46] and others can provide generic abstractions to be composed with problem specific ones.

In practice, the program analyzer contains a *generator* reading the program text and producing equations or constraints whose solution is a computer representation of the program abstract semantics. A *solver* is then used to solve these abstract equations/constraints. A popular resolution method is to use iteration. Of the numerical abstractions considered in Sec. 2.6, only the sign and simple congruence abstractions ensure the finite convergence of the iterates. If the limit of the iterates is inexistent (which may be the case e.g. for the polyhedral abstraction) or it is reached after infinitely many iteration steps (e.g. interval and octagonal abstractions), the convergence may have to be ensured and/or accelerated using a *widening* to over estimate the solution in finitely many steps followed by a *narrowing* to improve it [10,17,26].

In *abstract compilation*, the generator and solver are directly compiled into a program which directly yields the approximate solution.

This solution is an approximation of the abstract semantics which is then used by a *diagnoser* to check the specification. Because of the loss of information, the diagnosis is always of the form "yes", "no", "unknown" or "irrelevant" (e.g. a safety specification for unreachable code). The general structure of program analyzers is illustrated in Fig. 12. Besides diagnosis, static program analysis is also used for other applications in which case the diagnoser is replaced by an *optimiser* (for compile-time optimization), a *program transformer* (for partial evaluation [43]), etc.

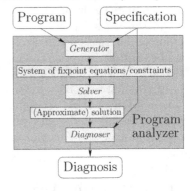

Fig. 12. Principle of Program Analysis

3.2   Shortcomings of Static Program Analysis

Static program analysis can be used for large programs (e.g. 220,000 lines of C) without user interaction. The abstractions are chosen to be of wide scope without specialization to a particular program. Abstract algebras can be designed and implemented into libraries which are reusable for different programming languages. The objective is to discover invariants that are likely to appear in many programs so that the abstraction must be widely reusable for the program analyzer to be of economic interest.

The drawback of this general scope is that the considered abstract specifications and properties are often simple, mainly concerning elementary safety properties such as absence of run-time errors. For example non-linear abstractions of sets of points are very difficult and very few mathematical results are of practical interest and directly applicable to program analysis. Checking termination and similar liveness properties is trivial with finite state systems, at least from a theoretical if not algorithmic point of view (e.g. finding loops in finite graphs). The same problem is much more difficult for infinite state systems because of fairness [48] or of potentially infinite data structures (as considered e.g. in partial evaluation) which do not amount to finite cycles so that termination or inevitability proofs require the discovery of *variant functions on well-founded sets* which is very difficult in full generality.

Even when considering restricted simple abstract properties, the semantics of real-life programming languages is very complex (recursion, concurrency, modularity, etc.) whence so is the corresponding abstract interpreter. The abstraction of this semantics, hence the design of the analyzer is mostly manual (and beyond the ability of casual programmers or theorem provers) whence costly. The considered abstractions must have a large scope of application and must be easily reusable to be of economic interest.

From a user point of view, the results of the analysis have to be presented in a simple way (for example by pointing at errors only or by providing abstract counter-examples, or less frequently concrete ones). Experience shows that the cases of uncertainty represent 5 to 10 % of the possible cases. They must be handled with other empirical or formal methods (including more refined abstract interpretations).

3.3   Applications of Static Program Analysis

Among the numerous applications of static program analysis, let us cite *data flow analysis* [52,28]; *program optimization and transformation* (including partial evaluation and program specialization [43] and data dependence analysis for the parallelisation of sequential languages); *set-based analysis* [27]; *type inference* [12] (including undecidable systems and soft typing); verification of *reactive* [39,42], *real-time* and *(linear) hybrid systems* including state space reduction; *cryptographic protocol* analysis; *abstract model-checking* of infinite systems [28]; *abstract debugging*, testing and verification ; *cache and pipeline behavior prediction* [34]; *probabilistic analysis* [49]; *communication topology analysis* for mobile/distributed code [35,40,57]; *automatic differentiation* of numerical programs; *abstract simulation* of temporal specifications; Semantic tattooing/*watermarking* of software [54]; etc.

Static program analysis has been intensively studied for a variety of programming languages including procedural languages (e.g. for alias and pointer analysis [32,33,53,58]), functional languages (e.g. for binding time [56], strictness [4,50] and comportment analysis [25], exception analysis [59]), parallel functional languages, data parallel languages, logic languages including Prolog [1,22,31] (e.g. for groundness [9], sharing [7], freeness [5] and their combinations [6], parallelizatiion [3], etc.), database programming languages, concurrent logic languages, functional logic languages, constraint logic languages, concurrent constraint logic languages, specification languages, synchronous languages, procedural/functional concurrent/parallel languages [21], communicating and distributed languages [20] and more recently object-oriented languages [2,55].

Abstract interpretation based static program analyses have been used for the static analysis of the embedded ADA software of the Ariane 5 launcher[1] and the

---

[1] Flight software (60,000 lines of Ada code) and Inertial Measurement Unit (30,000 lines of Ada code).

ARD[2] [44]. The static program analyser aims at the automatic detection of the *definiteness, potentiality, impossibility* or *inaccessibility* of run-time errors such as scalar and floating-point overflows, array index errors, divisions by zero and related arithmetic exceptions, uninitialized variables, data races on shared data structures, etc. The analyzer was able to automatically discover the Ariane 501 flight error. The static analysis of embedded safety critical software (such as avionic software [51]) is very promising [30].

3.4   Industrialization of Static Analysis by Abstract Interpretation

The impressive results obtained by the static analysis of real-life embedded critical software [44,51] is quite promising for the industrialization of abstract interpretation.

This is the explicit objective of AbsInt Angewandte Informatik GmbH (www.absint.com) created in Germany by R. Wilhelm and C. Ferdinand in 1998 commercializing the program analyzer generator PAG and an application to determine the worst-case execution time for modern computer architectures with memory caches, pipelines, etc [34].

Polyspace Technologies (www.polyspace.com) was created in France by A. Deutsch and D. Pilaud in 1999 to develop and commercialize ADA and C program analyzers.

Other companies like Connected Components Corporation (www.concmp.com) created in the U.S.A. by W.L. Harrison in 1993 use abstract interpretation internally e.g. for compiler design [41].

4   Grand Challenge for the Next Decade

We believe that in the next decade the software industry will certainly have to face its responsibility imposed by a computer-dependent society, in particular for safety critical systems. Consequently, *Software reliability*[3] will be a grand challenge for computer science and practice.

The grand challenge for formal methods, in particular abstract interpretation based formal tools, is both the large scale industrialization and the intensification of the fundamental research effort.

General-purpose, expressive and cost-effective abstractions have to be developed e.g. to handle floating point numbers, data dependences (e.g. for parallelization), liveness properties with fairness (to extend finite-state model-checking to software), timing properties for embedded software, probabilistic properties, etc. Present-day tools will have to be enhanced to handle higher-order compositional modular analyses and to cope with new programming paradigms involving complex data and control concepts (such as objects, concurrent threads,

---

[2] Atmospheric Reentry Demonstrator.
[3] other suggestions were "trustworthiness" (C. Jones) and "robustness" (R. Leino).

distributed/mobile programming, etc.), to automatically combine and locally refine abstractions in particular to cope with "unknow" answers, to interact nicely with users and other formal or informal methods.

The most challenging objective might be to integrate formal analysis by abstract interpretation in the full software development process, from the initial specifications to the ultimate program development.

Acknowledgements I thank Radhia Cousot and Reinhard Wilhelm for their comments on a preliminary version of this paper. This work was supported by the DAEDALUS [30] and TUAMOTU [54] projects.

References

1. R. Barbuti, R. Giacobazzi, and G. Levi. A general framework for semantics-based bottom-up abstract interpretation of logic programs. *TOPLAS*, 15(1):133–181, 1993.

2. B. Blanchet. Escape analysis for object-oriented languages: Application to Java. *OOPSLA '99. SIGPLAN Not. 34(10):20–34*, 1999.

3. F. Bueno, M.J. García de la Banda, and M.V. Hermenegildo. Effectiveness of abstract interpretation in automatic parallelization: A case study in logic programming. *TOPLAS*, 21(2):189–239, 1999.

4. G.L. Burn, C.L. Hankin, and S. Abramsky. Strictness analysis of higher-order functions. *Sci. Comput. Programming*, 7:249–278, 1986.

5. M. Codish, D. Dams, G. Filè, and M. Bruynooghe. Freeness analysis for logic programs – and correctness? *Proc. ICLP '93*, pp. 116–131. MIT Press, 1993.

6. M. Codish, H. Søndergaard, and P.J. Stuckey. Sharing and groundness dependencies in logic programs. *TOPLAS*, 21(5):948–976, 1999.

7. A. Cortesi and G. Filé. Sharing is optimal. *J. Logic Programming*, 38(3):371–386, 1999.

8. A. Cortesi, G. Filé, R. Giacobazzi, C. Palamidessi, and F. Ranzato. Complementation in abstract interpretation. *TOPLAS*, 19(1):7–47, 1997.

9. A. Cortesi, G. Filé, and W.H. Winsborough. Optimal groundness analysis using propositional logic. *J. Logic Programming*, 27(2):137–167, 1996.

10. P. Cousot. *Méthodes itératives de construction et d'approximation de points fixes d'opérateurs monotones sur un treillis, analyse sémantique de programmes*. Thèse d'État ès sciences mathématiques, Univ. of Grenoble, 1978.

11. P. Cousot. Constructive design of a hierarchy of semantics of a transition system by abstract interpretation. *ENTCS*, 6, 1997. http://www.elsevier.nl/locate/entcs/volume6.html, 25 pages.

12. P. Cousot. Types as abstract interpretations. 24th *POPL*, pp. 316–331. ACM Press, 1997.

13. P. Cousot. The calculational design of a generic abstract interpreter. In M. Broy and R. Steinbrüggen, editors, *Calculational System Design*, volume 173, pp. 421–505. NATO Science Series, Series F: Computer and Systems Sciences. IOS Press, 1999.

14. P. Cousot. Partial completeness of abstract fixpoint checking. *SARA '2000*, LNAI 1864, pp. 1–25. Springer-Verlag, 2000.

15. P. Cousot. Constructive design of a hierarchy of semantics of a transition system by abstract interpretation. *Theoret. Comput. Sci.*, To appear (Preliminary version in [11]).

16. P. Cousot and R. Cousot. Static determination of dynamic properties of programs. *2nd Int. Symp. on Programming*, pp. 106–130. Dunod, 1976.

17. P. Cousot and R. Cousot. Abstract interpretation: a unified lattice model for static analysis of programs by construction or approximation of fixpoints. *4th POPL*, pp. 238–252. ACM Press, 1977.

18. P. Cousot and R. Cousot. Automatic synthesis of optimal invariant assertions: mathematical foundations. *Symp. on Artificial Intelligence & Programming Languages*, SIGPLAN Not. 12(8):1–12, 1977.

19. P. Cousot and R. Cousot. Systematic design of program analysis frameworks. *6th POPL*, pp. 269–282. ACM Press, 1979.

20. P. Cousot and R. Cousot. Semantic analysis of communicating sequential processes. *7th ICALP*, LNCS 85, pp. 119–133. Springer-Verlag, 1980.

21. P. Cousot and R. Cousot. Invariance proof methods and analysis techniques for parallel programs. In A.W. Biermann, G. Guiho, and Y. Kodratoff, editors, *Automatic Program Construction Techniques*, ch. 12, pp. 243–271. Macmillan, 1984.

22. P. Cousot and R. Cousot. Abstract interpretation and application to logic programs[4]. *J. Logic Programming*, 13(2–3):103–179, 1992.

23. P. Cousot and R. Cousot. Abstract interpretation frameworks. *J. Logic and Comp.*, 2(4):511–547, Aug. 1992.

24. P. Cousot and R. Cousot. Inductive definitions, semantics and abstract interpretation. *19th POPL*, pp. 83–94. ACM Press, 1992.

25. P. Cousot and R. Cousot. Higher-order abstract interpretation (and application to comportment analysis generalizing strictness, termination, projection and PER analysis of functional languages). *Proc. 1994 ICCL*, pp. 95–112. IEEE Comp. Soc. Press, 1994.

26. P. Cousot and R. Cousot. Comparing the Galois connection and widening/narrowing approaches to abstract interpretation. *Proc. 4th PLILP '92*, LNCS 631, pp. 269–295. Springer-Verlag, 1992.

27. P. Cousot and R. Cousot. Formal language, grammar and set-constraint-based program analysis by abstract interpretation. *7th FPCA*, pp. 170–181. ACM Press, 1995.

28. P. Cousot and R. Cousot. Temporal abstract interpretation. *27th POPL*, pp. 12–25. ACM Press, 2000.

29. P. Cousot and N. Halbwachs. Automatic discovery of linear restraints among variables of a program. *5th POPL*, pp. 84–97. ACM Press, 1978.

30. DAEDALUS: *Validation of critical software by static analysis and abstract testing.* P. Cousot, R. Cousot, A. Deutsch, C. Ferdinand, É. Goubault, N. Jones, D. Pilaud, F. Randimbivololona, M. Sagiv, H. Seidel, and R. Wilhelm. Project IST-1999-20527 of the european 5th Framework Programme, Oct. 2000 – Oct. 2002.

31. S.K. Debray. Formal bases for dataflow analysis of logic programs. In G. Levi, editor, *Advances in Logic Programming Theory*, Int. Sec. 3, pp. 115–182. Clarendon Press, 1994.

32. A. Deutsch. Semantic models and abstract interpretation techniques for inductive data structures and pointers. *Proc. PEPM '95*, pp. 226–229. ACM Press, 1995.

---

[4] The editor of J. Logic Programming has mistakenly published the unreadable galley proof. For a correct version of this paper, see http://www.di.ens.fr/~cousot.

33. N. Dor, M. Rodeh, and M. Sagiv. Checking cleanness in linked lists. *Proc. SAS '2000*, LNCS 1824, pp. 115–134. Springer-Verlag, 2000.
34. C. Ferdinand, F. Martin, R. Wilhelm, and M. Alt. Cache behavior prediction by abstract interpretation. *Sci. Comput. Programming*, 35(1):163–189, 1999.
35. J. Feret. Confidentiality analysis of mobile systems. *Proc. SAS '2000*, LNCS 1824, pp. 135–154. Springer-Verlag, 2000.
36. R. Giacobazzi, F. Ranzato, and F. Scozzari. Making abstract interpretations complete. *J. ACM*, 47(2):361–416, 2000.
37. P. Granger. Static analysis of arithmetical congruences. *Int. J. Comput. Math.*, 30:165–190, 1989.
38. P. Granger. Static analysis of linear congruence equalities among variables of a program. 493, pp. 169–192. Springer-Verlag, 1991.
39. N. Halbwachs. About synchronous programming and abstract interpretation. *Sci. Comput. Programming*, 31(1):75–89, 1998.
40. R.R. Hansen, J.G. Jensen, F. Nielson, and H. Riis Nielson. Abstract interpretation of mobile ambients. *Proc. SAS '99*, LNCS 1694, pp. 134–138. Springer-Verlag, 1999.
41. W.L. Harrison. Can abstract interpretation become a main stream compiler technology? (abstract). *Proc. SAS '97*, LNCS 1302, p. 395. Springer-Verlag, 1997.
42. T.A. Henzinger, R. Majumbar, F. Mang, and J.-F. Raskin. Abstract interpretation of game properties. *Proc. SAS '2000*, LNCS 1824, pp. 220–239. Springer-Verlag, 2000.
43. N.D. Jones. Combining abstract interpretation and partial evaluation (brief overview). *Proc. SAS '97*, LNCS 1302, pp. 396–405. Springer-Verlag, 1997.
44. P. Lacan, J.N. Monfort, L.V.Q. Ribal, A. Deutsch, and G. Gonthier. The software reliability verification process: The ARIANE 5 example. *DASIA '98 – DAta Systems In Aerospace*, ESA Publications, 1998.
45. B. Le Charlier and P. Van Hentenryck. Experimental evaluation of a generic abstract interpretation algorithm for Prolog. *Proc. ICCL 92*, pp. 137–146. IEEE Comp. Soc. Press, 1992.
46. F. Martin. *Generating Program Analyzers*. Pirrot Verlag, Saarbrücken, 1999.
47. F. Masdupuy. Semantic analysis of interval congruences. *FMPA*, LNCS 735, pp. 142–155. Springer-Verlag, 1993.
48. L. Mauborgne. Tree schemata and fair termination. *Proc. SAS '2000*, LNCS 1824, pp. 302–321. Springer-Verlag, 2000.
49. D. Monniaux. Abstract interpretation of probabilistic semantics. *Proc. SAS '2000*, LNCS 1824, pp. 322–339. Springer-Verlag, 2000.
50. A. Mycroft. *Abstract Interpretation and Optimising Transformations for Applicative Programs*. Ph.D. Dissertation, CST-15-81, Univ. of Edinburgh, 1981.
51. F. Randimbivololona, J. Souyris, and A. Deutsch. Improving avionics software verification cost-effectiveness: Abstract interpretation based technology contribution. *DASIA '2000 – DAta Systems In Aerospace*, ESA Publications, 2000.
52. D.A. Schmidt and B. Steffen. Program analysis *as* model checking of abstract interpretations. *Proc. SAS '98*, LNCS 1503, pp. 351–380. Springer-Verlag, 1998.
53. J. Stransky. A lattice for abstract interpretation of dynamic (LISP-like) structures. *Inform. and Comput.*, 101(1):70–102, 1992.
54. TUAMOTU: *Tatouage électronique sémantique de code mobile Java*. P. Cousot, R. Cousot, and M. Riguidel. Project RNRT 1999 n° 95, Oct. 1999 – Oct. 2001.
55. R. Vallée-Rai, H. Hendren, P. Lam, É Gagnon, and P. Co. Soot - a Java^{tm} optimization framework. *Proc. CASCON '99*, 1999.
56. F. Védrine. Binding-time analysis and strictness analysis by abstract interpretation. *Proc. SAS '95*, LNCS 983, pp. 400–417. Springer-Verlag, 1995.

57. A. Venet. Automatic determination of communication topologies in mobile systems. *Proc. SAS '98*, LNCS 1503, pp. 152–167. Springer-Verlag, 1998.
58. A. Venet. Automatic analysis of pointer aliasing for untyped programs. *Sci. Comput. Programming*, 35(1):223–248, 1999.
59. Kwangkeun Yi. An abstract interpretation for estimating uncaught exceptions in standard ML programs. *Sci. Comput. Programming*, 31(1):147–173, 1998.

The electronic version of this paper includes additional material on static program analysis applications as well as a comparison with other formal methods (typing, model-checking and deductive methods) which, for lack of space, could not be included in this published version. A broader bibliography is available in its extended versior

Extended Static Checking: A Ten-Year Perspective

K. Rustan M. Leino

Compaq Systems Research Center
130 Lytton Ave., Palo Alto, CA 94301, USA
rustan.leino@compaq.com
http://research.compaq.com/SRC/personal/rustan/

Abstract. A powerful approach to finding errors in computer software is to translate a given program into a verification condition, a logical formula that is valid if and only if the program is free of the classes of errors under consideration. Finding errors in the program is then done by mechanically searching for counterexamples to the verification condition. This paper gives an overview of the technology that goes into such program checkers, reports on some of the progress and lessons learned in the past ten years, and identifies some remaining challenges.

0   Introduction

Software plays an increasingly important role in everyday life. We'd like software to be reliable, free of errors. The later an error is found, the more expensive it is to correct. Thus, we would like to detect software errors as early as possible in the software design process. Static program checkers analyze programs in search of errors and can be applied as soon as program development commences.

Many kinds of static program checkers are possible. To facilitate comparison between these from a user's perspective, it is useful to assess checkers along two dimensions, *coverage* and *effort*. The coverage dimension measures the proportion of errors in a program that are detected by the checker, giving a sense of what a user may expect to get out of the checker. The effort dimension measures how arduous it is to put the checker to use, giving a sense of what a user has to put in to benefit from the checker. Factors that contribute to the effort dimension include the time spent learning to use the checker, preparing a program to be input to the checker, waiting for the checker to complete, deciphering the checker's output, and identifying and suppressing spurious warnings.

Figure 0 shows some classes of static checkers along the two dimensions. In the lower left corner of the figure, depicting low coverage at low effort, we find checkers like type checkers and `lint`-like [17] checkers. Many programmers use checkers like these, because they perceive the benefit as outweighing the effort. The overall coverage may be low, but the kinds of errors caught by these checkers are common and relatively cheap to find.

In the upper right corner of the figure, depicting high coverage at high effort, we find full functional program verification. Here, the coverage approaches 100

R. Wilhelm (Ed.): Informatics. 10 Years Back. 10 Years Ahead, LNCS 2000, pp. 157–175, 2001.

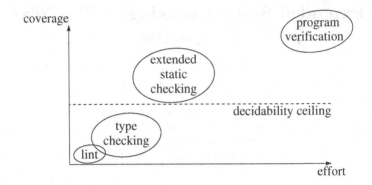

Fig. 0. Some classes of static checkers plotted along the two dimensions coverage and effort. The illustration is not to scale.

percent, but the effort required is tremendous, usually including tasks such as formalizing every detail of the program's desired behavior, axiomatizing mathematical theories that are often quite subtle, and hand-guiding a theorem prover through the proofs of correctness. Consequently, only for a small number of application areas, where programs are very small or where the cost of a software error could be devastating, does full functional program verification stand a chance of being cost effective.

Figure 0 includes a horizontal line labeled *decidability ceiling*. This is a limit along the coverage dimension below which the checker technology can provide certain mathematical guarantees. For example, the techniques applied below the decidability ceiling may run in, say, linear or cubic time, whereas the techniques required to achieve coverage above the decidability ceiling may have infeasible worst-time running times or may not even be decidable.

But giving up on the guarantees provided below the decidability ceiling may not be so bad in practice. By aiming to ascend above the decidability ceiling, one can explore uses of more powerful technology, hoping to find uses that will be reasonable for most of the programs given as input to the checker.

This paper focuses on a particular class of checker, an *extended static checker*, which (see Figure 1) analyzes a given program by generating *verification conditions*, logical formulas that, ideally, are valid if and only if the program is free of the kinds of errors under consideration, and passes these verification conditions to an automatic theorem prover which searches for counterexamples. Any counterexample context (predicate that, as far as the theorem prover can determine, is consistent and implies the negation of the verification condition) reported by the theorem prover is translated into a warning message that the programmer can understand. Extended static checking lies above the decidability ceiling in Figure 0, because it provides better coverage than traditional static checkers can achieve; and it lies way to the left of full functional program verification on the effort dimension, because the effort required to use it is considerably smaller.

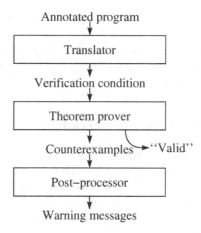

Fig. 1. Extended static checker architecture.

Early work with similar goals includes Dick Sites's PhD thesis [37] and Steve German's Runcheck verifier [15].

The present paper draws on the experience with building and using two extended static checkers during the last decade, both at the Compaq Systems Research Center (which belonged to Digital Equipment Corporation for most of that decade). Starting with some early experiments in 1991, the Extended Static Checking for Modula-3 (ESC/Modula-3) project developed the underlying checking technology in the years that followed [9]. By 1996, the checker proved usable for a number of systems modules, but by that time the pool of Modula-3 programmers in the world had dried up. In 1997, the Extended Static Checking for Java (ESC/Java) project began, seeking to build an extended static checker that would appeal to a large number of programmers [12,22]. ESC/Java adapted the technology developed for ESC/Modula-3, and made some significant changes in the annotation language in order to make the checker easier to use. Both of these checkers have been applied to thousands or tens of thousands of lines of code, and both have found errors in programs with many users.

Many research challenges were encountered during these two projects. For example: Which errors should the checker check for? Is there a suitable semantics for real (non-toy) programming languages? Can the theorem prover be automatic and fast enough? Can the theorem prover produce counterexample contexts, and can these be turned into useful warning messages? Is annotation of programs possible and can it avoid being onerous? This paper addresses these challenges and reports on the progress made toward overcoming the challenges as part of the two extended static checking projects. The paper then sketches some future challenges and possible research enterprises in this area of program checking for the next decade.

1   Challenges

In this section, I describe five major research challenges faced in the course of the two extended static checking projects and report on the status of our efforts to overcome these challenges.

1.0   Deciding Which Errors to Check for

A first research challenge in designing any kind of program checker is deciding what the checker is going to be good for. That is, what kinds of programming errors should the checker search for? This is an important decision, because some errors may occur more frequently than others, may have more disastrous effects than others, or may be more difficult than others to find using existing program checkers.

But this basic question immediately leads to another fundamental question that will no doubt send shivers down the spine of the purist: *So what about soundness?* Using the terminology of program verification, a checker is *sound* if it does not miss any errors in the program. Thus, deciding about which errors to check for means deciding how sound the checker should be. Why would we ever want to give up on soundness? Because soundness affects the complexity of the annotation language and the annotation burden, both of which contribute to the effort dimension of the checker.

Let me give an example. Suppose we were to check programs for arithmetic overflows. Precisely tracking the possible values of integer variables in all possible executions of a program is infeasibly difficult. The situation can be alleviated by using approximations [7] or relying on the programmer to supply hints in annotations. But the reason a particular integer operation does not overflow can easily be quite complicated. If the approximation machinery is not up to the task, the checker will produce many spurious warnings, which increases the effort in using the checker. Similarly, it takes an advanced annotation language to allow, say, writing down the precondition that guarantees that a matrix multiplication routine does not cause an overflow. The learning curve for such a language and the burden of actually annotating a program with the pertinent properties increase the effort in using the checker. And after all that effort, does, say, a caller of the matrix multiplication routine stand any chance of actually discharging the precondition? Is this effort worthwhile?

Even if we could do the analysis perfectly for arithmetic overflow, it's not certain that the result would be desirable in many applications. In some programs, it is conceivable that a non-negligible fraction of arithmetic operations may indeed overflow in certain runs of the program where the input is orders of magnitude larger than anticipated by the program designers and programmers. Then the many warnings produced by the checker may not be spurious after all, but the programmer would still have no interest in changing the program to properly handle such inputs—a sentence in the program's user manual would both be appropriate and require much less effort.

This example illustrates various design decisions that the designer of a program checker wrestles with daily. By introducing unsoundness in just the right places, the checker can achieve a better position in the coverage-to-effort design space.

We designed ESC/Modula-3 and ESC/Java to check for errors in three categories. First, they check for conditions for which the languages Modula-3 and Java prescribe run-time checks: null dereferences, array index bounds errors, type cast errors, division by zero, etc. Second, they are capable of checking for common synchronization errors: race conditions and deadlocks. Third, they check for violations of program annotations: for example, the checkers warn if a call site fails to meet a declared precondition or if a routine body fails to maintain a declared invariant.

Users can disable checking for any of the kinds of errors on a line-by-line basis by using a **nowarn** annotation or globally by using a command-line switch.

The checkers were designed not to look for problems with non-termination (because of the difficulty in providing appropriate annotations, and because some programs are designed to run continuously), arithmetic overflow, out of memory conditions (because of the flood of warnings of doubtful utility that this would produce), and various kinds of "leaking" and "rep exposure" problems (see, *e.g.*, [8,24,22]). One of the changes from ESC/Modula-3 to ESC/Java is that ESC/Java does not enforce **modifies** clauses (specifications that limit which variables a routine is allowed to modify), because of the requirements that **modifies** checking places on the annotation language [20,21] and on the user of the checker.

One final note about designing which errors to check for: by not checking for one kind of error, other errors may be masked. For example, consider the following (Java) program fragment:

$$
\begin{array}{l}
\textbf{if } (0 \leq x \ \&\& \ 0 \leq y) \ \{ \\
\quad \textbf{int } z = x + y; \\
\quad \textbf{int}[] \ a = \textbf{new int}[z]; \\
\qquad \vdots \\
\}
\end{array}
$$

The call to **new** allocates an integer array of size z, so z is required to be non-negative. In ordinary mathematics, this follows from the fact that z is the sum of two non-negative integers, but due to the possibility of arithmetic overflow (or addition modulo 2^{32}, which is what Java uses), z may actually be negative. Thus, even if the checker generally looks for negative-size array allocation errors, it may miss some such errors by not considering arithmetic overflow.

1.1 Defining Formal Semantics for Modern Languages

To build a static program checker that is capable of finding semantic errors in programs, one needs a formal semantics for the source language. Through the formal semantics, one can translate a given program into a set of verification conditions. But modern programming language like Modula-3 and Java include not just loops and procedures (which sometimes are considered difficult in their own right), but also object-oriented features like objects (which are references to data records and method suites), subtypes, dynamically dispatched methods, information hiding, and even concurrency features! Are these not difficult, or impossible, to model?

Indeed, if these features were to be used in unrestricted ways, untangling the mess into a formal semantics appears to be an impossible task [4]. Luckily, good programmers impose a structure on the way they use the features of the language; they follow a *programming methodology*. This helps them manage the complexity of their programs. Not only can a program checker take advantage of the fact that programmers use methodology, but it may also be a good idea for the program checker to enforce certain parts of the methodology.

The general concept of using *specifications* is fundamental to good programming methodologies. A specification is a contract that spells out how certain variables, procedures, or other constructs are to be used within the program. Once they are part of the source language, specifications help define the semantics of the language. For example, by using the programming methodology of associating a specification with every procedure, the formal semantics of a procedure call can be defined in terms of the procedure's specification alone, independent of the procedure's implementation. When making use of such a methodology, it seems prudent also to enforce the methodology, which is done by checking that every procedure implementation meets its specification. This old and fundamental idea [33] too often seems to be forgotten.

Making use of programming methodology overcomes the impossibility of designing a formal semantics, but the task may still seem unwieldy. To manage this complexity, we have found it convenient to translate the source language into a small intermediate language whose formal semantics is easy to define. Such a translation task is comparable to the compiler task of translating a source language into a more primitive intermediate language (like three-address codes [0]). We have used a variation of Dijkstra's guarded commands [10] as our intermediate language [23].

An intermediate language is good at capturing the essence of executable code in the source language, but may not be well suited for capturing all important information in the source language, especially if the intermediate language lacks declarations and types. We have found that we can encode the remaining information into a logical formula that we refer to as the *background predicate*. The background predicate, which is used as an antecedent of the verification condition, formalizes properties of the source language's expression operators and type system. (For a full description of the background predicate of a small object-oriented language, see Ecstatic [19].)

By giving a small example, I will attempt to convey a flavor of the translation of source-language programs into verification conditions. Consider the following Java class declaration:

$$\textbf{class } T \textbf{ extends } S \ \{ \ \dots \ \}$$

which introduces T as a subclass of S, and consider the following Java program fragment:

$$t = (T)s\,;$$

where t is a variable of static type T and s is a variable of static type S, and where the Java type-cast expression "$(T)s$" returns the value of s after checking that this value is assignable to type T. The background predicate includes a relation $<:_1$ ("direct subtype") on class names, and the Java class declaration above contributes the following part of the definition of that relation:

$$T <:_1 S$$

The background predicate defines a relation $<:$ as the reflexive transitive closure of $<:_1$. It also includes a predicate is, where $is(o, U)$ means that the value o is assignable to type U. This predicate is defined as follows:

$$(\,\forall o, U \,::\, is(o, U) \;\equiv\; o = \mathbf{null} \vee typeof(o) <: U \,)$$

where $typeof$ maps non-null objects to their (dynamic) types. The translation of the assignment statement in the Java program fragment above produces the intermediate-language command

$$\mathbf{assert}\ is(s, T)\ ;\ \ t = s$$

That is, before the actual assignment of s to t, the command explicitly checks that the value of s is assignable to type T. After applying the semantics of the intermediate language, for example using *weakest preconditions* [10], the verification condition takes the shape

$$\ldots T <:_1 S \wedge (\,\forall o, U \,::\, is(o, U) \equiv \ldots\,)\ldots \;\Rightarrow\; \ldots is(s, T) \wedge \ldots$$

This illustrates that one needs to prove $is(s, T)$ from the background predicate and from what is known about s.

As alluded to above, ESC/Modula-3 and ESC/Java reason about each call in terms of the specification of the callee. This allows the checkers to perform *modular checking*, which means that to check one module (or class) M, the checker only needs the declarations and specifications in the modules (or classes) that M imports (that is, builds on or uses). In particular, the implementations of the imported modules (or classes) are not needed. Consequently, one can check code that calls into a library module whose implementation details are hidden, and one can check the uses and implementation of a class without needing all its future subclasses. Modular checking is an important asset of the checkers; unfortunately, as we shall see later, it is also a liability.

1.2   Using a Theorem Prover

Once a verification condition has been produced, the next checker task is to attempt to find counterexamples to it. In many ways, the structure of verification conditions mimics that of the statement and expression constructs of the program. Typical verification conditions thus include many cases to be checked, but each case tends to be mathematically shallow. This makes the task ideally suited for a mechanical theorem prover.

The desire to keep the effort of using the program checker low places three requirements on the theorem prover. First, the theorem prover must run entirely automatically, with no user interaction. Any degree of user interactivity would mean that users of the program checker would need to learn to operate the theorem prover, something which takes a lot of training. Second, the output of the theorem prover needs to include a list of counterexample contexts. When a program contains errors and the verification condition is invalid, it would be unacceptable if the theorem prover's failure to prove the verification condition were not accompanied with a reason for the failure. Third, the theorem prover must be reasonably fast, because any program checker that is to be part of the program development process will need to be run frequently. Can these three requirements be met?

In our experience, we have found that it is indeed feasible to use a theorem prover in a program checker to do semantic analysis. Our theorem prover, called *Simplify*, works on the kinds of formulas that our extended static checkers produce as verification conditions, is entirely automatic, outputs counterexample contexts, and usually performs well. We have used the same theorem prover for both ESC/Modula-3 and ESC/Java.

The theorem prover Simplify is based on the Nelson-Oppen algorithm for cooperating decision procedures [30,31]. Simplify's decision procedures include an Egraph for the theory of equality including congruence closure, a simplex solver for linear arithmetic, a backtracking search for disjunctions, a matcher for universally quantified formulas, and an ordering-theory procedure for various partial orders. When Simplify was built as part of the ESC/Modula-3 project, we developed various heuristics that make it work well for the kinds of formulas that arise as verification conditions. We have since added some theorem prover features that have allowed us to enhance the output of ESC/Java, but the built-in heuristics have remained the same as they were for ESC/Modula-3.

There are many mathematically equivalent ways in which one can formulate verification conditions. Alternative formulations may differ dramatically in how they impact the theorem prover's performance. In building an extended static checker, one must pay ample attention to crafting the verification conditions carefully, and doing so requires both expertise with and experimentation with the underlying theorem prover.

An important desideratum of a program checker is that it not get stuck for too long (or forever!) in trying to find errors in some part of the given program. Consequently, we impose a time limit for each verification condition in ESC/Java (the default is 5 minutes, which is occasionally reached).

In Section 1.0, I emphasized the importance of allowing unsoundness into the design space of program checkers. However, unsoundness should be confined to areas that can be explained in the checker's user manual, so that programmers can understand the limitations. This suggests that it is prudent not to design unsoundness into the underlying theorem prover, because it may be hard to predict where such unsoundness may strike and to explain what the programmer can do to avoid the unsoundness.

1.3   Producing Meaningful Warning Messages

The next challenge is to turn verification-condition counterexample contexts, as output by the theorem prover, into meaningful warning messages. Users of the program checker should not be required to grok the theorem prover or the particular encoding of verification conditions in order to understand the checker's warning messages.

Because the structure of verification conditions mimics the structure of the program, particular parts of the verification condition correspond to checks being made at particular points in the program. By tracking which parts of a verification condition the theorem prover uses in the counterexample contexts it reports, we have found that one can accurately recover the kind of error (null dereference, array index bounds errors, etc.) and source location of the error, even an execution trace leading to the error, from the theorem prover's output.

Tracking the parts of the verification condition that the theorem prover is currently considering can be done in several ways. One effective way involves a theorem-prover *labeling* mechanism. The theorem prover Simplify allows subpredicates to be labeled and outputs with its counterexample context the labels of those labeled subpredicates that somehow contributed to the counterexample context. For example, consider a Java program that contains the following assignment statement:

$$p.f = 10;$$

Ordinarily, this would be translated into an intermediate-language command like

$$\textbf{assert } p \neq \textbf{null} ; \ p.f = 10$$

which in turn would give rise to a verification condition of the form

$$\ldots \Rightarrow \ldots p \neq \textbf{null} \wedge \ldots$$

To use the labeling mechanism, the subpredicate $p \neq \textbf{null}$ in this verification condition is instead written as the logically equivalent

$$(\textbf{label } L: \ p \neq \textbf{null})$$

where L is a fresh label that encodes which program check the subpredicate represents. If the theorem prover outputs the label L with a counterexample context, the checker will report a warning of a possible null dereference in the Java assignment statement above.

We have found that the error kind, source location, and execution trace usually suffice to diagnose a warning produced by the checker. Therefore, the default in ESC/Java is to hide the theorem prover's full counterexample context from the user. However, there are times when the rest of the counterexample context does contain useful information. Though we have tried, we have not succeeded in finding a general scheme for automatically extracting all interesting parts of a counterexample context. Instead, we have focused on detecting a couple of common situations that without further information can be quite confusing to users [28].

1.4   Grappling with Annotations

The last of the five big challenges regards program annotation. Is program annotation a task that programmers can reasonably be expected to perform? Are annotations understandable? Is the task of adding annotations too big a burden?

For both of the extended static checkers and their (different) annotation languages, we have found that the annotations describe programmer design decisions. That is, the annotations give properties that are relevant to the program's correctness, not obscure hints to the checking machinery that enable it to grind through the analysis of the given program. For example, an annotation may describe the decision that a particular method parameter should never be passed in as null or that the value of a particular integer field should always lie between 0 and the size of some array. This is good, because it means that programmers can understand what they write down as annotations. Moreover, the annotations serve as useful program documentation. And, unlike documentation written in a natural language, which can get out of sync with the program text, annotations can be mechanically checked to agree with the program text.

There are choices in the creation of a program checker's annotation language, because there are several different kinds of annotations that can be used to describe the same programmer design decisions. An important example of this choice is found in how the annotation languages of the two extended static checkers support writing down how data structures are represented. In ESC/Modula-3, the annotation language included abstract variables (fictitious variables whose values are given as functions of program variables) and abstraction dependencies (declarations that specify which program variables may be used in the representation of which abstract variables) [21,18]. An annotation idiom commonly used in ESC/Modula-3 is to introduce an abstract field called *valid* in each object type, with the meaning that an object is valid if it has been properly initialized and its fields are in a consistent state [21,9]. The field *valid* is then used as an explicit precondition of every routine that operates on such objects. To reduce the annotation burden involved in writing these pre- and postconditions, ESC/Java dispensed with abstract variables and abstraction dependencies in favor of object invariants, which declare what it means for the fields of an object to be in a consistent state, and which are then automatically used as preconditions of methods. The design choice to use object invariants led to further design choices, for example choosing when exactly an object invariant is supposed to hold. With its present object-invariant design, ESC/Java gives up on soundness in several ways where the abstract-variable design in ESC/Modula-3 did not have to. But the overall effect seems to be that the ESC/Java annotation language is easier to use. Trade-offs like this are essential to making more usable program checkers.

A critically important feature of the annotation language of an extended static checker is an escape hatch that suppresses the static checking performed, to be used when the checker issues spurious warnings that otherwise would be difficult or impossible to eliminate. Such escape hatches exist in traditional program checkers as well. For example, both Modula-3 and Java include type-cast expressions, which circumvent the strictness of the static type checker. To ensure the type safety of the running program, such type casts in Java and in the safe subset of Modula-3 are checked at run-time. Since ESC/Modula-3 and ESC/Java don't introduce run-time checks, their escape hatches belong under the rubric of unsound features.

For example, consider the following Java program fragment:

$$y = x * x + 2 * x + 1;$$
$$z = \textbf{new int}[y];$$

Because of properties of integers, y is always assigned a non-negative value (ignoring issues of arithmetic overflow), so the subsequent array allocation will never result in a negative-size array allocation error. However, an extended static checker is not likely to be equipped with the appropriate integer properties to deduce this fact automatically, so it will spuriously issue a warning. This warning can be suppressed in ESC/Java by adding a **nowarn** annotation on the line of the allocation:

$$y = x * x + 2 * x + 1;$$
$$z = \textbf{new int}[y]; \quad //@ \textbf{ nowarn}$$

or by instructing the checker to blindly assume the condition $0 \leq y$ after the assignment to y:

$$y = x * x + 2 * x + 1;$$
$$//@ \textbf{ assume } 0 \leq y;$$
$$z = \textbf{new int}[y];$$

In this example, the escape hatch is needed because of the checker's limited support for non-linear arithmetic. In other situations, an escape hatch may be used as an alternative to writing down some complex program invariant. When an escape hatch is used, the user takes responsibility for those execution paths that are not checked by the checker.

We have found that annotating a program increases its number of source lines by about 10 percent. For programming teams that are serious about building quality into their software, this number does not seem excessively high. Programmers on such teams are already accustomed to writing similar annotations in natural language comments. But the start-up cost is still too high. For programming teams with large amounts of already written code, the initial investment of adding annotations to the legacy code seems daunting. The argument that the checker performs modular checking, which means one can annotate a class at a time, does not make the situation compelling enough, judging from our limited experience with programmers outside our projects. Even for programming teams that are just starting a new project, there's still the initial training cost before the team acquires at least one expert at the new checker. The fact that the technology is still new means the risk of using an extended static checker is higher than if its use were common.

Like type declarations, extended static checking annotations impose stronger invariants on the program. Decades ago, when the benefits of static type checking weren't generally accepted, the type checking community faced problems similar to the ones I've outlined above. But with the continued design and use of statically typed programming languages, the fact that type declarations must be given explicitly no longer poses a barrier to entry for such languages. (When was the last time you heard, "I don't want to use Java, because the burden of writing explicit type declarations is just too large"?) This piece of history gives hope to extended static checking technology, but more research is called for.

2   Future Challenges

In the last ten years, the two extended static checking projects saw many research challenges, the first tier of which were overcome. More research challenges remain. In this section, I mention four of these and refer to some related work.

2.0   Reduce Annotation Burden

Although annotations capture programmer design decisions and provide a stylized way to record these, the reluctance to cope with the burden of annotating programs remains the major obstacle in the adoption of extended static checking technology into practice. Are there ways to use this more powerful checking technology at a reduced annotation cost?

One way to reduce the annotation burden is to not insist on modular checking. By spanning routine and module boundaries, the checker will need fewer annotations. Even if such a checker comes at a price of increased demand for computational resources (time, memory, disk space) or more complicated analysis techniques, it may reduce the overall effort of using the checker. Recently, an annotation-less static program checker called PREfix [34] has achieved good success in this area. Abstract interpretation [6,5] is another program analysis technique that can find errors in whole programs without requiring annotation.

Another way to reduce the annotation burden is to develop *annotation assistants*, which infer annotations automatically from the program text. A tool called Daikon [11], which uses a mix of static and dynamic analysis techniques, infers likely invariants of a given program. An annotation assistant for ESC/Java, called Houdini [14,13], is under development at Compaq SRC.

2.1   Understand Sound Modular Checking

The input to a program checker includes not just the routine or class implementations to be checked, but also the declarations given in the *scope* of such routines and classes. For example, if the implementation of a routine r calls another routine p, then conventional programming-language rules for resolving names ensure that the declaration of p is in the scope of r's implementation. On the other hand, other procedure declarations, and the implementation of p, may not be in the scope of r's implementation. Modular checking can be performed so long as the input to the checker includes the scopes of the routines or classes to be checked. But is this modular checking meaningful? Is a verification condition produced in a limited scope somehow related to the verification condition that would have been generated if the whole program were in scope?

Modular checking is *sound* with respect to a verification-condition generator, if it doesn't miss any errors that the same verification-condition generator would have detected if given the whole program [18,21]. For example, consider a limited scope M that's part of a program P, and consider an implementation r in M. (In Modula-3, the limited scope M corresponds to a module closed under imports, and P corresponds to all of the modules in the program.) Then, a theorem of *sound modular checking* takes the form

$$M \subseteq P \wedge WellFormed(M, P) \wedge r \in M \wedge Pass(r, M) \Rightarrow Pass(r, P)$$

where for any (limited or whole-program) scope X, the predicate $Pass(r, X)$ means that the checker issues no complaints about r when the checking is performed in the context of X. Soundness of modular checking is non-trivial and doesn't hold unless one restricts the programs under consideration. The predicate $WellFormed(M, P)$ says that module M and program P obey such restrictions.

In ESC/Modula-3, we tried hard to achieve sound modular checking. In contrast, we deliberately gave up on this chivalrous goal in ESC/Java, because it was not clear that the increased coverage that sound modular checking provides justifies the extra effort that it entails. But even if the extra coverage doesn't justify the extra effort, it may be enlightening to understand what sound modular checking really involves. As it stands, the soundness of modular checking for modern programming languages is an open problem [21].

2.2   Investigate More-than-Types Systems

Static type systems have had considerable success in popular programming languages. Consequently, the type checker helps enforce program invariants like "this variable is **null** or contains the address of a data record of type T". Experience has shown that the invariants imposed by a type system are easy to teach to programmers, helpful in finding common errors, and flexible enough for large classes of programs that programmers actually want to write. The flexibility comes in part from the fact that certain checks are not performed statically, but are instead enforced by simple dynamic checks. What are some stronger invariants that a programming language can reasonably enforce by a combination of static and dynamic checks? Can we do better than traditional type systems?

Extended static checking is a technique for finding errors in a program, not for providing guarantees about the program. Nonetheless, as a gedanken experiment, let us consider the possibility of making up for the (deliberate) unsoundness in ESC/Java's static checking by prescribing dynamic checks. Recall from Section 1.0 that by not checking for one kind of error, a checker may miss errors of others kinds, too. Thus, to guarantee any program invariant at all, we must examine every kind of unsoundness in the static checking.

One unsoundness in ESC/Java stems from **assume** annotations. The annotation statement **assume** p inhibits, from that program point onwards, ESC/Java's static checking for those program executions that reach the **assume** statement when p does not hold. An obvious way to make sure the inhibited checking is immaterial is to dynamically check p at the point of the annotation (reporting an error and halting the program if p does not hold). To keep the dynamic check simple may require restricting the annotation language, for example forbidding universal and existential quantifications.

Another unsoundness stems from the fact that ESC/Java does not enforce **modifies** clauses. For proper checking of the caller of a routine, one needs to know what parts of the program state the callee may modify. This is specified in **modifies** clauses, which require some form of abstraction in the annotation language [20,21]. Lacking such support for abstraction (as in ESC/Java), one can turn to some form of approximation, but this gets tricky. Overestimating what the callee modifies results in spurious warnings in the caller; overestimating what the caller assumes to go unchanged by the call results in spurious warnings in the callee. To reduce spurious warnings, ESC/Java uses declared **modifies** clauses when reasoning about calls, but omits the corresponding checking for the callee. Using dynamic checking to make up for the lack of static **modifies** checking is difficult. Naively, it would require taking a snapshot of the entire program state on entry to a routine and then comparing the snapshot with the program state on exit from the routine. To implement more efficient checks may require enforcing a stricter programming methodology or restricting the expressiveness of the programming language.

A third unsoundness in ESC/Java stems from the relaxed rules about where object invariants are checked to hold. On entry to a call, ESC/Java assumes that all object invariants hold for all objects. But at call sites, ESC/Java checks the object invariants only for the actual parameters of the call. Adding dynamic checks to restore soundness would involve analyzing the program to determine which variables and object fields the callee may read or write. If this analysis is to be precise enough, one may need to rely on additional annotations or programming methodologies that restrict which objects may be reached from where. Several methodologies have been proposed to restrict "aliasing" of objects (see, *e.g.*, [3,32,38,16,1,29]), but it seems there is still no practical and checkable solution to the part of this problem known as "rep exposure" or "abstract aliasing" [8].

Clearly, judging even from just the three kinds of unsoundness above, there are several hard problems to be solved before dynamic checking could complement extended static checking to achieve a sound system. Trying to increase the strength of guaranteed program invariants by instead adding static checks to systems that already prescribe dynamic checks can lead to similar problems.

Many programming systems can dynamically check user-supplied assertions (see, for example, the pioneering work by Satterthwaite [35]). The object-oriented programming language Eiffel [27] and the Ada annotation language Anna [26] provide facilities for systematically introducing dynamic checks of assertions like preconditions and object invariants, but these languages have not been designed for the purpose of supporting complementary static checking. In fact, neither language includes **modifies** clauses, and in neither language is it possible to infer, from the specifications visible to a caller, what conditions the caller is responsible for establishing prior to a call (*cf.* [18]). So is there any hope of increasing the strength of program invariants that programming-language designs can incorporate and enforce?

A simple measure for increasing the strength of program invariants is to augment object-oriented type systems with *may-be-null types*. A may-be-null type is a variant record representing either the special value **null** or a value of some (non-null) object type. A deference expression $E.f$, where f is an object field, is then defined only when the static type of the expression E is a non-null object type. An expression of a may-be-null type can be cast to the corresponding non-null type; the cast fails (dynamically) if the expression evaluates to **null**. May-be-null types were used in CLU [25], but they seem mostly to have been forgotten since.

Another possible measure for increasing the strength of program invariants enforced by a programming language is to augment the type system with *dependent types* (see, *e.g.*, [2,39]). These are essentially record, map, array, or object types with additional invariants. There is a temptation to stay within the realm of invariants whose checking is decidable, but I say why not leap above the decidability ceiling: by suitably restricting the annotation language, if an invariant cannot be checked statically, one can either fall back on dynamic checking or rely on the programmer to supply an **assume** statement (which may also require dynamic checking).

There are still problems with dependent types. One problem is the question of when to enforce the invariants. This problem is reminiscent of the problem of when to enforce object invariants, described above. Maybe one can restrict operations on values of dependent types in such a way that it becomes clear when the invariants should be enforced. Another problem with dependent types is the need for **modifies** clauses. To reason about particular program variables, one generally needs to know which variables may be modified by a call, but this leads to the problems with enforcing **modifies** clauses described above. It is possible that one could restrict the regions of a program where variables of dependent types are updated, in such a way that one does not rely on the exact values of these variables on entry to the regions, thereby possibly avoiding the need for **modifies** clauses. Another possible way out is to restrict one's attention to a functional language (in which variables are never changed), an approach explored by Augustsson in Cayenne [2] and by Xi and Pfenning [39].

In summary, the gap between the program invariants enforced by traditional type systems and the program invariants that extended static checkers check a program against seems to be wide. In response, I suggest investigating "more-than-types systems" which aspire to guarantee stronger program invariants than those guaranteed by traditional type systems, and which may rely on a combination of static checking above the decidability ceiling and dynamic checking. The research challenge is to investigate this space of programming-language designs to determine if there are more-than-types systems that are substantially more useful than traditional type systems. (In this volume, Schneider, Morrisett, and Harper discuss the combination of various static and dynamic checking techniques to enforce stronger security policies [36].)

2.3   Teach

One of the barriers to entry for extended static checking is that a regrettably large number of programmers don't really understand preconditions and invariants. When these concepts are taught in computer science curriculums, students tend to practice them only on paper. There's a large difference between turning in a homework assignment that is returned graded a week later and getting instant feedback from a mechanical checker. It seems to me that the current state of the art in extended static checkers, although designed to support programming in the large, would be quite instructional to use along with the compiler and type checker in early (and more advanced) programming classes. Even if the students wouldn't continue using an extended static checker outside the classes, the experience of using one with their programming assignments may teach them to think in terms of preconditions and invariants, which is likely to breed a new, better generation of programmers.

3   Conclusions

After a decade of research in the area of extended static checking, the first tier of research challenges has been overcome. Extended static checking seems promising as a technique to improve the quality of programs produced while programming in the large. However, challenges remain before extended static checking technology will be used routinely in program development in practice. As with the adoption of anything new, there are political and cultural barriers to break through. But I think there are also technical research challenges in getting the technology adopted. By investigating more-than-types systems, we may design programming languages that enforce stronger program invariants. By working on reducing the annotation burden and otherwise improving the user experience in applying extended static checking, we may produce better program checkers. By teaching a new generation of computer science students, we may raise better programmers. We can then hope for a future in which computer programs are more reliable.

Acknowledgments

ESC/Modula-3 was developed by Dave Detlefs, Greg Nelson, Jim Saxe, and the author, from the first half of the 1990's until 1996. ESC/Java was developed by Cormac Flanagan, Mark Lillibridge, Greg Nelson, Jim Saxe, Raymie Stata, and the author, starting in 1997. Damien Doligez, George Necula, Rajeev Joshi, Todd Millstein, and Silvija Seres worked on or with the extended static checking projects as SRC research interns. The projects also benefited from the help of other colleagues at Compaq SRC, including Rajeev Joshi, Steve Glassman, Allan Heydon, Marc Najork, and Caroline Tice. Rajeev Joshi, Greg Nelson, Jim Saxe, and Reinhard Wilhelm provided helpful comments on drafts of this paper.

References

0. Alfred V. Aho, Ravi Sethi, and Jeffrey D. Ullman. *Compilers: Principles, Techniques, and Tools.* Addison-Wesley, 1986.
1. Paulo Sérgio Almeida. Balloon types: Controlling sharing of state in data types. In Mehmet Akşit and Satoshi Matsuoka, editors, *ECOOP'97—Object-oriented Programming: 11th European Conference*, volume 1241 of *Lecture Notes in Computer Science*, pages 32–59. Springer, June 1997.
2. Lennart Augustsson. Cayenne — a language with dependent types. In *Proceedings of the 1998 ACM SIGPLAN International Conference on Functional Programming (ICFP '98)*, volume 34, number 1 in *SIGPLAN Notices*, pages 239–250. ACM, January 1999.
3. John Boyland. Alias burying: Unique variables without destructive reads. *Software—Practice & Experience.* To appear.
4. Edmund Clark. Language constructs for which it is impossible to obtain good Hoare-like axioms. *Journal of the ACM*, 26(1):129–147, January 1979.
5. Patrick Cousot. Progress on abstract interpretation based formal methods and future challenges. In *Informatics—10 Years Back, 10 Years Ahead*, volume 2000 of *Lecture Notes in Computer Science*. Springer-Verlag, 2000.
6. Patrick Cousot and Radhia Cousot. Abstract interpretation: a unified lattice model for static analysis of programs by construction or approximation of fixpoints. In *Conference Record of the Fourth Annual ACM Symposium on Principles of Programming Languages*, pages 238–252, January 1977.
7. Patrick Cousot and Nicolas Halbwachs. Automatic discovery of linear restraints among variables of a program. In *Conference Record of the Fifth Annual ACM Symposium on Principles of Programming Languages*, pages 84–96, January 1978.
8. David L. Detlefs, K. Rustan M. Leino, and Greg Nelson. Wrestling with rep exposure. Research Report 156, Digital Equipment Corporation Systems Research Center, July 1998.
9. David L. Detlefs, K. Rustan M. Leino, Greg Nelson, and James B. Saxe. Extended static checking. Research Report 159, Compaq Systems Research Center, December 1998.
10. Edsger W. Dijkstra. *A Discipline of Programming.* Prentice Hall, Englewood Cliffs, NJ, 1976.
11. Michael D. Ernst, Adam Czeisler, William G. Griswold, and David Notkin. Quickly detecting relevant program invariants. In *ICSE 2000, Proceedings of the 22nd International Conference on on Software Engineering*, pages 449–458, 2000.

12. Extended Static Checking for Java home page, Compaq Systems Research Center. On the web at `http://research.compaq.com/SRC/esc/`.

13. Cormac Flanagan, Rajeev Joshi, and K. Rustan M. Leino. Annotation inference for modular checkers. *Information Processing Letters*. To appear.

14. Cormac Flanagan and K. Rustan M. Leino. Houdini, an annotation assistant for ESC/Java. Technical Note 2000-003, Compaq Systems Research Center, 2000.

15. Steven M. German. Automating proofs of the absence of common runtime errors. In *Conference Record of the Fifth Annual ACM Symposium on Principles of Programming Languages*, pages 105–118, 1978.

16. John Hogg. Islands: Aliasing protection in object-oriented languages. In Andreas Paepcke, editor, *Object-Oriented Programming Systems, Languages, and Applications (OOPSLA'91)*, pages 271–285. ACM Press, October 1991.

17. S. C. Johnson. Lint, a C program checker. Computer Science Technical Report 65, Bell Laboratories, Murray Hill, NJ 07974, 1978.

18. K. Rustan M. Leino. *Toward Reliable Modular Programs*. PhD thesis, California Institute of Technology, 1995. Technical Report Caltech-CS-TR-95-03.

19. K. Rustan M. Leino. Ecstatic: An object-oriented programming language with an axiomatic semantics. In *The Fourth International Workshop on Foundations of Object-Oriented Languages*, January 1997. Proceedings available from `http://www.cs.williams.edu/~kim/FOOL/`.

20. K. Rustan M. Leino. Data groups: Specifying the modification of extended state. In *Proceedings of the 1998 ACM SIGPLAN Conference on Object-Oriented Programming, Systems, Languages, and Applications (OOPSLA '98)*, volume 33, number 10 in *SIGPLAN Notices*, pages 144–153. ACM, October 1998.

21. K. Rustan M. Leino and Greg Nelson. Data abstraction and information hiding. Research Report 160, Compaq Systems Research Center, 2000.

22. K. Rustan M. Leino, Greg Nelson, and James B. Saxe. ESC/Java user's manual. Technical Note 2000-002, Compaq Systems Research Center, October 2000.

23. K. Rustan M. Leino, James B. Saxe, and Raymie Stata. Checking Java programs via guarded commands. In Bart Jacobs, Gary T. Leavens, Peter Müller, and Arnd Poetzsch-Heffter, editors, *Formal Techniques for Java Programs*, Technical Report 251. Fernuniversität Hagen, May 1999. Also available as Technical Note 1999-002, Compaq Systems Research Center.

24. K. Rustan M. Leino and Raymie Stata. Checking object invariants. Technical Note 1997-007, Digital Equipment Corporation Systems Research Center, January 1997.

25. Barbara Liskov and John Guttag. *Abstraction and Specification in Program Development*. MIT Electrical Engineering and Computer Science Series. MIT Press, 1986.

26. David C. Luckham. *Programming with Specifications: An Introduction to ANNA, a Language for Specifying Ada Programs*. Texts and Monographs in Computer Science. Springer-Verlag, 1990.

27. Bertrand Meyer. *Object-oriented Software Construction*. Series in Computer Science. Prentice-Hall International, New York, 1988.

28. Todd Millstein. Toward more informative ESC/Java warning messages. In James Mason, editor, *Selected 1999 SRC Summer Intern Reports*, Technical Note 1999-003. Compaq Systems Research Center, 1999.

29. Naftaly H. Minsky. Towards alias-free pointers. In Pierre Cointe, editor, *ECOOP'96—Object-Oriented Programming: 10th European Conference*, volume 1098 of *Lecture Notes in Computer Science*, pages 189–209. Springer, July 1996.

30. Greg Nelson. Combining satisfiability procedures by equality-sharing. In W. W. Bledsoe and D. W. Loveland, editors, *Automated Theorem Proving: After 25 Years*, volume 29 of *Contemporary Mathematics*, pages 201–211. American Mathematical Society, 1984.

31. Greg Nelson and Derek C. Oppen. Simplification by cooperating decision procedures. *ACM Transactions on Programming Languages and Systems*, 1(2):245–257, October 1979.

32. James Noble, Jan Vitek, and John Potter. Flexible alias protection. In Eric Jul, editor, *ECOOP'98—Object-oriented Programming: 12th European Conference*, volume 1445 of *Lecture Notes in Computer Science*, pages 158–185. Springer, July 1998.

33. D. L. Parnas. A technique for software module specification with examples. *Communications of the ACM*, 15(5):330–336, May 1972.

34. PREfix. Intrinsa, Mountain View, CA, 1999.

35. E. Satterthwaite. Debugging tools for high level languages. *Software—Practice & Experience*, 2(3):197–217, July–September 1972.

36. Fred B. Schneider, Greg Morrisett, and Robert Harper. A language-based approach to security. In *Informatics—10 Years Back, 10 Years Ahead*, volume 2000 of *Lecture Notes in Computer Science*. Springer-Verlag, 2000.

37. Richard L. Sites. *Proving that Computer Programs Terminate Cleanly*. PhD thesis, Stanford University, Stanford, CA 94305, May 1974. Technical Report STAN-CS-74-418.

38. Mark Utting. Reasoning about aliasing. In *Proceedings of the Fourth Australasian Refinement Workshop (ARW-95)*, pages 195–211. School of Computer Science and Engineering, The University of New South Wales, April 1995.

39. Hongwei Xi and Frank Pfenning. Dependent types in practical programming. In *Conference Record of POPL'99: The 26th ACM SIGPLAN-SIGACT Symposium on Principles of Programming Languages*, pages 214–227, January 1999.

Compaq SRC Research Reports and Technical Notes are available on the web from `http://research.compaq.com/SRC/publications/`.

Progress on the State Explosion Problem in Model Checking*

Edmund Clarke[1], Orna Grumberg[2], Somesh Jha[3], Yuan Lu[4], and Helmut Veith[5]

[1] School of Computer Science, Carnegie Mellon University, USA
edmund.clarke@cs.cmu.edu
[2] Computer Science Department, Technion, Haifa, Israel
orna@cs.technion.ac.il
[3] Computer Sciences Department, University of Wisconsin, Madison, USA
jha@cs.wisc.edu
[4] Network Switch Department, Broadcom Co, USA
ylu@broadcom.com
[5] Institute of Information Systems, Vienna University of Technology, Austria
veith@dbai.tuwien.ac.at

Abstract. Model checking is an automatic verification technique for finite state concurrent systems. In this approach to verification, temporal logic specifications are checked by an exhaustive search of the state space of the concurrent system. Since the size of the state space grows exponentially with the number of processes, model checking techniques based on explicit state enumeration can only handle relatively small examples. This phenomenon is commonly called the "State Explosion Problem". Over the past ten years considerable progress has been made on this problem by (1) representing the state space symbolically using BDDs and by (2) using abstraction to reduce the size of the state space that must be searched. As a result model checking has been used successfully to find extremely subtle errors in hardware controllers and communication protocols. In spite of these successes, however, additional research is needed to handle large designs of industrial complexity. This aim of this paper is to give a succinct survey of symbolic model checking and to introduce the reader to recent advances in abstraction.

1 Introduction

During the last two decades, temporal logic model checking [12,13] has become an important application of logic in computer science. Temporal logic model checking is a technique for verifying that a system satisfies its specification by (i) representing the

* This research is sponsored by the Semiconductor Research Corporation (SRC) under Contract No. 97-DJ-294, the National Science Foundation (NSF) under Grant No. CCR-9505472, the Defense Advanced Research Projects Agency (DARPA) under Air Force contract No. F33615-00-C-1701, the Max Kade Foundation and the Austrian Science Fund Project N Z29-INF. Any opinions, findings and conclusions or recommendations expressed in this material are those of the authors and do not necessarily reflect the views of SRC, NSF, or the United States Government.

R. Wilhelm (Ed.): Informatics. 10 Years Back. 10 Years Ahead, LNCS 2000, pp. 176–194, 2001.

system as a Kripke structure, (ii) writing the specification in a suitable temporal logic, and (iii) algorithmically checking that the Kripke structure is a model of the specification formula. Model checking has been successfully applied in hardware verification, and is emerging as an industrial standard tool for hardware design. For extensive overviews of model checking, please refer to [10,11].

Model checking has several important advantages over mechanical theorem provers or proof checkers for verification of circuits and protocols. The most important is that the procedure is completely automatic. Typically, the user provides a high level representation of the model and the specification to be checked. The model checking algorithm will either terminate with the answer *true*, indicating that the model satisfies the specification, or give a counterexample execution that shows why the formula is not satisfied. The counterexamples are particularly important in finding subtle errors in complex transition systems. The procedure is also quite fast and often produces an answer in a matter of minutes. Since partial specifications can be checked, it is unnecessary to specify the circuit completely before useful information about its correctness can be obtained. Finally, the logics used for specifications can directly express many of the properties that are needed for reasoning about concurrent systems.

The main technical challenge in model checking is the *state explosion* which can occur if the system being verified has many components which make transitions in parallel. A fundamental breakthrough was made in the fall of 1987 by Ken McMillan, who was then a graduate student at Carnegie Mellon. He argued that larger systems could be handled if transition relations were represented implicitly with ordered binary decision diagrams (BDDs) [3]. By using the original model checking algorithm with the new representation for transition relations, he was able to verify some examples that had more than 10^{20} states [6,25]. He made this observation independently of the work by Coudert et al [16] and Pixley [28,29,30] on using BDDs to check equivalence of deterministic finite-state machines. Since then, various refinements of the BDD-based techniques by other researchers have pushed the state count up to more than 10^{120} [5]. The widely used symbolic model checker SMV [25] is based on these ideas.

Despite the success of symbolic methods, the state explosion problem remains a major hurdle in applying model checking to large industrial designs. *Abstraction* is among the most important techniques for tackling this problem. In fact, abstraction based methods have been essential for verifying designs of industrial complexity. Currently, abstraction is typically a manual process, often requiring considerable creativity. In order for model checking to be used more widely in industry, automatic techniques are needed for generating abstractions.

This paper is intended as an overview of a recently developed *automatic abstraction technique* [9] which extends the general framework of *existential abstraction* [14]. Existential abstraction computes an *upper approximation* of the original model. When a specification in the temporal logic ACTL is true in the abstract model, it will also be true in the concrete design. However, if the specification is false in the abstract model, the counterexample may be the result of some behavior in the approximation which is not present in the original model. When this happens, it is necessary to refine the abstraction so that the behavior which caused the erroneous counterexample is eliminated. The main contribution of [9] is an efficient automatic refinement technique which uses information obtained from erroneous counterexamples. The refinement algorithm keeps the size of the abstract state space small due to the use of abstraction functions which distinguish many degrees of abstraction for each program variable. Practical experiments including a large Fujitsu IP core design with about 500 latches and 10000 lines of SMV code demonstrate the utility of this approach. Although our current implementation is based on NuSMV [8], it is in principle not limited to the input language of SMV and can be applied to other languages.

Organization of the Paper. The paper is organized as follows: Section 2 contains an introduction to model checking, temporal logic and the state explosion problem. In Sections 3 and 4, a succinct overview of symbolic verification, and a more detailed overview of our recent counterexample-guided abstraction methodology [9] are given. Directions for future research are outlined in Section 5.

2 Fundamentals of Model Checking

In this section, we outline important notions which are necessary to understand the subsequent discussion of the state explosion problem. A more rigorous and detailed introduction can be found in [10].

Kripke Structures. In model checking, the system to be verified is formally represented by a finite *Kripke structure*. Essentially, a Kripke structure is a directed graph whose vertices are labeled by sets of atomic propositions. Vertices and edges are called *states* and *transitions* respectively. One or more states are considered to be *initial states*. Consider for example the Kripke structures in Figure 1 which represent traffic lights in the US and Austria, respectively.

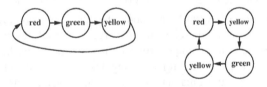

Fig. 1. US and Austrian Traffic Lights as Kripke Structures

Thus, a Kripke structure over a set of atomic propositions A is a tuple $K = (S, R, L, I)$ where S is the set of states, $R \subseteq S^2$ is the set of transitions, $I \subseteq S$ is the non-empty set of initial states, and $L : S \to 2^A$ labels each state by a set of atomic propositions. Note that more complicated definitions of Kripke structures are also used in the literature. In particular, it is common to label the transitions of a Kripke structure by *actions*. As demonstrated by the traffic light example, a Kripke structure can be viewed as a kind of automaton.

A *path* is an infinite sequence of states, $\pi = s_0, s_1, \ldots$ such that for $i \geq 0$, $(s_i, s_{i+1}) \in R$. Given a path π, π^i denotes the infinite path $s^i, s^{i+1}, \ldots$ We assume that the transition relation R is *total*, i.e., that all states have positive outdegree. Therefore, each finite path can be extended into an infinite path. Figure 2 indicates how a Kripke structure is unwound into an infinite tree such that the paths in the Kripke structure and the infinite tree coincide.

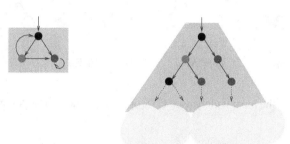

Fig. 2. Unwinding a Kripke Structure. The incoming arrows indicate the initial states.

Computation Tree Logics. CTL* is an extension of propositional logic obtained by adding *path quantifiers* and *temporal operators*.

1. **Path quantifiers**:
   A   "for every path"
   E   "there exists a path"
2. **Temporal Operators**:
   $\mathbf{X}p$ "p holds next time"
   $\mathbf{F}p$ "p holds sometime in the future"
   $\mathbf{G}p$ "p holds globally in the future"
   $p\mathbf{U}q$ "p holds until q holds"

In the computation tree logic **CTL** each temporal operator must be immediately preceded by a path quantifier. Thus, CTL can be viewed as a temporal logic based on the compound operators $\mathbf{AX}, \mathbf{EX}, \mathbf{AF}, \mathbf{EF}, \mathbf{AG}, \mathbf{EG}, \mathbf{AU}, \mathbf{EU}$. Let s_0 be a state in K. The formal semantics of $\mathbf{EX}, \mathbf{EG}$ and $\mathbf{EU}$ is defined as follows:

$s_0, K \models \mathbf{EX}\varphi$ iff there exists a path $\pi = s_0, s_1, \ldots$ such that $K, s_1 \models \varphi$
$s_0, K \models \mathbf{EG}\varphi$ iff there exists a path $\pi = s_0, s_1, \ldots$ such that
    for all $i \geq 0$, $K, s_i \models \varphi$
$s_0, K \models \mathbf{E}\varphi\mathbf{U}\psi$ iff there exists a path $\pi = s_0, s_1, \ldots$ and an $i \geq 0$ such that
    for all $0 \leq j < i$, $K, s_j \models \varphi$, and $K, s_i \models \psi$.

The remaining CTL operators are defined by abbreviations as follows:

$$\mathbf{EF}\varphi \equiv \mathbf{E}(\text{true}\mathbf{U}\varphi) \quad \mathbf{AG}\varphi \equiv \neg\mathbf{EF}\neg\varphi$$
$$\mathbf{AF}\varphi \equiv \neg\mathbf{EG}\neg\varphi \quad \mathbf{AX}\varphi \equiv \neg\mathbf{EX}\neg\varphi$$
$$\mathbf{A}\varphi\mathbf{U}\psi \equiv \neg\mathbf{E}(\neg\psi\mathbf{U}(\neg\varphi \wedge \neg\psi)) \wedge \neg\mathbf{EG}\neg\psi$$

Four important CTL operators are illustrated in Figure 3 by typical computation trees. Each computation tree has s_0 as its root.

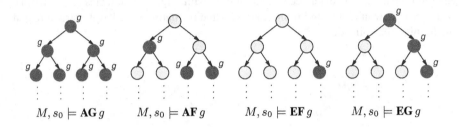

$$M, s_0 \models \textbf{AG}\, g \qquad M, s_0 \models \textbf{AF}\, g \qquad M, s_0 \models \textbf{EF}\, g \qquad M, s_0 \models \textbf{EG}\, g$$

Fig. 3. Example of the most widely used CTL operators. The dark states are states where g holds true.

Example 1. The following list contains some typical CTL formulas:

- **EF**(*Started* ∧ ¬*Ready*): it is possible to get to a state where *Started* holds but *Ready* does not hold.
- **AG**(*Req* ⇒ **AF** *Ack*): if a *Request* occurs, then it will be eventually *Acknowledged*.
- **AG**(**AF** *DeviceEnabled*): *DeviceEnabled* holds infinitely often on every computation path.
- **AG**(**EF** *Restart*): from any state it is possible to get to the *Restart* state.

ACTL is the fragment of CTL where only the operators involving **A** are used, and negation is restricted to atomic formulas. An important feature of ACTL is the existence of counterexamples. For example, the CTL specification **AF**p denotes *"On all paths, p holds sometime in the future."* If the specification **AF**p is violated, then there exists an infinite path where p never holds. This path is called a counterexample of **AF**p. In this paper, we will focus on counterexamples which are finite or infinite paths.

For a formal definition of related temporal logics such as CTL* and LTL, please refer to [10].

Explicit State Model Checking. Given a Kripke structure $K = (S, R, I, L)$ and a specification φ in a temporal logic such as CTL, the *model checking problem* is the problem of finding all states s such that

$$K, s \models \varphi$$

and checking if the initial states are among these. An explicit state model checker is a program which performs model checking directly on a Kripke structure.

Theorem 1. *[13,15] Explicit state CTL model checking has time complexity* $O(|K||\varphi|)$.

Besides linear time complexity, CTL has a number of other remarkable properties including decidability and the finite model property. Recent research in logic and databases has generalized the favorable properties of CTL and other temporal logics to fragments of first order and fixed point logics [1,20] and database query languages [18].

Model checking algorithms are usually fixed point algorithms which exploit the fact that temporal formulas can be expressed by fixed point formulas. For example, the set of states Y where the formula $\mathbf{EF}\varphi$ holds, can be defined inductively as follows:

- If $s \models \varphi$, then $s \in Y$.
- If $s \in Y$ and $R(s', s)$ then $s' \in Y$.
- Nothing else is in Y.

This gives rise to the fixed point characterization

$$\mathbf{EF}\varphi \equiv \mu Y.\varphi \vee \mathbf{EX}\,Y$$

where μ is the least fixed point operator. The fixed point extension of temporal logic is called the μ-calculus, and has been studied extensively. It is easy to see that all CTL and CTL* formulas can be expressed using only least fixed points, propositional logic, and the temporal operator $\mathbf{EX}$. Note that $\mathbf{EX}$ is also known as $\diamond$ in modal logic. Explicit state model checking for the μ-calculus is known to be in NP $\cap$ coNP, but the existence of a polynomial time algorithm is a famous open problem.

State Explosion. In practice, systems are described by programs in finite state languages such as SMV or VERILOG. These programs are then compiled into equivalent Kripke structures.

Example 2. In the verification system SMV, the state space S of a Kripke structure is given by the possible assignments to the system variables. Thus, a system with 3 variables $x, y, reset$ and variable domains $D_x = D_y = \{0, 1, 2, 3\}$ and $D_{reset} = \{0, 1\}$ has state space $S = D_x \times D_y \times D_{reset}$, and $|S| = 32$.

The binary transition relation R is defined by transition blocks which for each variable define its possible next value in the next time cycle, as in the following example:

init$(reset) := 0;$	**init**$(x) := 0;$	**init**$(y) := 1;$
next$(reset) := \{0, 1\};$	**next**$(x) := $ **case**	**next**$(y) := $ **case**
	$\quad reset = 1 : 0;$	$\quad reset = 1 : 0;$
	$\quad x < y : x + 1;$	$\quad (x = y) \wedge \neg(y = 2) : y + 1;$
	$\quad x = y : 0;$	$\quad (x = y) : 0;$
	$\quad$ **else** $: x;$	$\quad$ **else** $: y;$
	esac;	**esac**;

Here, **next**$(reset) := \{0, 1\}$ means that the value of $reset$ is chosen nondeterministically. Such situations occur frequently when $reset$ is controlled by the environment, or when the model of the system is too abstract to determine the values of $reset$. For details about the SMV input language, we refer the reader to [25]. Typical CTL properties to be verified by the system include the following:

CTL   *Informal Semantics*

AG EF $reset = 1$ *"From all reachable states, it is possible to reset the system in the future."*

EF AG $x = 1$ *"There exists a reachable state, after which $x = 1$ becomes an invariant."*

The main practical problem in model checking is the so-called **state explosion problem** caused by the fact that the Kripke structure represents the *state space* of the system under investigation, and thus it is of size *exponential* in the size of the system description. Therefore, even for systems of relatively modest size, it is often impossible to compute their Kripke structures.

In the rest of this paper, we will focus on two techniques, *symbolic verification* and *abstraction* which alleviate the state explosion problem.

- **Symbolic verification** is a conservative approach where the Kripke structure is represented by succinct data structures (in particular, Binary Decision Diagrams) without losing information.
- **Abstraction techniques** in contrast employ knowledge about the structure and the specification in order to model only relevant features in the Kripke structure.

3   Symbolic Model Checking

In *symbolic verification*, the transition relation of the Kripke structure is not explicitly constructed, but instead a Boolean function is computed which represents the transition relation. Similarly, sets of states are also represented by Boolean functions. Then, the fixed point algorithms mentioned above are applied to the Boolean functions rather than to the Kripke structure. Since in many practical situations the space requirements for Boolean functions are exponentially smaller than for explicit representation, symbolic verification is able to alleviate the state explosion problem in these situations.

In the remainder of this section, we introduce the main ingredients of symbolic model checking, and discuss the theoretical limitations of BDD based methods.

Ordered Binary Decision Diagrams. Let A be a set of propositional variables, and $\prec$ a linear order on A. An *ordered binary decision diagram* (BDD) $\mathcal{O}$ over A is an acyclic graph (V, E) whose non-terminal vertices (*nodes*) are labeled by variables from A, and whose edges and terminal nodes are labeled by 0, 1. Each non-terminal node v has out-degree 2, such that one of its outgoing edges is labeled 0 (the *low edge* or *else-edge*), and the other is labeled 1 (the *high edge* or *then-edge*). If v has label a_i and the successors of v are labeled a_j, a_k, then $a_i \prec a_j$ and $a_i \prec a_k$. In other words, for each path, the sequence of labels along the path is strictly increasing with respect to $\prec$.

Each BDD node v represents a Boolean function $\mathcal{O}_v$. The terminal nodes of $\mathcal{O}$ represent the constant functions given by their labels. A non-terminal node v with label a_i whose successors at the high and low edges are u and w respectively, defines the function $\mathcal{O}_v := (a_i \wedge \mathcal{O}_u) \vee (\neg a_i \wedge \mathcal{O}_w)$.

As the following example shows, BDDs are related to Boolean decision trees.

Example 3. The Boolean decision tree of Figure 4 represents the Boolean function $x \wedge$ $(y \vee z)$. The BDD in Figure 5 represents the same Boolean function in a more succinct way. Note that the BDD can be obtained from the decision tree by merging isomorphic subtrees, and removing redundant edges. The variable ordering is $x \prec y \prec z$.

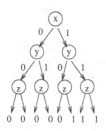

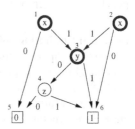

Fig. 4. Decision tree for $x \wedge (y \vee z)$.

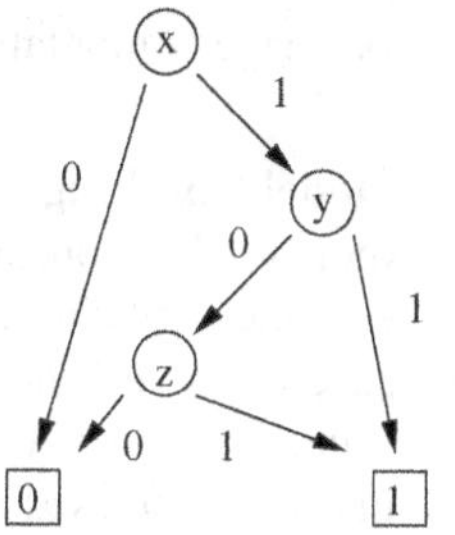

Fig. 5. A BDD for function $x \wedge (y \vee z)$.

Fig. 6. A shared BDD.

The size of a BDD is the number of nodes of the BDD. The size of a BDD in general depends on the variable order $\prec$, and may be exponential in $|A|$. However, it is well-known [3,4] that for every variable order $\prec$ and Boolean function f there exists a *unique minimal* BDD $\mathcal{O}$ over A which represents the Boolean function f. Given any BDD for f which respects $\prec$, $\mathcal{O}$ can be computed in polynomial time. Note that $\mathcal{O}$ contains at most two non-terminal nodes, and no two nodes of $\mathcal{O}$ describe the same Boolean function.

In practice, *shared BDDs* are used to represent several Boolean functions at once. For example, in the BDD of Figure 6, the nodes $1, 2$ and 3 represent the Boolean functions $x \wedge (y \vee z)$, $\neg x \wedge (y \vee z)$ and $y \vee z$ respectively.

Effective algorithms for handling BDDs have been described in the literature [3] and highly effective BDD libraries such as CUDD [31] have been developed.

Symbolic Verification Algorithms. A symbolic verification algorithm is an algorithm whose variables denote not single states, but *sets of states* which are represented by Boolean functions (usually as BDDs). Therefore, symbolic algorithms use only such operations on sets which can be translated into BDD operations. For example, union and intersection of sets correspond to disjunction and conjunction respectively. Binary Decision Diagrams have been a particularly useful data structure for representing Boolean functions; despite their relative succinctness they provide canonical representations of Boolean functions, and therefore expressions of the form $S_1 = S_2$, which are important in fixed point computations, can be evaluated very efficiently.

Image computation is the task to compute for a given set Q of states the set of states

$$\mathbf{EX}(Q) := \{ s : \exists s'. R(s, s') \wedge s' \in Q \}.$$

Recall that CTL can be expressed in fixed point logic with a temporal operator **EX**. Therefore, image computation is a central task in symbolic verification.

Image computation is one of the major bottlenecks in verification. Part of the reason for this, ironically, is the fact that it is in general not feasible to construct a single BDD for R. Instead, R is represented as the conjunction of several BDDs. The problem then arises how to compute **EX**(Q) without actually computing R. In a recent series of papers [7,26,27], improved algorithms for image computation have been investigated.

Theoretical Limitations of Symbolic Model Checking. Potentially, the BDD representation of a Kripke structure may be exponentially more succinct than the explicit representation. Practical experience with symbolic verification demonstrates that in many cases BDDs indeed yield a significant space improvement.

A classic information theoretic argument shows that only a small fraction of all finite Kripke structures can be exponentially compressed [23]. Of course, the general limitation applies to compression by BDDs as well. On the other hand, we know that the large Kripke structures encountered in model checking usually have small descriptions in terms of hardware description languages. This indicates that BDDs or more advanced data structures can in principle be used to obtain exponentially succinct representations of Kripke structures, at least for those Kripke structures in which we are interested.

Practical experiments show that the performance of symbolic methods is highly unpredictable. This phenomenon can be partially explained by complexity theoretic results which state that BDD representation does not improve worst case complexity. In fact, it has been shown [17,33] that representing a decision problem in terms of exponentially smaller BDDs usually increases its worst case complexity exponentially. For example, the problem of deciding **EF**p (reachability) is complete for nondeterministic logspace NL, while in BDD representation it becomes complete for PSPACE. Similar results can be shown for other Boolean formalisms and are closely tied to principal questions in structural complexity theory [19,32,34]. We conclude that symbolic verification is a very powerful method but needs to be complemented by more aggressive techniques. The following section deals with abstraction, one such technique.

4   Abstraction

Existential Abstraction. Intuitively speaking, existential abstraction amounts to partitioning the states of a Kripke structure into clusters, and treating the clusters as new abstract states, cf. Figure 7.

Formally, an abstraction function h is described by a surjection $h : S \to \widehat{S}$ where $\widehat{S}$ is the set of *abstract states*. The surjection h induces an equivalence relation $\equiv$ on the domain S in the following manner: let d, e be states in S, then

$$d \equiv e \quad \text{iff} \quad h(d) = h(e).$$

Since an abstraction can be represented either by a surjection h or by an equivalence relation $\equiv$, we sometimes switch between these representations.

The *abstract Kripke structure* $\widehat{M} = (\widehat{S}, \widehat{I}, \widehat{R}, \widehat{L})$ corresponding to the abstraction function h is defined as follows:

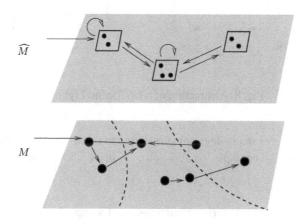

Fig. 7. Existential Abstraction. M is the original Kripke structure, and $\widehat{M}$ the abstracted one. The dotted lines in M indicate how the states of M are clustered into abstract states.

1. $\widehat{I}(\widehat{d})$ iff $\exists d(h(d) = \widehat{d} \wedge I(d))$.
2. $\widehat{R}(\widehat{d_1}, \widehat{d_2})$ iff $\exists d_1 \exists d_2(h(d_1) = \widehat{d_1} \wedge h(d_2) = \widehat{d_2} \wedge R(d_1, d_2))$.
3. $\widehat{L}(\widehat{d}) = \bigcup_{h(d)=\widehat{d}} L(d)$.

An atomic formula f *respects* an abstraction function h if for all d and d' in the domain S, $(d \equiv d') \Rightarrow (d \models f \Leftrightarrow d' \models f)$. Let $\widehat{d}$ be an abstract state. $\widehat{L}(\widehat{d})$ is *consistent*, if all concrete states corresponding to $\widehat{d}$ satisfy all labels in $\widehat{L}(\widehat{d})$, i.e., collapsing a set of concrete states into an abstract state does not lead to contradictory labels.

Spurious Counterexamples. It is easy to see that $\widehat{M}$ contains less information than M. Thus, model checking the structure $\widehat{M}$ potentially leads to wrong results. The following theorem shows that at least for ACTL, specifications which are correct for $\widehat{M}$ are correct for M as well.

Theorem 2. *Let h be an abstraction and φ be an ACTL specification where the atomic subformulas respect h. Then the following holds: (i) $\widehat{L}(\widehat{d})$ is consistent for all abstract states $\widehat{d}$ in $\widehat{M}$; (ii) $\widehat{M} \models \varphi \Rightarrow M \models \varphi$.*

On the other hand, the following example shows that if the abstract model invalidates an ACTL specification, *the actual model may still satisfy the specification.*

Example 4. Assume that for a US traffic light controller (see Figure 8), we want to prove $\psi = \mathbf{AG}\,\mathbf{AF}(state = red)$ using the abstraction function $h(red) = \widehat{red}$ and $h(green) = h(yellow) = \widehat{go}$. It is easy to see that $M \models \psi$ while $\widehat{M} \not\models \psi$. There exists an infinite abstract trace $\langle \widehat{red}, \widehat{go}, \widehat{go}, \dots \rangle$ that invalidates the specification.

Fig. 8. Abstraction of a US Traffic Light.

If an abstract counterexample does not correspond to some concrete counterexample, we call it *spurious*. For example, $\langle \widehat{red}, \widehat{go}, \widehat{go}, \ldots \rangle$ in the above example is a spurious counterexample.

The Fine Structure of Abstraction Functions. As Example 2 shows, the set of states S of a Kripke structure is typically obtained as the product $D_1 \times \cdots D_n$ of smaller domains. In this situation, an abstraction function h can be described by surjections $h_i : D_i \to \widehat{D_i}$, such that $h(d_1, \ldots, d_n)$ is equal to $(h_1(d_1), \ldots, h_n(d_n))$, and $\widehat{S}$ is equal to $\widehat{D_1} \times \cdots \widehat{D_n}$. The equivalence relations $\equiv_i$ corresponding to the individual surjections h_i induce an equivalence relation $\equiv$ over the entire domain $S = D_1 \times \cdots \times D_n$ in the obvious manner:

$$(d_1, \cdots, d_n) \equiv (e_1, \cdots, e_n) \ \text{ iff } \ d_1 \equiv_1 e_1 \wedge \cdots \wedge d_n \equiv_n e_n$$

4.1   Counterexample-Guided Abstraction

Recall that for a Kripke structure M, and an ACTL formula φ, our goal is to check whether the Kripke structure M corresponding to P satisfies φ. Our methodology consists of the following steps, cf. Figure 9.

1. *Generate the initial abstraction:* We generate an initial abstraction h by examining the transition blocks corresponding to the variables of the program which describes M, cf. Example 2. A detailed description of the initial abstraction is given in [9].
2. *Model-check the abstract structure:* Let $\widehat{M}$ be the abstract Kripke structure corresponding to the abstraction h. We check whether $\widehat{M} \models \varphi$. If the check is affirmative, then we can conclude that $M \models \varphi$ (see Theorem 2). Suppose the check reveals that there is a counterexample $\widehat{T}$. We ascertain whether $\widehat{T}$ is an actual counterexample, i.e., a counterexample in the unabstracted structure M. If $\widehat{T}$ turns out to be an actual counterexample, we report it to the user, otherwise $\widehat{T}$ is a spurious counterexample, and we proceed to step 3.
3. *Refine the abstraction:* We refine the abstraction function h by partitioning a *single equivalence class* of $\equiv$ so that after the refinement the abstract structure $\widehat{M}$ corresponding to the refined abstraction function no longer admits the spurious counterexample $\widehat{T}$. We will discuss partitioning algorithms for this purpose in Section 4.3. After refining the abstraction function, we return to step 2.

Using counterexamples to refine abstract models has been investigated by a number of other researchers beginning with the *localization reduction* of Kurshan [21]. He

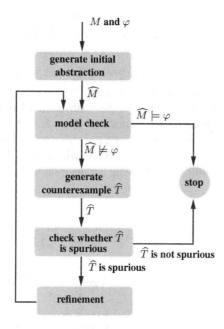

Fig. 9. Counterexample based refinement.

models a concurrent system as a composition of L-processes $L_1, \dots, L_n$ (L-processes are described in detail in [21]). The localization reduction is an iterative technique that starts with a small subset of relevant L-processes that are topologically close to the specification in the *variable dependency graph*. All other program variables are abstracted away with nondeterministic assignments. If the counterexample is found to be spurious, additional variables are added to eliminate the counterexample. The heuristic for selecting these variables also uses information from the variable dependency graph. A similar approach has been described by Balarin in [2,22].

4.2 Model Checking the Abstract Model

We use standard symbolic model checking procedures to determine whether $\widehat{M}$ satisfies the specification φ. If it does, then by Theorem 2 we can conclude that the original Kripke structure also satisfies φ. Otherwise, assume that the model checker produces a counterexample $\widehat{T}$ corresponding to the abstract model $\widehat{M}$. In the rest of this section, we will focus on counterexamples which are either *finite paths* or *infinite paths (loops)*.

Identification of Spurious Finite Path Counterexamples First, we will tackle the case when the counterexample $\widehat{T}$ is a finite path $\langle \widehat{s_1}, \cdots, \widehat{s_n} \rangle$. Given an abstract state $\widehat{s}$, the set of concrete states s such that $h(s) = \widehat{s}$ is denoted by $h^{-1}(\widehat{s})$, i.e., $h^{-1}(\widehat{s}) = \{s | h(s) = \widehat{s}\}$. We extend h^{-1} to sequences in the following way: $h^{-1}(\widehat{T})$ is the set of concrete finite paths given by the following expression

$$\{\langle s_1, \cdots, s_n\rangle | \bigwedge_{i=1}^{n} h(s_i) = \widehat{s_i} \wedge I(s_1) \wedge \bigwedge_{i=1}^{n-1} R(s_i, s_{i+1})\}.$$

We will occasionally write h_{path}^{-1} to emphasize the fact that h^{-1} is applied to a sequence. Next, we give a *symbolic* algorithm to compute $h^{-1}(\widehat{T})$. Let $S_1 = h^{-1}(\widehat{s_1}) \cap I$ and R be the transition relation corresponding to the unabstracted Kripke structure M. For $1 < i \leq n$, we define S_i in the following manner: $S_i := Img(S_{i-1}) \cap h^{-1}(\widehat{s_i})$. Recall that $Img(S_{i-1})$ is the forward image of S_{i-1} with respect to the transition relation R. The sequence of sets S_i is computed symbolically using BDDs and the standard image computation algorithm. The following lemma establishes the correctness of this procedure.

Lemma 1. *The following are equivalent:*

  (i) *The finite path $\widehat{T}$ corresponds to a concrete counterexample.*
  (ii) *The set of concrete finite paths $h^{-1}(\widehat{T})$ is non-empty.*
  (iii) *For all $1 \leq i \leq n$, $S_i \neq \emptyset$.*

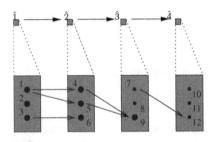

Algorithm SplitPATH

$S := h^{-1}(\widehat{s_1}) \cap I$
$j := 1$
while $(S \neq \emptyset$ and $j < n)$ {
    $j := j + 1$
    $S_{\text{prev}} := S$
    $S := Img(S) \cap h^{-1}(\widehat{s_j})$ }
if $S \neq \emptyset$ **then** output counterexample
else output j, S_{prev}

Fig. 10. An abstract counterexample

Fig. 11. SplitPATH checks spurious finite paths.

Example 5. Consider a program with only one variable with domain $S = \{1, \cdots, 12\}$. Assume that the abstraction function h maps $x \in S$ to $\lfloor (x-1)/3 \rfloor + 1$. There are four abstract states corresponding to the equivalence classes $\{1, 2, 3\}$, $\{4, 5, 6\}$, $\{7, 8, 9\}$, and $\{10, 11, 12\}$. We call these abstract states $\widehat{1}$, $\widehat{2}$, $\widehat{3}$, and $\widehat{4}$. The transitions between states in the concrete model are indicated by the arrows in Figure 10; small dots denote non-reachable states. Suppose that we obtain an abstract counterexample $\widehat{T} = \langle \widehat{1}, \widehat{2}, \widehat{3}, \widehat{4} \rangle$. It is easy to see that $\widehat{T}$ is spurious. Using the terminology of Lemma 1, we have $S_1 = \{1, 2, 3\}$, $S_2 = \{4, 5, 6\}$, $S_3 = \{9\}$, and $S_4 = \emptyset$. Notice that S_4 and therefore $Img(S_3)$ are both empty.

It follows from Lemma 1 that if $h^{-1}(\widehat{T})$ is empty (i.e., if the counterexample $\widehat{T}$ is spurious), then there exists a minimal i ($2 \leq i \leq n$) such that $S_i = \emptyset$. The symbolic Algorithm **SplitPATH** in Figure 11 computes this number and the set of states in S_{i-1}. In this case, we proceed to the refinement step (see Section 4.3). On the other hand, if the conditions stated in Lemma 1 are true, then **SplitPATH** will report a "real" counterexample and we can stop.

Identification of Spurious Loop Counterexamples. Now we consider the case when the counterexample $\widehat{T}$ includes a loop, which we write as $\langle \widehat{s_1}, \cdots, \widehat{s_i} \rangle \langle \widehat{s_{i+1}}, \cdots, \widehat{s_n} \rangle^\omega$. The loop starts at the abstract state $\widehat{s_{i+1}}$ and ends at $\widehat{s_n}$. Since this case is more complicated than the finite path counterexamples, we first present an example in which some of the typical situations occur.

Example 6. We consider a loop $\langle \widehat{s_1} \rangle \langle \widehat{s_2}, \widehat{s_3} \rangle^\omega$ as shown in Figure 12. In order to find out if the abstract loop corresponds to concrete loops, we unwind the counterexample as demonstrated in the figure. There are two situations where cycles occur. In the figure,

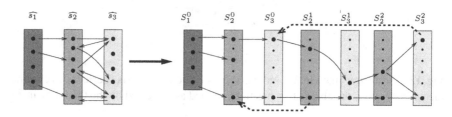

Fig. 12. A loop counterexample, and its unwinding.

for each of these situations, an example cycle (the first one occurring) is indicated by a fat dashed arrow. We make the following important observations: (i) A given abstract loop may correspond to several concrete loops of *different size*. (ii) Each of these loops may start at different stages of the unwinding. (iii) The unwinding eventually becomes periodic (in our case $S_3^0 = S_3^2$), but only after several stages of the unwinding. The size of the period is the least common multiple of the size of the individual loops, and thus, in general *exponential*.

We conclude from the example that a naive algorithm may have exponential time complexity due to an exponential number of loop unwindings. However, it is shown in [9] that a minor modification of the algorithm **SplitPATH** can be used to analyze abstract loop counterexamples effectively. For easy reference we shall refer to this algorithm as **SplitLOOP**.

4.3 Refining the Abstraction

In this section we explain how to refine an abstraction to eliminate the spurious counterexample. Let us first consider the situation outlined in Figure 13. We see that the abstract path does not have a corresponding concrete path. Whichever concrete path we go, we will end up in state D, from which we cannot go further. Therefore, D is called a *deadend state*. On the other hand, the *bad state* is state B, because it made us believe that there is an outgoing transition. It is easy to see that the algorithm **SplitPath** of the previous section will output the set of deadend states. The question now arises how to partition the abstract state in such a way that the spurious counterexample is eliminated.

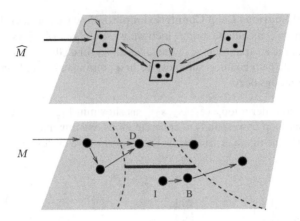

Fig. 13. The abstract path in $\widehat{M}$ (indicated by the thick arrows) is spurious. To eliminate the spurious path, the abstraction has to be refined as indicated by the thick line in M.

Since we know from the previous section that loop counterexamples can be treated in a very similar way as finite path counterexamples, we will concentrate on finite path counterexamples. Let us formally consider the case when the counterexample $\widehat{T} = \langle \widehat{s_1}, \cdots, \widehat{s_n} \rangle$ is a finite path. Since $\widehat{T}$ does not correspond to a real counterexample, by Lemma 1 (iii) there exists a set $S_i \subseteq h^{-1}(\widehat{s_i})$ with $1 \leq i < n$ such that $Img(S_i) \cap h^{-1}(\widehat{s_{i+1}}) = \emptyset$ and S_i is reachable from initial state set $h^{-1}(\widehat{s_1}) \cap I$. Since there is a transition from $\widehat{s_i}$ to $\widehat{s_{i+1}}$ in the abstract model, there is at least one transition from a state in $h^{-1}(\widehat{s_i})$ to a state in $h^{-1}(\widehat{s_{i+1}})$ even though there is no transition from S_i to $h^{-1}(\widehat{s_{i+1}})$. We partition $h^{-1}(\widehat{s_i})$ into three subsets $S_{i,D}$, $S_{i,B}$, and $S_{i,I}$ as follows (compare Figure 14):

Deadend States	$S_{i,D} = S_i$
Bad States	$S_{i,B} = \{s \in h^{-1}(\widehat{s_i}) \mid \exists s' \in h^{-1}(\widehat{s_{i+1}}).R(s,s')\}$
Irrelevant States	$S_{i,I} = h^{-1}(\widehat{s_i}) \setminus (S_{i,D} \cup S_{i,B}).$

Thus, we have partitioned the abstract state $h^{-1}(\widehat{s_i})$ according to the above discussion. For illustration, consider again the example in Figure 10. Note that $S_1 = \{1, 2, 3\}$, $S_2 = \{4, 5, 6\}$, $S_3 = \{9\}$, and $S_4 = \emptyset$. The deadend state is $S_{3,D} = \{9\}$, the bad state is $S_{3,B} = \{7\}$, and the irrelevant state is $S_{3,I} = \{8\}$. Since $S_{i,B}$ is not empty, there is a spurious transition $\widehat{s_i} \rightarrow \widehat{s_{i+1}}$. This causes the spurious counterexample $\widehat{T}$. Hence in order to refine the abstraction h so that the new model does not allow $\widehat{T}$, we need a refined abstraction function *which separates the two sets* $S_{i,D}$ *and* $S_{i,B}$, i.e., we need an abstraction function, in which no abstract state simultaneously contains states from $S_{i,D}$ and from $S_{i,B}$. In Figure 13, such a refinement of the partition is indicated by a thick line.

It is natural to describe the needed refinement in terms of equivalence relations: Recall from our discussion about the *fine structure of abstraction functions* that $h^{-1}(\widehat{s})$ is an equivalence class of $\equiv$ which has the form $E_1 \times \cdots \times E_n$, where each E_i is an equivalence class of $\equiv_i$. Thus, the refinement $\equiv'$ of $\equiv$ is obtained by partitioning the equivalence classes E_j into subclasses, which amounts to refining the equivalence relations $\equiv_j$. The *size of the refinement* is the number of new equivalence classes. Ideally, we would like to find the coarsest refinement that separates the two sets, i.e., the separating refinement with the smallest size. We can show however that this is computationally intractable.

Theorem 3. *(i) The problem of finding the coarsest refinement is NP-hard; (ii) when $S_{i,I} = \emptyset$, the problem can be solved in polynomial time.*

Thus, we conclude that it is the existence of the irrelevant states which makes the problem hard. (Intuitively, the existence of irrelevant states increases the number of possible solutions, and therefore, it is hard to identify the optimal one.)

The polynomial time symbolic algorithm **PolyRefine** corresponding to case (ii) of Theorem 3 is described in Figure 15. The algorithm uses the following notation: Let P_j^+, P_j^- be two projection functions, such that for $s = (d_1, \ldots, d_m)$, $P_j^+(s) = d_j$ and $P_j^-(s) = (d_1, \ldots, d_{j-1}, d_{j+1}, \ldots, d_m)$. Then $proj(S_{i,D}, j, a)$ denotes the *projection* set $\{P_j^-(s) \mid P_j^+(s) = a, s \in S_{i,D}\}$.

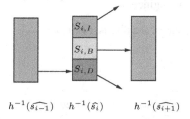

Algorithm PolyRefine
for j := 1 to m {
    $\equiv'_j := \equiv_j$
    for every $a, b \in E_j$ {
        if $proj(S_{i,D}, j, a) \neq proj(S_{i,D}, j, b)$
            then $\equiv'_j := \equiv'_j \setminus \{(a, b)\}$ }}

Fig. 14. Three sets $S_{i,D}, S_{i,B}$, and $S_{i,I}$

Fig. 15. The algorithm **PolyRefine**

In the implementation [9], we use the following heuristics: We merge the irrelevant states in $S_{i,I}$ into $S_{i,B}$, and use the algorithm **Polyrefine** to find the coarsest refinement that separates the sets $S_{i,D}$ and $S_{i,B} \cup S_{i,I}$. The equivalence relation computed by **PolyRefine** in this manner is not optimal, but it is a correct refinement which separates $S_{i,D}$ and $S_{i,B}$, and eliminates the spurious counterexample. This heuristic has given good results in our practical experiments.

Our procedure continues to refine the abstraction function by partitioning equivalence classes until a real counterexample is found, or the ACTL property is verified. The partitioning procedure is guaranteed to terminate since each equivalence class must contain at least one element. Thus, our method is complete.

Theorem 4. *Given a model M and an ACTL specification φ whose counterexample is either a finite path or a loop, our algorithm will find a model $\widehat{M}$ such that $\widehat{M} \models \varphi \Leftrightarrow M \models \varphi$.*

5   Directions for Future Research

Despite the progress in model checking made during the last twenty years, additional research is needed to realize the full potential of the method. Some particularly fertile research directions are listed below:

- Investigate the use of *abstraction*, *compositional reasoning*, and *symmetry* to reduce the state explosion problem.
- Develop methods for verifying *parametrized systems*, i.e., systems with arbitrarily many identical components.
- Develop practical tools for *real-time* and *hybrid* systems. Such systems involve both discrete variables and variables that change continuously with time.
- Investigate alternatives to BDDs for symbolic model checking, such as the use of efficient SAT procedures like GRASP [24].
- Combine model checking with *deductive verification*, i.e., automated theorem proving.
- Extend current model checking techniques to *software*, in particular safety-critical embedded systems that involve both hardware and software.
- Develop *tool interfaces* suitable for system designers. Temporal logic may not be the most perspicuous specification language for engineers.

Many of these topics, along with appropriate references, are discussed in [10].

References

1. H. Andréka, J. van Benthem, and I. Németi. Modal languages and bounded fragments of predicate logic. *Journal of Philosophical Logic*, 27:217–274, 1998.
2. F. Balarin and A. L. Sangiovanni-Vincentelli. An iterative approach to language containment. In *Computer-Aided Verification*, volume 697 of *LNCS*, pages 29–40, 1993.
3. R. E. Bryant. Graph-based algorithms for boolean function manipulation. *IEEE Transaction on Computers*, pages 35(8):677–691, 1986.
4. R. E. Bryant. On the complexity of VLSI implementations and graph representations of boolean functions with application to integer multiplication. *IEEE Transaction on Computers*, pages 40:205–213, 1991.
5. J. R. Burch, E. M. Clarke, and D. E. Long. Symbolic model checking with partitioned transition relations. In A. Halaas and P. B. Denyer, editors, *Proceedings of the 1991 International Conference on Very Large Scale Integration*, Aug. 1991. Winner of the Sidney Michaelson Best Paper Award.
6. J. R. Burch, E. M. Clarke, and K. L. McMillan. Symbolic model checking: 10^{20} states and beyond. *Information and Computation*, 98:142–170, 1992.
7. P. Chauhan, E. Clarke, S. Jha, and H. Veith. Efficient image computation. Manuscript, 2000.
8. A. Cimatti, E. Clarke, F. Giunchiglia, and M. Roveri. NuSMV: a new symbolic model checker. *Software Tools for Technology Transfer*, 1998.
9. E. Clarke, O. Grumberg, S. Jha, Y. Lu, and H. Veith. Counterexample-guided abstraction refinement. In *Computer-Aided Verification (CAV) 2000*, volume 1855 of *LNCS*. Springer, 2000. Full version available as Technical Report CMU-CS-00-103, Carnegie Mellon University.
10. E. Clarke, O. Grumberg, and D. Peled. *Model Checking*. MIT Publishers, 1999.

11. E. Clarke and H. Schlingloff. Model checking. In J. Robinson and A. Voronkov, editors, *Handbook of Automated Reasoning*. Elsevier, 2000. to appear.

12. E. M. Clarke and E. A. Emerson. Synthesis of synchronization skeletons for branching time temporal logic. In *Logic of Programs: Workshop*, LNCS, 1981.

13. E. M. Clarke, E. A. Emerson, and A. P. Sistla. Automatic verification of finite-state concurrent system using temporal logic. In *Proceedings of the Tenth Annual ACM Symposium on Principles of Programming Languages (POPL)*, January 1983.

14. E. M. Clarke, O. Grumberg, and D. E. Long. Model checking and abstraction. *ACM Transactions on Programming Languages and System (TOPLAS)*, 16(5):1512–1542, September 1994.

15. E. M. Clarke Jr., E. A. Emerson, and A. P. Sistla. Automatic verification of finite-state concurrent systems using temporal logic specifications. *ACM TOPLAS*, 8(2):244–263, Apr. 1986.

16. O. Coudert, C. Berthet, and J. C. Madre. Verification of synchronous sequential machines based on symbolic execution. In J. Sifakis, editor, *Proceedings of the 1989 International Workshop on Automatic Verification Methods for Finite State Systems, Grenoble, France*, volume 407 of *Lecture Notes in Computer Science*. Springer-Verlag, June 1989.

17. J. Feigenbaum, S. Kannan, M. Y. Vardi, and M. Viswanathan. Complexity of problems on graphs represented as OBDDs. *Chicago Journal of Theoretical Computer Science*, 1999.

18. G. Gottlob, E. Grädel, and H. Veith. Datalog LITE: a deductive query language with linear time model checking. *ACM Transactions on Computational Logic (TOCL)*, 2001. Accepted for publication.

19. G. Gottlob, N. Leone, and H. Veith. Succinctness as a source of complexity in logical formalisms. *Annals of Pure and Applied Logic*, 97(1–3):231–260, 1999.

20. E. Grädel and I. Walukiewicz. Guarded fixed point logic. In G. Longo, editor, *Proc. 14th IEEE Symp. on Logic in Computer Science*, pages 45–54, 1999.

21. R. P. Kurshan. *Computer-Aided Verification of Coordinating Processes*. Princeton University Press, 1994.

22. Y. Lakhnech. personal communication. 2000.

23. M. Li and P. Vitányi. *An introduction to Kolmogorov Complexity and its applications*. Spinger Verlag, New York, 1993.

24. J. Marques-Silva and K. A. Sakallah. GRASP: A search algorithm for propositional satisfiability. *IEEE Transactions on Computers*, 48(5):506–521, 1999.

25. K. L. McMillan. *Symbolic Model Checking*. Kluwer Academic Publishers, 1993.

26. I. Moon, J. H. Kukula, K. Ravi, and F. Somenzi. To split or to conjoin: The question in image computation. In *Proceedings of the 37th Design Automation Conference (DAC'00)*, pages 26–28, Los Angeles, June 2000.

27. I. Moon and F. Somenzi. Border-block triangular form and conjunction schedule in image computation. In *Proceedings of the Formal Methods in Computer Aided Design (FMCAD'00)*, November 2000. To appear.

28. C. Pixley. A computational theory and implementation of sequential hardware equivalence. In R. Kurshan and E. Clarke, editors, *Proc. CAV Workshop (also DIMACS Tech. Report 90-31)*, Rutgers University, NJ, June 1990.

29. C. Pixley, G. Beihl, and E. Pacas-Skewes. Automatic derivation of FSM specification to implementation encoding. In *Proceedings of the International Conference on Computer Desgin*, pages 245–249, Cambridge, MA, Oct. 1991.

30. C. Pixley, S.-W. Jeong, and G. D. Hachtel. Exact calculation of synchronization sequences based on binary decision diagrams. In *Proceedings of the 29th Design Automation Conference*, pages 620–623, June 1992.

31. F. Somenzi. CUDD: CU decision diagram package. http://vlsi.colorado.edu/ fabio/.

32. H. Veith. Languages represented by boolean formulas. *Information Processing Letters*, 63:251–256, 1997.
33. H. Veith. How to encode a logical structure as an OBDD. In *Proc. 13th Annual IEEE Conference on Computational Complexity (CCC)*, pages 122–131. IEEE Computer Society, 1998.
34. H. Veith. Succinct representation, leaf languages and projection reductions. *Information and Computation*, 142(2):207–236, 1998.

From Research Software to Open Source

Susan L. Graham

University of California, Berkeley, CA 94720, USA
`graham@cs.berkeley.edu`

Abstract. It is a longstanding practice that software researchers share their source code with the research community, allowing other researchers to inspect their work and to build on it. Many widely used software systems originated as code distributions from research projects. Early examples include Berkeley UNIX, sendmail, TEX, Emacs, and many others. The distribution practices of the research community evolved into the free software movement initiated by Richard Stallman, and the more recent open source and libre software movements. Eric Raymond has argued eloquently in "The Cathedral and the Bazaar" that the development processes that stem from these approaches to software development and distribution lead to higher quality software than the traditional proprietary approaches. There is much talk about open source in the commercial arena. In this paper we review the issues that surround the open source approach to software development. We consider the impact of open source on industry, on government, and on the research environment from which it emerged.

1 Introduction

In the early days of computer science research, many researchers in academia and in industrial research laboratories made their experimental software available to researchers outside their own organization, usually in source code form. Some of that software achieved widespread use. As the commercial value of software increased, the practice of distributing source code became less widespread, particularly within industry. That change did not go un-noticed. Under Richard Stallman's leadership, the Free Software Foundation [5] played a major role both in raising the issue and in making available a variety of systems software in source code form. Recently, the Open Source movement has raised the issue in a way that is influencing the commercial world to adopt some open source practices. That change is resulting, in part, from the arguments made by Eric Raymond, and others that an open source development process results in higher quality software [19]. The purpose of this paper is to provide some historical context and to consider the present-day implications for software research and development.

R. Wilhelm (Ed.): Informatics. 10 Years Back. 10 Years Ahead, LNCS 2000, pp. 195–208, 2001.

2   Why Share Source Code?

From a research perspective, there are many reasons to release software to the research community. The most important are the integrity of the scientific method of inquiry and the collective research advantage of building on an existing software base.

2.1   Validating Research Results

In order to reproduce results, researchers must have an explanation of the research methodology, access to the same experimental setting, the same instruments, and the same data. In software research, the detailed description of the experiment is the source code - execution of the target code may provide some insight into characteristics of the solution, such as performance, robustness, and behavior on other inputs, but it often does not suffice to understand exactly how the results are achieved.

In the days when programs were smaller, and many of the research results were algorithms rather than complex systems, the Communications of the ACM published algorithms, including both the documentation and the source code. Sometimes algorithm publication was accompanied by publication of a research paper explaining the ideas behind the algorithm. Even before the advent of widely available networking, the algorithms were made available in computer-readable form. There was an additional form of publication called a certification, in which the author reported the results of using the documentation and testing the algorithm. Certification was a form of validation of the published software, but also served to validate the underlying research contribution. As programs became larger, it became infeasible (and perhaps less useful) to publish the source code in printed form in a journal. Nevertheless, the role of both source code and data in enhancing understanding and validating results remains.

2.2   Software Research Infrastructure

Software research is often concerned with creating new ways to solve problems that exist within a wider context. For example, in the realm of compiler construction, the researcher might want to experiment with a new dataflow algorithm, a new intermediate representation, or a new cache management strategy. In order to evaluate the effect of the new method in practice, the researcher might wish to embed it within a compiler for a widely used programming language such as Java. It is preferable to be able modify an existing Java compiler, rather than to develop a new one. One reason is that creating a new compiler requires a substantial amount of effort, much of which might be peripheral to the research goals. Another important reason is that in order to evaluate the performance of the new method in a controlled way, it might be necessary to hold other factors constant, which is difficult to do in a new implementation of the entire compiler. Thus, modifying an existing software artifact provides both improved efficiency for the researcher and improved integrity of the results.

In re-implementing well-understood methods in order to use them as tools or components, the researcher also introduces both unreliability and inefficiency. Widely used software artifacts are likely to have fewer bugs and better performance than software written in the heat of the moment by the researcher. The sharing of mathematical libraries, parser generators, user interface toolkits, and the like has a long history in software-enabled research and is still widely practiced today.

3   Widely Used Research Software

If the purpose of making source code available were only to reveal the details of the solution to other researchers and to share the software base with people working on similar problems, then software distribution would be successful even if it only reached a relatively small peer group. However, software also represents a realization of ideas, of new ways of providing useful services and techniques. Sometimes, a community of users puts those ideas into practice by widespread use of research software and by collective improvement. As the research software becomes useful infrastructure, it undergoes development that goes beyond the needs of its research creator. Often, other people or other organizations do that development.

There are many well-known examples. Among them are Berkeley UNIX [12], TEX [11], sendmail [3], Emacs [23], the X window system [22], and, more recently, the user interface scripting language and toolkit TCL/Tk [16], and the UNIX-based GNU/Linux operating system [9]. In every case, the distributed source code has been a vehicle for research and education, as well as a software base for widely shared tools and services. The following section discusses the software distribution of Berkeley UNIX – an example chosen both because the author has first-hand experience with it, and because the example includes within it a variety of smaller tools and services.

4   How Berkeley UNIX Came About

UNIX was originally the child of a research project at AT&T to build a simple, clean operating system for the Digital Equipment Corp. PDP-11 [21].[1] In 1974, the Berkeley Computer Science Division, EECS Dept., acquired a PDP-11, to be shared with the departments of Mathematics and Statistics as a research machine. Under the guidance of then-assistant professor Robert Fabry, we chose to use UNIX in preference to the Digital Equipment Corp. operating system. The INGRES research project [8] was one of the early users of the system for large-scale software development. In the fall of 1975, Ken Thompson arrived from Bell Labs as a visiting professor, and Bill Joy arrived as a new graduate student. Thompson initiated work on a Pascal interpreter, which we subsequently

---

[1] The same project produced the C systems implementation language [20], designed specifically for UNIX, and the Portable C Compiler [10].

completed, extended with a compiler and improved to the point that it became the system of choice for teaching programming for many years [6]. That system was the basis for the first Berkeley Software Distribution, initiated by Joy in 1977. Once we had a distribution, it became convenient to add other software that we wanted to share.[2] The Second Berkeley Software Distribution (2BSD) contained not only the Pascal system, but Joy's ex and vi text editors.

When we acquired a Digital Equipment Corp. VAX-11 in late 1978, we first used the Bell Labs 32/V port of UNIX to the VAX, but shortly thereafter Özalp Babaoglu, a graduate student, and Joy developed a virtual memory UNIX system [1]. Our first VAX UNIX distribution, together with ports of Pascal, ex, vi, the C shell, and other tools, went out in late 1979. Shortly thereafter, the U.S. Defense Advanced Projects Research Agency (DARPA) contracted with Berkeley, in particular, with the Berkeley Computer Systems Research Group (CSRG) for us to develop enhancements to Berkeley UNIX for the research community, including an implementation of the TCP/IP networking protocols, the Berkeley Internet Name Domain package (BIND) and a fast file system. That contract enabled us to hire a staff distribution manager. It also stimulated the incorporation of additional contributed software into the Berkeley distribution, some of it contributed by people outside Berkeley, some of it stemming from Berkeley projects (e.g. sendmail [3] and gprof [7]). CSRG provided periodic releases of the Berkeley Software Distribution (BSD). Over time, CSRG took on the role not only of making technical enhancements to BSD UNIX, but also serving as system integrators, quality assurance managers, and coordinators of the many external contributors.

The success of BSD UNIX also led us into licensing. Berkeley UNIX was based on the AT&T Bell Laboratories UNIX and contained some AT&T code. AT&T had provided that code to us for research purposes under a licensing agreement. Consequently, by agreement with AT&T, we could only distribute UNIX source code to sites that demonstrated to us that they held a UNIX license from AT&T. That led to a Berkeley distribution agreement (i.e. a license) that, in addition, provided some protection for the University against liability. Appropriate copyright notices were affixed to the code. As the popularity of Berkeley UNIX grew, it also became necessary to charge a fee to recover the costs of tapes, mail and license processing. Our concern about intellectual property was primarily that the authors of contributed software, many of whom were students, get credit for their work by having their names on the documentation and manual pages.

As the popularity of UNIX grew, AT&T realized that there was a potential business market for UNIX and released a commercial version called UNIX System V. For much of the 1980's, BSD enhancements were carried over to System V. In 1989, we pulled out the networking code we had written as a separate distribution that did not require the increasingly expensive AT&T source code license. That was followed by a community effort to re-implement much of the UNIX system, to free it from the need for dual licensing. The commercialization of UNIX eventually led to a lawsuit against the University (see McKusick [13]), a

---

[2] Recall that there was no Internet. Software was distributed by mailing tapes.

suit that the University won, but that took considerable time away from research and was a significant factor in ending the Berkeley project in 1995.

The Berkeley UNIX experience was an important example for the themes of this discussion in two respects. First, it demonstrated the value of source code availability for making progress in research and for improving software quality. And secondly, it illustrated the difficulty in combining the open distribution of source code with commercial interests. In some respects, the research endeavor was better off before software became commercial.

5   Richard Stallman and the Free Software Movement

Richard Stallman joined the MIT A.I. Laboratory in the early 1970's. He wrote the Emacs editor while still an undergraduate. He too did his work in an environment of shared and available source code. As commercial interests caused more and more software to become proprietary and inaccessible, he developed a philosophical view that software should be free, in the sense of available to use and modify (although not necessarily without cost), and that developers should have the right to make their enhancements (so-called *derived works*) available to others as well.

In 1984, Stallman set out to create a UNIX-compatible free operating system called GNU (for "GNU's not UNIX"), using free software tools and components, such as the X window system where possible. What emerged from this effort was a lot of widely used software. Among the software is GNU Emacs, the GNU compiler collection (gcc), the debugger gdb, the GNU C library, and a variety of other UNIX libraries and utilities. Eventually, the operating system was completed by the emergence of the Linux kernel. Stallman also founded the Free Software Foundation (FSF) [5], a non-profit umbrella for free software development.

Not only was (and is) GNU software widely used for research, it was also used commercially, primarily by companies whose primary business was something other than selling systems software. A service industry grew up around GNU software, providing the software support that was essential in the commercial world, and providing enhancements that then found their way back into the available source code base. For example Cygnus Support (now part of Red Hat) retargeted the GNU C compiler to a number of vendor hardware platforms. Many groups benefited from that activity. The clients who paid for the compiler got the ability to run their applications on that vendor's platform, the vendor had a potentially larger customer base, and the user community had access to the source code for the new compiler.

6   Mid-80's to Mid 90's

During the decade or so after the advent of the free software movement, there were multiple tracks for software distribution. Many researchers continued to make their source code available to other researchers. However, many of their institutions began to understand the potential of software as a source of licensing income, and also the potential liability to the institution stemming from software distribution. The limitations some institutions placed on distribution of research software have caused the availability of such software to become less common than it was. Free software (in the FSF sense) continued to flourish, although many advocates of the free software approach also resorted to licensing as a means of insuring the freeness of derived works. And meanwhile, the amount of mostly-commercial proprietary software grew rapidly.

7   The Cathedral and the Bazaar

In 1997 Eric Raymond distributed his highly influential paper "The Cathedral and the Bazaar" on the Internet.[3] In that paper, Raymond argues for the benefits of variants of the bottom-up grass-roots model of software development that we had experienced with Berkeley UNIX. He describes the *cathedral* model of software development as the more traditional process in which software is carefully crafted by an expert team under a top-down management-driven process, and is only released when it is of sufficiently high quality. He contrasts that with the process he had observed Linus Torvalds to have followed in the early development of Linux. In that *bazaar* model, software is developed by a community process in which there is extensive user participation, frequent releases of systems containing user-contributed code, and source code availability for all.

Raymond argues that if one cultivates users to serve as co-developers, then many benefits accrue. The inclusive strategy creates a large talent pool for further development. The user/developers are often contributors of very good ideas, both for the design, and for solving technical problems. The participation of a large group of enthusiastic developers will cause problems to be detected more readily and, more importantly, to be fixed better and more quickly because *someone* in the community is bound to understand the solution. In summary, a system can evolve more rapidly and more robustly given that open developer community.

Of course, the frequent releases are what enable the changes to get out to the user/developer community rapidly. Clearly, it is only the infrastructure provided by the Internet and the Web that make that practice possible - it was much more difficult to provide frequent releases before it became possible to download them from the Web. It is also the Internet and the Web that facilitates the participation of a wide community of geographically and institutionally diverse developers, all of whom are able to keep themselves current without logistical difficulties.

8   What Is the Bazaar Development Model?

Raymond goes on to summarize two important preconditions for bazaar-style development - an existing software artifact and a talented coordinator/integrator.

---

[3] It has subsequently been revised and published more formally [19].

He observes that the bazaar style presumes an existing software base. It would be difficult to do *ab initio* software development in that fashion, or to create a co-developer community without a body of software from which to start. Indeed, all of the examples we have cited stemmed from novel and useful software created by one person or a small group. Other people joined in because they wanted to improve a software system that they already found to be useful and valuable.

The role of the coordinator/integrator is crucial to the success of an open source endeavor. One or two people must decide what goes into a release, manage the release process, rally the developers, and keep the process moving. The coordinator/integrator need not be the original developer. Inevitably, the successful coordinator/integrator will be involved in ongoing development and enhancement and will be intimately familiar with the system. But as Raymond observes, an equally important characteristic of the coordinator/integrator is *taste* - the ability to recognize and appreciate the good ideas of other developers. Interpersonal skills are also important. The coordinator/integrator is leading a community of volunteers, some of whom are difficult to work with and almost all of whom have other demands on their time. He or she must be able to attract talented co-developers and keep them engaged, while still maintaining the quality and integrity of the collectively developed system.

Some critics have argued that open source development efforts are unreliable - in particular, that they will not yield high quality software. The GNU/Linux experience seems to contradict that. If the self-selected co-developers are also users, then their own self-interest drives them to improve the software quality. In contrast to the separate quality assurance departments found in cathedral-style development, in the bazaar the quality assurance group is found within the co-developer community.

9   The Open Source Movement

According to the Open Source Initiative [15], the term *open source* was coined in 1998, as part of a nascent effort by a well-respected group of software developers (including Raymond) to take advantage of the announced public release of the source code to the Netscape browser to popularize the advantages of an open development process for commercial software. The goal of the evangelists of open source software was pragmatic - to promote the use of an open process by explaining the self-interest for the commercial world, i.e. by "making the business case". Part of the pragmatism was to relax some of the requirements of the free software movement. In essence, all free software (in the FSF sense) is open source, but the converse is not true.

The open source evangelists have been successful in popularizing the notion of open source software, and there are signs that its use is increasing as well. The primary example of widespread adoption is the use of GNU/Linux, which provides a UNIX system for PC platforms. Several companies provide GNU/Linux distribution and support services. Several major computer vendors are promoting GNU/Linux as an important system for their hardware platforms, and are building products to run on GNU/Linux.

10   The Evolution of Widely Used Research Software

It is instructive to see how some of the widely distributed software mentioned earlier fared during this period. The history of Berkeley UNIX has been summarized already. Both free and commercial versions of BSD UNIX are available [2]. The research version of the INGRES software created under Berkeley UNIX was made available, but a commercial version based on the research prototype was developed that eventually supplanted the research version.

The TEX system for formatting and typesetting technical documents was developed by Professor Donald Knuth of Stanford, a prolific author. Early on, the American Mathematical Association adopted TEX as a standard for its publications. Over time, some authors switched to more automated systems such as Microsoft Word, and others moved to more advanced commercial systems. However, many people in the research community stayed with TEX.[4] Today there are both free and commercial providers of TEX software.

The `sendmail` system developed by Eric Allman at Berkeley remained publicly available until well into the 1990's. Today there are both open source and commercial versions available, but `sendmail` is still a *de facto* standard.

Emacs remains popular in the academic community, and continues to be available from the Free Software Foundation. The X Window System, developed at MIT, the TCL/Tk software developed by Prof. John Ousterhout when he was at Berkeley and the Linux operating system kernel originally developed by Linus Torvalds are all available under open source. Commercial support is available for each system as well.

11   Open Source and the Commercial World

The examples we have looked at so far illustrate a variety of ways to make money from open source software. Cygnus Support was primarily a GNU service provider, supplying installation, maintenance, porting, enhancements, classes, and the like to commercial users of GNU software, while preserving the free software nature of that software. Many GNU/Linux-based and BSD-based companies have followed that model as well. Some companies sell proprietary enhancements to open-source software. Others sell proprietary software that uses open source components or operating system platforms. Still others charge high prices for commercial source-code availability, but provide source code to researchers at little or no cost.

It is in the business interest of commercial users of open source software to see that software flourish. That can be good news for open source efforts. Critics sometimes deride open source projects as being dependent on volunteers, who

---

[4] TEX was used to typeset this paper.

are unmanageable, unreliable, and unwilling to do programming tasks they find uninteresting. However, it has often been the case that contributors to open source projects have been paid to work on those projects, and have done so to further the goals of their employers. For example, the Cygnus staff were responding to the needs of their customers at the same time they were improving the community software base. In the later years of the Berkeley UNIX project, professional programmers were hired to insure that the DARPA research community was well served. To the extent that computer vendors such as IBM are using GNU/Linux platforms, they are employing their own highly-skilled and well-paid staff as co-developers, so that their own needs get prompt attention. As long as the community consensus-building and coordinator/integrator processes are working, such co-developers do not have undue influence on design decisions.

12   Licensing and Intellectual Property

It is generally agreed that people should be given credit for their ideas and for their creative work. When their ideas are embodied in software, and when that software has potential commercial value, there are competing forces that complicate the sharing of source code.

Two important motives for licensing source code that is intended to be widely available have been to limit liability stemming from the use of the software and to assert copyright protection. Variations among licenses arise from differing rules about further redistribution of the original work, distribution of derived work, continued availability of source code versions of the work, and distribution fees. Some of the issues are summarized here. Deutsch has provided an excellent discussion of the issues [4]. The opensource.org Web site [14] is another source of licensing information.

In general, limitations of liability and requirements for copyright notice are passed on when source code is redistributed. In some cases, redistribution is limited to research and not-for-profit organizations; in other cases not. There is normally no usage fee for not-for-profit use of the software, but usage fees are sometimes charged for commercial use. Recovery of reproduction or distribution expenses is normally allowed. Some license agreements, such as the Free Software Foundation GNU General Public License (GPL), require that any redistribution include the availability of source code. Other license agreements, such as the one used for Berkeley UNIX, also allow redistribution exclusively in binary form.

Either implicitly or explicitly, licensing agreements usually allow users to modify licensed source code for their own use. Differences occur when those users want to share their modifications with others. It is common practice to document the fact that software that is re-distributed is derived, i.e. that it differs from the original. Sometimes the derived work contains a patch file or other detailed summary of changes; sometimes it also must have a new name. The GNU General Public License (GPL) requires that the source code for derived works be made available in any distribution of derived work. The Berkeley UNIX agreement, and some other open source distributions, allow binary-only distribution of derived work.

A middle ground arises when the free or open source software is to be used as a component of a larger system - for example, a package that runs on an open source version of UNIX or a system that uses the C runtime library (`glibc`). In situations like that, in which the open source components are not modified, but are used through standard interfaces such as function calls, it is often permissible to distribute the larger system in a restricted way, provided the open source software distribution and use conforms to its licensing rules. For example, the Free Software Foundation created the Lesser General Purpose License (LGPL) to serve that need.

Despite the attempts to serve both the needs and desires of the developers and the needs of the users, difficulties remain in establishing licensing agreements. Here are just a few of them.

One of the ways in which people attempt to improve software quality and increase software productivity is to assemble systems from high-quality components and to re-use components in new systems. Since different distributors of source code have different values and goals, a variety of licensing agreements are used. It can be challenging to combine components with different licensing agreements into a system while still satisfying the sometimes-conflicting conditions of the various licenses.

Many open source software systems have lasted a long time; two examples are the various UNIX systems and TEX. Integrators of open source releases normally request written permission from contributors and co-developers to incorporate their work, so that the integrators can distribute the new release under the same terms as the previous one. However, occasionally, developers have incorporated material, perhaps inadvertently, for which someone else holds or comes to hold copyright or patent rights. That inclusion may become a problem years later, when the other individual asserts previously unknown rights.

The use of licensing agreements is based on law. Since business in general and software distribution in particular is an international activity, licensing is complicated by the differing laws that exist in different countries to which software is distributed. The fact that software is easily passed on via the Internet complicates the situation even more.

13   Government Policy and Open Source Software

The U.S. government and the governments of many other countries invest significant amounts of money both in research in how to build and maintain software and in research for which software is used as a tool. Many governments have an interest in having that research software shared both with other researchers and with government agencies. Governments are also major consumers of research, both for defense and for almost every other area of government. A recent report from an advisory committee to the U.S. government addresses the potential to use open source software for high-end computing. A recent report to the European Commission addresses the role of open source and free software in Europe.

13.1   Open Source for High-End Software

In the fall of 1999, following the submission of a report to President Clinton concerning U.S. investment in information technology research and development [17], the President's Information Technology Advisory Committee (PITAC), on which I serve, convened a panel to study the use of open source software for high-end computing. The study was motivated by the fact that although high-end computing is very important as a tool for research, for defense, and for many other purposes, the high-end computing market is growing much more slowly than other computing markets that compete for the talents of information technology professionals, and consequently the number of suppliers is diminishing. The panel was charged with charting a vision of how the U.S. government might support open source activities for high-end computing, defining a policy framework, identifying policy, legal, and administrative barriers to the use of open source, and identifying potential roles for public institutions.

The panel concluded that open source was a promising avenue to create and maintain the software base needed at the high end. The panel report also identified some potential difficulties, among them the need to change funding, management, and procurement practices, the need to provide access to high-end development platforms, the need for a shared repository and clearinghouse for information about open source projects, and the importance of multi-agency cooperation and coordination.

The panel made three recommendations, together with some further elaboration [18]:

1. The [U. S.] Federal government should encourage the development of open source software as an alternate path for software development for high end computing.
2. The Federal government should allow open source development efforts to compete on a "level playing field" with proprietary solutions in government procurement of high end computing software.
3. An analysis of existing open source licensing agreements should be undertaken, and the results should be distributed to all agencies funding high end computing.

An interagency working group is currently studying the recommendations.

13.2   Working Group on Libre Software

The working group on Libre software was created by the Information Society Directorate General of the European Commission.[5] The working group prepared

---

[5] The use of the term "libre" rather than the English word "free" dispels the ambiguity between absence of limitation and absence of cost.

a comprehensive report concerning free and open source software that was submitted to the Director General in April 2000 [24]. The report contains a list of fourteen recommendations:

1. Technical issues
    (a) Promotion of open source reference implementations for any protocol standard.
    (b) Endorsement of neutral data formats and open source tools for managing them.
    (c) Promotion of projects to improve quality of free software.
    (d) Promotion of free software in precompetitive research projects financed with public money.
2. Organization and support
    (a) Services for organization of information related to open source.
    (b) Funding of open source projects, including the provision of general facilities for open source development.
    (c) Promotion of projects related to documentation, translation and localization of free software.
3. Legal issues
    (a) Fight software patents at all levels.
    (b) Ensure the freedom to build free software implementations which can interoperate with proprietary interfaces.
    (c) Improve the legal framework so that calls for tenders are open to free software solutions.
4. Training, promotion and explanation of benefits
    (a) Promotion of training and education on free software products.
    (b) Creation of an office to help institutions take advantage of free software.
    (c) Specific recommendations of use of free software.
    (d) Research about the economic and social impact of open source software.

The report concludes "... Our feeling is that open source software has already started to modify the rules in the information technology industry, which will produce enormous changes in the years to come. Given these facts, it is clear to us that those countries and companies that adopt open source technologies in the short term will have a huge competitive advantage, and that society in general can benefit a lot from this early adoption. ..."

13.3   Comments

Both the PITAC report and the Libre software report appear to be receiving favorable consideration. Some government officials are realizing that proprietary software is expensive, both because of the lower likelihood of common solutions across multiple agencies, and because of the difficulties of customization for special needs. Both reports make clear that open source software is not without cost. For example, programmers on government contracts need to be paid for the time they spend contributing to open source projects. However, the government investment can be money well spent.

14   Final Observations

We have given a research argument for source code availability and a software quality argument. We have briefly summarized philosophical issues, intellectual property issues, commercial issues, and government issues. The open source movement and the more wide-spread availability of source code is in a state of rapid change and it is difficult to make predictions about the future. Many interesting questions are as yet unanswered.

- Does the open source process really provide better software quality than proprietary development? There are some arguments and some examples that suggest that it does, but no research has been done to support the claims.
- Is it the bazaar model of development that provides improved quality, rather than the public openness? If so, is this a better model for large proprietary development projects to use? Can the model flourish in a corporate setting, in which top-down management is the traditional norm? If so, how does the manager's role change? Again, there are conjectures, but no real data.
- Is this development style more suited to systems software and tools than to applications? For example, one can note that the widely used data base systems are both proprietary and expensive. Is that an accident of history or is there something more fundamental going on?
- To what extent can and will the research community retain its tradition of sharing source code? Are we already losing that tradition in areas in which commercial potential exists? Will the open source movement help to restore that tradition?

References

[1] Ö. Babaoglu and W. N. Joy. Converting a swap-based system to do paging in an architecture lacking page-referenced bits. In *Proceedings of the Eighth ACM Symposium on Operating Systems Principles*, pages 78–86, December 1981.

[2] bsd.org. http://www.bsd.org//.

[3] Bryan Costales and Eric Allman. *Sendmail*. O'Reilly & Associates, Inc., November 1993. Second Edition, January 1997.

[4] L. Peter Deutsch. Licensing alternatives for freely redistributable software. In *Proceedings of the First Conference on Freely Redistributable Software*, Cambridge, MA, February 1996. Free Software Foundation.

[5] The Free Software Foundation. http://www.gnu.org/fsf/fsf.html/.

[6] Susan L. Graham, Charles B. Haley, and William N. Joy. *Berkeley Pascal User's Manual*. Computer Science Division, University of California at Berkeley, September 1977. 54 pages.

[7] Susan L. Graham, Peter B. Kessler, and Marshall K. McKusick. An execution profiler for modular programs. *Software–Practice & Experience*, 13(8):671–685, August 1983.

[8] G. D. Held, M. Stonebraker, and E. Wong. INGRES–A relational data base management system. In *National Computer Conference*, volume 44, pages 409–416, Anaheim, CA, May 1975. AFIPS Press.

[9] Linux International. Linux history. http://www.li.org/linuxhistory.php.

[10] S. C. Johnson. A portable compiler: Theory and practice. In *Conference Record of the Fifth Annual ACM Symposium on Principles of Programming Languages*, pages 97–104. Association for Computing Machinery, January 1978.

[11] D. E. Knuth. *TEX and METAFONT, New Directions in Typesetting*. Digital Press, Billerica, MA, 1979.

[12] Samuel J. Leffler, Marshall Kirk McKusick, Michael J. Karels, and John S. Quarterman. *The Design and Implementation of the 4.3BSD UNIX Operating System*. Addison-Wesley Publishing Co., 1989.

[13] Marshall Kirk McKusick. Twenty years of Berkeley Unix: From AT&T-owned to freely redistributable. In Chris DiBona, Sam Ockman, and Mark Stone, editors, *Open Sources: Voices from the Open Source Revolution*. O'Reilly & Associates, Inc., January 1999.

[14] The open source initiative. http://www.opensource.org/.

[15] History of the open source initiative. http://www.opensource.org/history.html.

[16] John K. Ousterhout. Tcl: An embeddable command language. In *Proceedings of the Winter 1990 USENIX Conference*, pages 133–146, Washington, DC, USA, January 1990. USENIX Association.

[17] President's Information Technology Advisory Committee. *Information Technology Research: Investing in Our Future*. Report to the President, February 1999. Available from http://www.itrd.gov/ac/.

[18] President's Information Technology Advisory Committee. *Developing Open Source Software to Advance High End Computing*. Report to the President, September 2000. Available from http://www.itrd.gov/ac/.

[19] Eric S. Raymond. *The Cathedral & The Bazaar*. O'Reilly & Associates, Inc., October 1999.

[20] D. M. Ritchie, S. C. Johnson, M. E. Lesk, and B. W. Kernighan. The C programming language. *The Bell System Technical Journal*, 57(6):1991–2019, July-August 1978.

[21] D. M. Ritchie and K. Thompson. The UNIX time-sharing system. *Communications of the ACM*, 17(7):365–75, July 1974.

[22] Robert W. Scheifler and Jim Gettys. The X window system. *ACM Transactions on Graphics*, 5(2):79–109, April 1986.

[23] Richard M. Stallman. Emacs: The extensible, customizable, self-documenting display editor. In *Proceedings, ACM SIGPLAN/SIGOA Symposium on Text Manipulation*, pages 147–156, Portland, Oregon, June 8-10, 1981. Published as SIGPLAN Notices 16(6), June 1981.

[24] Working group on Libre Software. *Free Software/Open Source: Information Society Opportunities for Europe?* April 2000. Available from http://eu.conecta.it/.

Microprocessors — 10 Years Back, 10 Years Ahead

Gurindar S. Sohi

Computer Sciences Department
University of Wisconsin-Madison
1210 W. Dayton St. Madison, WI 53706
sohi@cs.wisc.edu

1 Introduction

Continuing improvements in semiconductor technology — as characterized by
Moore's law — have provided computer architects with an increasing number
of faster transistors with which to build microprocessors. In the past decade,
architects have seized these opportunities to build microprocessors that bear little resemblance to the microprocessors of the 1970s and 1980s. With Moore's
law projected to hold beyond the next decade, microprocessor architects will
have even larger transistor budgets with which to build innovative microprocessors; the microprocessor circa 2010 is likely to bear little resemblance to today's
microprocessor.

The driving force behind the innovation in microprocessors for the past two
decades has been the quest for higher performance. Arguably the best way to
achieve this goal is an integrated approach that combines innovation in all
aspects of the problem: algorithms, software, and hardware. Computer architects typically work with a given algorithm, and concern themselves with hardware and software. Within this context, the best technical solution is perhaps
an integrated software/hardware solution, where a compiler works in concert
with the architecture and implementation, possibly with changes to the hard-
ware/software interface (*i.e.*, the instruction set architecture). However, this approach has not proven to be viable in the long term for a variety of reasons, both
technical and non-technical. Perhaps the most compelling (non-technical) reason
is that it is not practical to change the instruction set frequently. Radical changes
to instruction sets for general-purpose processors happen infrequently, perhaps
only once every few decades (*e.g.*, DEC's change from VAX to Alpha), with incremental changes/additions (*e.g.*, Intel's MMX enhancements to IA-32) being
more common. This changes the model for achieving the desired goal of higher
performance: both software and hardware are forced to work within the constraints of a fixed (or nearly fixed) software/hardware interface. Consequently,
many of the innovations in microprocessors have been in the microarchitecture,
the building blocks of a microprocessor. A circa 1990 microprocessor (*e.g.*, the
Intel 486) and a circa 2000 microprocessor (*e.g.*, the Intel Pentium IV) of the
same family have essentially the same instruction set architecture, but radically
different microarchitectures.

R. Wilhelm (Ed.): Informatics. 10 Years Back. 10 Years Ahead, LNCS 2000, pp. 209–218, 2001.

To understand the innovations in microarchitecture, let us start out with the CPU performance equation: $Time = N \times CPI \times T$, where $Time$ is the time taken to execute a program, N is the number of instructions executed dynamically, CPI is the number of cycles per instruction, and T is the clock cycle time. Improving execution time means reducing the three terms on the right-hand side of the equation. The microprocessor architect typically has little influence over the first term — that is the realm of instruction set designers and compiler writers — so the emphasis is on decreasing the second and third terms.

Semiconductor technology allows faster transistors, and these translate into a faster clock cycle. The clock cycle can be made even faster by pipelining the logic into more stages. Since not all technologies improve at the same rate (*e.g.*, logic speeds have increased much faster than memory speeds), a faster clock cycle results in increasing (relative) latencies of operations, which translates into an increase in CPI. The role of the microprocessor architect is then to develop microarchitectural features that not only prevent an increase in CPI as the clock cycle is reduced, but even decrease it. The additional transistors provide ample resources for implementing new features that aim to achieve this goal.

2   10 Years Back: The Emergence of Speculative Execution Microarchitectures

To decrease CPI, parallelism is used to overlap the processing of instructions. For a microprocessor architect, this has meant *fine-grain*, or *instruction-level parallelism (ILP)*, leaving more coarse-grain parallelism to be exploited by multiprocessors. Exploiting ILP is a cost-effective way of making use of chip real estate and improving performance. Many of the techniques in the microprocessor architect's toolbox increase the exploitation of ILP in a program's execution.

Techniques to exploit ILP can either be static — those used in EPIC [8], or they can be dynamic — those used by superscalar processors such as Compaq's Alpha 21264, Intel's Pentium II, and others. We will limit our discussion to dynamically-scheduled superscalar processors since these dominated the 1990s, whereas general-purpose microprocessors using statically-scheduled ILP techniques were only announced towards the end of the 1990s.

The processing of an instruction requires many steps, and we want to overlap as many steps as possible to increase throughput; more overlap requires more ILP. To understand the increasing demand for ILP, consider the increase in the number of instructions that can be "in flight" at a given time in a microprocessor. In the 1970s, microprocessors executed one instruction at a time, taking many clock cycles to execute that instruction — there was only one instruction in flight. The 1980s were the decade of pipelining; a typical pipeline had 5 stages, processing a single instruction per clock cycle, resulting in up to 5 instructions in flight. The 1990s were characterized by deeper pipelines, and wider instruction issue (processing multiple instructions per cycle): a 2-issue, 5-stage pipeline Pentium processor, a 3-issue, 10-stage pipeline Pentium II, and a 3-issue, 20-stage pipeline Pentium IV, have about 10, 30, and 60 instructions (more accurately, operations) in flight, respectively.

A strategy that relies on keeping many instructions in flight can only succeed if many "useful" instruction can be kept in flight, and this requires the processor to identify the path that will be taken through the program. Since a branch instruction occurs every 5 to 6 instructions in typical programs, techniques to prevent branches from stalling instruction fetching had to be developed: the flow of instructions cannot be stopped when a branch is encountered. (With 50-60 instructions in flight there are likely to be about 10 branch instructions in flight, so clearly branches cannot be processed sequentially.) Early machines proposed *predicting* the direction of a branch and fetching instructions from the predicted path [1]. But fetching alone is not enough, since the number of pipeline stages devoted to instruction fetching constitute only a fraction of the pipeline. This then bring up the notion of *speculative execution*: instructions from a predicted path of a branch must also be executed so that more instructions can be kept in flight, and overlap in processing increased.

The 1990s were the decade of speculative execution, *i.e.*, the decade where speculative execution processors entered the mainstream of processor design. Today it is more apt to call the above *control speculation*, since the speculation is on the outcome of a control (branch) instruction. Other forms of speculation have since appeared. With control speculation, the outcome of a branch instruction is predicted, and instructions from the predicted path executed in a speculatively. If the prediction turns out to be incorrect, the speculative instructions are *squashed* (or *aborted*). Control speculative execution necessitates microarchitectural mechanisms to support it [17, 24]. These include mechanisms to guide the speculation: branch predictors, and mechanisms to recover from a misspeculation: physical registers, register renaming, and precise exceptions.

The branch predictor is a key component, since the accuracy of the predictor directly determines the utility of the instructions being executed speculatively. The 1990s saw a lot of research in the design of branch predictors. Early processors used simple 2-bit predictors [22], which quickly gave way to 2-level adaptive predictors [32], as transistor resources increased. Processors of the late 1990s even employ multiple branch predictors since experiments suggested that different prediction automaton work better on different types of branches [14].

The first major component of speculative execution hardware is *storage* where results of (speculatively-executed) instructions can reside — typically only non-speculative values can reside in the logical (or architectural) register file and the memory system. Storage is needed to hold values until they are consumed, or *committed* to architectural state. This storage can be provided in several ways, including reservations stations, reorder buffers, and physical register files.

The second major component is a *precise exception mechanism*. The program which the processor executes is written with the assumption of sequential execution — instructions are executed one at a time. Thus while a processor may overlap the execution of instructions in a pipeline, execute instructions out of program order, and even execute instructions speculatively, it must appear to an outside observer (*e.g.*, the creator of the program) that the instructions executed sequentially. In particular, it must be possible to recover the precise state of the program at any given time. A precise state at an arbitrary point in a program's execution corresponds to the state that would result if all instructions prior to the point of interest have completed execution (and updated machine state), and no subsequent instructions have affected machine state. There are several mechanism to recover a precise machine state. These include *reorder buffers, history buffers* (or *checkpoints*), and *future files* [21].

The third major component is a *register renaming mechanism*. With many in-flight instructions, there may be many distinct values associated with a logical register; register renaming helps find the correct value. With a renaming mechanism values that would reside in a logical register at different points in time during the execution of a program (*e.g.*, results of two instructions separated by a branch) can reside in different physical storage elements, thereby allowing the execution of the two instructions to be overlapped. Without different storage elements to hold the results, and an accompanying register renaming mechanism, only one of the instructions could be processed at a time.

Different dynamically-scheduled superscalar processors of the 1990s used different combinations of mechanisms to support speculative execution (*e.g.*, physical register files with history buffers for precise exceptions, or reservation stations and reorder buffer) — no two processors implement the same functionality in the same way. Some processors even used different mechanisms for recovering precise versions of different state (*e.g.*, reorder buffers for registers, and history buffers for register rename mappings). Collectively, the mechanisms allow instructions to be scheduled dynamically to maximize overlap in instruction processing, yet retain the appearance of sequential execution. Many microprocessor architects have viewed the constraint of maintaining the appearance of sequential execution as an asset rather than a liability: sequential execution provides a precise definition of a total order in which events have to occur, and this facilitates debugging and verification of hardware. Without a total order, it can be difficult to verify and debug hardware and software, since the sequence of events that creates a problem cannot be repeated. Thus, even though out-of-order execution and register renaming was proposed in the 1960s (albeit, without speculative execution) [28], the lack of precise state recovery mechanisms, and the consequent difficulties of debugging, had cast a shadow on these techniques.

The increased processing rate brought on by microarchitectural innovations has placed increasing demands on the memory system. Already handicapped by a widening gap between logic and memory speeds, more innovation was needed to deal with the increasing latency, as well as with increasing bandwidth demands. Multi-level caches arose to plug the latency gap; most high-performance microprocessors today have two levels of cache on the chip, and many have an additional level of cache off chip. To meet the bandwidth demands, the upper levels of the cache hierarchy (the ones closer to the CPU) became *non-blocking*, allowing requests to be overlapped, *i.e.*, allowing misses to be overlapped with hits, and with other misses [12, 25]. In addition, to service multiple hits per cycle, caches have recently become multi-ported [25]. The impact of the increasing bandwidth demands has stretched all the way to the main memory, with high-bandwidth Rambus DRAMs (RDRAMs) replacing traditional DRAMs for high performance applications.

3 Current: The Blossoming of Speculative Execution Microarchitectures

While there was resistance to speculative execution and dynamic scheduling in the late 1980s and early 1990s, this resistance was overcome, and today high-end processors from most companies support both. Having implemented microarchitectural mechanisms to support these techniques within existing transistor budgets, microarchitects asked: (i) what else could these microarchitectural mechanisms be used for, (ii) how to use the additional transistors made available by Moore's law? These lead to an "obvious" question: could we use speculation to overcome other constraints? The basic mechanisms to support one form of speculation could possibly support other forms of speculation as well, and additional resources can be used both to increase the amount of speculative execution, as well as to improve the accuracy of different forms of speculation.

Processors that have been announced circa 2000 extend speculation beyond the basic control speculation model of the 1990s. In control speculation, a speculation was made on the outcome (taken or not taken) of a branch instruction. Modern microprocessors extend the notion of speculation to include *data speculation*, where the data values, or instruction relationships that are based upon data values, are speculated. Data speculation can be used to overcome arbitrary dependence constraints, including ambiguous- and true-dependence constraints. In its most general form, speculation could be applied to predict the value of arbitrary data items, *e.g.*, the result of an address calculation operation [2], or the value loaded from memory [13]. There has been a significant amount of research on this subject recently, but the prediction accuracies for the general form of data value speculation are currently not sufficient to allow this technique to achieve performance improvements; in many cases performance actually degrades. However, data speculation can be used profitably in other forms. Two forms used in circa 2000 microprocessors are described next.

Ambiguous dependences constrain the scheduling of load instructions. Without speculation, a load instruction cannot be (dynamically) scheduled to execute before a prior store instruction, because they might access the same memory location. This restriction, which unnecessarily constrains parallelism, can be overcome with *data dependence speculation* — speculating that the ambiguous dependence is actually not a dependence, *i.e.*, the load is independent of prior stores (whose store addresses are unknown). When a dependence exists, however, the speculation is incorrect; speculation accuracy can be improved by speculating when the ambiguous dependence is likely to resolve to no dependence, and not speculating otherwise. One way to improve the speculation is to predict the addresses which the store (and load if need be) will access, and use these predictions to assess if a true dependence is likely to be violated. This technique is cumbersome, due to the need for predicting different store addresses, and not very accurate. An alternative is to use *data dependence prediction*, where the dependence relationships (between stores and loads) are predicted. Recent work has shown that these dependence relationships are very stable, and can be predicted with very high accuracy [4, 15]. Dependence prediction and speculation is being used in several processors that are being designed circa 2000.

Another form of data speculation is used in Intel's Pentium IV processor [7]. Traditionally a cache operation is carried out atomically: data is accessed from the cache data array and the cache tags are checked to see if the correct data is being accessed. Typically these two sub-operations take different amounts of time. An atomic cache access means waiting for the slower operation (typically tag matching) to complete, increasing the latency of the overall operation. Speculation can be used to reduce the expected latency of a cache access as follows: the access is divided into its two constituent operations, data access and tag matching. Data is read from the data arrays, a speculation is made that it is a cache hit, and the data returned to the processor immediately. Later when the tags are checked, the speculation is verified. If the speculation was incorrect, *i.e.*, the reference was a cache miss, the offending instruction, and instructions dependent on it, are replayed. (Another way of looking at this speculation is as a load value speculation, with the cache serving as the "value predictor," and the tag matching logic providing the verification.)

In addition to the two new forms of speculation described above, other forms of speculation are being researched, and are likely being considered for processors that are being designed. These new forms of speculation are also resulting in refinements of techniques to recover from misspeculations. For example, for control speculation, machines typically squashed all instructions following a misspeculated branch, since these instructions were unlikely to contain instructions that were control- and data-independent of the misspeculated branch. However, for data speculation, a brute-force squashing is likely to squash useful instructions (instructions that are independent of the offending instruction). Accordingly, *selective squashing* or *selective recovery/replay* mechanisms have been invented.

4   Near Future: The Emergence of Clustered and Multithreaded Microarchitectures

The coming decade will bring even more challenges, as well as opportunities, for microprocessor architects. The challenges will include *ease of design and verification*, the growing importance of *wire delays*, and the increase in *power consumption*. Monolithic designs occupying many tens or hundreds of millions of transistors will be very difficult to design, debug, and verify, and increasing wire delays will make intra-chip communication and clock distribution costly. These technology constraints suggest designs that are made of replicated components, where each component may be as much as a complete processing element. Distributed, replicated organizations can "divide and conquer" the complexities of design, debug and verification, and can exploit localities of communication to deal with wire delays. The impact of power consumption on microarchitecture is still being investigated, but some researchers believe that distributed, replicated microarchitectures are likely to have better power/performance characteristics that centralized microarchitectures. Meanwhile, opportunities will be provided by even more transistor resources, and by the emergence of multithreaded workloads. Important workloads, such as server workloads, are being written as multithreaded applications, inviting microprocessor architects to use multithreading to improve the overall processing effectiveness.

The challenges and opportunities of the next decade are likely to lead to microprocessors with clustered microarchitectures that are capable of running multiple threads of code simultaneously. Several multithreaded processor models are currently being explored. *Simultaneous multithreading (SMT)* [5, 11, 30, 31] extends a "traditional" dynamically-scheduled superscalar processor to support the simultaneous execution of multiple programs. *Chip multiprocessing (CMP)* [9], as the name implies, proposes a distributed design, along the lines of a more traditional multiprocessor, on a single chip. The distinction between the SMT and CMP microarchitectures is likely to blur over time. Increasing wire delays will require decentralization of most critical processor functionality, while flexible resource allocation policies will enhance the appearance of resource sharing. In either case, multithreaded processors will logically appear to be collections of processing elements with support for speculative execution. In this context, microprocessors are expected to employ *thread-level speculation* to overcome barriers to traditional methods of parallelizing a single program. Thus, in addition to executing conventional parallel threads, the logical processors could execute *single programs that are divided into speculative threads*. Speculative multithreaded processors will provide not only high throughput but also high single-program performance when needed.

5   10 Years Ahead: The Blossoming of Speculative Multithreaded Microarchitectures

With support for both speculation and multithreading, novel techniques for using speculative threads are likely to be discovered. Research into some of these techniques is already in progress, and the expectation is that some of these research discoveries will be implemented in circa 2010 microprocessors. We briefly review some of this ongoing research below.

Threads can broadly be classified into *control-driven* and *data-driven* threads, depending on whether threads are divided primarily along control-flow or data-flow boundaries. Each category can be further sub-categorized as either *non-speculative* — the threads are completely independent from the point of view of the processor and any dependence is explicitly enforced using architectural synchronization constructs, or *speculative* — the threads may not be perfectly independent, or synchronized, and it is up to the hardware to detect and potentially recover from violations of the independence assumptions.

Despite extensive research, compiler generated non-speculative threads (*e.g.*, those generated by parallelizing compilers) have not held much promise beyond numeric programs because of the difficulties of statically dividing a program into such threads. The analysis required to create threads statically has too many unknowns (*e.g.*, ambiguous dependences), thwarting parallelization efforts. Again, speculation can be used to overcome constraints imposed by unknown information, and a program *dynamically parallelized* into speculative threads. Thus a program will appear to be sequential, statically, but speculatively execute in parallel, dynamically. Speculation is likely to be applied to both control- and data-driven threads.

Speculative control-driven multithreading has been the subject of academic research in the 1990's [10, 23, 27] and is slowly finding its way into commercial products. Sun's MAJC architecture [29] supports such threads, via its Space Time Computing (STC) model. More recently, NEC's Merlot chip [16] uses speculative control-driven multithreading to parallelize the execution of code that cannot be parallelized by other known means. We expect that more processors will make use of speculative control-driven threads in the coming decade, as this technology moves from the research phase into commercial implementations.

Speculative data-driven threads are likely to be employed as "helper" threads which assist the "main" program thread. These helper threads that run ahead and *pre-execute* or "solve" performance-degrading problem instructions before they have a chance to cause stalls in the main program thread. There has been a fair amount of research into this issue recently [3, 6, 18, 19, 20, 26, 33], with commercial adoptions likely over the course of the next decade.

6   Summary

The microarchitecture of microprocessors has seen a dramatic change in the past decade; the same is expected for the next decade. The most significant transition of the past decade is that simple in-order processing microarchitectures have given way to dynamic-scheduling, out-of-order execution, and speculative execution. Speculative execution, initially applied to overcome control dependences, is now being used in a variety of ways, to overcome ambiguous- and even true-dependence constraints. The coming decade is expected to result in even more innovation in microprocessor microarchitectures, as microprocessors begin to support multithreaded execution, and as even more novel uses of speculation are found. A promising model for next decade microprocessors is thread-level speculation, where speculation is applied to parallelize the execution of programs that defy traditional methods of parallelization.

Acknowledgements

The author would like to thank various organizations that have supported his research over the years, including the National Science Foundation (NSF), the Defense Advanced Projects Agency (DARPA), companies such as Intel and Sun

Microsystems, and the University of Wisconsin Graduate School. The contributions of various graduate students is also gratefully acknowledged.

References

[1] D. W. Anderson, F. J. Sparacio, and R. M. Tomasulo. The IBM System/360 Model 91: Machine Philosophy and Instruction-Handling. *IBM Journal of Research and Development*, pages 8–24, Jan. 1967.

[2] Todd M. Austin, Dionisios N. Pnevmatikatos, and Gurindar S. Sohi. Streamlining data cache access with fast address calculation. In *Proceedings of the 22nd Annual International Symposium on Computer Architecture*, pages 369–381, June 1995.

[3] R.S. Chappell, J. Stark, S.P. Kim, S.K. Reinhardt, and Y.N. Patt. Simultaneous Subordinate Microthreading (SSMT). In *Proc. 26th International Symposium on Computer Architecture*, May 1999.

[4] G.Z. Chrysos and J.S. Emer. Memory Dependence Prediction using Store Sets. In *Proc. 25th International Symposium on Computer Architecture*, pages 142–153, Jun. 1998.

[5] J. Emer. Simultaneous Multithreading: Multiplying Alpha's Performance. Microprocessor Forum, Oct. 1999.

[6] A. Farcy, O. Temam, R. Espasa, and T. Juan. Dataflow Analysis of Branch Mispredictions and Its Application to Early Resolution of Branch Outcomes. In *Proc. 31st International Symposium on Microarchitecture*, pages 59–68, Dec. 1998.

[7] P. Glaskowsky. Pentium 4 (Partially) Previewed. *Microprocessor Report*, 14(8), Aug. 2000.

[8] Linley Gwennap. Intel, HP Make EPIC Disclosure. *Microprocessor Report*, 11(14), Oct. 1997.

[9] L. Hammond, B.A. Nayfeh, and K. Olukotun. A Single-Chip Multiprocessor. *IEEE Computer*, 30(9):79–85, Sep. 1997.

[10] L. Hammond, M. Willey, and K. Olukotun. Data speculation support for a chip multiprocessor. In *Proc. 8th International Conference on Architectural Support for Programming Languages and Operating Systems*, pages 58–69, Oct. 1998.

[11] H. Hirata, K. Kimura, S. Nagamine, Y. Mochizuki, A. Nishimura, Y. Nakase, and T. Nishizawa. An Elementary Processor Architecture with Simultaneous Instruction Issuing from Multiple Threads. In *Proc. 19th Annual International Symposium on Computer Architecture*, pages 136–145, May 1992.

[12] D. Kroft. Lockup-Free Instruction Fetch/Prefetch Cache Organization. In *Proc. 8th Annual International Symposium on Computer Architecture*, pages 81–87, May 1981.

[13] M.H. Lipasti, C.B. Wilkerson, and J.P. Shen. Value Locality and Load Value Prediction. In *Proc. 7th International Conference on Architectural Support for Programming Languages and Operating Systems*, pages 138–147, Oct. 1996.

[14] Scott McFarling. Combining Branch Predictors. Technical Report WRL Technical Note, TN-36, Digital Equipment Corporation, Jun. 1993.

[15] A. Moshovos, S.E. Breach, T.N. Vijaykumar, and G.S. Sohi. Dynamic Speculation and Synchronization of Data Dependences. In *Proc. 24th International Symposium on Computer Architecture*, pages 181–193, Jun. 1997.

[16] N. Nishi, T. Inoue, M. Nomura, S. Matsushita, S. Toru, A. Shibayama, J. Sakai, T. Oshawa, Y. Nakamura, S. Shimada, Y. Ito, M. Edahiro, M. Mizuno, K. Minami, O. Matsuo, H. Inoue, T. Manabe, T. Yamazaki, Y. Nakazawa, Y. Hirota, and

Y. Yamada. A 1 GIPS 1 W Single-Chip Tightly-Coupled Four-Way Multiprocessor with Architecture Support for Multiple Control-Flow Execution. In *Proc. 47th International IEEE Solid-State Circuits Conference*, Feb. 2000.

[17]   Y. N. Patt, S. W. Melvin, W. W. Hwu, and M. Shebanow. Critical issues regarding hps, a high performance microarchitecture. In *Proc. 18th Annual Workshop on Microprogramming*, pages 109–116, Dec. 1985.

[18]   A. Roth, A. Moshovos, and G.S. Sohi. Dependence Based Prefetching for Linked Data Structures. In *Proc. 8th Conference on Architectural Support for Programming Languages and Operating Systems*, pages 115–126, Oct. 1998.

[19]   A. Roth, A. Moshovos, and G.S. Sohi. Improving Virtual Function Call Target Prediction via Dependence-Based Pre-Computation. In *Proc. 1999 Internation Conference on Supercomputing*, pages 356–364, Jun. 1999.

[20]   A. Roth and G.S. Sohi. Speculative Data-Driven Multithreading. In *Proc. 7th International Symposium on High-Performance Computer Architecture*, Jan. 2001.

[21]   J. E. Smith and A. R. Pleszkun. Implementation of Precise Interrupts in Pipelined Processors. In *Proc. 12th Annual International Symposium on Computer Architecture*, Jun. 1985.

[22]   J.E. Smith. A Study of Branch Prediction Strategies. In *Proc. 8th International Symposium on Computer Architecture*, pages 135–148, May 1981.

[23]   G.S. Sohi, S. Breach, and T.N. Vijaykumar. Multiscalar Processors. In *Proc. 22nd International Symposium on Computer Architecture*, pages 414–425, Jun. 1995.

[24]   G.S. Sohi and S. Vajapeyam. Instruction Issue Logic for High-Performance Interruptable Pipelined Processors. In *Proc. 14th International Symposium on Computer Architecture*, pages 27–34, May 1987.

[25]   Gurindar S. Sohi and Manoj Franklin. High-Bandwidth Data Memory Systems for Superscalar Processors. In *Proc. 4th Conference on Architectural Support for Programming Languages and Operating Systems*, pages 52–62, Apr. 1991.

[26]   Y.H. Song and M. Dubois. Assisted Execution. Technical Report #CENG 98-25, Department of EE-Systems, University of Southern California, Oct. 1998.

[27]   J.G. Steffan and T.C. Mowry. The Potential for Using Thread Level Data-Speculation to Facilitate Automatic Parallelization. In *Proc. 4th International Symposium on High Performance Computer Architecture*, Feb. 1998.

[28]   R.M. Tomasulo. An Efficient Algorithm for Exploiting Multiple Arithmetic Units. *IBM Journal of Research and Development*, pages 25–33, Jan. 1967.

[29]   M. Tremblay. MAJC: An Architecture for the New Millenium. In *Proc. Hot Chips 11*, pages 275–288, Aug. 1999.
http://www.sun.com/microelectronics/MAJC/documentation/docs/HC99sm.pdf.

[30]   D.M. Tullsen, S.J. Eggers, J.S. Emer, H.M. Levy, J.L. Lo, and R.L. Stamm. Exploiting Choice: Instruction Fetch and Issue on an Implementable Simultaneous Multithreading Processor. In *Proc. 23rd International Symposium on Computer Architecture*, pages 191–202, May 1996.

[31]   W. Yamamoto and M. Nemirovsky. Increasing Superscalar Performance Through Multistreaming. In *Proc. 1995 Conference on Parallel Architectures and Compilation Techniques*, Jun. 1995.

[32]   T-Y. Yeh and Y.N. Patt. Two-level Adaptive Training Branch Prediction. In *Proc. 24th International Symposium on Microarchitecture*, pages 51–61, Nov. 1991.

[33]   C.B. Zilles and G.S. Sohi. Understanding the Backward Slices of Performance Degrading Instructions. In *Proc. 27th International Symposium on Computer Architecture*, pages 172–181, Jun. 2000.

The Quantum Computing Challenge

Paul Vitányi*

CWI
Kruislaan 413, 1098 SJ Amsterdam, The Netherlands.
paulv@cwi.nl

Abstract. The laws of physics imposes limits on increases in computing power. Two of these limits are interconnect wires in multicomputers and thermodynamic limits to energy dissipation in conventional irreversible technology. Quantum computing is a new computational technology that promises to eliminate problems of latency and wiring associated with parallel computers and the rapidly approaching ultimate limits to computing power imposed by the fundamental thermodynamics. Moreover, a quantum computer will be able to exponentially improve known classical algorithms for factoring, and quadratically improve every classical algorithm for searching an unstructured list, as well as give various speed-ups in communication complexity, by exploiting unique quantum mechanical features. Finally, a quantum computer may be able to simulate quantum mechanical systems, something which seems out of the question for classical computers, thus reaching the ultimate goal of replacing actual quantum mechanical experiments with simulated ones. On the downside, for some problems quantum mechanical computers cannot significantly improve the performance of classical computers.

1 Introduction

Apparently, the earliest mention of quantum computing is by Paul Benioff [14] who demonstrated how to implement a classical Turing machine using quantum mechanical processes. In 1982 Richard Feynman raised the question of simulating elementary quantum mechanical systems by computer. A quantum mechanical system with 2^n basis states—for example an n-bit memory—has pure quantum states that consist of a superposition of all of the basis states. Every basis state in this superposition has a probability amplitude (a complex real) that indicates the probability of observing this basis state in an appropriate measurement. To simulate the evolution of such a system, one needs to track the evolution of the 2^n probability amplitude parameters per simulated step. It is not known how to do this classically in time less than exponential in n. To overcome this problem, Feynman [17] suggested to fight fire with fire: A quantum mechanical computer may possibly be able to simulate every quantum mechanical system

---

* Partially supported by the European Union through NeuroCOLT II Working Group and the QAIP Project. The author is also affiliated with the University of Amsterdam.

R. Wilhelm (Ed.): Informatics. 10 Years Back. 10 Years Ahead, LNCS 2000, pp. 219–233, 2001.

in polynomial time since it operates on the same principles. In a way this boils down to the time-honored method of analogue computing, where an appropriate model of the simulated system is built—like wind tunnels to test turbulence and experimental simulation of water systems. The next step to digital quantum computing was taken by David Deutsch [16] who defined a quantum mechanical version of the classical Turing machine and in turn raised the question whether such computers could possibly speed up classical digital computations significantly over what is achievable by classical computers. The field attracted some interest but remained esoteric: Problems were formulated that benefitted from the quantum mechanical approach but they looked rather contrived. The field gained momentum in 1994 when Peter Shor proposed a fast quantum factoring algorithm [12]. This algorithm (probabilistically) factors a composite l-bit number in slightly over l^2 steps, while the best known classical algorithm, the number field sieve, takes $2^{cl^{1/3}\log^{2/3}l}$ (c constant) steps [19]. The apparent difficulty of factoring composite numbers with only large factors is the basis of almost all commonly used cryptographic systems in financial bank transactions and internet security. The fact that a quantum computer (if it can be build) will compromise such systems galvanized the physics and computer science research communities. A subsequent quantum mechanical algorithmic improvement to searching an unstructured data base excited the interest even further. Apart from some other less straightforward improvements (below), however, these remain the only genuine successes of quantum algorithmics today. Worse, it can be shown that for many problems quantum mechanical methods don't help significantly [3,2,9], like, for example, with binary search [1]. While the jury is still out whether quantum mechanical computing is the greatest thing in computing since the invention of personal computing, it seems evident that the advent of the quantum computer is unavoidable since improvement of computing by parallellizing and further miniaturizing of classical methods runs into problems. The purpose of this writing is to give an outline of the area of quantum computing without going into much detail—a general textbook treatment of both the theory and experimental realization is [9].

1.1   Wither Classical Computing?

In performance analysis of classical sequential computation such as performed by a Turing machine or a von Neumann architecture computer—the common computer—one can safely ignore many physical aspects of the underlying computer system and analyze the computational complexity of an algorithm or program in a purely logical fashion. One cannot always ignore the reality of the physical world we live in to such an extent. The appropriateness of the analysis may stand or fall with the account taken of physical reality: Nonclassical or nonstandard physical realizations of computers may have totally unexpected properties, such as, for example, the quantum computer. To see why quantum computing may be the natural next step in computing technology, let us analyze some problems attending the further improvement of classical computing. Two natural ways to improve classical computing are continued miniaturization and large-scale parallellization.

The Cooking Problem Computers increasingly pervade our society. This increasing influence is enabled by their ever increasing power, which has roughly doubled every 18 months for the last half-century (Moore's law). The increase in power, in turn, is primarily due to the continuing miniaturization of the elements of which computers are made, resulting in more and more elementary gates with higher and higher clock pulse per unit of silicon, accompanied by less and less energy dissipation per elementary computing event. Roughly, a linear increase in clock speed is accompanied by square increase in elements per silicon unit—so if all elements compute all of the time, then the dissipated energy per time unit rises cubicly (linear times square) in absence of energy decrease per elementary event. The continuing dramatic decrease in dissipated energy per elementary event is what has made Moore's law possible. But there is a foreseeable end to this: There is a minimum quantum of energy dissipation associated with elementary events. This puts a fundamental limit on how far we can go with miniaturization, or does it?

Both classical and quantum physics are believed to be strictly reversible at the fundamental level: A complete description of the microscopic state of the system uniquely determines the earlier and future states of the system—this holds not only in Newtonian mechanics but for example also for the unitary evolution of every quantum mechanical system. Currently, computations are commonly irreversible, even though the physical devices that execute them are fundamentally reversible. This irreversibility is due to the fact that information tends to be erased all the time: computing a function like $a + b = c$ one inputs a and b and obtains output c. From c one cannot uniquely retrieve a and b. The contrast between the physics of the computing machinery which is reversible and the executed irreversible computation is only possible at the cost of efficiency loss by generating thermal entropy into the environment. With computational device technology rapidly approaching the elementary particle level this effect gains in significance to the extent that efficient operation (or operation at all) of future computers requires them to be reversible. The 'logically irreversible' operations in a physical computer necessarily dissipate $kT \ln 2$ energy by generating a corresponding amount of entropy for every bit of information that gets irreversibly erased; the logically reversible operations can in principle be performed dissipation-free. Here k is Boltzmann's constant and T the absolute temperature in degrees Kelvin, so that $kT \approx 3 \times 10^{-21}$ Joule at room temperature.

Extrapolations of current trends show that the energy dissipation per binary logic operation needs to be reduced below kT (thermal noise) within 15 years. Even at kT level, a future laptop containing 10^{13} gates operating at 100 gigahertz dissipates 3,000 watts. For thermodynamic reasons, cooling the operating temperature of such a computing device to almost absolute zero (to get kT down) must dissipate at least as much energy in the cooling as it saves for the computing.

Especially Landauer [18] has argued that it is only the *irreversible* elementary events (like erasing information) that necessarily dissipate energy; there is no physical law that requires *reversible* events (like negation) to dissipate energy. It has been shown that all irreversible computations can be performed logically reversibly at the cost of possibly increasing computation time and memory [4]. It remains to develop the technology to implement the physical reversible execution of the logically reversible computation in a dissipation-free manner. Reversible computers can be implemented using quantum-mechanical technologies; quantum-mechanical computers are reversible except for the observation phases. So far the development of computation machinery is mostly based on the principles of classical physics and irreversible components. At the basic level, however, matter is governed by quantum mechanics, which is reversible. Further miniaturization will very soon reach scales where quantum mechanical effects take over and classical laws cease to apply accurately. The mismatch of computing organization and reality will express itself in friction: increasingly powerful computers will dissipate increasing and unsustainable amounts of energy unless their mode of operation becomes quantum mechanical (and thus reversible). That is, harnessing quantum mechanical effects may be essential for further miniaturization and hence acceleration of classical computing methods.

There is an added bonus: once we get involved in quantum effects, it appears we can go further than just miniaturizing classical computers to the quantum scale. Quantum mechanics may actually spawn a *qualitatively new* kind of computing: a kind which profits from quantum effects to boost computation to such an extent that things are achieved that would forever be out of reach of classical computers, even if these could be miniaturized to the same level.

The Spaghetti Problem Parallel computation that allows processors to randomly access a large shared memory, or rapidly access a member of a large number of other processors, will necessarily have large latency. If we use n processing elements of, say, unit size each, then the tightest they can be packed is in a 3-dimensional sphere of volume n. Assuming that the units have no "funny" shapes, assume for example they are spherical, some units are at distance equal to the radius R from one another,

$$R = \left(\frac{3n}{4\pi}\right)^{1/3} \tag{1}$$

Because of the bounded speed of light, it is impossible to transport signals over n^α ($\alpha > 0$) distance in $o(n)$ time. In fact, the assumption of the bounded speed of light says that the lower time bound on *any* computation using n processing elements is linear in $n^{1/3}$ outright.

The *spaghetti* problem is as follows: We illustrate the approach with a popular architecture, say the *binary d-cube*. Recall, that this is the network with $n = 2^d$ nodes, each of which is identified by a d-bit name. There is a two-way communication link between two nodes if their identifiers differ by a single bit. The network is represented by an undirected graph $C = (V, E)$, with V the set of nodes and $E \subseteq V \times V$ the set of edges, each edge corresponding with a communication link. There are $d2^{d-1}$ edges in C. Let C be embedded in 3-dimensional Euclidean space, each node as a sphere with unit volume. The distance between two nodes is the Euclidean distance between their centers.

Lemma 1. *The average Euclidean length of the edges in the 3-space embedding of C is at least $7R/(16d)$.*

One can derive a general theorem that gives similar lower bounds that are optimal in the sense of being within a constant multiplicative factor of an upper bound for several example graphs of various diameters, [24]. At present, many popular multicomputer architectures are based on highly symmetric communication networks with small diameter. Like all networks with small diameter, also asymmetric ones like complete binary trees, such networks will suffer from the communication bottleneck above, necessarily contain *some* long interconnects (embedded edges). However, the desirable fast permutation routing properties of symmetric networks don't come free, since they require that the average of *all* interconnects is long. Then, the ratio between the volume of the combined processing elements and the required volume of the wires vanishes—even for moderate numbers the processors become needles in a haystack of wires. Here we have not yet taken into account that longer wires need larger drivers and have a larger diameter, that the larger volume will again cause the average interconnect length to increase, and so on, which explosion may make embedding altogether impossible with finite length interconnects as exhibited in a related context in [23]. It appears that the "spaghetti" problem too may be resolved—in a fashion—by the inherent parallellism of coherent quantum computation.

2   Quantum Computation

The quantum computer as first advocated in [14] is currently aimed to exploit the standard physical model that quantum evolution of an appropriate system consists in a superposition of many (potentially infinitely many) simultaneous computation paths. It is theoretically possible that through the specific quantum mechanical rules of interference of the different paths one can boost the probability associated with desirable evolutions and suppress undesirable ones. Upon observation of the system state one of the states in superposition is realized. By quantum specific algorithmic techniques the idea is to observe the desired outcome with appropriately large positive probability, or to compute the desired outcome from the observed data with high probability.

This coherent quantum computing (CQC) approach will partially alleviate the wiring problem (Section 1.1) because an exploding number of different computation paths will be simultaneously followed (with appropriate probability amplitudes, to be sure) by the same single physical apparatus requiring but a tiny amount of physical space. This may be the substance of R. Feynman's dictum "there is room at the bottom" in the context of his proposal of CQC, [17]. Of course, since the different computation paths of a quantum computation cannot communicate as is often a main feature in a parallel distributed computation, it is only a very special type of room which is available at the bottom.

Since the quantum evolution in a computation if unobstructed by observation and decoherence is reversible, the pure form of CQC, apart from the irreversible observation phase, can be energy dissipation free. CQC seems to a very large extent to achieve the optimal thermodynamic neutral computation aimed for in Section 1.1. Although there seems to be agreement that energy gets dissipated in the irreversible observation phase, to the author's knowledge it is not yet clear how much.

Through a sequence of proposals [14], [17], [16], [7], there has emerged a Turing machine model of quantum coherent computing. There is also the closely related and in often more convenient quantum circuit model, see [9]. In this introduction we only aim at outlining basic principles, algorithmic improvements, and technological problems attending the quantum computing challenge. Details can be found in the references.

2.1   Background: Probabilistic Turing Machines

The simplest way to introduce quantum computing seems by way of probabilistic computing. Suppose we consider the well known probabilistic Turing machine which is just like an ordinary Turing machine, except that at each step the machine can make a probabilistic move which consists in flipping a (say fair) coin and depending on the outcome changing its state to either one of two alternatives. This means that at each such probabilistic move the computation of the machine splits into two distinct further computations each with probability $\frac{1}{2}$. Ignoring the deterministic computation steps, a computation involving m coinflips can be viewed as a binary computation tree of depth m with 2^m leaves, where the set of nodes at level $t \leq m$ correspond to the possible states of the system after t coinflips, every state occurring with probability $1/2^t$. For convenience, we can label the edges connecting a state x directly with a state y with the probability that a state x changes into state y in a single coin flip (in this example all edges are labeled '$\frac{1}{2}$').

For instance, given an arbitrary Boolean formula containing m variables, a probabilistic machine can flip its coin m times to generate each of the 2^m possible truth assignments and subsequently check deterministically wether the assignment makes the formula true. If there are k distinct such assignments then the probabilistic machine finds that the formula is satisfiable with probability at least $k/2^m$—since there are k distinct computation paths leading to a satisfiable assignment.

Now suppose the probabilistic machine is hidden in a black box and the computation proceeds without us knowing the outcomes of the coin flips. Suppose that after m coin flips we open part of the black box and observe the bit which denotes the truth assignment for variable x_5 ($5 \leq m$). Before we opened the black box all 2^m initial truth assignments to variables $x_1, \ldots, x_m$ were still equally possible, each with probability $1/2^m$. After we observed the state of variable x_5, say 0, the probability space of possibilities has collapsed to the truth assignments which consist of all binary vectors with a 0 in the 5th position each of which has probability renormalized to $1/2^{m-1}$.

2.2   Quantum Turing Machines

A quantum Turing machine can be viewed as a generalization of the classical probabilistic Turing machine. Consider the same computation tree. In the probabilistic computation there is a probability $p_i \geq 0$ associated with each node i (state of the system) at the same level in the tree, such that $\sum p_i = 1$, summed over the nodes at the same level. In a quantum mechanical computation there is a "probability amplitude" α_i associated with each basis state $|i\rangle$ of the system. The "bra-ket" notation is due to P. Dirac and is the standard quantum mechanics notation. The "bra" $\langle x|$ denotes a row vector with complex entries, and "ket" $|x\rangle$ is the column vector consisting of the conjugate transpose of $\langle x|$ (columns replaced by rows and the imaginary part of the entries negated, that is, $\sqrt{-1}$ is replaced by $-\sqrt{-1}$). For convenience consider the simple case (corresponding to the probabilistic example) where i runs through the classical values 0 through $2^m - 1$, so that $|i\rangle$ is an m-bit binary column vector. The amplitudes are complex numbers satisfying $\sum ||\alpha_i||^2 = 1$, where if $\alpha_i = a + b\sqrt{-1}$ then $||\alpha_i|| = \sqrt{a^2 + b^2}$, and the summation is taken over all distinct states of the observable at a particular instant. The transitions are governed by a matrix U which represents the program being executed. Such a program has to satisfy the following constraints. Denote the set of possible configurations of the Turing machine by X, where X is the set of m-bits column vectors (the basis states) for simplicity. Then U maps the column vector $\underline{\alpha} = (\alpha_x)_{x \in X}$ to $U\underline{\alpha}$. Here $\underline{\alpha}$ is a vector of amplitudes of the quantum superposition of the basis states before the step, and $U\underline{\alpha}$ the same after the step concerned. The special property which U needs to satisfy in quantum mechanics is that it is *unitary*, that is, $U^\dagger \cdot U = I$ where I is the identity matrix and $U^\dagger$ is the conjugate transpose of U (as with the bra-ket, "conjugate" means that all $\sqrt{-1}$'s are replaced by $-\sqrt{-1}$'s and 'transpose' means that the rows and columns are interchanged). In other words, U is unitary iff $U^\dagger = U^{-1}$.

The unitary constraint on the evolution of the computation enforces two facts.

1. If $U^0\underline{\alpha} = \underline{\alpha}$ and $U^t = U \cdot U^{t-1}$ then $\sum_{x \in X} ||(U^t\underline{\alpha})_x||^2 = 1$ for all t (discretizing time for convenience).
2. A quantum computation is reversible (replace U by $U^\dagger = U^{-1}$).

The quantum version of a single bit is a superposition of the two basis states a classical bit can have:

$$|\Psi\rangle = \alpha \, |0\rangle + \beta \, |1\rangle,$$

where $||\alpha||^2 + ||\beta||^2 = 1$. Such a state $|\psi\rangle$ is called a quantum bit or *qubit*. It consists of partially the basis state $|0\rangle$ and partially the basis state $|1\rangle$. The states are denoted by the column vectors of the appropriate complex probability amplitudes. For the basis states the vector notations are: $|0\rangle = \binom{1}{0}$ (that is, $\alpha = 1$ and $\beta = 0$), and $|1\rangle = \binom{0}{1}$ (that is, $\alpha = 0$ and $\beta = 1$).

Physically, for example, the state $|\psi\rangle$ can be the state of a polarized photon, and the basis states are horizontal or vertical polarization, respectively. Upon measuring according to the basis states, that is, passing the photon through a medium that is polarized either in the horizontal or vertical orientation, the photon is observed with probability $||\alpha||^2$ or probability $||\beta||^2$, respectively.

Consider a sample computation on a one-bit computer executing the unitary operator:

$$S = \frac{1}{\sqrt{2}} \begin{pmatrix} 1 & 1 \\ -1 & 1 \end{pmatrix}. \tag{2}$$

It is easy to verify, using common matrix calculation, that

$$S\,|0\rangle = \frac{1}{\sqrt{2}}\,|0\rangle - \frac{1}{\sqrt{2}}\,|1\rangle,\ S\,|1\rangle = \frac{1}{\sqrt{2}}\,|0\rangle + \frac{1}{\sqrt{2}}\,|1\rangle$$

$$S^2\,|0\rangle = 0\,|0\rangle - 1\,|1\rangle = -\,|1\rangle,\ S^2\,|1\rangle = 1\,|0\rangle + 0\,|1\rangle = |0\rangle$$

If we observe the computer in state $S\,|0\rangle$, then the probability of observing state $|0\rangle$ is $(\frac{1}{\sqrt{2}})^2 = \frac{1}{2}$, and the probability to observe $|1\rangle$ is $(-\frac{1}{\sqrt{2}})^2 = \frac{1}{2}$. However, if we observe the computer in state $S^2\,|0\rangle$, then the probability of observing state $|0\rangle$ is 0, and the probability to observe $|1\rangle$ is 1. Similarly, if we observe the computer in state $S\,|1\rangle$, then the probability of observing state $|0\rangle$ is $(\frac{1}{\sqrt{2}})^2 = \frac{1}{2}$, and the probability to observe $|1\rangle$ is $(\frac{1}{\sqrt{2}})^2 = \frac{1}{2}$. But now, if we observe the computer in state $S^2\,|1\rangle$, then the probability of observing state $|0\rangle$ is 1, and the probability to observe $|1\rangle$ is 0. Therefore, the operator S inverts a bit when it is applied twice in a row, and hence has acquired the charming name *square root of 'not'*. Note that there is no classical unconditional Boolean operator that has the effect of S; this is one difference between quantum computation and probabilistic computation.

In computing the above amplitudes, subsequent to two applications of S, according to matrix calculus we found that

$$S^2\,|1\rangle = \frac{1}{\sqrt{2}}\left(\frac{1}{\sqrt{2}}(\,|0\rangle - |1\rangle) + \frac{1}{\sqrt{2}}(\,|0\rangle + |1\rangle)\right)$$

$$= \tfrac{1}{2}(\,|0\rangle - |1\rangle + |0\rangle + |1\rangle) = |0\rangle.$$

In a probabilistic calculation, flipping a coin two times in a row, we would have found that the probability of each computation path in the complete binary computation tree of depth 2 was $\frac{1}{4}$, and the states at the four leaves of the tree were $|0\rangle$, $|1\rangle$, $|0\rangle$, $|1\rangle$, resulting in a total probability of observing $|0\rangle$ being $\frac{1}{2}$, and the total probability of observing $|1\rangle$ being $\frac{1}{2}$ as well.

The principle involved is called *interference*, similar to the related light phenomenon in the seminal "two slit experiment:" If we put a screen with a single small enough hole in between a light source and a target, then we observe a gradually dimming illumination of the target screen, the brightest spot being colinear with the light source and the hole. If we put a screen with *two* small holes in between, then we observe a diffraction pattern of bright and dark stripes due to interference. Namely, the light hits all of the screen via two different routes (through the two different holes). If the two routes differ by an even number of half wave lengths, then the wave amplitudes at the target are added, resulting in twice the amplitude and a bright spot, and if they differ by an odd number of half wave lengths then the wave amplitudes are in opposite phase and are subtracted resulting in zero and a dark spot. Similarly, with quantum computation, if the quantum state is

$$|\Psi\rangle = \alpha \, |x\rangle + \beta \, |y\rangle,$$

then for $x = y$ we have a probability of observing $|x\rangle$ of $||\alpha + \beta||^2$, rather than $||\alpha||^2 + ||\beta||^2$ which it would have been in a probabilistic fashion. For example, if $\alpha = \frac{1}{\sqrt{2}}$ and $\beta = -\frac{1}{\sqrt{2}}$ then the probability of observing $|x\rangle$ is 0 rather than $\frac{1}{2}$, and with the sign of β inverted we observe $|x\rangle$ with probability 1.

2.3   Multi-qubit States

Above, a qubit takes a value in $\mathcal{C}^2$ where $\mathcal{C}$ is the set of complex real numbers. To generalize this to strings of n qubits, we consider the quantum state space $\mathcal{C}^N$ with $N = 2^n$. The basis vectors $e_0, \ldots, e_{N-1}$ of this space are parametrized by binary strings of length n, so that e_0 is shorthand for $e_{0\ldots0}$ and e_{N-1} is shorthand for $e_{1\ldots1}$. Mathematically, $\mathcal{C}^N$ is decomposed into a tensor product of n copies of $\mathcal{C}^2$, and an n-qubit state $|a_1 \ldots a_n\rangle$ in bra-ket notation can also be written as the tensor product $|a_1\rangle \ldots |a_n\rangle$, a string of n qubits, the qubits being distinguished by position.

2.4   Input and Output

We restrict ourselves to the case where the quantum computer has a classical input. If the input x has k bits, and the number of qubits used by the computation is $n \geq k$ (input plus work space), then we pad the input with nonsignificant 0's and start the quantum computation in an initial state (which must be in $\mathcal{C}^N$) $e_{x0\ldots0}$. When the computation finishes the resulting state is a unit vector in $\mathcal{C}^N$, say $\sum_i \alpha_i e_i$ where i runs through $0, \ldots, N - 1$ and the probability amplitudes α_i's satisfy $\sum_i ||\alpha_i||^2 = 1$. The output is obtained by performing a measurement with as possible outcomes the basis vectors. The observed output is probabilistic: we observe basis vector e_i, that is, the n bit string i, with probability $||\alpha_i||^2$. A typical scenario is as follows. Suppose there are "right" and "wrong" answers and we can verify whether an answer is "right", as in the case when we receive a purported factor of a composite number. Suppose further that the probability of obtaining a "right" answer is at least $\frac{1}{2}$. Then running the algorithm t times, the probability of receiving t "wrong" answers is at most 2^{-t}.

2.5   Quantum Algorithmics

A quantum algorithm corresponds to a unitary transformation U that is built up from elementary unitary transformations, every one of which only acts on one or two qubits. The algorithm applies U to an initial classical state containing the input and then makes a final measurement to extract the output from the final quantum state. The algorithm is "efficient" if the number of elementary operations is "small", which usually means at most polynomial in the length of the input. Quantum computers can do everything a classical computer can do probabilistically — and more.

3   What Quantum Computers Can Do

A readable brief introduction to quantum algorithms is [13]. The biggest success so far — and the event which ignited the current explosive growth of the field of quantum computing — was Peter Shor's 1994 discovery of an efficient quantum algorithm for finding the prime factors of large composite integers [12].

Fast Factoring All fast factoring algorithms are based on the following idea: To factor a composite integer M it suffices to obtain two integers x and y such that $x^2 \equiv y^2 \pmod{M}$ but $x \not\equiv \pm y \pmod{M}$. Then $(x-y)(x+y) \equiv 0 \pmod{M}$ but neither factor in the left-hand side is divisible by M. Hence, $x + y$ contains one factor of M and $x - y$ another one. To obtain a factor we determine the greatest common divisor of $x+y$ and M, for example by Euclid's algorithm which runs in polynomial time. In the quantum algorithm we try to find the period r of a random x modulo M with $1 < x < M$. That is, $x^r \equiv 1 \pmod{M}$. If r is even then $(x^{r/2} + 1)(x^{r/2} - 1) \equiv 0 \pmod{M}$. If also $x^{r/2} \not\equiv -1 \pmod{M}$ then we can determine a proper factor of M by the gcd algorithm as above. Number theory tells us that at least half of all x's yield a proper prime factor this way. Hence, repeating this process k times, the probability is at least $1-1/2^k$ that we find a proper factor of M. Thus, the problem of factoring M reduces to finding the order r. This is done by judicious use of the so-called quantum Fourier transform, the details of which can be found in Shor's articles referred to above or the textbook [9].

The trick is to first use a sequence H_n of n one-qubit unitary operations, the Hadamard transform,

$$H = \frac{1}{\sqrt{2}} \begin{pmatrix} 1 & 1 \\ 1 & -1 \end{pmatrix}$$

on the successive bits of a register of n bits originally in the all–0 state $|\Psi\rangle = |00\ldots0\rangle$. The result is a superposition of

$$H_n |\Psi\rangle = \sum_{x \in \{0,1\}^n} 2^{-n/2} |x\rangle$$

of all the 2^n possible states of the register, each with amplitude $2^{-n/2}$ (and hence probability of being observed of 2^{-n}.)

The Hadamard transform is ubiquitous in quantum computing; its singlefold action is similar to that of the transform S of eq. (2) with the the roles of "0" and

"1" partly interchanged. In contrast to S^2 that implements the logical "not," we have $H^2 = I$ with I the identity matrix.

Now the computation proceeds in parallel along the exponentially many computation paths in quantum coherent superposition. A sequence of tricky further unitary operations, for example the "quantum Fourier transform," and observations serves to exploit interference (and so-called entanglement) phenomena to effect a high probability of eventually observing outcomes that allow us to determine the desired period r.

One principle that is used in many quantum algorithms (and also in factoring) is as follows. If A is a classical algorithm for computing some function f, possibly even irreversible like $f(x) \equiv x \pmod 2$, then we can turn it into a unitary transformation which maps classical state $|x, 0\rangle$ to $|x, f(x)\rangle$. Note that we can apply A to a superposition of all 2^n inputs:

$$A\left(2^{-n/2} \sum_x |x, 0\rangle\right) = 2^{-n/2} \sum_x |x, f(x)\rangle.$$

In some sense this state contains the results of computing f for *all* possible inputs x, but we have only applied A once to obtain it. This effect shows one of the advantages of quantum over classical computing and is called *quantum parallelism*.

By making clever use of superpositions, interference, quantum parallelism, and some classical number theory, Shor's algorithm finds a factor of a number M in time roughly the square of the length of the input (which is $l = \log M$ bits). In contrast, every known classical algorithm requires exponential time asymptotically in excess of $2^{l^{1/3}}$ (see Introduction) to factor an l-bit number. Since factoring is one of the most elementary aspects of number theory, the oldest mathematical discipline, and centuries of efforts by the greatest mathematicians have not yielded better methods, it is widely believed that such better methods either do not exist or are prohibitively difficult to find. In fact, this belief underlies most of current public-key cryptography, notably the RSA system, ubiquitously used on the Internet and in the financial world. Such crypto-systems can be broken if one can factor large numbers fast. Accordingly, the advent of quantum computing compromises all such systems: if a quantum computer can be built, then most of current cryptography becomes totally insecure, and, for example, electronic money can be forged.

Cryptography What quantum computing takes away with one hand (classical public-key crypto), it gives back in another form with the other (quantum secret-key crypto) albeit only in part. Already in 1984, Bennett and Brassard found a scheme which allowed two distant parties to obtain a shared secret key via quantum mechanical communication [5]. Their scheme was believed to be fully secure against any type of spy or eavesdropper, and this has indeed been formally proven. The security relies on the basic tenet of quantum mechanics that one cannot observe a quantum state consisting of a superposition of basic states without destroying it and a state in superposition cannot be copied—hence an eavesdropper cannot tamper with a message consisting of such states without this being detectable if the sender and receiver exchange classical information (which can be done in such a way that it gives zero information about the quantum message to the eavesdropper). On the other hand, some other parts of electronic transactions, like unforgeable signatures, appear to be beyond the power of quantum methods.

Rapid Search A third application is Grover's 1996 algorithm for searching databases [11]. Consider finding some specific record in a large unordered database of N items. Classically, there is no smarter method than just to go through all records sequentially, which will requires expected $N/2$ time steps for a record in general position. Grover's algorithm, however, uses quantum superpositions to examine all records "at the same time", and finds the desired record in roughly $\sqrt{N}$ steps. Examining 10^{12} records with unit microsecond probes, this is the difference between about two months of computing and one second of computing! His algorithm also allows to solve the widespread and notoriously hard NP-complete problems (such as the traveling salesman problem) quadratically faster than known classical methods—reducing say exponential time with exponent N to exponential time with exponent $N/2$.

Communication Complexity A fourth application deals with the setting where two separated parties, Alice and Bob, want to compute some function $f(x, y)$ depending on x (only known to Alice) and y (only known to Bob). A simple scheme would be for Alice to send her x to Bob and then let Bob do all the work by himself, but this may take a lot of bits of communication and often there are much more clever schemes requiring less communication. The field of *communication complexity* examines the optimal number of bits that have to be communicated in order to compute the function at hand. What happens if we generalize this setting to the quantum world and allow Alice and Bob the use of quantum computers and qubit-communication? It turns out that some tasks can be solved with significantly less communication if we allow such quantization [10] — and this despite a fact known as "Holevo's theorem" stating that quantum bits cannot contain more information than classical bits! It turns out there are similar advantages by sticking to classical communication, but allowing Alice and Bob the use of pre-established "entangled" qubits. Physically, such entangled qubits appear in the Einstein-Podolsky-Rosen paradox, capable of a paradoxical spooky instantaneous action at a distance. While such action can't exchange information since that would violate the speed of light bound, the mentioned results establish the unexpected fact that it can *save* on exchanged information. The first results using pre-established entangled qubits and classical communication were obtained by Cleve and Buhrman [8]. Both approaches beat the limits provable for just classical communication.

Simulating Quantum Matter Finally, some indications have been given that quantum mechanical computers may be able to simulate quantum mechanical systems at acceptable speeds, [26], just as envisioned by Feynman [17] in his original suggestion of the possibility and use of quantum mechanical computing.

Limitations The above developments suggested the vision that *all* computation can be enormously sped up by quantum computers. But not so! There are strong and general *limitations* of quantum computers as well. Recall that Grover's algorithm is quadratically faster than classical search algorithms. It was already known that such a quadratic speed-up is the best quantum computers can achieve for searching a database, so exponential speed-ups cannot be obtained for this problem. Recently, it was shown that the same holds for *all* problems in the database-setting of Grover's algorithm: for all such problems, quantum computers can be at most polynomially faster than classical computers [3]. Other lower bounds showing that for certain problems quantum mechanical methods do not improve significantly on classical methods have been given in [1] for binary search, [2,9] for other problems. The polynomial lower bound approach has been partially extended to quantum communication complexity as well, but there have also been exhibited some new (polynomial) speed-ups, both in Grover's setting and in communication complexity.

Limiting results like the above, of course, do not preclude exponential speed-ups in different settings, like Shor's, or a clever future setting as yet unknown. Exploring this potential of quantum computation remains an exciting and important task for computer scientists and physicists alike. The current state of knowledge resembles the situation of a person in a dark room, knowing by touch some isolated objects. Somebody has to turn on the light.

4   How Quantum Computers Do It

How about actually building quantum computers that can run the fast algorithms like Shor's, Grover's, or communication complexity algorithms? To date only very small quantum algorithms (and larger quantum crypto devices) have been implemented. On the one hand, quantum cryptographical systems work fine over fiber optics interconnects and even over common co-axial TV cables over considerable distances like 40 km, sufficient for a local area network. This application essentially works by transmitting single polarized photons—in superposition of two orthogonal polarizations. Technological difficulties and system noise apparently give a very low yield in useful bits of, say, one in 10,000.

Currently, the most sophisticated experimental quantum computer is the five qubit NMR based computer built by the team of Isaac Chuang, [22], at IBM Almaden's Research Center. While there are larger qubit assemblies extant, with this five qubit computer the experimenters succeeded in executing the quantum mechanical step in Shor's fast factoring algorithm—the order-finding step—for every example in its range, while a conventional computer would require repeated steps to solve the problem.

One problem with physical realizations that we need to perform logical operations on pairs of intact pure quantum states, which means that we have to bring them together, operate on them, and transmit the result, all without destroying the superposition. Generally, physical realizations of CQC will have to struggle with the fact that the coherent states of the superposition will tend to deteriorate by interaction with each other and the universe, a phenomenon called *decoherence*, see for example [27]. The larger the scale of the coherent superposition the faster decoherence. Of course, the gain one hopes to make with quantum computing over classical computing must come out of the scale of the superposition. In [21] it is calculated that that CQC calculations using physical realizations based on spin lattices will have to be finished in an extremely short time. For example, factoring a 1000 bit number in square quantum factoring time we have to perform 10^6 steps in less than the thermal time scale $\hbar/kT$ which at 1 K is of order 10^{-9} seconds. Such a CQC computation would need to proceed at optical frequencies. Other technologies have more favorable characteristics, see [9] Chapter 7. Quantum versions of error-correcting codes have been developed recently which may solve this problem in theory, but not yet in the brittle practice of the physical lab (let alone the brittle practice of our desktops). This is related to development of Quantum Information Theory—the quantum extension of classical information theory. For a survey see [6]. Similarly, classical Kolmogorov complexity (algorithmic information theory) [20] can be extended to a quantum mechanical approach [25]. Actually building large quantum computers presents formidable problems to experimental physicists reminiscent of the initial barriers to classical computing: unreliable components, physically large components, memory, organisation, communication, programming. This has the effect that hitherto unexplored areas of quantum mechanical theory are suddenly put in the limelight. In fact, the theory of quantum mechanics experiences a renaissance, and is being extended, for example with respect to the algebraic analysis of "quantum entanglement"—a vital notion in many quantum algorithms, not yet thoroughly investigated in quantum theory, [15].

References

1. A. Ambainis, A better lower bound for quantum algorithms searching an ordered list, *Proc. 40th IEEE Symp. Foundat. Comput. Sci.*, 352–357, 1999.
2. A. Ambainis, Quantum lower bounds by quantum arguments, *Proc. 32nd ACM Symp. Theor. Comput.*, 2000.
3. R. Beals, H. Buhrman, R. Cleve, M. Mosca, and R. de Wolf. Quantum lower bounds by polynomials. In *Proc. 39th IEEE Symp. Foundat. Comput. Sci.*, 1998, 352–361.
4. C.H. Bennett. Logical reversibility of computation. *IBM J. Res. Develop.*, 17(1973), 525–532.
5. C.H. Bennett, F. Bessette, G. Brassard, L. Salvail and J. Smolin, Experimental quantum cryptography, *J. Cryptology*, 5:1(1992), 3-28; C.H. Bennett, G. Brassard and A. Ekert, Quantum cryptography, *Scientific American*, Oct. 1992, 50-57.
6. C.H. Bennett and P.W. Shor, Quantum information theory, *IEEE Trans. Inform. Th.*, IT-44:6(1998), 2724–2742.
7. E. Bernstein and U. Vazirani, Quantum complexity theory, *SIAM J. Comput.*, 26:5(1997), 1411–1473.

8. R. Cleve and H. Buhrman, Substituting quantum entanglement for communication, Physical Review A, 56:2(1997),1201-1204.

9. M.A. Nielsen and I.L. Chuang, *Quantum Computation and Quantum Information*, Cambridge University Press, 2000.

10. H. Buhrman, R. Cleve, and A. Wigderson. Quantum vs. classical communication and computation. In *Proc. 30th ACM Symp. Theor. Comput.*, 1998, 63–68.

11. L. K. Grover. A fast quantum mechanical algorithm for database search. In *Proc. 28th ACM Symp. Theor. Comput.*, 1996, 212–219.

12. P. W. Shor. Polynomial-time algorithms for prime factorization and discrete logarithms on a quantum computer. *SIAM Journal on Computing*, 26:5(1997), 1484–1509.

13. P.W. Shor, Introduction to quantum algorithms, http://xxx.lanl.gov/abs/quant-ph/0005003

14. P. Benioff, J. Stat. Phys., 22(1980), 563–591, also *J. Math. Phys.*, 22(1981), 495–507, *Int. J. Theoret. Phys.*, 21(1982), 177–201, *Phys. Rev. Letters*, 48(1982), 1581–1585, *J. Stat. Phys.*, 29(1982), 515–546, *Phys. Rev. Letters*, 53(1984), 1203, *Ann. New York Acad. Sci.*, 480(1986), 475–486.

15. D.P. DiVincenzo, T. Mor, P.W. Shor, J.A. Smolin, B.M. Terhal, Unextendible Product Bases, Uncompletable Product Bases and Bound Entanglement, http://xxx.lanl.gov/abs/quant-ph/9908070

16. D. Deutsch, Quantum theory, the Church-Turing principle and the universal quantum computer. *Proc. Royal Society London, Series A*, 400(1985), 97–117; see also *Proc. Royal Society London, Series A*, 425(1989), 73–90; with R. Josza, *Proc. Royal Society London, Series A*, 439(1992), 553–558.

17. R.P. Feynman, Simulating physics with computers, *Int. J. Theoret. Physics*, 21(1982), 467–488; Quantum mechanical computers. *Foundations of Physics*, 16(1986), 507–531. (Originally published in *Optics News*, February 1985); Tiny Computers Obeying Quantum Mechanical Laws. In: *New Directions in Physics: The Los Alamos 40th Anniversary Volume*,, N. Metropolis and D. M. Kerr and G. Rota, Eds.,Academic Press,, Boston, 1987, 7–25.

18. R. Landauer. Irreversibility and heat generation in the computing process. *IBM J. Res. Develop.*, 5(1961), 183–191.

19. A.K. Lenstra and H.W. Lenstra, Jr. (Eds.), *The Development of the Number Field Sieve*, Lecture Notes in Mathematics, Vol. 1554, Springer-Verlag, Berlin, 1993.

20. M. Li and P.M.B. Vitányi, *An Introduction to Kolmogorov Complexity and Its Applications*, 2nd Edition, Springer-Verlag, New York, 1997.

21. Unruh, W. G., Maintaining coherence in quantum computers, *Physical Review A*, 51(1995), 992–.

22. L.M.K. Vandersypen, M. Steffen, G. Breyta, C.S. Yannoni, R. Cleve, I. L. Chuang, Experimental realization of order-finding with a quantum computer, http://xxx.lanl.gov/abs/quant-ph/0008065

23. P.M.B. Vitányi, Area penalty for sublinear signal propagation delay on chip, *Proc. 26th IEEE Symp. Foundat. Comput. Sci.*, 1985, 197–207.

24. P.M.B. Vitányi, Locality, communication and interconnect length in multicomputers, *SIAM J. Computing*, 17 (1988), 659–672.

25. P.M.B. Vitányi, Quantum Kolmogorov Complexity Based on Classical Descriptions, *IEEE Trans. Inform. Th.*, To appear.

26. C. Zalka, Efficient simulations of quantum mechanical systesms by quantum computers, *Proc. Royal Soc. London, Ser. A*, 454(1998), 313–322.

27. W.H. Zurek, Decoherence and the transition from quantum to classical, *Physics Today*, 44(1991), 36–44.

Parallel Computation: MM +/- X

Lawrence Snyder

University of Washington, Seattle

Abstract. Accomplishments from the past decade of parallel computation research are reviewed. The present state of the art is described, and critical problems for future researchers are identified.

1 Introduction

Parallel computation was an extremely active research area across the world during the decade of the '90s. Components such as interconnection networks and routers were studied, architectures were invented and built, languages were defined and compilers constructed, algorithms were developed, and applications programmed. It is impossible to assess all of that research fairly and faithfully in a few pages. Rather, as a mechanism for focusing our review of progress in parallel computation, we ask the question, "Why after so much progress has the adoption of parallel computation been so slow?"

The 1980s ended with a widely held belief that using parallel computers would soon be the norm, though few were in production then. David Mizell [19], wanting to characterize "blue collar" parallel programs, i.e. parallel codes working in daily production, polled the community for examples at the time and found none. Today users do run parallel programs in production, but it is only a small group of elite "power users," not the whole community. Why has adoption been so slow?

The possible explanations are numerous, ranging from the dramatic speed improvements of standard sequential computers, to the absence of a general-purpose parallel programming language. But, a unifying feature of many of the explanations is that the deep intellectual challenges presented by parallelism were not widely appreciated at the start of the decade. Bringing a scalable amount of processing power to bear on a single problem is difficult. It is affected by the architecture of the parallel computer, which in turn is sensitive to a host of technological issues. It is affected by the programming language, which in turn is influenced by the abstract machine model, the programming model, the compiler, system support and libraries. And it is affected by algorithms and the programmer's sophistication, which in turn depend on a clear understanding of resource costs and is enabled by experience. Applying parallelism is complex. Despite that fact, parallelism is effectively applied today, reflecting favorably on the research progress of the past decade.

Our naivete about the intellectual challenge of parallel computation is evidenced most clearly by the many "one-answer" approaches over the decade for

R. Wilhelm (Ed.): Informatics. 10 Years Back. 10 Years Ahead, LNCS 2000, pp. 234–250, 2001.

"solving" parallel computation. The proponents of these approaches saw a single impediment to the adoption of parallelism, and then proceeded to overcome that problem. The research pushed our understanding tremendously in the topic areas. Since parallelism is influenced by many factors, as just indicated, these solutions contributed but were not sufficient. However, they also provide an effective organizing principle for reporting on the progress of the past decade. In the following a series of "single dimension" assertions about parallel computation will be adopted as topic headings. Though written in quotes, they are fictionalized embodiments of the prevailing sentiment in 1990. The quotes approximate phrases I recall hearing around that time, but they were not necessarily spoken by any of the cited authors.

2   Technology: "Performance of CMOS Processor Chips Will Soon Peak"

Of all of the assumptions current at the start of the '90s, perhaps the one that has been most thoroughly revised was that CMOS microprocessors were close to their peak performance. It is probably impossible to quantify the advance in processor speed over that period, since the art and science of assessing performance evolved rapidly during the decade. But, from September 1995 to September 2000 the peak single processor performance of the SPECInt95 integer benchmark suite grew from 7.33 to 50.0 [25]. Though this is slightly less than the factor of 8 performance improvement predicted by Moore's "Law" (performance doubles every 1.6 years), it represents observed, rather than potential, performance. SPECInt95 numbers are not available for machines of 1990 vintage, but it is likely that observed performance over the first half of the decade advanced by at least a factor of 7 or 8, probably faster.

With single processor performance over the decade improving by approximately 50 times, the challenge to parallel processing was substantial. A user had little motivation to invest any effort in parallel programming or money in parallel computers while sequential computers were getting faster so fast. If one's performance appetite could be limited to a factor of 2 every year-and-a-half, sequential computing would keep up. Unquestionably, sequential computer performance improvements are the most significant factor in explaining the slow adoption of user level parallelism.

Of course, since parallel computer designers can and usually do use these same sequential processors as "node machines," this performance advancement aided parallel computing, too. There can be no doubt that the goal of achieving sustained parallel performance in excess of 10^9 floating-point operations per second, 1 TF, was significantly assisted by the speed improvements of CMOS sequential processors. When that performance was achieved on December 17, 1996, it was CMOS processors that did it [14,31]. The achievement would have been substantially more difficult had it been attempted using last decade's technology.

It is important that CMOS was sufficient to the task of parallel computer components. In the years around 1990 with computer designers concerned about

CMOS speeds architects at Cray and Tera thought emitter-coupled logic (ECL) and gallium arsenide (GaAs) technologies would be essential for high-speed parallel designs. But with CMOS speeds competitive and densities extremely high, CMOS remained the technology of choice. Parallel computers were able to ride the technology wave carrying sequential computers. A consequence of CMOS's primacy was that one didn't have to be an expert in exotic technologies to design a fast parallel computer. This fact had significant architectural implications, as we now consider.

3   Architecture: "The One Feature Essential for All Parallel Computers Is ..."

The '90s were dominated by many parallel architectures that can unfairly be described as "one idea" computers. The characterization is unfair and inaccurate because in every case the architects solved a myriad of problems demanding many new ideas and creative designs. But, because "promoting" a parallel computer, whether to customers, funding agencies or our technical colleagues, requires that we lead with the "biggest" idea, the computer soon becomes branded as an implementation of that idea. The most unjust and unfortunate consequence of this phenomenon is that for many observers the idea's merit becomes bound to the computer's success. Computer architecture is much more than a single idea and a computer's success depends on much more than just its architecture.

Perhaps the most egregious cases of branding a parallel computer by one single feature are those that focus on the machine's interconnection network. During the decade there were mesh machines, hypercube machines, fat-tree machines, 3D torus machines, etc. These machines had many other interesting properties from which the single focus on topology tended to distract us. One tangible problem with elevating topology to a defining property of the computer is that it seems to encourage "programming to the topology," i.e. embedding topological properties into user programs [10]. Such an approach can dramatically reduce the program's portability, since the next computer many not have that topology. Though the topology is an important aspect of a parallel architecture, it is largely irrelevant to users.

The point of mentioning the "one idea" phenomenon is to observe that it overemphasizes variety in parallel computer design. Though variety is unquestionably plentiful, focusing on a single feature masks the fact that machines divide into two basic classes: Those with hardware supported shared memory, and those without. With the exception of Single Instruction Stream Multiple Data Stream (SIMD) computers, which had become all but obsolete by 1990 due to cheap memory (replicating programs ceased to be expensive) and their inherent inflexibility, all computer designs of the decade can be neatly compartmentalized into the Shared and Nonshared Memory Multiple Instruction Stream Multiple Data Stream (MIMD) parallel computer classes. These will be the basis for our discussion, though not all members in each class can be reviewed in these few pages. [22].

3.1   Shared Memory Parallel Computers

In sequential computing architects have largely preserved the ideal of a flat, uniformly fast, randomly accessible memory of arbitrary size through the use of virtualization, paging and caching. The illusion, though not perfect, is close enough that few programmers worry about memory. Applying these ideas in a parallel context is direct and equally effective, provided there is still a single reference stream, i.e. the processors do not share memory. With each processor having a private view of memory and its own reference stream, the standard caching techniques apply to speed performance. But, when processors share memory, the standard techniques do not suffice. Nevertheless, it is widely assumed that sharing memory is desirable.

The problem is this. As programmers we believe that a single memory image evolving through a computation is essential to programming, mostly to manage complexity. It's difficult to imagine trusting the results of parallelism without it. When multiple processors reference the same location, however, they can potentially make independent changes to that location creating different memory states. The crux of supporting shared memory is to allow the processors to reference the location while guaranteeing a single evolving memory image: In the presence of memory conflicts the computer should produce a rational, predictable result.

The simplest solution is to outlaw the problem, prohibiting different processors from referencing the same location at the same time, but this greatly complicates the task of separate threads cooperating to solve a problem and it tends to shift the burden to rapid synchronization. [However, see Nonshared Memory below.] A more realistic solution is to treat the global RAM memory as a literal specification of the single memory image and to resolve reference conflicts to preserve its integrity. This approach was fashionable in the 1980s, with machines like the BBN Butterfly, the Ultracomputer and RPP-3, Cedar, etc. The Saarland PRAM machine is a recent example of such an approach [21]. Though the conflict resolution techniques differ tremendously, the key point is not to allow (writable) memory to be cached, and to serialize conflicting changes to the global memory state. However, as processor speeds have increased, the penalty for not caching locations has become too burdensome.

To mitigate the penalty, hardware multithreading was intensively studied during much of the decade. The idea is to overlap the interpretation of multiple instructions coming from different instruction streams so as to pipeline their memory references. Though the latency of interpreting any given instruction is still the sum of the fetch, decode, memory reference and execution times, concurrent interpretation and pipelining can give excellent throughput. The Tera MTA was the most aggressive implementation of this idea, but it was also applied in Alewife, SMT processors, etc. Though promising, the jury is still out on multithreading's performance, motivating other approaches.

If all processors can "see" all global memory references, say because they are attached to a common memory bus, then the caching problem is easily solved, at least in principle. Any processor can cache a private copy of any memory location. While it computes, it also "snoops" the common connection, watching the memory locations requested by other processors. If it recognizes a reference to a location it has cached, it raises a signal to notify the other processor and the conflict is resolved by some protocol. Such techniques, known as cache coherency protocols, received intensive study in the 1990s. They are extremely effective, being the basis for the symmetric multiprocessor (SMP) architecture. They solve the problem for small numbers of processors, e.g. 16. But, the (global) memory references, which must be serialized on the bus, become a performance bottleneck, preventing the approach from scaling directly to many processors.

The most dramatic assault on the shared memory problem came with directory-based cache coherency mechanisms [11]. These approaches replace the bottleneck of the shared memory bus with a decentralized scheme in which processors sharing an interest in a specific location cooperate directly. The idea foregoes the global RAM memory as a literal specification of the memory image, and virtualizes it. That is, there is a single logical memory image evolving through time, but it may not literally exist.

In a typical directory scheme each memory location stores a record of the other processors having a copy of that location. As long as the copy stored in the location is valid, a processor can get a cacheable copy by visiting the location and having its processor ID added to the list. When an owner of a cached copy wants to change its value, invalidation messages must be sent to all processors having a copy, notifying them that the value is no longer current. In order to maintain a single evolving state the processor making the change is constrained to wait for acknowledgments from the other processors holding copies before committing the change. Protocols differ in detail as to how the process is implemented [8]

The key points regarding the directory-based schemes are that a per-location record of other owners replaces the globally visible sequence of references, and that changes to a cached location cannot take place until all owners have acknowledged that they've invalidated their copies. The former introduces a memory overhead and the latter introduces a performance overhead. For very small latencies (measured in terms of processor cycles) and a moderate number of processors the results are promising. The scalability of the scheme is in doubt because of the impact of increased latencies and greater potential sharing caused by more processors.

Finally, return to the original assumption, that hardware supported shared memory is desirable. Though widely held, the assumption is losing adherents. First, programming shared memory can be subtle. To improve performance relaxed consistency models have been advocated [8]. Further, it is easy to introduce race situations. Race detecting program analyzers, a new development in the decade, assist programmers but assuring correctness remains difficult. Second, to achieve good performance, focus on locality is essential, and doing so is rather more difficult with a flat, unstructured memory abstraction [8]. Third, of greatest value to parallel programmers is a global view of the computation, which is not synonymous with shared memory and can be achieved without it [35]. And, parallelizing compilers, the greatest motivators for hardware supported shared memory, have not been as effective as originally hoped. When one considers the engineering and hardware costs of hardware supported shared memory, it is worth considering the alternative.

3.2 Nonshared Memory Parallel Computers

Nonshared memory machines are designed without automatic hardware for global memory reference. The terms "distributed memory" and "message passing" have been used to describe such machines, but independent of sharing support all recent parallel computer designs (except small bus-based designs) distribute memory with the processors and pass messages, making those terms imprecise. So, "nonshared" will be used. Also, notice that fast communication hardware improves both shared and nonshared memory computers.

There are two milestone accomplishments for nonshared memory computers: communication primitives and clusters. When the decade dawned the standard communication primitives were synchronous and asynchronous message passing. These primitives are heavyweight in the sense of requiring repeated message copying, kernel calls, interrupts and acknowledgments. "Lightweight messaging" avoided some of the overhead, but new ideas were needed to speed communication. Two primitives that emerged were active messages and one-sided communication.

Active messages carry not only the destination processor address, but also the name of an event handler [9]. When a message arrives at a processor, it doesn't get stuffed into a buffer to wait passively to be processed, but rather the message causes the event handler to be activated. This process can perform any activity, including loading the information into a buffer to be passively processed. Generally, active messages are used to build more complex behaviors such as the "combining" operation for global summation. Such flexibility enables active messages to implement communication protocols, making them an ideal communication primitive.

One-sided communication refers to the ability of a processor to **get** data from or **put** data into another processor without its intervention. There is no mechanism to keep the memory coherent. The scheme generally requires a global address space so each processor can refer to any memory location. (In the Cray T3 implementation there are additional memory mapping constraints [7].) This is trivially accomplished by using the high-order bits of a memory address to encode the processor number. One-sided communication can be fast because of the limited involvement of the other processor. And, like active messages, one-sided communication is an ideal primitive for building more complex communication protocols.

The other major accomplishment in nonshared memory computers in the decade was cluster computers. With processor boards and interconnection technology readily available, researchers began assembling their own parallel computers [1]. In many instances the interconnect medium was standard LAN technology such as Ethernet, but some machines were built with more sophisticated point-to-point interconnect technology. Clusters became extremely common, providing many laboratories with inexpensive parallel computing power. Clusters have not supplanted parallel computers because the latter have more highly optimized interprocessor communication facilities – higher bandwidth and lower latency – and therefore deliver high performance.

In summary, both shared and nonshared memory architectures are available, though clusters are very widespread.

4   Programming Languages: "Program to Exploit the Machine's Features"

Though the advice to exploit a machine's features was still common when the decade began, many programmers soon discovered that doing so bound their code too tightly to a platform. When, as regularly happened, a (completely) new parallel computer became available, one's program was no longer "optimal" if it ever was. Indeed, the program likely relied on features that now worked differently or were no longer available. Programmers learned not to exploit a machine's features, but to distance themselves from its idiosyncrasies – their new synonym for "features." Portability became important to programmers.

Programming languages are perhaps the most effective way to distance programmers from hardware idiosyncrasies, since the compiler implements the computer-specific customizations. Had an adequate parallel programming language existed when the need for portability became evident, that language would clearly have become standard. Instead of having a finished language ready for wider adoption, however, parallel programming language researchers had only just begun working on the problem. During the decade dozens, perhaps a hundred parallel programming languages were invented worldwide. Few were ever used to program a parallel computer, and fewer still ever ran the application fast. In the meantime users simply continued with sequential programming languages (Fortran, C, C++), augmenting them with message passing libraries (PVM, MPI). This result was not unexpected [29]. The message passing approach, though more portable than a machine-specific language, gets its portability from the wide availability of the libraries, not from abstraction. Message passing remains too low-level to avoid embedding machine specifics, which differ from platform-to-platform and so have significant performance implications. The problem – portable parallel programming – remains unsolved in general.

Though the full problem has not been solved, considerable progress has been made. A brief review will highlight a few of the many achievements.

4.1   Parallelizing Compilers

The task of converting a program written in a sequential language into an equivalent parallel program was an active research area at the start of the decade [33]. There was substantial progress, including the SUIF compiler [16], which formed the basis of a community-wide compiler infrastructure. But, measured against the original goal of automatically parallelizing existing sequential programs without significant user assistance, the success was modest [15]. The goal was perhaps too ambitious in the first place, and researchers began to entertain the idea that a modest amount of user input, say in the form of compiler directives, or hints, could enable them to be successful. Such hints might not be too burdensome and achieve good parallel performance on legacy programs.

By 1993 the High Performance Fortran Forum [13], a committee of compiler, language and high performance computing specialists from academia, industry and government, was meeting to define a set of compiler directives with which to augment Fortran 90, a standard array extension of Fortran 77. The directives assisted the compiler with both program analysis and the details of parallel execution. Unlike the automatic parallelizing compiler research that relied on shared memory architectures, High Performance Fortran sought to target non-shared memory parallel computers as well. Compilers were permitted to follow or ignore the directives, and since the Forum had industrial participation, industrial strength compilers were expected to follow the yearlong language definition effort. And, indeed, IBM, Applied Parallel Research and the Portland Group soon produced compilers for much of the HPF language. Researchers at labs and universities also pursued compiler implementations. Programmers, however, found the language difficult to use. Ignoring the usual "new software instabilities," the fundamental reasons seemed to be [30] that the language had no underlying machine model and following the directives were optional for the compiler. Accordingly, programmers were never certain what the compiler was doing, or whether they were using parallelism effectively or not. Few HPF programs were written, and by decade's end most users and researchers had moved on to other approaches.

4.2   Language Extensions

An alternative to optional language directives is to give programmers explicit parallel programming facilities for which the compiler must generate code. These could form an entirely new language, but many researchers, mindful of the programmer aversion to adopting a new language, chose instead to extend an existing language with parallel constructs. And, because object oriented programming was maturing during the period, many of the extensions were applied to OO languages. So, for example, there were CC++, HPC++, etc. in addition to Cilk, BSP and many others.

In terms of advancing the state-of-the-art, language extensions were largely practical efforts designed to explore a specific capability. So, for example, Cilk [6] augmented C with the ability to fork a thread of computation on a procedure call, and CC++ focused on the problem of composing modules in a parallel context. With compilers, programmers skilled in the base language and an extant software base – extended languages include all programs of the base language as trivially extended – rapid development and evaluation were possible. Accordingly, extended languages were usually implemented to a point where application programs could run in parallel. In additional to solving implementational details, these experiments gave insight regarding the use and value of the extension.

Though a good research vehicle, the language extension approach did not produce a widely used parallel programming language. Several explanations can be conjectured. In some cases portability was a problem because to appropriate existing compiler technology and exploit the software base, languages required a shared memory platform. A more serious problem common to all extension approaches is a semantic conflict between the sequential semantics of the base language and the parallel semantics of the extensions. Though the relationship is clear to the language inventors, allowing them to be successful programmers, regular users are often unsure of the relationship between the two, leaving them unsure how to achieve good parallel results. Another issue might be called completeness. Extension languages as a class usually focus on one aspect of parallel programming, neglecting many others. Problems that match, work well, but many do not. For whatever the reason extension languages did not catch on.

4.3   New Languages

A new language can solve the problems handicapping other approaches. The language can have powerful abstractions that simplify parallel programming. Further, it can have clean, consistent semantics that incorporate recent language and compiler research. And there are no legacy programs forcing designers to preserve mistakes of the past. But, breaking from the past comes at a huge price: There are no programs and no programmers.

Nevertheless, many researchers explored new language designs over the decade. Because of the tremendous effort required to build a compiler, supporting software and documentation for a new language, few were implemented completely enough to assess fairly. Two that were were NESL [2] and ZPL [35]. The former, a clean functional language structured around the parallel prefix (scan) operator, targeted shared memory platforms, while the latter, a clean imperative language structured around a new region concept, targeted both shared and nonshared platforms. In both languages programmers were presented with a global view of the computation together with abstractions freeing them from implementing the concurrency or communication required for parallel execution. The interpreter or compiler, respectively, did all the work. These languages are powerful tools for those who know and understand them. But, to use them, one must learn them. And it may be that people's reluctance to learn a new language explains their limited adoption, though other explanations surely apply, too.

4.4   Libraries

The benefits of software reuse motivated many researchers to advocate library solutions to parallelism. Libraries like ScaLAPACK [24] sought to extend the tradition of scientific subroutines to parallel computers. Other researchers, recognizing the special problems introduced by dynamic and irregular data structures, offered a variety of solutions that emphasized runtime support. Examples include PARTI [23] and LPARX [18]. Object libraries were also the basis for still other approaches [17]. Typically, libraries provide good solutions to some, but not all, of the problems confronting the applications programmer, and without sufficient support for the other parts, libraries didn't generate a following commensurate with the investment.

5   Models: "Start with the PRAM Model, and Refine to a More Realistic Model"

Though there were tremendous advances in technology, architecture, programming systems and algorithms – not surveyed here because they are more problem-specific – the unifying research problem of the decade was to identify an effective model of parallel computation. Only a few of the thousands of published papers explicitly mentioned this topic in their titles or abstracts, but it was implicitly the subject of most studies, being the subtext for the research. An architecture is the embodiment of a more abstract machine, generalizing its specific details. The constructs of a programming language express operations relative to some virtual execution engine. An algorithm's formulation and analysis are relative to the costs, behaviors and resources of an idealized computer. For practical success these models must align as they do with the von Neumann model of sequential computation [28]. But there was no consensus about which model is best at the start of the decade [29], so, much of the research can be viewed as exploring the effectiveness of various abstractions.

Much was learned about the threads, PRAM and BSP models of shared memory and the CTA, message passing, and LoGP models of nonshared memory. But, no "winner" can be declared. Message passing reigns as the practical choice for large-scale parallel computing, while threads are the medium of choice for SMP multiprocessors. It is not unheard of for both models to be applied simultaneously – threads on shared memory for "node computations" and message passing among them. It may be that such a hybrid approach could become standard, though one hopes for further progress.

It is impossible in this space to review all of the insights gained regarding the above-mentioned models, but it is worth observing why the hybrid approach – threads + message passing – would make sense to some programmers. The problem the shared memory approaches have not solved is the exploitation of locality. Thus, while all memory accesses are cheap, as on SMPs, the shared models are efficient, but when communication costs dominate as they must by the laws of nature, nonlocal references are penalized and performance plummets. Conversely, message passing exploits locality to avoid communication latency and the overhead of both message construction and synchronization. Thus, while high latency costs reward using communication sparingly, message passing is efficient, but when cheap communication on small SMPs magnifies the overhead of the abstraction, performance is no longer competitive. That trade-off, though oversimplified, summarizes the import of much of the research on the models of computation.

Two simple examples emphasize the point. The quotation of this section advising the refinement from the PRAM model seemed rational when proposed. But the approach foundered because exploiting locality is both difficult and the essence of practical performance; the PRAM contributed little to that task. In the nonshared memory world, message passing, focused on the mechanism of communication rather than the fundamental property of locality. Then, when faster, one-sided communication came along, having little affect on locality, but significant affect on mechanism, the programs had to be rewritten. So, studying the models has revealed fundamentals in many different ways.

6   The Present

The foregoing discussion has been honest about the limitations of many of the research paths pursued during the last decade. They didn't solve the "big problem" – making parallel computation convenient, fast and portable – and so there is a tendency to presume that the whole enterprise has been unsuccessful. On the contrary, there are many dimensions in which it has been successful. For example, sustained TeraFLOPS-level performance (10^9 floating point operations per second) has been demonstrated [31]. Parallel computations are in everyday production use. And aggressive parallel computers continue to be produced.

Based on the foregoing review of the last decade's major accomplishments, the most pressing open problem is the lack of an effective general-purpose parallel programming language. What is the present status of achieving that goal? It is difficult to say since the path to the solution is unknown. Nevertheless, it is possible to assess progress based on less general parallel programming languages. Accepting that the desired language must be convenient, meaning that it has abstractions to make programming simple and effective, fast, meaning that the programs are as fast as programs produced by lower-level means, and portable, meaning that the programs run on all parallel platforms, then the best results to date have been demonstrated by ZPL [35]. ZPL supports only data parallelism and a limited form of threading, and thus fails the standard for "general purpose." However, it meets the other conditions of convenient, fast and portable.

Figure 1 shows sample performance from a recent paper measuring the NAS Multigrid benchmark computation [27]. MG computes over a hierarchy of arrays, the base being a 512x512x512 array of doubles and the other arrays being 1/2 size in all dimensions for each successive level. The results shown are for Co-array Fortran [3], ZPL and MPI message passing [20] on the Cray T3E. Co-array Fortran, being a Cray proprietary alternative to message passing, provides few abstractions and no portability. The numbers suggest, and the full paper demonstrates more conclusively, that the convenience of ZPL's high level abstractions are available at no performance penalty. The extent of that convenience can be indicated by data also provided in the paper [27] showing the number of productive lines of code (no comments or white space) of various types:

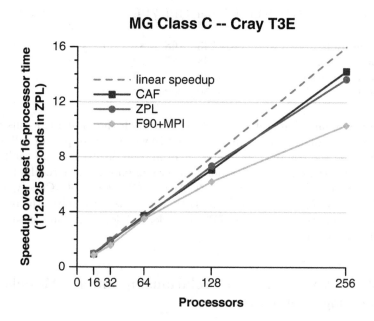

Fig. 1. Performance of three programs on the Cray T3E for the NAS MG Class C benchmark. The base array size is 512 x 512 x 512.

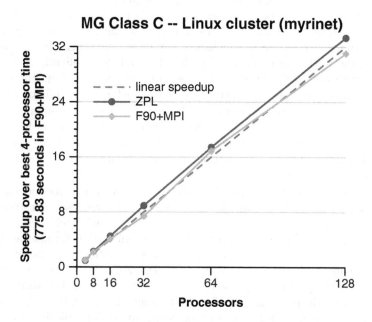

Fig. 2. Performance of two programs on the Los Alamos Cluster computer (Myrinet interconnect) for the NAS MG Class C benchmark.

	Co-Array Fortran	MPI	ZPL
Declarations	243	168	87
Computation	238	237	70
Communication	669	587	0
Total	1150	992	157

The communication statements, which are both the most numerous in the "local view" languages and the most difficult to write, are not part of ZPL source code, because the compiler generates them automatically. A more challenging architecture is the Los Alamos Linux Cluster computer, whose results for these same programs are shown in Figure 2. Again, ZPL does well. Clearly, for the limited domain of parallel programming that it treats, ZPL solves the big problem. (ZPL's successor, Advanced ZPL, is under development and contains more parallel abstractions.)

7   WYSIWYG: The Interrelationship among Models, Languages, Architectures

In the progress review above only a few of the most accessible accomplishments and impediments were discussed by topic area. Such isolated treatment allows the significant milestones to be cited, but it overlooks the cross-topic achievements. This interdisciplinary research was surprisingly abundant, involving projects connected with using Transputer machines, Dash, CM-5 and others. Being multidisciplinary, the work is more involved to describe and the implications are somewhat more subtle. In the interest of space, only one example from the author's research will be illustrated as a representative of such interdisciplinary projects.

The topic concerns the interrelationships between the programming language, the machine model and practical parallel computers. It is important for explaining how a high-level language (ZPL) can compete with low-level approaches (MPI), as explained in the last section. To understand the issues, recall quickly how ZPL was designed [12].

ZPL is a new language founded on the CTA parallel machine model. Being "founded on" means first that the semantics of the language's constructs are explained in terms of how they behave on the CTA virtual machine, and second that the ZPL compiler logically targets the CTA. Since the CTA abstracts practical parallel computers, programs can port to these different platforms simply by customizing back-end details of the compiler and support libraries. This approach solves the portability problem for classes of computers well abstracted by the CTA. From the point of view of understanding programs, the CTA's role for ZPL programmers is analogous to the von Neumann model's role for Fortran and C programmers for sequential computation. They imagine program execution as it would be on these idealized machines. This is sufficient for a clear behavioral understanding of a computation. But, there is more.

A programming language implements a *programming model* on top of the machine model [32]. That is, because the machine model is typically low-level, it is advantageous to add further abstractions that assist programmers with common operations. Fortran, C, etc. implement what might be called the imperative-procedural model, supporting array data structures, procedures with parameters, various forms of control flow, etc. These capabilities are not part of the machine model, but they are extremely useful in programming. More importantly, the machine model explains their operation. The programming model ZPL implements is called the *Phase Abstractions* model [32]. It includes various kinds of arrays, collective operations, procedures with parameters, control flow, etc.

When programmers write code whose performance matters, they must make decisions about alternative solutions. In a language like C they apply their understanding of how the object machine, represented by the von Newmann model, will execute the code to predict which of two solutions is better. Their knowledge cannot be exact, i.e. measured in nanoseconds, because C runs on many machines with different characteristics. But, relative knowledge is sufficient to make the choice. Their understanding of the behavior includes facts like shifts are faster than divides, a property from the machine model, as well as facts like passing pointers to values is generally cheaper than passing the values themselves, a property of the programming model. It is difficult to imagine writing an efficient program without this kind of information.

ZPL is unique among parallel languages for providing such performance information to programmers. The model is known as the what-you-see-is-what-you-get or WYSIWYG performance model [34], because it reveals performance-related information through syntactic cues in the source program. Using the cues, programmers can estimate the performance of their code relative to alternatives, and thus develop efficient solutions. How does it work?

Scalar computations on the CTA are performed by nodes abstracted as von Neumann processors. Thus, since the compiler is a source-to-source translator, ZPL to C, the scalar part of any ZPL program has its performance defined "as it would be in C." Said another way, a ZPL program running on one processor performs as the equivalent sequential C program.

The parallel activity of ZPL is more complex since it requires a clear understanding of the program's concurrency, how the compiler will allocate data across the processors, and how it will generate communication. In the WYSIWYG model, programmers are told how the facilities of their source programs will affect concurrency, data allocation and communication relative to the CTA. They will know that certain operations, like squaring the elements of an array

```
A := A * A;
```

will use no communication and be fully parallel, that a related operation of computing the sum of adjacent neighbors

```
A := A@east + A@west;
```

will use point-to-point communication and be fully parallel, and that finding the global sum of all elements

```
sum := +<<A;
```

will have communication and parallelism properties of the parallel prefix algorithm. The costs are specified in terms of the CTA, enabling one to estimate performance qualitatively, i.e. in terms of concurrent operations, though not quantitatively, i.e. in nanoseconds.

How do programmers use WYSIWYG performance information? They explore alternative solutions by reasoning through the probable cost of each solution. Since the compiler implements ZPL via the CTA onto practical machines, the predictions are correct in their gross characteristics. Such analysis has been illustrated for the Cannon [4] and SUMMA [26] matrix multiplication algorithms [34]. Though the two programs perform the same floating point operations and are of similar length, the Cannon program uses point-to-point communication and local data motion, while the SUMMA program relies on broadcast communication (flooding). These are sufficiently different characteristics that it would be impossible to compare them without some guidance about the relative costs of the features. Using the WYSIWYG model, it is possible to infer that the SUMMA should be the faster program, a prediction that has been verified across a series of parallel platforms [34]. Such analysis is the daily activity of ZPL programmers, and is a significant contributor to the language's good performance.

To summarize, there is a comprehensible connection between the program source code and the program execution based on how the compiler maps the source to the physical machine via the CTA abstraction. Using this knowledge allows programmers to control the behavior of any parallel machine modeled by the CTA, but because of the convenient high level abstractions, all of the work – specifying the parallelism, generating the communication commands, allocating and managing the data structures – is off-loaded to the compiler. Without such low-level details over-constraining the source code, the program can be efficiently retargeted to different machines, assuring that the performance model behaves as promised, completing the cycle.

8   The Future

At the start of the decade grand challenges in parallel computation seemed to be to build the ideal parallel architecture, create an efficient general purpose parallel programming language, formulate an optimal model of parallel computation, and discover the most efficient parallel algorithms for every interesting problem. We have come a long way towards achieving these goals, though none is fully solved. But, our understanding is deep and we are homing in on the solutions. So, for example, though the standard parallel architecture has not yet fully emerged, trends suggest it will have SMP nodes with one-sided communication among the nodes over a global address space; its communication network will be as fast as possible consistent with scaling to large numbers, since latency remains a significant cost; and without the need for shared memory, only moderate network bandwidth will be necessary.

The remaining grand challenge is the creation of an efficient, general-purpose parallel programming language. Since efficient languages covering limited forms of parallelism exist, such as ZPL, a general understanding of how to proceed is known. And, abstractions are known for many the kinds of parallelism that a general-purpose language would support. What is not known is how these forms of parallelism interact. At the language level how should one express a computation that is a mix of, say, tasks, pipelining and data parallelism? At the compiler level how can the different forms of parallelism be exploited to assure smooth execution with minimal overhead. These are the problems that must be solved over the next decade.

References

1. D. Becker, T. Sterling, D. Savarese, E. Dorbond, U. Ranawake, C. Parker: BE-OWULF A Parallel Workstation for Scientific Computation. Int'l Conf. on Parallel Processing (1995) 11-14
2. G. Blelloch, S. Chatterjee, J. Hardwick, J. Sipelstein, M. Zagha: Implementation of a Portable Nested Data-Parallel Language. J. Parallel and Distributed Computing (1994) 4-14
3. R. Niewerich, J. Reid: Co-array Fortran for Parallel Programming. Technical Report RAL-TR-1998-060. Rutherford Appleton Laboratory, Oxon UK (1998)
4. L. Cannon: A Cellular Computer to Implement the Kalman Filter Algorithm. Ph.D. Thesis, Montana State University (1969)
5. K. M. Chandy, C. Kesselman: CC++: A Declarative Concurrent Object Oriented Programming Notation. Technical Report CS-TR-92-01, Caltech (1993)
6. M. Frigo, C. Leiserson, K. Randall: The Implementation of the Cilk-5 Multi-threaded Language. ACM Conference on Programming Languages (1998)
7. Cray Inc. T3E Supercomputer. www.cray.com/products/systems/crayt3e/
8. D. Culler, J. Singh: Parallel Computer Architecture. Morgan-Kaufmann (1999)
9. W. Dally, J. Fiske, W. Horwat, J. Keen, J. Larivee, R. Lethin, P. Nuth: The Message Driven Processor: A Multicomputer Processing Node with Efficient Mechanisms. IEEE Micro (1992) 23–39
10. G. Fox, M. Johnson, G. Lyzenga, S. Otto, J. Salmon, D. Walker: Solving Problems on Concurrent Processors. Prentice Hall (1988)
11. D. Lenoski, K. Gharachorloo, A. Gupta, J. Hennessy: The Director-based Cache Coherency Protocol for the DASH Multiprocessors. 17th ISCA (1990) 148–159
12. L. Snyder: Foundations of Practical Parallel Programing Languages. In J. Ferranti, A. Hey (eds.): Portability and Performance for Parallel Processing. John Wiley (1993)
13. High Performance Fortran Forum: HPF Language Specification. Scientific Programming (1993) 2(1):1-270
14. Intel Corporation: www.intel.com/pressroom/archive/releases/cn1217.html
15. D. Kuck: High Performance Computing: Challenges for Future Systems. Oxford University Press (1996)
16. M. Hall, J. Anderson, S. Amarasinghe, B. Murphy, S.-W. Liao, E. Bugnion, M. Lam: Maximizing Multiprocessor Performance with the SUIF Compiler. IEEE Computer (1996)

17. S. Karmesin, J. Crotinger, J. Cummings, S. Haney, W. Humphrey, J. Reynders, S. Smith, T. Williams: Array Design and Expression Evaluation in POOMA II. Lecture Notes in Computer Science, Vol. 1505. Springer-Verlag (1998) 231-238

18. LPARX Programming System: www-cse.ucsd.edu/groups/hpcl/lparx.html

19. Mizell, D.: Personal communication. August (2000)

20. Message Passing Interface Forum. MPI A Message Passing Interface Standard. Int. J. of Supercomputing Applications (1994) 8(314):169-416

21. A. Formella, J. Keller, T. Walle: HPP: A High Performance PRAM. Euro-Par 96. Lecture Notes in Computer Science, Vol. 1124. Springer-Verlag (1996)

22. D. Lerman, L. Rudolph: Parallel Evaluation of Parallel Processors. Plenum Press, (1993)

23. A. Sussman, J. Saltz, R. Das, S. Gupta, D. Mavriplis, R. Ponnusany, K. Crowley: PARTI Primitives for Unstructured and Block Structured Problems. Computer Systems Engineering (1992) 3(1):73-86

24. L. Blackford, et al.: ScaLAPACK: A Linear Algebra Library for Message-Passing Computers. SIAM Conference on Parallel Processing (1997)

25. Standard Performance Evaluation Corporation, www.spec.org

26. R. von de Geijn, J. Watts: SUMMA Scalable Universal Matrix Multiplication Algorithm. Technical Report TR-95-13, University of Texas Austin (1995)

27. B. Chamberlain, S. Deitz, L. Snyder: A Comparative Study of the NAS MG Benchmark across Parallel Languages and Architectures. Proc. of the 2000 ACM/IEEE Supercomputing Conference on High Performance Networking and Computing. November (2000)

28. L. Snyder: Experimental Validation of Models of Parallel Computation. In: A. Hofmann, J. van Leeuwen (eds.): Lecture Notes in Computer Science, Vol. 1000. Springer-Verlag (1995) 78-100

29. L. Snyder: Type architecture, shared memory and the corollary of modest potential. Annual Review of CS (1986) I:289-317

30. T. Ngo, L. Snyder, B. Chamberlain: Portable Performance of Data Parallel Languages. Supercomputing '97 (1997)

31. University of Tennessee Top 500: netlib2.cs.utk.edu/benchmark/top500/.html

32. G. Alverson, W. Griswold, C. Lin, D. Notkin, L. Snyder: Abstractions for Portable Scalabel Parallel Programming. IEEE TPDS (1998) 9(1):71-86

33. M. Wolfe: Optimizing Supercompilers for Supercomputers. MIT Press (1989)

34. B. Chamberlain, S.-E. Choi, E Lewis, L. Snyder, D. Weathersby: ZPL's WYSIWYG Performance Model. IEEE 3rd Workshop on High-level Parallel Programming Models and Supportive Environments (1998) 50-61

35. L. Snyder: Programmer's Guide to ZPL. MIT Press (1999)

Computational Complexity and Mathematical Proofs

Juris Hartmanis

Cornell University
Ithaca, NY 14853
U.S.A.

Abstract. This paper discusses how the major computational complexity classes, P, NP and PSPACE, capture different computational properties of mathematical proofs and reveal new quantitative aspects of mathematics.

1 Proof Finding and Checking

One of the most important open problems in computer science is the P versus NP problem, where P designates all the languages accepted by a *deterministic* Turing machine in polynomial-time and NP designates the languages accepted by a *nondeterministic* Turing machine in polynomial-time. It is well known that NP contains a rich variety of very important computational problems for which we do not know any deterministic polynomial-time solutions. The P versus NP problem is to determine if P is or is not different from NP.

The importance of this problem has been dramatically emphasized by a recent announcement by the Clay Mathematics Institute of the seven Millennium Prize Problems in mathematics. The P versus NP problem is one of these seven problems and the solution of each of these problems will earn a million dollar prize.

The P versus NP problem is clearly an important problem for computer science and for practical computing, but here we want to emphasize that it is also a fundamental problem about the nature of mathematics. In particular, we want to illustrate how computational complexity concepts allow us to formulate new quantitative questions about the nature of proofs and gain new insights about mathematics.

To make this claim more precise, let $\mathcal{F}$ be a sound axiomatizable mathematical proof system. That means that $\mathcal{F}$ proves only true theorems and that the set of provable theorems is recursively enumerable. The key concept in the definition of "formal system" is how a proof is presented and verified. For simplicity, in our definition of formal system we insist that the proof must be presented as a sequence of horizontal lines written on a two dimensional page. Each line is a string over a fixed alphabet and is written in a left-justified form directly below the proceeding line. Moreover, we insist that the proof can be checked by a deterministic finite automaton (DFA) in the following way. The DFA proof checker

R. Wilhelm (Ed.): Informatics. 10 Years Back. 10 Years Ahead, LNCS 2000, pp. 251–256, 2001.

starts at the top-left corner of the page and reads two adjacent symbols at a time from the first two lines of the proof. The DFA scans the input in an oblivious manner; it reads (compares) the first two lines, scanning from left to right, and returns to the left margin to read (compare) the second and third lines, left to right, and so forth. When the DFA reaches the bottom right corner, it accepts or rejects. The proofs of the formal system are exactly those sequences of lines accepted by the DFA proof checker, and the theorems of the formal system are the first lines of the proof. That is, we assume that all proofs start with the statement of the theorem and end with Q.E.D.

Equivalently, the proof in $\mathcal{F}$ could be presented in a straight line with a two-head finite automaton proof checker which reads the proof scanning from left to right.

At first glance, our definition of formal system may seem too restrictive. But it is actually quite robust since more powerful proof checkers do not change the classes defined below [3].

Let $\mathcal{F}$ be a formal system and $D_{\mathcal{F}}$ be the corresponding proof checker, as described above.

Definition 1. *The* width *of a proof in $\mathcal{F}$ is the length of the longest line (or the maximal separation of the two reading heads of the two-head proof checker). The* width *of a theorem* T *in $\mathcal{F}$, is the width of the narrowest proof of* T *in $\mathcal{F}$. The* length *of the proof is the number of symbols in the proof.*

We now define the class of theorems with polynomially-wide proofs.

Definition 2. *We say that a language $\mathcal{L}$ is in PWT, that is, $\mathcal{L}$ is a set of* polynomially-wide theorems, *if there exist a* k $\geq$ 1 *and a formal system $\mathcal{F}$, such that* T *is in $\mathcal{L}$ if and only if* T *has a proof in $\mathcal{F}$ of width less or equal to* $|T|^k$.

Theorem 1 *PWT=PSPACE.*

Proof. (This proof is included to illustrate the interaction between the recursively enumerable set of theorems, the proof checker and the width of theorems). Let $\mathcal{L}$ be in PWT. Then, using our definition of a formal system, there exists a constant k and a deterministic finite automaton, the proof checker, such that T is in $\mathcal{L}$ if and only if T is a theorem of $\mathcal{F}$ with a proof of width less or equal to $|T|^k$.

To verify that the desired proof exists, on input T, a nondeterministic Turing machine M can guess a width m less or equal to $|T|^k$, guess successive lines of length less or equal to m and use the proof checker to verify that these are successive lines of the proof of T in $\mathcal{F}$. If such proof is found T is accepted. Thus T is in $\mathcal{L}$ if and only if M(T) accepts.

Since NPSPACE is contained in PSPACE, we see that $\mathcal{L}$ is in PSPACE.

Conversely, suppose that $\mathcal{L}$ is in PSPACE. Then there is a Turing machine M which accepts $\mathcal{L}$. We can define a formal system that uses the instanteous descriptions (ID) of M's computation as lines of the proof. Since the ID's change only near the tape head, a deterministic finite automaton can check if one ID follows another according to the transition table of M. Moreover, the length of the ID's are polynomial in the length of the input string T, so the width of the proof is polynomial in length of T. Thus there is a formal system which proves exactly the strings in $\mathcal{L}$ using polynominially-wide proofs. Therefore,

$$\text{PWT} = \text{PSPACE}.$$

□

We can now state the relation of mathematical proofs to the complexity classes P, NP, PSPACE and PWT.

Let $\mathcal{F}$ be a sound axiomatizable system sufficiently strong to formulate and prove at least elementary facts in number theory and automata construction.

Theorem 2 *Let $k \geq 1$ be an integer. Then*
$L_1 = \{Th.\ x.\ Proof : y \ \Box \mid |y| \leq |x|^k$ *and y is a proof of x in $\mathcal{F}\}$*
is a P-complete set.
$L_2 = \{Th.\ x.\ Proof : \#^t \ \Box \mid$ *there is a proof y of x in $\mathcal{F}$ with $|y| = t \leq |x|^k\}$*
is a NP-complete set.
$L_3 = \{Th.\ x.\ Proof : \#^t \ \Box \mid t \leq |x|^k$ *and there is a proof y of x in $\mathcal{F}$ of width $t\}$*
is a PSPACE-complete set.

Informally, we can say that checking the correctness of proofs in $\mathcal{F}$ is a P-complete problem and thus characterizes P and that finding proofs of bounded-length for theorems in $\mathcal{F}$ characterizes NP. Similarly, finding proofs of bounded-width for theorems in $\mathcal{F}$ characterizes PSPACE.

It is interesting to observe that the PSPACE = PWT result emphasizes that the polynomially-wide theorems are exactly those theorems whose proofs can be presented to an intelligent student (or proof checker with finite memory) on a polynomially-wide black board. On the blackboard the proof is presented few successive lines at a time. By the end of the proof the student will be convinced that a proof exists, but may not remember it (just as a DFA proof checker).

Thus the basic questions about the difficulty of checking proofs, finding proofs or determining if there is a proof that can be presented in a given space (or found in this space) correspond to and characterize the three most important computational complexity classes.

As a matter of fact, by choosing our proof systems accordingly, we can represent languages in NP as the sets of theorems for which there exist polynomially-long proofs, and PSPACE as the sets of theorems for which there exist polynomially-wide proofs.

Intuitively, from all our experience with proving theorems and checking proofs, we believe that the difficulty increases dramatically as we go from checking of proofs, to finding proofs, to finding proofs that can be presented in a given space (with erasing). Still there is no proof that these tasks (or families of sets) are different. We sincerely believe that the resolution of these problems is going to give deep insights about the complexity of computational problems as well as a deeper understanding of the nature of mathematics and, indirectly, creative work.

2   Interactive Proofs

In this section we discuss the possibility to give interactively convincing evidence that a theorem is provable in $\mathcal{F}$ without showing the complete proof, which may be too long to read.

Clearly, if we do not give a complete proof to a verifier (that does not have the power or time to generate and check the proof), then we cannot expect the verifier to be completely convinced that the theorem is provable. This led to a very fascinating problem: how can a verifier be convinced *with high probability* that a given theorem is provable without seeing the whole proof, and how rapidly can this be done?

This problem has been formulated and extensively studied in terms of *interactive protocols* [Gol89]. Informally, an interactive protocol consists of a *Prover* and a *Verifier*. The prover is an all powerful Turing Machine (TM) and the Verifier is a TM which operates in time polynomial in the length of the input. In addition, the Verifier has a random sourc e (e.g., a fair coin) not visible to the Prover. In the beginning of the interactive protocol the Prover and the Verifier receive the same input string. Then, the Prover tries to convince the Verifier, through a series of queries and answers, that the input string belongs to a given language. The Prover succeeds if the Verifier accepts with probability greater than 2/3. The probability is computed over all possible coin tosses made by the Verifier. However, the Verifier must guard against imposters masquerading as the real Prover. That is, the Verifier must not be convinced to accept a string **not** in the language with probability greater than 1/3, even if the Prover lies. By repeating this process the probabilities can be improved to any desired degree. We summarize this in the next definition.

Definition 3. *Let* V *be a probabilistic polynomial-time TM and let* P *be an arbitrary TM.* P *and* V *share the same input tape and communicate via a communication tape.* P *and* V *form an interactive protocol for a language* $\mathcal{L}$ *if*

1. x in $\mathcal{L} \Longrightarrow Prob[$P-V *accepts* x $] > 2/3$.
2. x not in $\mathcal{L} \Longrightarrow \forall P^*, \ Prob[P^*$-V *accepts* x$] < 1/3$

A language $\mathcal{L}$ *is in IP if there exist* P *and* V *which form an interactive protocol for* $\mathcal{L}$.

Clearly, IP contains all NP languages, because in polynomial-time the Prover can give the Verifier the entire proof. In such a protocol, the Verifier cannot be fooled and never accepts a string not in the language. To illustrate how randomness can generalize the concept of a proof, we look at an interactive protocol for a language not known to be in NP. Consider GNI, the set of pairs of graphs that are not isomorphic. GNI is known to be in co-NP and believed not to be in NP. However, GNI does have an interactive protocol [1]. For small graphs, the Verifier can easily determine if the two graphs are not isomorphic. For sufficiently large graphs, the Verifier solicits help from the Prover to show that G_i and G_j are not isomorphic, as follows:

1. The Verifier randomly selects G_i or G_j and a random permutation of the selected graph. This process is independently repeated n times, where n is the number of vertices in G_j. If the graphs do not have the same number of vertices, they are clearly not isomorphic. This sequence of n randomly chosen, randomly permuted graphs is sent to the Prover. Recall that the Prover has not seen the Verifier's random bits. This assumption is not necessary, but simplifies the exposition.
2. The Verifier asks the Prover to determine, for each graph in the sequence, which graph, G_i or G_j, was the one selected. If the Prover answers correctly, then the Verifier accepts.

Suppose the two original graphs are not isomorphic. Then, only one of the original graphs is isomorphic to the permuted graph. The Prover simply answers by picking that graph. If the graphs are isomorphic, then the Prover has at best 2^{-n} chance of answering all n questions correctly. Thus, the Verifier cannot be fooled often. Therefore, GNI $\in$ IP.

Note that GNI is believed to be an incomplete set in co-NP. So, the preceding discussion does not show that co-NP $\subseteq$ IP. In fact, the computational power of interactive protocols was not fully appreciated until Lund, Fortnow, Karloff and Nisan [4] showed that IP actually contains the entire Polynomial Hierarchy. This result then led Shamir [5] to completely characterize IP.

Theorem 3 *IP = PSPACE.*

We recall that PSPACE = PWT and therefore we see that the ability to convince a verifier that with high probability a theorem has a proof, quite surprisingly, depends on the width of the theorem and not on its length which could be exponentially bigger. It is very interesting that this result focuses our attention on a new dimension of proofs and yields quantitative results in terms of this new dimension - the width of proofs.

Though we do not yet have a definition of *ease of understanding proofs*, intuitively, we expect that among equally long theorems the ones with narrow proofs are more easily understood.

3   Conclusion

We believe that these results, in particular the IP = PSPACE result in the IP = PWT interpretation, reveal new and interesting insights about the quantitative nature of mathematical proofs and thus about the fundamental nature of mathematics. The two dimensional shape of the proof determines how rapidly one can give overwhelming evidence that there is a proof without showing the whole proof. These results also add to the importance of resolving the P versus NP problem and the related P versus PSPACE and NP versus PSPACE problems.

Acknowledgement

This paper is based on the concepts in [3].

References

[1] O. Goldreich, S. Micali, and A. Widgerson. Proofs that yield nothing but their validity and a methodology of cryptographic protocol design. In *IEEE Symposium on Foundations of Computer Science*, pages 174 – 187, 1986.

[2] S. Goldwasser. Interactive proof systems. In *Proceedings of Symposia in Applied Mathematics*, pages 108 – 128. American Mathematical Society, 1989.

[3] J. Hartmanis, D. Ranjan R. Chang, and P. Rohatyi. On IP = PSPACE and theorems with narrow proofs. *EATCS-Bulletin*, 41:166 – 174, 1990.

[4] C. Lund, L. Fortnow, H. Karloff, and N. Nisan. Algebraic methods for interactive proofs. In *Proceedings 31st IEEE Symp. on the Foundations of Computer Science*, pages 1 – 10, 1990.

[5] A. Shamir. IP = PSPACE. In *Proc. 31st IEEE Symp. on the Foundations of Computer Science*, pages 11 – 15, 1990.

Logic for Computer Science: The Engineering Challenge*

Wolfgang Thomas

RWTH Aachen, Lehrstuhl für Informatik VII,
52056 Aachen, Germany
thomas@informatik.rwth-aachen.de

Abstract. This essay is a reflection on the roles which logic played and can play in computer science. We recall the obvious merits of mathematical logic as a parent discipline of computer science, from which many fields in theoretical computer science emerged, but then address some unresolved issues in connection with the engineering tasks of computer science. We argue that logic has good perspectives here, following a tradition which is closer to Leibniz than to Hilbert and Gödel.

1 Introduction

Logic is a cornerstone of scientific methodology and thus belongs to the foundation of every scientific discipline. For computer science, logic plays a still more central role:

- Logic is a parent discipline of computer science; historically computer science emerged from problems and methods which were developed in mathematical logic.
- Logic is a basic constituent of the computer science curriculum; in fact, there is agreement that it is required in a stricter sense in computer science education than, for example, in mathematics.
- Logic has produced a large reservoir of methods and theories for computer science (which are often typical for this application area and no more to be counted to mathematical logic itself).

The present paper starts with an elaboration on these aspects.

But beyond these merits and contributions of "logic in computer science", there is also a deeper (and I think more problematic) level of the relation between logic and its computer science context. In the never-ending discussion of the role of "theory" in computer science, and why (for instance) logic should continue to be taught in the way it is, I find implicit criticisms and challenges which are rarely made explicit. Much of this discussion is due to the different viewpoints which scientists and engineers have. For classical mathematics (especially, for

---

* Transcription of a lecture given at the Dagstuhl Anniversary Conference, Saarbrücken, August 2000

R. Wilhelm (Ed.): Informatics. 10 Years Back. 10 Years Ahead, LNCS 2000, pp. 257–267, 2001.

analysis), it is generally accepted that engineers have a legitimate special view and use of the subject. For the concepts and techniques of logic, which today are used (mostly in an implicit way, unfortunately) in the daily work of hundreds of thousands of software engineers, an engineering view has not yet emerged as natural and legitimate. Today, engineers usually have a rather distorted view of logic; many use the term "logic" just to mean a circuit, i.e. a realization of a Boolean formula. But logic has the potential to offer much more, namely to supply another basic "calculus" with a core of techniques which should be known and applied by every professional systems engineer. This would involve a certain move in the orientation of logic, from "logic *in* computer science" to what I would call "logic *for* computer science". In the second half of this paper I will try to explain these challenges in more detail, in which way they deviate from the focus of classical mathematical logic (and even of classical theoretical computer science), and why I find them to be promising tracks on which logic can contribute to progress in computer science.

2   Mathematical Logic as an Origin

There is not a single event which can be called the birth of computer science; indeed, this new discipline evolved by a complicated interaction between engineers, mathematicians, and also logicians. But there are eminent single contributions which surely were essential in forming this new scientific field, several of them from mathematical logic. Among them, Alan Turing's paper of 1936 *On computable numbers, with an application to the Entscheidungsproblem* is a prominent example. In this paper, one finds a proposal to capture in precise terms the most fundamental notion of computer science ("algorithm"), one finds the idea of a universal machine (anticipating the concept of programmable processor), and also first unsolvability results, showing principal limitations of the algorithmic method.

Turing's paper was a contribution to mathematical logic; it showed that the most famous problem of the subject at the time, "Hilbert's Entscheidungsproblem", is algorithmically unsolvable. Let us briefly recall these logical origins of computer science.

Mathematical logic is a relatively new branch of logic which took shape in the second half of the nineteenth century. At first, the aim was to join logic with the ideas of arithmetic and algebra, in order to make logic accessible to the powerful algebraic techniques of formula manipulation. In the works of Boole and Schröder, interesting parts of deductive reasoning were cast in algebraic formalisms (in "Boolean algebra" and Schröders "Algebra der Logik").

But these formalisms covered only small fragments of mathematical language and inference methods. In his pioneering monograph *Begriffsschrift*, Gottlob Frege overcame these deficits. He proposed a universal formal language (in particular, involving quantifiers), in which one could express all ordinary mathematics, and he developed a syntactic proof calculus which was strong enough to imitate mathematical proofs.

This success suffered from a drawback and some irritation which originated in Cantorian set theory by the set theoretic paradoxes, for example, by the paradox of the set of sets which are not an element of itself (discovered independently by Zermelo and Russell). Cantor himself had been aware of the subtleties which had to be observed when dealing with infinite sets (and he had spoken of consistent and inconsistent sets). But for a formal reconstruction of the foundations of mathematics, as designed by Frege, the Zermelo-Russell paradox came as a surprise and a shock. Hilbert, who felt like Cantor, was concerned about the perspective that mathematics might be put into doubt. He proposed what is called "Hilbert's Program": to get rid of the worries about the foundations of mathematics in two steps:

- by simulating ordinary mathematics in a sufficiently strong formal system (with a syntactic proof calculus),
- by showing with elementary means ("finitist methods", which were not subject to doubt) that in this formal system a contradiction like $0 = 1$ could not be derived.

Part of the second item was "Hilbert's Entscheidungsproblem": it asked for a procedure by which it could be decided whether a given formula (like $0 = 1$) is or is not derivable in the proof calculus.

In pursuing this program, mathematical logicians clarified a concept which proved to be central in the subsequent formation of computer science, namely the concept of a formal system, with a clear separation of syntax and semantics, with the notion of a formal proof calculus (defining "computational steps"), and its properties of soundness, completeness, and consistency. The master example of such a formal system was first-order logic (or predicate logic). Later, in computer science, formal systems were created in hundreds of different versions, for example in the definition of specification languages, process calculi, and programming languages. But in the original context of first-order logic, the breakthrough results of mathematical logic were established:

- Gödel's completeness theorem, showing that a first-order formula is valid (true in every model) iff it can be derived in the proof calculus,
- Gödel's incompleteness theorem, which states that the sentences which are true in the fixed model of arithmetic cannot be generated completely by an axiom system (like the axioms of first-order Peano arithmetic),
- Church's and Turing's clarification of the notion of algorithm and the proof that Hilbert's Entscheidungsproblem is undecidable for first-order logic.

The last two results meant that the second part of Hilbert's Program could not be carried out in the form as originally envisaged. On the other hand, the admirable and tedious work of Frege, Russell, Whitehead, and many others had produced the astonishing fact that the first part of Hilbert's program was indeed realizable, first in systems of higher-order logic, and finally, with the development of set theory, even in first-order logic (based on the first-order axiom system ZFC, "Zermelo-Fraenkel set theory with the axiom of choice").

The idea of coding a significant part of science in such a formal manner was not new: Two hundred years earlier, Gottfried Wilhelm Leibniz had formulated the far-reaching vision of a *characteristica universalis*, a universal language in which knowledge could be expressed and manipulated in a computational fashion:

> It should be possible to set up a kind of alphabet of human thoughts, and to invent and to decide everything by a combination of its letters and by the analysis of the words composed from them.

Leibniz had overoptimistic views about the realizability of his project (maybe typical for scientists who have to raise funds):

> It would cost no more work than what is already now invested in many treatises and encyclopedias. I think that some selected persons can do the job within five years, but that after two years they are already able to master by an unfallible calculus the disciplines which are required most for life, i.e., moral and metaphysics. [1]

At first sight, Leibniz's vision looks much too ambitious to be feasible, even when restricted to the domain of mathematics; indeed, I do not know of any mathematician or philosopher who agreed to Leibniz in that his program might be worth trying. Leibniz himself could provide only very small technical steps towards his goal (among them the sketch of a fragment of Boolean algebra). Nevertheless, only two centuries later the program was realized for the domain of mathematics.

However, an important difference has to be noted: The aim of mathematical logic was to clarify a very general methodological question, that of consistency of mathematical assumptions and reasoning; so it was sufficient to code mathematics *in principle*, without any claims on a practical use of the formalization. On the other hand, Leibniz took the approach of a knowledge engineer who wanted to set up a *practical calculus of information processing*. Only in the continuation of logic within computer science, this practical aspect began to play a role again, when logic programming and automated theorem proving were developed. These two views of logic, that of a foundational discipline as perceived by Hilbert and Gödel and that of a framework for practical computation as suggested by Leibniz, point precisely to the question which profile logic should have today in the context of computer science.

The great success of mathematical logic was first seen in the fact that a number of new mathematical subjects came into existence, among them recursion theory, model theory, set theory, and proof theory. The *Handbook of Mathematical Logic* [2] gives a first impression of their beauty and strength. These new mathematical subjects were created in the very short time of only two or three generations, and they helped to establish new connections between logic and other mathematical subjects (for example, algebra). On the elementary level, a core theory emerged which is now part of the undergraduate curriculum:

---

[1] Quotations from [5] (my translation from Latin)

Propositional logic, syntax and semantics of first-order logic, a proof calculus, its soundness and completeness, basic undecidability and incompleteness results, and expressiveness results (like the compactness theorem or separation results on the expressive power of logics).

3   Logic in Computer Science

Apart from the new subjects created within mathematical logic, many areas in theoretical computer science developed as offsprings of logic. For example, the above-mentioned logic subjects of recursion theory, model theory, and proof theory all gave rise to new disciplines in theoretical computer science with a new specific orientation: From recursion theory, the area of complexity theory emerged, addressing the quantitative refinement of computability, with many new concepts and methods. Similarly, model theory took a specific shift in response to "the challenge of computer science" (see Gurevich's paper [3]), by focussing on finite models and establishing the new field of descriptive complexity theory. Finally, the subject of proof theory had many continuations in computer science, notably type theory, which itself plays a central role e.g. in programming language semantics.

Today it seems impossible to give a complete list all fields in computer science which are rooted in logic. Here is an excerpt (and the reader may consult the *Handbook of Logic in Computer Science* [1] to get a more detailed picture):

- programming language semantics,
- type theory, linear logic, categorical theories,
- λ-calculus, π-calculus,
- specification logics, e.g., dynamic logic, Hoare logic, temporal logic, systems like VDM, Z,
- finite model theory, data base theory,
- term rewriting, unification, logic programming, functional programming,
- automated theorem proving,
- program verification,
- process calculi and concurrency theory,
- modal logic, logics of knowledge

This list is to be complemented by families of concrete software systems which were designed as direct outgrowths of theories of logic. Among these "practical successes" of logic, there are the following:

- Systems for circuit design,
- Relational data base systems,
- Expert systems,
- Model checkers and theorem provers.

Despite this rich landscape of theoretical subjects and concrete systems, the status of logic in computer science is under dispute (e.g., regarding its role in the curriculum), and logic faces criticism of practitioners as being too formal and too remote from the world of software (or systems) development practice. When leafing through the proceedings of logic conferences in computer science, one gets the feeling that this nice and deep research is not terribly influential in mainstream computer science. A standard reply to this is that the practice of computer science is not yet scientific and that some time in the future the relevance of the precise methods will be appreciated. I think that this kind of reply makes things too easy and avoids facing some challenges which in fact can prove very fruitful for logic.

4   Some Challenges in the Context of Engineering

A characteristic feature of mathematical logic is its concentration on formal systems as a whole. Usually, a logical framework is a formal system, and the statements and claims made are concerned with global properties, like consistency or completeness, expressiveness in comparison with other formal systems, or questions of decidability and complexity of algorithmic problems about these systems. Often, this involves the reduction of the phenomena under consideration to the "atomic level", on which the technical work is then performed. This applies not only to classical mathematical logic but also to most of the above-mentioned logic-oriented areas in theoretical computer science.

Some well-known examples might illustrate this. In Turing's analysis of the notion of algorithm, one finds a reduction of the conceivable computational processes to the most elementary units, the Turing machine moves, and these units are argued to be "complete" for discrete computation. Similarly, in the conception of a first-order proof calculus, some very elementary proof steps are isolated and formulated as proof rules, and the calculus as a whole is shown to be sound and complete. Similar statements can be made about other calculi, like the λ-calculus or the π-calculus, and many more formalisms (see, for example, the concluding section of Milner's Turing Award Lecture [4]). The maturity and experience which logic has gained in setting up, analyzing, and comparing formal systems allows today such studies of high subtlety and scholastic refinement; it is fun to play on this stage. (In other branches of theoretical computer science, like the theory of formal languages, the same tendency is to be seen, only different types of formal systems are studied.)

The study of formal systems and their global properties corresponds to the situation in the natural sciences where one also tries to reduce existing phenomena to elementary units (facts and laws) such that the observed phenomena can be explained from them. This scientific analysis is useful and essential also in computer science for a deeper understanding of the "natural laws" of information processing, but it is somewhat opposite to the interests of an engineer. He is less concerned with the extreme reduction of processes or objects, but more with the synthesis of systems from "usable" components which very rarely are "atomic", and he needs a clear terminological framework which supports this synthesis. This explains why the computer science professional usually handles units which are of a quite different nature than the structures which he sees in his undergraduate courses, say in logic or theoretical computer science. The (software or systems) engineer would appreciate from logic *concepts and techniques as thinking tools* [2], *which are clean, adequate, and convenient, to support him (or her) in describing, reasoning about, and constructing complex software and hardware systems.*

This is different from the conception of uniform general theories; it emphasizes construction rather than reduction. In the present landscape of logic, such constructive and useful tools exists. Let us mention some of them:

- Propositional logic and ordered binary decision diagrams,
- temporal logic and model-checking,
- Horn clause logic and logic programming,
- the relational data model.

But these concepts and techniques are just mosaic pieces of a more comprehensive "discrete system theory" which an engineer could use. Much has to be done to complete this mosaic. To give some more detailed perspective, I list five general challenges, the first four being more of methodological nature, the last giving a kind of research direction.

4.1   Pragmatics Is Important

The clients of classical mathematical logic were mathematicians with an interest in the foundations of mathematics. This is a small, excellently qualified audience. In computer science, logic is (or should be) applied by hundreds of thousands of average software engineers. It is obvious that the two communities need rather different presentations of logic. Moreover, the impact of the software engineers' logic education is (via the quality of their software products) by far greater than the impact which logic has ever reached in foundational studies. Logic should respond to this challenge, and it would gain a much higher significance by a tighter connection to engineering. The pragmatics of logic formalisms, i.e., their suitability for everyday use, is here more important than classical criteria like completeness.

Let me illustrate this with a very small example. Propositional temporal logic of linear time is known to be expressively equivalent to the first-order language over labelled orderings of order type ω. For a logician or a mathematician it is trivial to use first-order formulas rather than temporal formulas. But in practice, it makes a difference whether one has to write down explicitly the variables for time points (as is necessary in first-order logic) or whether one may use temporal operators which spare this. Experience shows that engineers prefer very much the variable-free framework over first-order logic. Such aspects are irrelevant in classical logic but have to be addressed if a widespread use of a formalism is important.

---

[2] This term is due to C. Jones; see his contribution to this volume.

4.2   Building a New Model Theory

In classical model theory, one considers first-order structures and relations and operations like extension, elementary extension, the formation of products, etc. Usually, one considers one model at a time. An average software engineer, modelling some application say in the object-oriented UML-framework ("Unified Modelling Language"), may handle hundreds of structures at the same time, of different sorts, and with much more complicated interactions like instantiation, multiple references, inheritance, etc. Neither is there (up to now) a well-defined semantics for the full range of the UML language, nor is there a clear and unambiguous terminology which would guarantee a consistent use of the object-oriented framework. To supply a clean and clear way of handling this chaotic world of models is both a very practical and theoretically demanding task. A student who compares the models of his logic course to the complexities of the models which he has to treat in his software engineering project work may come to the conclusion that theory is not very useful for him.

4.3   Merging the Languages of Formulas and Diagrams

There are two basic approaches to the specification of systems and their behaviour: Formula based frameworks (like temporal logic, VDM, Z) and diagram based formalisms (like SDL, UML, Statecharts). Both have their typical advantages. By their conception, formula based frameworks are "compositional"; their formulas or terms are constructed inductively, and the definition of the semantics usually follows this inductive structure. On the other hand, diagrams and graph-like objects are usually more flexible in use, and also algorithmic problems like satisfiability or simplification ("minimization") are often solved more easily here than over formulas. Classical results giving a precise connection between the two approaches are, for instance, the equivalence between Boolean formulas and ordered binary decision diagrams, and the equivalence between regular expressions (or monadic second-order logic over words) and finite automata. The large-scale use of specifications by diagrams seems to be typical for computer science (and probably is another aspect of pragmatics). Theories which support merging diagram-based languages with term- or formula-based ones would help in designing better specification languages.

4.4   Taking Hierarchy Seriously

The description of large (software or hardware) systems is only possible by referring to their hierarchical structure, often reflecting different levels of abstraction. A "specification" is often more a kind of book than a kind of formula. The basic models of logic (and of theoretical computer science), like first-order structures or automata, are flat, and their measure of complexity is often simply their size (number of elements or states). This is highly inadequate in the study of nontrivial systems; "hierarchy level" should be a first-class parameter. There are promising theoretical models supporting hierarchical descriptions and constructions, like communicating or hierarchical state-machines, statecharts, or Gurevich's abstract state machines. But the theory of their behaviour is not yet well developed, and more work has to be invested to make it accessible to engineers.

The systems of computer science cover such a wide range of levels of hierarchy today that it even seems doubtful to try to cover them by just one methodology. In natural science, it is agreed that different levels of organization require different concepts and laws, as seen in the division of science into fields like physics, chemistry, and biology. The hierarchical world of information processing systems has reached a richness where the same question arises. An example may illustrate this aspect: It is clear that in the memory cells of a processor a single bit matters. But on the level of the world-wide web this is no more true; there, it usually does not even matter whether a whole server is down. So, in teaching "foundations of computer science", it is probably no more appropriate to map everything (in principle) to the flat world of finite automata or Turing machines. This is like trying to explain chemical or biological phenomena just with the concepts and laws of physics.

4.5   The Challenge of the Web

In the past ten years, the development of the world-wide web has caused a revolution in the world of information processing. The framework for the publication and exchange of scientific results is changing deeply and rapidly. Today, a large part of scientific knowledge is avalaible not only in symbolic form (i.e., in texts), but also in a format which supports machine-based search, analysis, and composition. This gives a completeley new perspective to Leibniz's project of a universal framework for the management of knowledge. It is rather clear that new kinds of "inference" and "composition of propositions" have to be developed to handle the potentials of the web adequately. Leibniz would probably be enthusiastic about this wonderful new arena for logic. But in academic logic, these practical Leibnizian tasks do not attract much interest. Instead, computer scientists, in particular data base researchers, are addressing these questions. [3] Sometimes I have the impression that we are living in a golden age of logic but that logic does not know it.

5   Conclusion

In the sections above, I argued that computer science gives to logic new challenges and perspectives, in particular, to develop clean, adequate, and convenient methods for modelling and constructing discrete systems (software and hardware systems). For achieving this, logic would no more stay just a foundational science, but also function as an engineering-oriented (however theoretical!) discipline. It should give to system engineers mathematical tools which they require in any constructions which are done "according to professional standards".

---

[3] see the paper of G. Weikum in this volume

For other parts of mathematics, it is agreed which methods and tools belong to such a standard: For example, every engineer has to know how to use linear differential equations and the Laplace transform. This is part of what is called "mathematical modelling". The restriction of this term to continuous models is no more adequate today, because highly nontrivial discrete systems, especially software systems, occur in the daily practice of virtually every engineer (not only in software engineering). In an evolving discipline of "discrete modelling" and "discrete system theory", logic has a significant part (together with other fields like data structures, automata theory, algorithmics). In the long run, this discrete system theory should provide a "calculus" which is to be applied in any professionally performed construction of software systems.

When this challenge is taken seriously, the focus of logic will be shifted beyond the scope of classical mathematical logic, even more as it already did during the formation of theoretical computer science. Some mathematical logicians will say that these tasks should be carried out by computer scientists, and some logicians in computer science may say that data base theorists, programming language researchers, or software specialists will do the job. Anyway, if logicians of any flavour would agree that challenges like the ones mentioned above are interesting and not just an outgrowth of a fashion, then their expertise would contribute to a much faster progress. Moreover, there would be less discussion whether logic institutes be closed or logic professorships cancelled. The best response to the challenges raised above is an intensive cooperation between logicians, computer scientists, and engineers.

A word of caution seems to be in order. The idea to develop a new way of teaching logic to engineers does not mean to throw all the treasures away which logic has given us. Especially for basic courses it is important to present coherent and lucid theory, as it was developed in logic by a long process of scientific effort. At the present time, it seems that a comprehensive and polished treatment of "logic for engineers" does not yet exist. Many more steps are needed to arrive at it, especially to separate the lasting principles from the hot but sometimes not so deep topics.

The task of shaping clean, adequate, and convenient theoretical frameworks which can be taught to and are usable by engineers, is hard and requires the study of engineering practice. It will not be funded much, will for a long time not share the glory of industrial partnerships (as many "applied" projects do), and it will be progressing slowly. But the long-term impact will be high, and I am certain that over the coming decades the demand for this kind of research will grow, in the same way as the demand for reliable and manageable software systems will grow.

6   Acknowledgment

I thank several colleagues for their helpful comments on a draft of this paper, in particular Heinz-Dieter Ebbinghaus, Jörg Flum, Erich Grädel, and Reinhard Wilhelm.

References

1. S. Abramsky, D. M. Gabbay, T.S.E. Maibaum (eds.) *Handbook of Logic in Computer Science*, Vols. I - IV, Clarendon Press, Oxford 1992-1995.
2. J. Barwise (ed.), *Handbook of Mathematical Logic*, North-Holland, Amsterdam 1977.
3. Y. Gurevich, Logic and the challenge of computer science, in: *Current Trends in Theoretical Computer Science* (E. Börger, ed.), Computer Science Press, 1988, pp. 1-57.
4. R. Milner, Elements of interaction - Turing Award Lecture, *Comm. ACM* 36(1), 1993, pp. 78-89.
5. G.W. Leibniz, Anfangsgründe einer allgemeinen Charakteristik (Latin original untitled), in: *Die philosophischen Schriften von Gottfried Wilhelm Leibniz* (C. I. Gerhardt, ed.), Vol. VII, Berlin 1890, p. 185 ff.

From Algorithm to Program to Software Library

Kurt Mehlhorn

Max-Planck-Institut für Informatik, 66123 Saarbrücken, Germany
http://www.mpi-sb.mpg.de/~mehlhorn

The area of algorithmics has made significant progress over the past ten years.

- *New concepts were invented and flourished*: probabilistically checkable proof, non-approximability, approximation algorithms, on-line algorithms, to name some of them. The books [Hoc96, ACG+99, BEY98] give accounts.
- *Many improved algorithms were found*, for example, the $O(nm)$ barrier for maximum network flow, which resisted for more than three decades, was finally broken [GR98].
- *Programs became first class citizens*. Ten years ago, algorithmicists considered programs only as an afterthought. Our work was done, when algorithms were formulated and analyzed. Today, algorithmicists also think about implementations, develop software libraries, and experiment with algorithms. Many algorithms are now available in software libraries. Think of CPLEX, MAPLE, MATHEMATICA, CGAL, LEDA, ILOG-solver. I was involved in the design of LEDA [LED] and CGAL [CGA] and want to share with you some of the experiences made. A much more detailed account can be found in [MN99].

I concentrate on four aspects: (1) algorithms are usually designed for a machine that can compute with real numbers (in the sense of mathematics). That's a problem in general, it is a big problem for geometric algorithms. (2) Programmers are not perfect, they make mistakes. (3) RAMs, our model for theoretical analysis, differ from real machines in many ways. (4) Libraries must be simple to use.

Implementing Geometric Algorithms: Geometric algorithms rely on geometric predicates for their flow of control. Examples of geometric predicates are the orientation predicate for three points or the incircle predicate for four points. The evaluation of geometric predicates usually amounts to computing the sign of an arithmetic expression in the coordinates of the points involved. For example, three points p, q, r form a left-turn, lie on a straight-line, form a right-turn iff the sign[1] of $q_x r_y - q_y r_x - p_x r_y + p_y r_x + p_x q_y - p_y q_x$ is positive, zero, or negative, respectively. When evaluated with floating point arithmetic (or more generally, any arithmetic that may incur roundoff error), the wrong sign may be obtained and hence the geometric predicate may be decided incorrectly. *What*

---

[1] We use p_x and p_y to denote the Cartesian coordinates of point p and analogously for the other points.

R. Wilhelm (Ed.): Informatics. 10 Years Back. 10 Years Ahead, LNCS 2000, pp. 268–273, 2001.

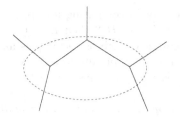 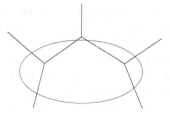

is so bad about this? After all, numerical analysis has dealt with roundoff errors for decades. The problem is that decisions in geometric algorithms are not independent. The figures on the next page illustrate the problem.

The figures illustrate an update step in an incremental Voronoi diagram computation; for the argument to follow, the reader needs only a superficial knowledge of Voronoi diagrams. A Voronoi diagram is a graph like structure embedded into the plane. It can be constructed incrementally. In an update step, part of the current diagram is removed; in the figure on the left the current diagram is drawn solid and the part to be removed is enclosed in a dashed ellipse. It is a theorem that the part to be removed forms a subtree of the current graph structure. The update algorithm uses geometric predicates to determine the part of the diagram to be removed. In particular, it is determined, which vertices of the current graph structure are to be removed. Assume now that (inexact) evaluation of geometric predicates tells us to remove precisely the vertices indicated in the right part of the figure, contradicting the theorem that the subgraph to be removed is a tree and hence connected. Most implementations of the update algorithm will go astray when faced with this situation.

There are two approaches to the problem: one can either reformulate the algorithms [SOI90, Mil88, FM91, GSS93] or one can resort to exact arithmetic [KLN91, FvW96, YD95, MN94]. We use the latter approach in LEDA and CGAL. The exact arithmetic approach proved to be very successful for computations staying within the rational numbers. Efficient filter technology and effective special purpose algorithms for particular predicates were developed [FvW96, MN94, BBP98, BFS98, Cla92, ABDP97, BEPP97].

The situation is less clear as soon as non-rational algebraic numbers are required. Algebraic numbers are, for example, needed to handle curves and surfaces, and for problems involving distances. LEDA's sign computations for algebraic numbers are based on the following lemma [BFMS00, MS00b]. Similar theorems were shown in [KLPY99, LY00].

Let E be an expression with integer operands and operators $+$, $-$, $*$ and $\sqrt{\ }$. Let $u(E)$ be the value of E after replacing $-$ by $+$ and let $k(E)$ be number of distinct square roots in E. Then

$$E = 0 \qquad or \qquad E \% \ \geq B = \frac{1}{u(E)^{2^{k(E)}}}$$

Sign computation for an expression E amounts to computing an approximation $\tilde{E}$ of E with $E - \tilde{E}\% < B/2$: if $\tilde{E}\% < B/2$ then $E = 0$ and if $\tilde{E}\% \geq B/2$ then $sign(E) = sign(\tilde{E})$. Numerical analysis techniques and arbitrary precision floating point arithmetic are used to obtain an approximation of the required quality. An interesting alternative approach stays within the integers [BMS94, DFMT00].

A challenge for the next ten years is to develop methods that can efficiently handle curves and surfaces.

Program Result Checking: In LEDA we had a planarity test starting in 91. A planarity test takes a graph and outputs "Yes", if the graph is planar, and outputs "No", otherwise. Several years later, we were sent a graph that our implementation declared non-planar. The planarity of the graph was witnessed by a planar drawing. When Stefan Näher and I analyzed the situation, we concluded that we should try to make our programs "convincing". They should not only output the desired result, but also a "proof", which makes it easy to check that the program worked correctly on a particular input. In the case of the planarity test, this meant to output a so-called combinatorial embedding in the case of a planar graph and a Kuratowski subgraph in the case of a non-planar graph. We also wrote programs that check the proofs. The proof checkers are typically so simple that their correctness is "obvious". We refer the reader to [WB97, MN99] for a more detailed discussion of program result checking.

A challenge for the coming years is to combine program result checking and program proving.

Consider the following example[2]: A sorting routine working on a set S

(a) must not change S and
(b) must produce a sorted output.

The first property is hard to check (provably as hard as sorting), but usually trivial to prove, e.g., if the sorting algorithm uses a *swap*-subroutine to exchange items. The second property is easy to check by a linear scan over the output, but hard to prove (if the sorting algorithm is complex).

RAMs and Real Machines: In the machine model used for the theoretical analysis of algorithms, instructions and memory accesses are unit cost. Real machines are different, they have pipelines, memory hierarchies, ... ; the distance between the model and real machines will further increase and hence the predictive value of theoretical analysis will further decrease. The area of external memory algorithms [Vit98] addresses the issue for the high-end of the memory hierarchy. A study of the algorithmic aspects of cache memories is emerging [LL97, FLPR99, MS00a].

The challenge for the coming years is to make more aspects of real machines amenable to theoretical analysis. Another challenge is to combine theoretical analysis and experimental evaluation of algorithms.

---

[2] The author does not recall where he learned about this example.

Software Engineering: LEDA is by now widely used. This is certainly partly due to its broad scope and the fact that the algorithms and data structures in LEDA are correct[3] and efficient. The main reason for the wide use of LEDA is probably its ease of use[4]. The architecture of LEDA boils down to small number of concepts: items, iterators, graphs, ... We refer the reader to the discussion in [MN99, Chapter II] for details. Ease of use and flexibility or generality are goals that are frequently in conflict. LEDA is usually siding with the ease of use side, CGAL [CGA] and STL [MS96] are siding with the generality side.

A challenge is to combine the ease of use of LEDA with the generality of STL and CGAL.

Conclusion: An answer to the challenges formulated in the text above would allow us to build libraries of correct, efficient, predictable, certified, flexible implementations of data structures, combinatorial and geometric algorithms.

Remark: The slides for the talk given at the Dagstuhl 10th Anniversary Meeting are available at the author's web page.

References

[ABDP97]   F. Avnaim, J.-D. Boissonnat, O. Devillers, and F.P. Preparata. Evaluating signs of determinants with floating point arithmetic. *Algorithmica*, 17(2):111–132, 1997.

[ACG+99]   G. Ausiello, P. Crescenzi, G. Gambosi, V. Kann, A. Marchetti-Spaccamela, and M. Protasi. *Complexity and Approximation: Combinatorial Optimization Problems and their Approximability Properties.* Springer Verlag, 1999.

[BBP98]   H. Brönnimann, C. Burnikel, and S. Pion. Internal arithmetic yields efficient arithmetic filters for computational geometry. In *Proceedings of the 14th Annual Symposium on Computational Geometry (SCG'98)*, pages 165–174, 1998.

[BEPP97]   H. Brönnimann, I. Emiris, V. Pan, and S. Pion. Computing exact geometric predicates using modular arithmetic with single precision. In *Proceedings of 13th Annual ACM Symposium on Computational Geometry (SCG'97)*, pages 174–182, 1997.

[BEY98]   A. Borodin and R. El-Yaniv. *ONLINE COMPUTATION AND COMPETITIVE ANALYSIS.* Cambridge University Press, 1998.

[BFMS00]   C. Burnikel, R. Fleischer, K. Mehlhorn, and S. Schirra. A strong and easily computable separation bound for arithmetic expressions involving radicals. *Algorithmica*, 27:87–99, 2000.

[BFS98]   C. Burnikel, S. Funke, and M. Seel. Exact arithmetic using cascaded computation. In *Proceedings of the 14th Annual Symposium on Computational Geometry (SCG'98)*, pages 175–183, 1998.

---

[3] We have not had a bug report for any of the major algorithms in months.

[4] Correctness plays a major role here; we all know that there is little fun in using buggy software.

[BMS94]   C. Burnikel, K. Mehlhorn, and S. Schirra. How to compute the Voronoi di-
           agram of line segments: Theoretical and experimental results. In Springer,
           editor, *Proceedings of the 2nd Annual European Symposium on Algorithms
           - ESA'94*, volume 855 of *Lecture Notes in Computer Science*, pages 227–
           239, 1994.

[CGA]   CGAL (Computational Geometry Algorithms Library).
           www.cs.ruu.nl/CGAL.

[Cla92]   K.L. Clarkson. Safe and effective determinant evaluation. In *Proceed-
           ings of the 31st Annual Symposium on Foundations of Computer Science
           (FOCS'92)*, pages 387–395, 1992.

[DFMT00]   O. Devillers, A. Fronville, B. Mourrain, and M. Teillaud. Algebraic meth-
           ods and arithmetic filtering for exact predicates on circle arcs. In *16th
           ACM Symposium on Computational Geometry*, pages 139–147, 2000.

[FLPR99]   Frigo, Leiserson, Prokop, and Ramachandran. Cache-oblivious algorithms.
           In *FOCS: IEEE Symposium on Foundations of Computer Science (FOCS)*,
           1999.

[FM91]   S. Fortune and V.J. Milenkovic. Numerical stability of algorithms for
           line arrangements. In *Proceedings of the 7th Annual ACM Symposium on
           Computational Geometry (SCG'91)*, pages 334–341. ACM Press, 1991.

[FvW96]   S. Fortune and C. van Wyk. Static analysis yields efficient exact integer
           arithmetic for computational geometry. *ACM Transactions on Graphics*,
           15:223–248, 1996.

[GR98]   A.V. Goldberg and S. Rao. Beyond the flow decomposition barrier. *JACM*,
           45(5), 1998.

[GSS93]   L.J. Guibas, D. Salesin, and J. Stolfi. Constructing strongly convex ap-
           proximate hulls with inaccurate primitives. *Algorithmica*, 9:534–560, 1993.

[Hoc96]   D. S. Hochbaum, editor. *Approximation Algorithms for NP-Hard Prob-
           lems*. PWS Publishing Company, 1996.

[KLN91]   M. Karasick, D. Lieber, and L.R. Nackman. Efficient Delaunay triangula-
           tion using rational arithmetic. *ACM Transactions on Graphics*, 10(1):71–
           91, January 1991.

[KLPY99]   V. Karamcheti, C. Li, I. Pechtchanski, and Chee Yap. A core library for
           robust numeric and geometric computation. In *Proceedings of the 15th
           Annual ACM Symposium on Computational Geometry*, pages 351–359,
           Miami, Florida, 1999.

[LED]   LEDA (Library of Efficient Data Types and Algorithms).
           www.mpi-sb.mpg.de/LEDA/leda.html.

[LL97]   A. LaMarca and R.E. Ladner. The influence of caches on the performance
           of sorting. In *Proceedings of the 8th Annual ACM-SIAM Symposium on
           Discrete Algorithms (SODA'97)*, pages 370–379, 1997.

[LY00]   Z. Li and C.K. Yap. A new constructive root bound for algebraic expres-
           sions. 2000.

[Mil88]   V.J. Milenkovic. *Verifiable Implementations of Geometric Algorithms Us-
           ing Finite Precision Arithmetic*. PhD thesis, Carnegie Mellon University,
           1988.

[MN94]   K. Mehlhorn and S. Näher. The implementation of geometric algorithms.
           In *Proceedings of the 13th IFIP World Computer Congress*, volume 1,
           pages 223–231. Elsevier Science B.V. North-Holland, Amsterdam, 1994.
           www.mpi-sb.mpg.de/~mehlhorn/ftp/ifip94.ps.

[MN99]   K. Mehlhorn and S. Näher. *The LEDA Platform for Combinatorial and
           Geometric Computing*. Cambridge University Press, 1999. 1018 pages.

[MS96]   D. R. Musser and A. Saini. *STL Tutorial and Reference Guide: C++ Programming with the Standard Template Library.* Addison-Wesley, Reading (MA), USA, 1996.

[MS00a]   K. Mehlhorn and P. Sanders. Scanning multiple sequences via cache memory. `www.mpi-sb.mpg.de/~mehlhorn/ftp/cache.ps`, February 2000.

[MS00b]   K. Mehlhorn and S. Schirra. A generalized and improved constructive separation bound for real algebraic expressions. Technical Report MPI-I-2000-004, Max-Planck-Institut für Informatik, 2000. `www.mpi-sb.mpg.de/~{}mehlhorn/ftp/improved-sepbound.ps`.

[SOI90]   K. Sugihara, Y. Ooishi, and T. Imai. Topology-oriented approach to robustness and its applications to several voronoi-diagram algorithms. In *Proceedings of the 2nd Canadian Conference in Computational Geometry (CCCG'90)*, pages 36–39, 1990.

[Vit98]   J. S. Vitter. External memory algorithms. *Lecture Notes in Computer Science*, 1461:1–??, 1998.

[WB97]   H. Wasserman and M. Blum. Software reliability via run-time result-checking. *Journal of the ACM*, 44(6):826–849, 1997.

[YD95]   C.K. Yap and T. Dube. The exact computation paradigm. In *Computing in Euclidean Geometry II*. World Scientific Press, 1995.

Pervasive Speech and Language Technology

Wolfgang Wahlster

German Research Center for Artificial Intelligence, DFKI GmbH
Stuhlsatzenhausweg 3, 66123 Saarbrücken, Germany
wahlster@dfki.de
http://www.dfki.de/~wahlster

Abstract. Advances in human language technology offer the promise of pervasive access to on-line information and electronic services. Since almost everyone speaks and understands a language, the development of natural language systems will allow the average person to interact with computers anytime and anywhere without special skills or training, using common devices such as a mobile telephone. The latest results and component technologies for multilingual and robust speech processing, prosodic analysis, parsing, semantic analysis, discourse understanding, translation, and speech synthesis are reviewed using the Verbmobil system as an example. Verbmobil is a speaker-independent and bidirectional speech-to-speech translation system for spontaneous dialogs in mobile situations. It recognizes spoken input, analyses and translates it, and finally utters the translation. The multilingual system handles dialogs in three business-oriented domains, with context-sensitive translation between three languages (German, English, and Japanese). We will show that the most successful current systems are based on hybrid architectures incorporating both deep and shallow processing schemes. They integrate a broad spectrum of statistical and rule-based methods and combine the results of machine learning from large corpora with linguists' hand-crafted knowledge sources to achieve an adequate level of robustness and accuracy. We argue that packed representations together with formalisms for underspecification capture the uncertainties in each processing phase, so that these uncertainties can be reduced by linguistic, discourse and domain constraints as soon as they become applicable. We show that the current core technologies for natural language and speech processing enable us to create the next generation of information extraction and summarization systems for the Web, speech-based Internet access and multimodal communication assistants combining speech and gesture.

1 Introduction

Human language technology will become pervasive in our daily lifes (see Fig. 1). When you have breakfast in the morning you can control your coffee machine by speech commands. Before you drive to a meeting you can program your car navigation system and select a music CD via voice commands. While

R. Wilhelm (Ed.): Informatics. 10 Years Back. 10 Years Ahead, LNCS 2000, pp. 274–293, 2001.

you are stuck in traffic, you can dictate and send an email to one of your colleagues via your WAP-enabled cell phone. In your office, you can retrieve and extract information from digital recordings of television broadcast news stored in video databases available through the Internet. In contrast to traditional TV programs, such content-based video retrieval provides information on demand. Instead of taking notes during your business meetings, you store them on your personal audio memory device. Using audio mining technology your notes are converted into searchable text that is indexed to time code on your digital audio memory. You can use your cell phone as a speech-to-speech translation device, that recognizes your spoken input, analyses and translates it to Japanese, and finally utters the translation.

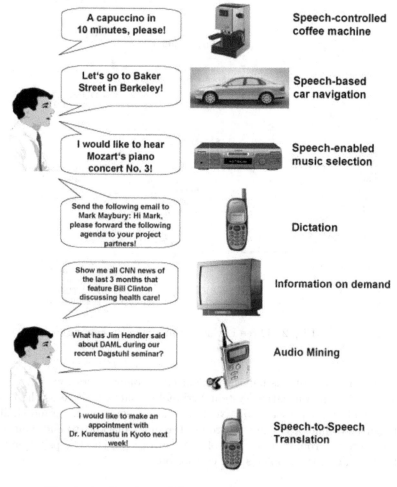

Fig. 1. Applications of Human Language Technology

Today, there exist operational demonstrators and prototypes for all the application scenarios mentioned above and some of them are being commercialized right now. This should not be misunderstood: Of course, there are many more open problems than solved ones in speech and language understanding. We will mention some of the most important open issues at the end of this paper.

Although great progress has been made in speech recognition over the past decade, the semantic level of speech analysis and the pragmatic level of speech understanding are only achieved by very few systems that work in narrowly restricted domains of discourse. Only on the the third level of language understanding all relevant ambiguities can be resolved by discourse and domain knowledge so that an unambiguous interpretation of a dialog contribution becomes possible (see Fig. 2).

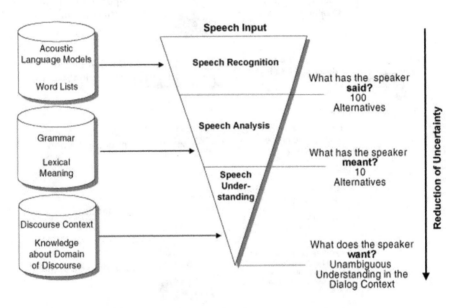

Fig. 2. Three Levels of Language Processing

The remainder of this paper is organized as follows. First, we introduce the speech-to-speech translation system Verbmobil that will serve as the concrete background of our presentation. Next, we discuss some of the grand challenges of language technology. Then we present the multi-blackboard and multi-engine approach to the robust processing of spontaneous speech. The paper ends with a discussion of open problems and conclusions.

2   The Speech-to-Speech-Translation System Verbmobil

Verbmobil is a software system that provides mobile phone users with simultaneous dialog interpretation services for restricted topics (see Wahlster, 1993, 2000). As the name Verbmobil suggests, the system supports verbal communication with foreign interlocutors in mobile situations. It recognizes spoken input, analyses and translates it, and finally utters the translation. The multilingual system handles dialogs in three business-oriented domains, with bidirectional translation between three languages (German, English, and Japanese).

In contrast to previous dialog translation systems that translate sentence-by- sentence, Verbmobil provides context-sensitive translations. Since Verbmobil must "hear between the words" — things that were communicated earlier and things about the topic being discussed — it uses an explicit dialog memory and exploits domain knowledge. Figure 3 illustrates the use of Verbmobil in the travel planning scenario.

It shows that the Verbmobil server translates the German word "nächste" into English either as "next" or "nearest" depending on a temporal or spatial question context. In Verbmobil, the dialog context is used to resolve ambiguities and to produce an adequate translation in a particular conversational situation.

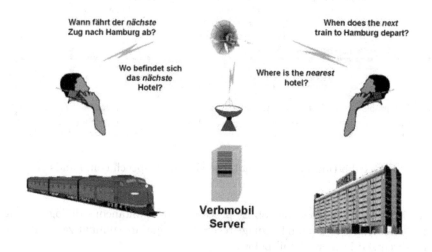

Fig. 3. Context-sensitive speech-to-speech translation

Verbmobil is the first speech-only dialog translation system. Verbmobil users can simply pick up a standard mobile phone and use voice dialing and speech commands in order to initiate a dialog translation session (see Figure 4). In contrast to previous versions of Verbmobil and other systems in the C-STAR consortium (see Woszczyna, 1999), the operation of the final Verbmobil system is completely hands-free without any push-to-talk button. Since the Verbmobil speech translation server can be accessed by GSM mobile telephones, the system can be used anywhere and anytime. No PC, notebook or PDA must be available to access the Verbmobil translation service, just a phone for each dialog participant. In addition, no waiting time for booting computers and keyboard or mouse input to start the Verbmobil system is needed — dialog translation can begin instantaneously. Although the primary goal of Verbmobil is to support face-to-face conversations, in which all participants use their mobile phones as translation devices, Verbmobil can also be used for conversations in which the participants cannot see one another.

Fig. 4. Setting up a Verbmobil session with speech commands

Verbmobil emphasizes the robust processing of spontaneous dialogs posing difficult challenges to human language technology, that are summarized in Figure 5 and discussed in more detail below.

3   Some Grand Challenges for Speech and Language Technology

Verbmobil is the only dialog translation system to date based on an open microphone condition. It is not a "push-to-talk" system which has to be told which chunks of the sound signal represent coherent contributions by individual speakers:

Verbmobil works that out for itself from the raw input signal. The signal may be of different qualities — not necessarily from a lab-quality close-speaking microphone, for instance it can be GSM (mobile phone) quality. Thus, Verbmobil includes different speech recognizers for 16 kHz and 8 kHz sampling rates. Verbmobil deals with spontaneous speech. This does not just mean continuous speech like in current dictation systems, but speech which includes realistic disfluencies and repair phenomena, such as changes of tack in mid-sentence (or mid-word), ums and ers, and cases where short words are accidentally left out in rapid speech. For example, in the Verbmobil corpus about 20% of all dialog turns contain at least one self-correction and 3% include false starts. Verbmobil uses a combination of shallow and deep analysis methods to recognize a speaker's slips and translate what he tried to say rather than what he actually said.

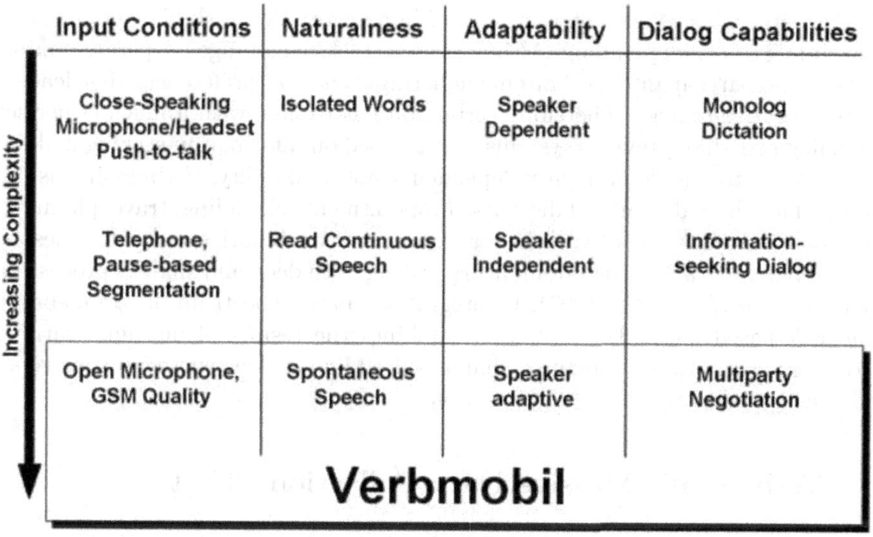

Input Conditions	Naturalness	Adaptability	Dialog Capabilities
Close-Speaking Microphone/Headset Push-to-talk	Isolated Words	Speaker Dependent	Monolog Dictation
Telephone, Pause-based Segmentation	Read Continuous Speech	Speaker Independent	Information-seeking Dialog
Open Microphone, GSM Quality	Spontaneous Speech	Speaker adaptive	Multiparty Negotiation

*(Left axis: Increasing Complexity; bottom label spanning: **Verbmobil**)*

Fig. 5. Some challenges for speech and language technology

At an early processing stage prosodic cues are used to detect self-corrections. A stochastic model is used to segment the repair into the "wrong" part (the so-called reparandum) and the correction. Then the corrected input is inserted as a new hypothesis into the word hypotheses graph. Thus, Verbmobil's repair processing is a filter between speech recognition and syntactic analysis. The word lattice is augmented by an additional path that does no longer contain those parts of the utterances that the speaker tried to correct. This transformation of the word lattice is used in addition to simple disfluency filtering, that eliminates sounds like "ahh" that users often make while speaking.

In addition to this shallow statistical approach, other forms of self-corrections are also processed at a later stage on the semantic level. A rule-based repair approach is applied during robust semantic processing to a chart containing possible semantic interpretations of the input (the so-called VIT Hypotheses Graph (VHG)).

Verbmobil applies various hand-crafted rules to detect repairs in semantic representations and to delete parts of the representation that corresponds to slips of the speaker. Verbmobil is a speaker-adaptive system, i.e. for a new speaker it starts in a speaker-independent mode and after a few words have been uttered it improves the recognition results by adaptation. A cascade of unsupervised methods, ranging from very fast adaptation during the processing of a single utterance to complex adaptation methods that analyze a longer sequence of dialog turns, is used to adjust to the acoustic characteristics of the speaker's voice, the speaking rate and pronunciation variants due to the dialectal diversity of the user community.

Verbmobil deals with mixed-initiative dialogs between human participants. Each partner has a clear interaction goal in a negotiation task like appointment scheduling or travel planning. Although these tasks encourage cooperative interaction, the participants have often conflicting goals and preferences that lead to argumentative dialogs. Therefore Verbmobil has to deal with a much richer set of dialog acts than previous systems that focused on information-seeking dialogs.

In order to ensure domain independence and scalability, Verbmobil was developed for three domains of discourse (appointment scheduling, travel planning, remote PC maintenance) with increasing size of vocabularies and ontologies.

Verbmobil is a hybrid system incorporating both deep and shallow processing schemes (see Bub et al., 1997). It integrates a broad spectrum of corpus-based and rule-based methods. Verbmobil combines the results of machine learning from large corpora with linguists' hand-crafted knowledge sources to achieve an adequate level of robustness and accuracy.

4   Verbmobil's Massive Data Collection Effort

A significant programme of data collection was performed during the Verbmobil project to extract statistical properties from large corpora of spontaneous speech. A distinguishing feature of the Verbmobil speech corpus is the multi-channel recording. The voice of each speaker was recorded in parallel using a close-speaking microphone, a room microphone, and various telephones (GSM phone, wireless DECT phone and regular phone), so that the speech recognizers could be trained on data sets with various audio signal qualities.

The so-called partitur (German word for musical score) format used for the Verbmobil speech corpora orchestrates fifteen strata of annotations: two transliteration variants, lexical orthography, canonical pronunciation, manual phonological segmentation, automatic phonological segmentation, word segmentation, prosodic segmentation, dialog acts, noises, superimposed speech, syntactic category, word category, syntactic function, and prosodic boundaries. In addition to the monolingual data, the multilingual Verbmobil corpus includes bilingual dialogs (from Wizard-of-OZ experiments, face-to-face dialogs with human in-

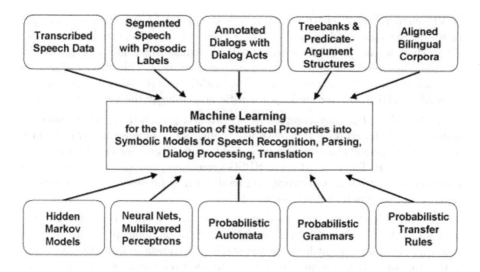

Fig. 6. Extracting statistical properties from large corpora

terpreters, or dialogs interpreted by various versions of Verbmobil) and aligned bilingual transliterations . Three treebanks for German, English and Japanese have been developed with annotations on three strata: morpho-syntax, phrase structure, and predicate-argument structure.

Various machine learning methods have been used to train Hidden Markov Models, neural nets, probabilistic automata, parsers, rule systems, translation methods and plan recognizers. The end-to-end evaluations of the various Verbmobil prototypes have shown clearly, that the robustness, coverage and accuracy of a speech-to-speech translation system for spontaneous dialogs depends critically on the quantity and quality of the training corpora.

5   The Main Components of Verbmobil

The screenshot of Verbmobil's control panel provides an overview of the main components of the system. The overall control and data flow is indicated by arrows pointing upwards on the left side of the screenshot, from left to right in the middle and downwards on the right side. On the bottom various input devices can be selected (Europeans call a cell phone a "handy"). Since Verbmobil is a multilingual system it incorporates three speech recognizers and three speech synthesizers for German, English and Japanese.

A distinguishing feature of Verbmobil is its multi-engine parsing architecture. Three parsers based on different syntactic knowledge sources are used to process the word hypotheses graphs (WHG) that are augmented by prosodic information extracted by the prosody module (see Section 5 below). All parsers use the multistratal VIT representation as an output format. Since in most cases the parsers produce only fragmentary analyses, their results are combined in a chart of VIT structures. A chart parser and a statistical LR parser are combined in a package that is visualized in the screenshot as "integrated processing". These shallow parsers produce trees that are transformed into VIT structures by a module called semantic construction (see Figure 7). This syntax-semantics interface is primarily lexically driven . The module with the label "deep analysis" is based on a HPSG parser for deep linguistic processing in the Verbmobil system.

Verbmobil is the only completely operational speech-to-speech translation system that is based on a wide-coverage unification grammar and tries to preserve the theoretical clarity and elegance of linguistic analyses in a very efficient implementation. The parser for the HPSG grammars processes the n best paths produced by the integrated processing module. It is implemented as a bidirectional bottom-up active chart parser.

The statistical translation module starts with the single best sentence hypothesis of the speech recognizer. Prosodic information about phrase boundaries and sentence mode are utilized by the statistical translation module. The output of this module is a sequence of words in the target language together with a confidence measure that is used by the selection module (not shown in the control panel) for the final choice of a translation result. Verbmobil includes two components for case-based translation. Substring-based translation is a method for incremental synchronous interpretation, that is based on machine learning methods applied to a sentence-aligned bilingual corpus. Substrings of the input for which a contiguous piece of translation can be found in the corpus are the basic processing units. Substring pairs are combined with patterns for word order switching and word cluster information in an incremental translation algorithm for a sequence of input segments. The other component for case-based translation is based on 30000 translation templates learned from a sentence-aligned corpus. Date, time and naming expressions are recognized by definite clause grammars (DCGs) and marked in the WHG. An A* search explores the cross-product graph of the WHG with the subphrase tags and the template graph. A DCG-based generator is used to produce target language output from the interlingual representation of the recognized date, time and naming expressions. These subphrases are used to instantiate the target language parts of translation templates.

Dialog-act based translation includes the statistical classification of 19 dialog acts and a cascade of more than 300 finite-state transducers that extract the main propositional content of an utterance. The statistical dialog classifier is based on n-grams and takes the previous dialog history into account. The recognized dialog act, the topic and propositional content are represented by a simplistic frame notation including 49 nested objects with 95 possible attributes covering the appointment scheduling and travel planning tasks. A template-based approach to generation is used to transform these interlingual terms into the corresponding target language. The shallow interlingual representation of an utterance is stored together with topic and focus information as well as a deep semantic representation encoded as a VIT in the dialog memory for further processing by the dialog and context evaluation component.

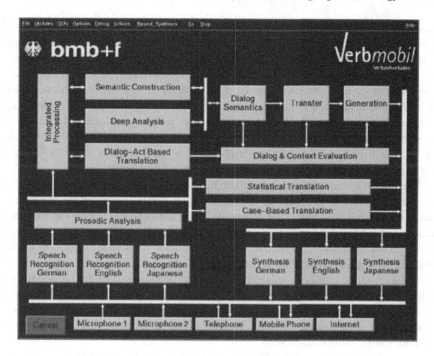

Fig. 7. A snapshot of Verbmobil's control panel

The dialog component includes a plan processor, that structures an ongoing dialog hierarchically in different dialog phases, games and moves. Dialog acts are the terminal nodes of the tree structure that represents the dialog structure. Information about the dialog phase is used eg. during the semantic-based transfer for disambiguation tasks. In addition, inference services are provided by the dialog and context component eg. for the completion of underspecified temporal expressions and the resolution of anaphora or ellipsis. Temporal reasoning is used for example to transform expressions like "two hours later" or "next week" into fully specified times and dates stored in the dialog memory for summarizing the results of a negotiation. The transfer module triggers contextual reasoning process only in cases where a disambiguation or resolution is necessary for a given translation task. For example the German noun "Essen" can be translated into "lunch" or "dinner" depending on the time of day, which can be derived by contextual reasoning. Disambiguation and resolution on demand is typical for Verbmobil's approach to translation, since various forms of underspecification and ambiguity can be carried over into target language, so that the hearer can resolve them.

The transfer component is basically a rewriting system for underspecified semantic representations using Verbmobil's VIT formalism. Semantic-based transfer receives a VIT of a source language utterance and transforms it into a VIT for the target language synthesis. This means that the transfer module abstracts away from morphological and syntactic analysis results. The final Verbmobil system includes more than 20000 transfer rules. These rules include conditions that can trigger inferences in the dialog and context evaluation module to resolve ambiguities and deal with translation mismatches, whenever necessary. The transfer component uses cascaded rule systems, first for the phrasal transfer of idioms and other non-compositional expressions and then for the lexical transfer. The translation of spatial and temporal prepositions is based on an interlingual representation in order to cut down the number of specific transfer rules. Semantic-based transfer is extremely fast and consumes on the average less than 1% of the overall processing time for an utterance.

Verbmobil's multilingual generator includes a constraint-based microplanning component and a syntactic realization module that is based on the formalism of lexicalized tree-adjoining grammars. The input to the microplanning component are VITs produced by the transfer module. A sentence plan is generated that consists basically of lexical items and semantic roles linking them together. The microplanner decides about subordination, aggregation, focus and theme control as well as anaphora generation. The syntactic realization component can either use LTAG grammars that are compiled from the HPSG grammars used for deep analysis or a hand-written LTAG generation grammar. For English and Japanese the grammars that were designed for analysis are usable for generation after an offline-compilation step.

The speech synthesizer for German and American English follows a concatenative approach based on a large corpus of annotated speech data. The word is the basic unit of concatenation, so that subword units are only used if a word is not available in the database.

The synthesizer applies a graph-based unit selection procedure to choose the best available synthesis segments matching the segmental and prosodic constraints of the input. Whenever possible the synthesizer exploits the syntactic, prosodic and discourse information provided by previous processing stages. Thus for the deep processing stream it provides concept-to-speech synthesis, whereas for the shallow translation threads it operates more like a traditional text-to-speech system resulting in a lower quality of its output.

6   Using Prosodic Information at All Processing Stages

Verbmobil is the first spoken-dialog interpretation system that uses prosodic information systematically at all processing stages. The results of Verbmobil's multilingual prosody module are used for parsing, dialog understanding, translation, generation and speech synthesis (see figure 8). This means that prosodic information in the source utterance is passed even through the translation process to improve the generation and synthesis of the target utterance. Prosodic differences in one language can correspond to lexical or syntactic differences in another; for instance, a German utterance beginning "wir haben noch ..." may be translated by Verbmobil into English either "as we still have ..." or as "we have another ..." depending whether noch is stressed. Although prosody is used in some other recent speech recognition systems, the exploitation of prosodic information is extremely limited in these approaches. For example, the ATR Matrix system (see Takezawa et al., 1998) uses prosody only to identify sentence mood (declarative vs. question). We believe that Verbmobil is the first system to make significant use of prosodic aspects of speech. The prosody module of Verbmobil uses the speech signal and the word hypotheses graph (WHG) produced by the speech recognizer as an input and outputs an annotated WHG with prosodic information for each recognized word. The system extracts duration, pitch, energy, and pause features and uses them to classify phrase and clause boundaries, accented words and sentence mood. A combination of a multilayer perceptron and a polygram-based statistical language model annotate the WHG with probabilities for the classified prosodic events.

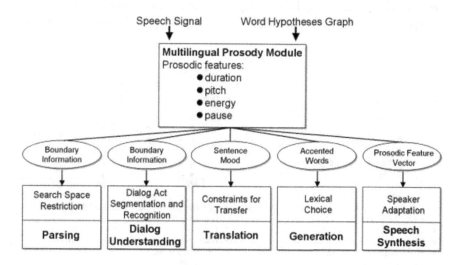

Fig. 8. The role of prosodic information in Verbmobil

Verbmobil uses the probabilistic prosodic information about clause boundaries to reduce the search space for syntactic analysis dramatically. During parsing, the clause boundary marks that are inserted into the WHG by the prosody module play the role of punctuation marks in written language. Dialog act segmentation and recognition is also based on the boundary information provided by the prosody module. Prosodic cues about sentence mood is often used in Verbmobil's translation modules to constrain transfer results, if there is not enough syntactic or semantic evidence for a certain mood (e.g. question). The information about word accent is used to guide lexical choice in the generation process. Finally, during speech synthesis the extracted prosodic features are used for speaker-adaptation.

7   The Multi-blackboard Architecture of Verbmobil

The final Verbmobil system consists of 69 highly interactive modules. The transformation of speech input in a source language into speech output in a target language requires a tremendous amount of communication between all these modules. Since Verbmobil has to translate under real-time conditions it exploits parallel processing schemes whenever possible. The non-sequential nature of the Verbmobil architecture implies that not only inputs and results are exchanged between modules but also top-down expectations, constraints, backtracking signals, alternate hypotheses, additional parameters, probabilities, and confidence values.

198 blackboards are used for the necessary information exchange between modules. A module typically subscribes to various blackboards. Modules can have several instances, e.g. in a multiparty conversation there may be two German speakers, so that two instances of the German speech recognition module are needed.

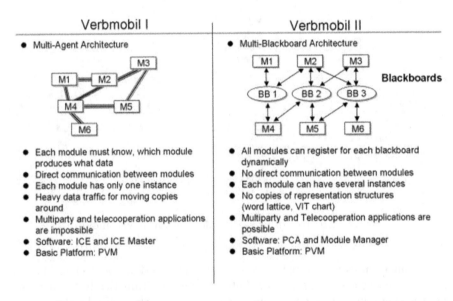

Fig. 9. A comparison of the architecture of Verbmobil I and II

The final Verbmobil system is based on a multi-blackboard architecture that pools processing modules around blackboards representing intermediate results at each processing stage. It turned out that such a multi-blackboard approach is much more efficient than the more general multi-agent architecture used in the first Verbmobil prototype. Due to the huge amount of interaction between modules a multi-agent architecture with direct communication among module agents would imply 2380 different interfaces for message exchanges between the

69 agents. Figure 9 summarizes the advantages of the multi-blackboard approach vs. the multi-agent approach for the Verbmobil architecture.

In a multi-blackboard architecture based on packed representations at all processing stages (speech recognition, parsing, semantic processing, translation, generation, speech synthesis) using charts with underspecified representations the results of concurrent processing threads can be combined in an incremental fashion. All results of concurrent processing modules come with a confidence value, so that selection modules can choose the most promising results at each processing stage or delay the decision until more information becomes available. Packed representations such as the WHG (Word Hypotheses Graph) and VHG (VIT Hypotheses Graph) together with formalisms for underspecification capture the non-determinism in each processing phase, so that the remaining uncertainties can be reduced by linguistic, discourse and domain constraints as soon as they become applicable.

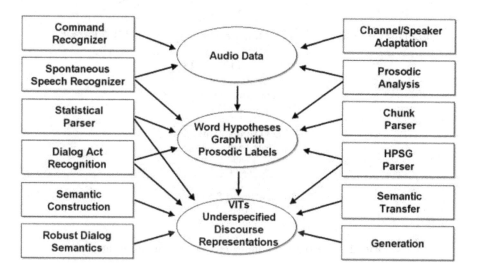

Fig. 10. Some key blackboards with their subscribing modules

VITs (Verbmobil Interface Terms) are used as a multi-stratal semantic representation by the central blackboards for the deep processing threads in Verbmobil. The semantic representation in a VIT is augmented by various features concerning morpho-syntax, tense, aspect, prosody, sortal restrictions and discourse information. VITs form the input and output of the modules for robust semantic processing and semantic-based transfer. The initial design of the VIT representation language was inspired by underspecified discourse representation structures. VITs provide a compact representation of lexical and structural ambiguities and scope underspecification of quantifiers, negations and adverbs. Figure

10 illustrates the role of VITs as a common semantic representation language
for the blackboards of Verbmobil.

8   Verbmobil's Multi-engine Approach

Verbmobil performs language identification, parsing and translation with several
engines simultaneously. Whereas the multi-engine parsing results are combined
and merged into a single chart, a statistical selection module chooses between
the alternate results of the concurrent translation threads, so that only a single
translation is used for generating the system's output.

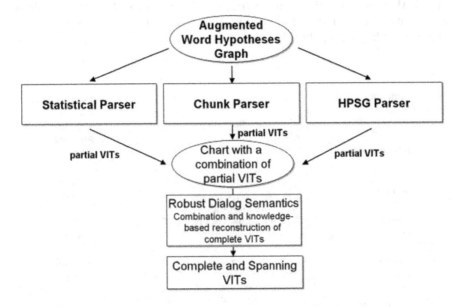

Fig. 11. Verbmobil's multi-engine parsing approach

Verbmobil uses three parallel parsing threads: an incremental chunk parser,
a probabilistic LR parser and a HPSG parser. These parsers cover a broad spectrum with regard to their robustness and accuracy. The chunk parser produces
the most robust but least accurate results, whereas the HPSG parser delivers
the most accurate but least robust analysis. All parsers process the same word
hypotheses graph with its prosodic annotations. The search for the best scored
path (according to the acoustic score and the language model) is controlled by
a central A* algorithm that guides the three parsers through the word hypotheses graph. The HPSG parser may return more than one analysis for ambiguous
inputs, whereas the chunk parser and statistical parser return always only one
result. Each parser uses a semantic construction component to transform its
analysis results into a semantic representation term. Even partial results of the

different parsing engines are integrated into a chart of VITs, that is further analyzed by the robust semantic processing component.

The final Verbmobil system includes five translation engines: statistical translation, case-based translation, substring-based translation, dialog-act based translation, and semantic transfer. These engines cover a wide spectrum of translation methods. While statistical translation is very robust against speech recognition problems and produces quick-and-dirty results, semantic transfer is computationally more expensive and less robust but produces higher quality translations (see Figure 12). However, it is one of the fundamental insights gained from the Verbmobil project, that the problem of robust, efficient and reliable speech-to-speech translation can only be cracked by the combined muscle of deep and shallow processing approaches.

The language identification component of Verbmobil uses also a multi-engine approach to identify each user's input language. The three instances of the multilingual speech recognizer for German, English, and Japanese run concurrently for the three first seconds of speech input. A confidence measure is used to decide which language is spoken by a particular dialog participant. The language identification component switches to the selected recognizer that produces a word hypotheses graph for the full utterance. Verbmobil's error rate for this type of language identification task is only 7.3% .

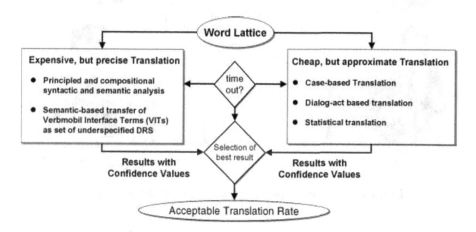

Fig. 12. Competing strategies for robust speech translation

9   Summarizing Dialogs

Another novel functional feature of Verbmobil is the ability to generate dialog summaries. Suppose that two speakers negotiate a travel plan: one can ask the system either to specify the final agreement, omitting the negotiating steps, or to summarize the steps of argument while leaving out irrelevant details of wording. A dialog summary can be produced on demand after the end of a conversation (see Figure 13). The summaries are based on the semantic representation of all dialog turns stored in the dialog memory of Verbmobil. It is interesting to note that dialog summaries are mainly a bye-product of the deep processing thread and the dialog processor of Verbmobil. The most specific accepted negotiation results are selected from the dialog memory. The semantic-based transfer component and the natural language generators for German and English are used for the production of multilingual summaries. This means that after a conversation over a cell phone the participants can ask for a written summary of the dialog in their own language. The dialog summary can be sent as a HTML document using email. In the context of business negotiations Verbmobil's ability to produce written dialog summaries of a phone conversation is an important valued-added service.

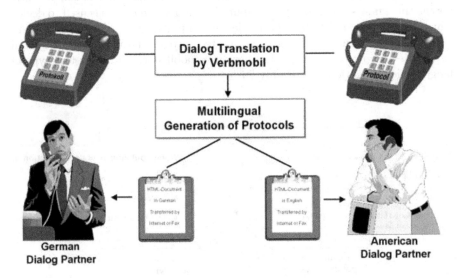

Fig. 13. The generation of a multilingual dialog summaries

10   Conclusion: Lessons Learned, Open Problems, and Future Impact

One of the main lessons learned from the Verbmobil project is that the problem of speech-to-speech translation of spontaneous dialogs can only be cracked by the combined muscle of deep and shallow processing approaches:

– deep processing can be used for merging, completing and repairing the results of shallow processing strategies

- shallow methods can be used to guide the search in deep processing
- statistical methods must be augmented by symbolic models to achieve higher accuracy and broader coverage
- statistical methods can be used to learn operators or selection strategies for symbolic processes

The final Verbmobil architecture supports large and robust dialog systems and maximizes the necessary interaction between processing modules:

- in a multi-blackboard and multi-engine architecture, that is based on packed representations on all processing levels and uses charts with underspecified multi-stratal representations, the results of concurrent processing threads can be combined in an incremental fashion
- all results of concurrent and competing processing modules come with a confidence value, so that statistically trained selection modules can choose the most promising result at each stage, if demanded by a following processing step-packed representations together with formalisms for underspecification capture the uncertainties in each processing phase, so that the uncertainties can be reduced by linguistic, discourse and domain constraints as soon as they become applicable.

10.1   Open Problems

Although the Verbmobil project has successfully met all project goals, many open problems in language technology remain that we must solve in the next decade. Current language technology relies heavily on machine learning approaches. But there are three major problems with the current corpus-based learning methods:

- data collection is very expensive
- the training data sets are cognitively unrealistic
- the data sparseness causes problems for important, but infrequent words

In addition, there are various problems with hand-crafted knowledge sources that are used in hybrid processing schemes to complement the statistical models:

- the methods are still quite brittle
- the knowledge sources are often domain dependent
- the scalability of hand-crafted knowledge sources is limited

Although enormous progress has been made during the past decade, most operational systems work only in restricted domains, with limited vocabularies, and for a single language only. Scaling up, rapid porting to new discourse domains, and achieving full multilinguality are key challenges for future research in language technology.

Fig. 14 surveys the mayor application areas for multilingual language technology for the next decade. In addition to dialog translation, multilingual access to huge video and audio archives has a great application potential. Speech-based web access will become increasingly important in mobile and hands-free situations. Finally, the synergistic use of speech and gesture recognition will lead to more intuitive user interfaces to advanced e-services. In SmartKom, the follow-up project to Verbmobil, we are working on such an intelligent multimodal interface agent.

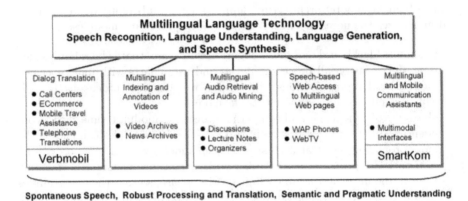

Fig. 14. International research trends in multilingual systems

10.2   Future Impact

In the next decade, speech technology will allow us to store retrieve and process spoken language like we are doing it today for written texts. Thus in many situations, writing and reading may be substituted by speaking and hearing. Meeting minutes, transcribed interviews, or lecture notes contain less information than the original spoken contributions, since the emotional colouring, the disambiguation and the focusing effects of prosody cannot be covered by the transcription. Thus important information about the speaker's affective state, the situative context and the speaker's intention are lost in textual transcriptions. When intelligent audio mining methods will allow us to easily retrieve every utterance that we have produced or heard during our lifetime, we may return to a more oral society like during the thousands of years before Gutenberg. However, these early oral societies had no mass storage for audio information, no automatic processing and no retrieval tools for spoken language. Today in our textual society, we pass news and knowledge mainly textually, since we have digital mass storage for texts and can easily process and retrieve texts on our computers. Let us conclude with a speculative claim: Human language technology will allow us to return from a textual knowledge society to a more oral knowledge society in about fifty years, when the digital storage, processing and retrieval of spoken language will be as easy, fast and widely available as it is today for written language. After all, it is well known that the human cognitive system is more adapted to speaking and hearing than to writing and reading.

References

1. Bub, T., Wahlster, W., and Waibel, A. *Verbmobil: The Combination of Deep and Shallow Processing for Spontaneous Speech Translation.* In Proceedings of the International IEEE Conference on Acoustics, Speech and Signal Processing, München, Germany (1997) 71–74
2. Cole,R., Mariani, J., Uszkoreit, H., Zaenen, A, Zue, V. (eds.) *Survey of the State of the Art in Human Language Technology.* Cambridge: Univ. Press (1998)
3. Jurafsky, D., Martin, J.H. Speech and Language Processing *An Introduction to Natural Language Processing, Computational Linguistics, and Speech Recognition.* New Jersey: Prentice-Hall (2000)
4. Manning, C.D., Schütze, H.: *Foundations of Statistical Natural Language Processing.* Cambridge: MIT Press (1999)
5. Maybury, M, Wahlster, W. (eds.): *Readings in Intelligent User Interfaces.* San Francisco: Morgan Kaufmann (1998)
6. Takezawa, T., Morimoto, T., Sagisaka, Y., Campbell, N., Iida, H., Sugaya, F., Yokoo, A., and Yamamoto, S. *A Japanese-to-English Speech Translation System: ATR-MATRIX.* In Proceedings of the ICSLP (1998) 957–960
7. Wahlster, W. *Verbmobil: Translation of Face-to-Face Dialogs.* In Proceedings of the Fourth Machine Translation Summit, Kobe, Japan (1993) 128–135
8. Wahlster, W. (ed.): *Verbmobil: Foundations of Speech-to-Speech Translation.* Berlin, Heidelberg, New York: Springer (2000)
9. Woszczyna, M. (ed.) *Proceedings of the C-STAR Workshop.* Schwetzingen, Germany (1999)

Embodied Artificial Intelligence
10 Years Back, 10 Years Forward

Rolf Pfeifer

Artificial Intelligence Laboratory,
Department of Information Technology,
University of Zurich, Winterthurerstrasse 190, CH-8057 Zurich, Switzerland
phone: +41 1 635 4320/4331, fax: +41 1 635 6809
pfeifer@ifi.unizh.ch
http://www.ifi.unizh.ch/~pfeifer

Abstract. In the early days of artificial intelligence the focus was on abstract thinking and problem solving. These phenomena could be naturally mapped onto algorithms, which is why originally artificial intelligence was considered to be part of computer science. Over time, it turned out that this view was too limited to understand natural forms of intelligence and that embodiment must be taken into account. As a consequence the focus changed to systems that are able to autonomously interact with their environment. The major implications of embodiment, dynamical and information theoretic, are illustrated in a number of case studies. Two grand challenges, evolving grounded intelligence and exploring ecological balance, i.e. the relation between task environment, morphology, materials, and control in an artificial organism, are discussed.

1 Introduction

Computer science has grown into an enormous discipline with many subfields and it is often hard to see how the different areas are still connected to form one discipline, except that they all, one way or other, deal with computers. What about Artificial Intelligence? For several decades, i.e. from the 50s until the mid-80s it was mostly concerned with algorithms, for example for playing chess, checkers (and other games), solving cryptarithmetic puzzles, or natural language processing of written text. Because of this perspective, it was considered a subdiscipline of computer science. As we will be arguing below, there have been severe limitations of this approach because of its focus on algorithms exclusively. Over time, it became clear that intelligence was not so much a question of algorithms but of the interaction of an agent with the real world and researchers started using robots as their workhorse. This change in orientation entails many new research issues that are well outside the field of computer science. Not all researchers in artificial intelligence have changed direction; many are continuing to pursue the algorithmic approach. Which direction one is interested in depends on the goals: If the goal is to find a solution to a problem, the algorithmic approach might be best (e.g. Wolfgang Wahlster, this volume). However, if it is to understand the principles underlying (naturally) intelligent

R. Wilhelm (Ed.): Informatics. 10 Years Back. 10 Years Ahead, LNCS 2000, pp. 294-310, 2001.

behavior, the alternative approach, i.e. the one of embodiment is better suited, as will be argued later.

We begin with a short history of artificial intelligence. Then we introduce the concept of embodiment and provide a set of case studies to illustrate the different kinds of implications. Next we attempt to characterize the state of the art in the field of embodied artificial intelligence. This is followed by an outline of some of the grand challenges.

2 A Brief History of Artificial Intelligence

The field of artificial intelligence has dramatically changed during the past 15 years-or-so. Initially, starting in the fifties, intelligence was essentially considered to be synonymous with thinking, i.e. with problem solving, reasoning, and logical deduction. Within this framework thinking could naturally be conceptualized as a sequence of steps, as algorithms. The main idea of the classical or traditional approach in artificial intelligence can be captured in the so-called cognitivistic paradigm which states that cognition can be viewed as computation, cognition being a very general term for mental processes. This implies that intelligence can be studied at the level of algorithms and there is no need to investigate the underlying physical processes. Thus, there is a deliberate abstraction from the physical level. This paradigm has spawned a host of research and artificial intelligence grew into a large discipline consisting of many different subfields, including knowledge representation, logic, planning, natural language processing, problem solving and reasoning, expert systems, qualitative reasoning about physical processes, theorem proving, and machine learning.

During the 1980s artificial intelligence was booming, in particular the field of so-called expert systems. There had been high hopes that we would soon have computer programs capable of solving real-world problems like medical diagnosis, configuration and repair of complex devices, scheduling, commercial loan assessment, etc. By the end of the 1980s it had become clear that expert systems had not been successful. The idea underlying expert systems, that human expertise – or intelligence if you like – could be captured in a possibly large set of logical rules that could then be run on a computer, proved to be an inappropriate model of the true nature of human expertise (for a review of the arguments see, e.g. Clancey, 1997; Pfeifer and Scheier, 1999; Vinkhuyzen, 1998; Winograd and Flores, 1986). One of the most fundamental problems with such systems was the lack of grounding. Grounding means that an expert's skills are built on top of a long history of interaction with a physical and social world during which sensory-motor and perceptual skills have evolved. An implication of grounded intelligence is that abstract concepts and symbols can be meaningfully interpreted vis-à-vis the real world. It became apparent that intelligence could not be sensibly conceived of in purely computational terms.

In addition to these developments, evidence for the problems with the cognitivistic approach to artificial intelligence came from another area. Around the same time, i.e. also during the 1980s, many people started building robots. The basic idea of the traditional approach to robotics has been and still is that the essence of intelligence is to be seen in the internal, symbolic processing. All that would be required, so the rationale, is to attach a camera and some actuators in order to have a system that can interact with the real world. One could then map the camera image onto an internal representation, a model of the real world, generate a plan of action that could then be executed by the robot. In the meantime, it is well-known that this approach which constitutes the standard approach to computer vision did not pan out in general. It only worked in well-defined settings like factory environments. The limitations of viewing intelligence as a computational phenomenon exclusively became obvious. Given these insurmountable problems a radically new approach was required. Rodney Brooks of the MIT Artificial Intelligence Laboratory suggested that we forget about logic and problem solving, that we do away with thinking and with what people call high-level cognition and focus on the interaction with the real world (Brooks, 1991a, b). This interaction is, of course, always mediated by a body, i.e. the proposal was that intelligence be "embodied". What originally seemed nothing more than yet another buzzword turned out to have profound ramifications and rapidly changed the research disciplines of artificial intelligence and cognitive science. It is currently beginning to exert its influence on psychology, neurobiology, and ethology, as well as engineering.

Research in artificial intelligence employs a synthetic methodology, i.e. an approach that can be succinctly characterized as "understanding by building": by developing artifacts that mimic certain aspects of the behavior of natural systems, a deeper understanding of that behavior can be acquired. There are three aspects to the synthetic methodology: (1) building a model of some aspect of a natural system, (2) abstracting general principles of intelligence, and (3) applying these abstract principles to the design of intelligent systems. The artifacts of interest are either computer programs, as in classical artificial intelligence, or robots as in embodied artificial intelligence. In the embodied approach simulations are used as well, but they are of a particular type and include models of an independent environment that have their own dynamics, as well as the agent's sensory and motor interactions with these surroundings. The synthetic methodology contrasts with the analytic one where a given system is analyzed in a top-down manner, as is the standard way of proceeding in science.

3 Embodiment

The goal of this section is to introduce the novel ideas that have been developed within the framework of embodied artificial intelligence. In particular we will show that embodiment means much more than simply "using a robot" – it requires an entirely new way of thinking, and it necessitates reflecting on the interaction with the real world; the latter is messy and not as neat as the world of the virtual machine. We start with a few comments on embodiment and then present a series of case studies.

3.1 Implications of Embodiment

Embodiment has two main types of implications, physical and information theoretic. The former are concerned with physical forces, inertia, friction, vibrations, and energy dissipation, i.e. anything concerned with the (physical) dynamics of the system, the latter with the relation between sensory signals, motor control, and neural substrate. Rather than focusing on the neural substrate only, the focus is now on the complete organism which includes morphology (shape, distribution and physical characteristics of sensors and actuators, limbs, etc.) and materials. One of the surprising consequences is that often, problems that seem very hard if viewed from a purely computational perspective, turn out to be easy if the embodiment and the interaction with the environment are appropriately taken into account. For example, given a particular task environment, if the morphology is right, the amount of neural processing required may be significantly reduced (e.g. case study 1). Because of this perspective on embodiment, entirely new issues are raised and need to be taken into account. An important one concerns the so-called "ecological balance", i.e. the interplay between the sensory system, the motor system, the neural substrate, and the materials used (Hara and Pfeifer, 2000; Pfeifer, 1996; Pfeifer, 1999, 2000; Pfeifer and Scheier, 1999). Ten years of research in this new field have generated a large number of fascinating results and unexpected insights.

3.2 Case Studies

We begin with a simple robotics experiment, the "Swiss Robots" and an example from artificial evolution which illustrate mostly the relation between behavior, sensor morphology, and internal mechanism. Then we discuss motor systems, in particular biped walking, and muscles where the exploitation of (physical) dynamics is demonstrated. Finally we will show how it all fits together.

Case Study 1: The "Swiss Robots"

The "Swiss Robots" (figure 1a) can clean an arena cluttered with Styrofoam cubes (figure 1b) (which is why they are called the "Swiss Robots"). They can do this, even though they are only equipped with a simple obstacle avoidance reflex based in infrared (IR) sensors. The reflex can be described as "stimulation of right IR sensor, turn left", "stimulation of left IR sensor, turn right". If a robot happens to encounter a cube head-on, there will be no sensory stimulation because of the physical arrangement of the sensors and the robot will move forward and at the same time push the cube until it encounters another one on the side (figure 1c) at which point it will turn away. If the position of the sensors is changed (figure 1d), the robots no longer clean the arena, although the control program is exactly the same (for more detail, the reader is referred to Maris and te Boekhorst, 1996; Pfeifer and Scheier, 1998; or Pfeifer, 1999). Another powerful idea which is illustrated by this example is that if the morphology is right, control can become much simpler (in this case a simple obstacle avoidance reflex leads to clustering behavior). This point will be further illustrated when we discuss the trade-off between morphology and control in the following case study on the evolution of the morphology of an "insect eye" on a robot.

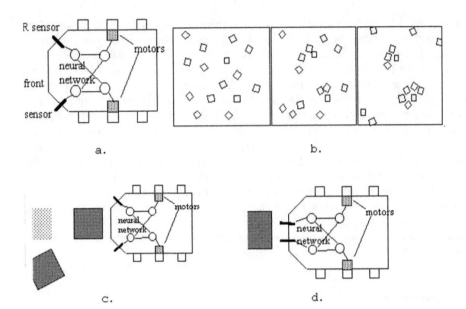

Fig. 1. The "Swiss Robots". (a) Robot with IR sensors and neural network implementing a simple avoidance reflex. (b) Clustering process. (c) Explanation of cluster formation. (d) Changed morphology: modified sensor positioning (details: see text).

Case Study 2: Evolving the Morphology of an "Insect Eye" on a Robot

When sitting in a train, looking out the window in the direction of the train, a light point, say a tree, will travel slowly across the visual field as long as the tree is well in front and far away. The closer we are getting, the more the tree will move to the side, and the faster it will move across the visual field. This is called the phenomenon of motion parallax; it is solely a result of the geometry of the system-environment interaction and does not depend on the characteristics of the visual system. If the agent is moving at a fixed lateral distance to an object with a constant speed we may want its motion detectors to deliver a constant value to reflect the constant speed. Assume now that we have an insect eye consisting of many facets or ommatidia. If they are evenly spaced, i.e. if the angles between them are constant (figure 2a), different motion detector circuits have to be used for each pair of facets. If they are more densely spaced toward the front (figure 2b), the same circuits can be used for motion detection in the entire eye. Indeed, this has been found to be the case in certain species of flies (Franceschini et al., 1992) where the same kind of motion detectors are used throughout the eye, the so-called EMDs, the Elementary Motion Detectors. Thus, if the cells are appropriately positioned much less computation has to be done. This is an illustration of how morphology can be traded for computation. Where this trade-off is chosen depends on the particular task environment, or in natural systems, on the ecological niche: natural evolution has come up with a particular solution because morphology and neural substrate have co-evolved.

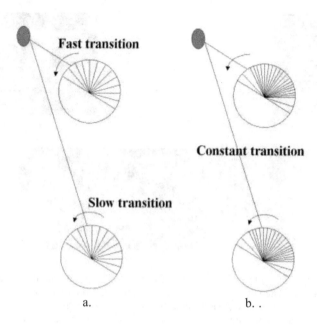

Fig. 2. Trading morphology for computation. (a) Evenly spaced facets imply different motion detection circuits for different pairs of facets. (b) Inhomogeneous distribution of facets implying that the same neural circuits can be used for motion detection throughout the entire eye.

In order to explore these ideas, Lichtensteiger and Eggenberger (1999) evolved the morphology of an "insect eye" on a real robot: They fixed the neural substrate, i.e. the elementary motion detectors which were taken to be the same for all pairs of facets were not changed during the experiment, and they used a flexible morphology where they could adjust at what angles the facets were positioned (figure 3c). They used an evolution strategy (Rechenberg, 1973) to evolve the angles for the task of maintaining a minimal lateral distance to an object. The results confirm the theoretical predictions: the facets end up with an inhomogeneous distribution with a higher density towards the front (figure 3b). The idea of space-variant sensing (e.g. Ferrari et al., 1995; Toepfer et al., 1998) capitalizes on this trade-off and is gaining rapid acceptance in the field of robot vision.

Fig. 3. Evolving the morphology of an "insect eye". (a) The Eyebot used for experiments on motion parallax. (b) The experiment seen from the top. The robot has to maintain a miminal lateral distance to an obstacle (indicated by the vertical light tube) by modifying its morphology, i.e. the positioning of the facet tubes. This is under the control of an evolution strategy. The same EMDs are used for all pairs of facets. (c) Final distribution of facets from three different runs. The front of the robot is towards the right. In all of runs, the distribution is more dense towards the front than on the side. In all of them, there are no facets directly in the front of the robot. This is because of the low resolution (the aperture) of the tubes.

Although these examples are very simple and obvious, they demonstrate the interdependence of morphology and control, a point that should always be explicitly taken into account but has todate not bee systematically studied.

Case Study 3: The Passive Dynamic Walker

Let us start with an example illustrating the relation between morphology, materials, and control. The passive dynamic walker (McGeer, 1990a, b), illustrated in figure 4, is a robot (or, if you like, a mechanical device) capable of walking down an incline without any actuation whatsoever. In other words, there are no motors and there is no control on the robot; it is brainless, so to speak. In order to achieve this task the passive dynamics of the robot, its body and its limbs, must be exploited. This kind of walking is very energy efficient but its "ecological niche" (i.e. the environment in which the robot is capable of operating) is extremely narrow: it only consists of inclines of certain angles. The strategy is to build a passive dynamic walker, and then to extend its ecological niche and have the robot walk on a flat surface (and later more complex environments) by only adding little actuation and control. Energy-efficiency is achieved because in this approach the robot is operated near one of its Eigenfrequencies.

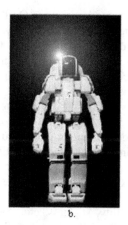

Fig. 4. Two approaches to robot building. (a) The passive dynamic walker, (b) the Honda robot.

A different approach has been taken by the Honda design team. There the goal was to have a robot that could perform a large number of movements. The methodology was to record human movements and then to reproduce them on the robot which leads to a relatively natural behavior of the robot. On the other hand control is extremely complex and there is no exploitation of the intrinsic dynamics as in the case of the passive dynamic walker. The implication is also that the movement is not energy efficient. It should be noted that even if the agent is of high complexity as the Honda robot, there is nothing that prevents the exploitation of its passive dynamics.

There are two main conclusions that can be drawn from these examples. First, it is important to exploit the dynamics in order to achieve energy-efficient and natural kinds of movements. The term "natural" not only applies to biological systems, but artificial systems also have their intrinsic natural dynamics. Second, there is a kind of trade-off or balance: the better the exploitation of the dynamics, the simpler the control, the less neural processing will be required and vice versa.

Case Study 4: Muscles – Control from Materials

Let us pursue this idea of exploiting the dynamics a little further and show how it can be taken into account to design actual robots. Most robot arms available today work with rigid materials and electrical motors. Natural arms, by contrast, are built of muscles, tendons, ligaments, and bones, materials that are non-rigid to varying degrees. All these materials have their own intrinsic properties like mass, stiffness, elasticity, viscosity, temporal characteristics, damping, and contraction ratio to mention but a few. These properties are all exploited in interesting ways in natural systems. For example, there is a natural position for a human arm which is determined by its anatomy and by these properties. Grasping an object like a cup with the right hand is normally done with the palm facing left, but could also be done – with considerable additional effort – the other way around. Assume now that the palm of your right hand is facing right and you let go. Your arm will immediately turn back into its natural position. This is not achieved by neural control but by the properties of the muscle-tendon system: On the one hand the system acts like a spring – the more you stretch it, the more force you have to apply and if you let go the spring moves back into its resting position. On the other there is intrinsic damping. Normally reaching equilibrium position and damping is conceived of in terms of electronic (or neural) control, whereas in this case, this is achieved (mostly) through the material properties.

These ideas can be transferred to robots. Many researchers have started building artificial muscles (for reviews of the various technologies see, e.g., Kornbluh et al., 1998 and Shahinpoor, 2000) and used them on robots, as illustrated in figure 5. ISAC, a "feeding robot", and the artificial hand by Lee and Shimoyama use pneumatic actuators, Cog the series elastic actuators, and the Face Robot shape memory alloys. Facial expressions also provide an interesting illustration for the point to be made here. If the facial tissue has the right sorts of material properties in terms of elasticity, deformability, stiffness, etc., the neural control for the facial expressions becomes much simpler. For example, for smiling, although it involves the entire face, the actuation is very simple: the "complexity" is added by the tissue properties.

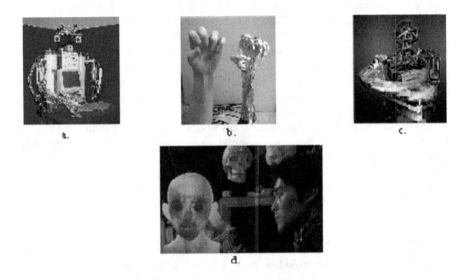

Fig. 5. Robots with artificial muscles. (a) The service robot ISAC by Peters (Vanderbilt University) driven by McKibben pneumatic actuators. (b) The artificial hand by Lee and Shimoyama (University of Tokyo), driven by pneumatic actuators. (c) The humanoid robot Cog by Rodney Brooks (MIT AI Laboratory), driven by series-elastic actuators. (d) The "Face Robot" by Kobayashi, Hara, and Iida (Science University of Tokyo), driven by shape-memory alloys.

Let us briefly summarize the ideas concerning the interplay between morphology, materials, and control. First, given a particular task environment, the (physical) dynamics of the agent can be exploited which leads not only to a natural behavior of the agent, but also to higher energy-efficiency. Second, by exploiting the dynamics of the agent, often control can be significantly simplified. And third, materials have intrinsic control properties.

We have now talked about ants, simple robots, insect eyes, simple biped walkers and artificial muscles. How does this all fit together and how does it relate to intelligence? These are not questions that can be answered now but they constitute in fact, the major challenges in the field for the next 10 years.

4 State-of-the Art

Typically when discussing the state-of-the-art in artificial intelligence questions of the following sort are addressed: In the classical approach we could do high-level problem solving like medical diagnosis, theorem proving, and natural language processing. With the embodied approach we are doing tasks suited for robots like obstacle avoidance, navigation, homing, perhaps sorting objects into categories or manipulating physical objects. Where are we now? Have we given up on the original goal of trying to understand what people call high-level cognition? The problem with these questions is that we have never really been able to do medical diagnosis, at least not in the same way that human physicians would do it, simply because we have not yet understood the nature of human expertise. What we have been able to do is define sets of rules that capture the formal aspects of diagnostic knowledge. As shown earlier, there is now widespread agreement, that this is not a realistic way of modeling human expertise. A similar point could be made about natural language. This implies that if we are interested in the foundations of high-level cognition, this "detour" is necessary because there is increasing evidence that high-level thinking must be grounded in the sensory-motor history of an individual's interaction with its environment. We put "detour" between quotation marks to indicate that this is not actually a detour but a necessary research activity. Getting there is one of the great challenges (see section 5).

During the mid-1980s Rodney Brooks argued on the basis of natural evolution that we first need to understand simpler forms of intelligence before we can tackle higher levels as we find them in humans and that we should begin by working on insect-like robots. He developed a series of highly interesting robots such as Genghis and Hannibal that imitated at some level insect walking. These robots could learn to walk and climb over obstacles, for example. By the early 1990s he claimed that these robots had achieved insect-level intelligence and that it was time to move to something more challenging like human-level intelligence and he engaged in the Cog project (e.g. Brooks et al., 1999; see below).

While Genghis and Hannibal are fascinating and are indeed capable of imitating certain aspects of insect behavior, they are far from "insect intelligence". Just imagine what other things insects are capable of doing: the are excellent navigators, i.e. they can find their way with great precision in very taxing environments; they reproduce, they care for their offspring; they have sophisticated sensory-motor abilities; they can distinguish food from non-food; they can find food efficiently in the environment; they build amazing structures; and they often form complex societies. In this perspective Ghenghis and Hannibal are not very insect-like, and it is, in our view, an exaggeration to talk about insect-level intelligence. Again, this by no means implies that they are not interesting; they simply have not yet achieved insect-level intelligence in general.

The Cog project has the ambitious goal to eventually achieve human-level intelligence. A developmental approach is taken to the problem (for more detail, see section 5.1). The idea of this approach is to equip the robot with "human-like" sophisticated sensory and motor systems: There is a torso with arms a head with a neck, an active vision system, an acoustic system, touch sensors, and proprioceptive sensors (for measuring joint angles and forces of the robot's limbs). As it interacts with the real physical and social world it learns to make distinctions (i.e. it forms categories) and it acquires communication skills. In this way – and the is the grand goal of this project – what we call high-level cognition can be bootstrapped from this embodied interaction with the real world. Anything the robot learns is thus "grounded", to use the jargon of the field. The conviction underlying this project and that we fully share, is that intelligence must be grounded in sensory-motor interactions. Perception is not mapping a sensory stimulation (e.g. a pixel array) onto an internal representation but a sensory-motor coordination (Dewey, 1896). Again, Cog is a fascinating robot and there is a lot of potential for research. However, talking about human-level would be an enormous exaggeration. While in the case of insects we might be inclined to believe that today's robots have achieved their level of intelligence, it is entirely obvious that this is not the case for humans – infants or adults.

The discussion about the state-of-the art in the field of robotics and artificial intelligence has always been difficult because of science fiction and horror scenarios. It is encumbered by numerous predictions that do not contribute to assessing what robots can and cannot do and how this will be in the future. Of course, nobody can predict the future, especially where technology is concerned. However, some scenarios are science fiction and do not belong into a scientific discourse.

5 Some Grand Challenges

It will be a long way until we reach the romantic vision of understanding intelligence, whatever that would exactly mean. And there are many grand challenges that need to be resolved along the way. We discuss two that we believe cover most of the issues in the synthetic study of intelligence that we are currently aware of. They are both tightly intertwined but can be separated for the purpose of dividing up the research into manageable chunks. The first one implies understanding how we can evolve an artificial real-world agent, i.e. a robot, for high-level cognition, the second comprehension of "ecological balance".

5.1 The First Challenge: Evolving Grounded Intelligence

One of the most fundamental abilities of agents—animals, humans, and robots—in the real world, is the capacity to make distinctions: food has to be distinguished from non-food, predators from con-specifics, the nest from the rest of the environment, and so forth. This ability is also called categorization and forms the basis of concept formation and ultimately high-level cognition. In order to elucidate the distinction between traditional computer models and embodied models, we briefly discuss a prominent traditional categorization model, ALCOVE (Kruschke, 1992). Indeed, ALCOVE is an excellent model: It can predict a large part of the experimental data published in the psychological categorization literature. In essence, ALCOVE is a connectionist model in which certain nodes, the category nodes, are activated whenever an instance of a particular category is encountered. In other words, these category nodes are representations of the categories. The task of ALCOVE can then be seen as one of mapping the input feature vector onto an internal representation of the category.

The main problem with ALCOVE, as is the problem with most models in classical cognitive psychology and classical artificial intelligence, is that it is not connected to the outside world: its inputs are feature vectors, its output activation levels of nodes in a neural network. In the real world, agents are exposed to a stream of continuously changing sensory stimulation, not to feature vectors, and they require a continuous stream of motor control. Moreover, there is the problem of object constancy, i.e. the phenomenon that the sensory stimulation from one and the same object varies enormously depending, for example, on distance, orientation, and lighting conditions. It turns out—and it has been discussed extensively in the literature—that categorization in the real world requires a completely different approach, as the history of computer vision teaches.

The insight that categorization in the real world is not an exclusively computational problem and requires that embodiment be taken into account is gaining increasing acceptance: It has been demonstrated that categorization is best viewed as a process of sensory-motor coordination (Edelman, 1987; Metta et al., 1998; Pfeifer and Scheier, 1997; Scheier, Pfeifer, and Kuniyoshi, 1997). The sensory stimulation that the neural system has to process depends on the physical characteristics and on the positioning of the sensors on the agent. But not only that, it also crucially depends on the agent's behavior. For example, touching a bottle with a stiff hand yields entirely different sensory stimulation than fully grasping the bottle with the entire hand bent around the bottle. Note that this is a change in the morphology of the hand which leads to a change in the sensory stimulation. So, there are two closely related factors influencing the sensory stimulation, morphology, and sensory-motor coordination.

The question we have to ask now is how this all connects to the study of high-level intelligence or cognition. how does cognition come about? What we have shown is the basic ways in which neural processing, morphology, and environment are interconnected. An increasing number of people are becoming convinced that if we are to explain cognition, we must understand how it evolves during ontogenetic development (e.g. Clark, 1997; Edelman, 1987; Elman et al., 1997; Thelen and Smith, 1994). Thelen and Smith argue that while in human infants behavior is initially highly sensory-motor and is directly coupled to the system-environment interaction, during development some processes become "decoupled" from the direct sensory-motor interaction, but the underlying mechanisms, the neural substrate, is exactly the same. The advent of the discovery of mirror neurons (see, e.g. Rizzolatti et al., 2000, for an overview), i.e. neurons that are equally activated when performing or just observing an action, adds validity to this view. The question of what the mechanisms are through which, over time, this "decoupling" from the environment takes place is, to our knowledge, an unresolved research issue.

The challenge for artificial intelligence is to build robots that can mimic the processes of human infant development. This will on the one hand help us uncover the mechanisms underlying development, and on the other we will be able to build highly complex and intelligent systems. Of course, given the current state-of-the art, it is an illusion to build a robot that actually (physically) grows. Perhaps with progress in nanotechnology this may eventually be possible. But for now we have to work with non-growing robots. Given this limitation, one approach is to build a humanoid robot, i.e. a robot that has some similarity with humans in terms of morphology (shape), sensory and motor systems. The human sensory and motor systems are extremely sophisticated. For example, the entire body is covered with many sensors, e.g. touch and temperature, there are different types of sensory channels (vision, hearing, touch, smell, taste), and there are many internal (proprioceptive) sensors. We have already discussed the complex properties of muscles. Building a complex robot implies, in addition to the conceptual challenges, technological ones in terms of actuators, "tissue", and sensors. A grand challenge indeed, requiring the cooperation of many scientific disciplines from computer science, developmental psychology, neuroscience, engineering and materials science. Mimicking human infants (or toddlers) is one of the goals of the Cog project that was mentioned above.

The drawback is that we are stuck with one particular design, a complex and sophisticated one perhaps, but still a given one. Artificial intelligence has additional possibilities in that we can explore designs that do not exist in nature. But how should we design our systems, then? In order to answer this question we need to understand "ecological balance". A good method to explore a problem space is artificial evolution. We will show how it can be used to understand and explore "ecological balance" in systematic ways.

5.2 The Second Challenge: Understanding and Exploring "Ecological Balance"

Using artificial evolution for design has a tradition in the field of evolutionary robotics. The standard approach there is to take a particular robot and use a genetic algorithm to evolve a control architecture for a particular task. However, if we want to explore ecological balance we must include morphology and materials into our evolutionary algorithms. The example of the Eyebot where the morphology of an "insect eye" was evolved, demonstrates another way in which evolution can be used: We fix the neural substrate and let evolution work on the morphology to solve the problem. Both of these approaches are not biologically plausible and can only be done in artificial systems.

The problem with including morphology and materials is that the search space which is already very large for control architectures, literally explodes. Moreover, if sophisticated shapes and sensors are to be evolved, the length of the genome which is required for encoding these shapes will grow very large and there is no hope that anything will ever converge. This issue can be approached in various ways, we just mention two. The first which we will not further discuss is to parameterize the shapes, thus bringing in biases from the designer on the types of shapes that are possible. In the eyebot the rods with the light-sensitive cells were given and only the angle could be adjusted, which makes the problem very simple, but then there is only little variation possible in the morphology. An example that has stirred a lot of commotion in the media recently is provided by Hod Lipson and Jordan Pollack's robots that were automatically produced (Lipson and Pollack, 2000). They decided that the morphology would consist of rods to which different types of joints could be attached. Rods can, for example, be parameterized as length, diameter, and material constants etc., thus limiting the space of possible shapes dramatically, but then the search space, even though it is still large, becomes manageable. While this example is impressive, it still implies a strong designer bias.

A more general and the more natural approach, is to not encode directly the structure of the organism in the genome but instead to encode the developmental processes. For example, it is not possible to encode the structure of the human brain in the genome because in the latter there is not enough information content. Once again, nature can be taken as a source of inspiration.

An illustration of how biological development might be modeled is given in Eggenberger (1997, 1999) who succeeded in growing 3-D shapes based on the Artificial Evolutionary System (AES). The AES implements the biological mechanisms of gene-based cell-to-cell communication. The final organism corresponds to an attractor of a highly complex dynamical system. Although these sorts of models are only in their initial stages, they will become increasingly important if we are to understand the principles of "ecological balance" and of agent design. The attempt behind the AES is to evolve entire organisms from one cell. The search space is, again, extremely vast and there is little hope that anything will converge within reasonable time. Natural systems have evolved mechanisms to impose constraints so that, for example, groups of genes couple together for certain periods of time during development (e.g. the hox genes) which enables, for example, the coordinated growth of organs or limbs.

If we have the mechanisms for co-evolving entire organisms' morphology, materials, and control, we have a powerful tool at hand by which we can explore the space of possible designs and thus "ecological balance". At the moment this is only possible in simulation; the experiments with artificial systems that can grow physically are only in their very initial stages. One way to get around this problem, at least to some extent, is on the one hand to have a good simulator that models the physics of an evolved individual and its interactions with the real world, on the other to have rapid robot building kits that enable the researchers to quickly build a robot to test some individuals in the real world. But even if done in simulation, evolving an organism from scratch is a grand challenge as well.

One of the problems with the examples and ideas presented in this paper is that they are mostly qualitative. Clearly, more quantitative statements will be required to make the story more compelling. But we hope that researchers will take up the challenges posed by embodiment.

6 Conclusions

We have tried to outline the history and the future of artificial intelligence, from its initial form as an algorithmic – cognitivistic – discipline all the way to its current embodied form. The big and frequently asked question is whether this embodied approach will indeed succeed to achieve in a bottom-up manner, higher levels of intelligence that go beyond direct sensory-motor tasks. We feel that this is indeed the case: It has been suggested, for example, that even abstract relationships like transitivity can be explained as emergent from embodied interactions with the environment (Linda Smith, pers. comm.). A similar argument has been made for mathematical concepts (e.g. Núñez and Lakoff, 1998). The jury is still out on whether this is a sound intuition or will turn out to be flawed; all we can do at the moment is outline a research program. But because embodiment provides a new perspective and many ideas for empirical studies on natural and artificial systems, as well as for new kinds of agents, we are optimistic that we can achieve a better understanding of intelligence in the future.

Acknowledgment

I would like to thank Reinhard Wilhelm for suggesting the topic of this paper and to the members of the Artificial Intelligence Laboratory for many discussions, in particular Lukas Lichtensteiger and Gabriel Gómez.

References

1.   Brooks, R. A. (1991a). Intelligence without representation. *Artificial Intelligence*, **47**, 139-160.

2.   Brooks, R. A. (1991b). Intelligence without reason. *Proceedings International Joint Conference on Artificial Intelligence-91*, 569-595.

3.   Brooks, R. A., Breazeal, C., Marjanovic, M., Scassellati, B., and Williamson, M. (1999). The Cog project: building a humanoid robot. http://www.ai.mit.edu/projects/cog/.

4.   Clancey, W.J. (1997). *Situated cognition. On human knowledge and computer representations*. Cambridge, UK: Cambridge University Press.

5.   Clark, A. (1998). *Being there: Putting brain, body, and world together again.* Cambridge, Mass.: MIT Press.

6.   Dewey, J. (1896). The reflex arc in psychology. *Psychol. Review*, **3**, 1981, 357-370. Reprinted in J.J. McDermott (eds.): *The Philosophy of John Dewey.* Chicago, IL: The University of Chicago Press, 136-148.

7.   Edelman, G.E. (1987). *Neural Darwinism. The theory of neuronal group selection.* New York: Basic Books.

8.   Eggenberger, P. (1997). Evolving morphologies of simulated 3d organisms based on differential gene expression. In: P. Husbands, and I. Harvey (eds.). *Proc. of the 4th European Conference on Artificial Life.* Cambridge, Mass.: MIT Press.

9. Eggenberger, P. (1999). *Evolution of three-dimensional, artificial organisms: simulations of developmental processes.* Unpublished PhD Dissertation, Medical Faculty, University of Zurich, Switzerland.

10. Elman, J.L., Bates, E.A., Johnson, M.H., Karmiloff-Smith, A., Parisi, D., and Plunkett, K. (1996). *Rethinking innateness. A connectionist perspective on development.* Cambridge, Mass.: MIT Press.

11. Ferrari, F., Nielsen, P.Q.J., and Sandini, G. (1995). Space variant imaging. *Sensor Review*, **15**, 17-20.

12. Franceschini, N., Pichon, J.M., and Blanes, C. (1992). From insect vision to robot vision. *Phil. Trans. R. Soc. Lond. B*, **337**, 283-294.

13. Hara, F., and Pfeifer, R. (2000). On the relation among morphology, material and control in morpho-functional machines. *In Proc. SAB 2000*, 33-40.

14. Kornbluh, R. D., Pelrine, R., Eckerle, J., and Joseph, J. (1998). Electrostrictive polymer artificial muscle actuators. In *Proc. 1998 IEEE Int. Conf. on Robotics and Automation.* New York, N.Y.: IEEE, 2147-2154.

15. Kruschke, J.K. (1992). ALCOVE: An exemplar-based connectionist model of category learning. *Psychological Review*, **99**, 22-44.

16. Lipson, H., and Pollack J. B. (2000), Automatic design and manufacture of artificial life forms. *Nature,* **406**, 974-978.

17. Lichtensteiger, L., and Eggenberger, P. (1999). Evolving the morphology of a compound eye on a robot. In: Proc. of Eurobot'99.

18. Maris, M., and te Boekhorst, R. (1996). Exploiting physical constraints: heap formation through behavioral error in a group of robots. In Proc. IROS'96, IEEE/RSJ International Conference on Intelligent Robots and Systems, 1655—1660.

19. McGeer, T. (1990a). Passive dynamic walking. *Int. Journal of Robotics Research*, **9**, 62-82.

20. McGeer, T. (1990b). Passive walking with knees. Proc. of the IEEE Conference on Robotics and Automation, 2, 1640-1645.

21. Metta, G., Sandini, G., and Konczak, J. (1998). A developmental approach to sensori-motor coordination in artificial systems. In *Proc. of IEEE Conference on System, Man and Cybernetics*, San Diego (USA), 11-14.

22. Núñez, R.E., and Lakoff, G. (1998). What did Weierstrass really define? The cognitive structure of natural and ε-δ continuity. *Mathematical Cognition*, **4**, 85-101.

23. Pfeifer, R. (1996). Building "Fungus Eaters": Design principles of autonomous agents. In P. Maes, M. Mataric, J.-A. Meyer, J. Pollack, and S.W. Wilson (eds.): *From Animals to Animats. Proc. of the 4th Int. Conf. on Simulation of Adaptive Behavior.* Cambridge, Mass.: A Bradford Book, MIT Press, 3-12.

24. Pfeifer, R. (1999). Dynamics, morphology, and materials in the emergence of cognition. *Proc. KI-99, Lecture Notes in Computer Science*. Berlin: Springer, 27-44.

25. Pfeifer, R. (2000). On the role of morphology and materials in adaptive behavior. *Proc. SAB 2000*, 23-32.

26. Pfeifer, R., and Scheier, C. (1997). Sensory-motor coordination: the metaphor and beyond. *Robotics and Autonomous Systems*, **20**, 157-178.

27. Pfeifer, R., and Scheier, C. (1998). Representation in natural and artificial agents: an embodied cognitive science perspective. *Zeitschrift für Naturforschung*, **53c**, 480-503.

28. Pfeifer, R., and Scheier, C. (1999). *Understanding intelligence. Cambridge,* Mass.: MIT Press.

29. Rechenberg, I. (1973). *Evolutionsstrategie: Optimierung technischer Systeme nach Prinzipien der biologischen Evolution.* Stuttgart: Frommann-Holzboog.

30. Rizzolatti, G., Fogassi, L., and Gallese, V. (2000). Cortical mechanisms subserving object grasping and action recognition: A new view of the cortical motor functions. In: M.S. Gazzaniga (ed.). *The new cognitive neurosciences.* Cambridge, Mass.: MIT Press.

31. Scheier, C., Pfeifer, R., and Kuniyoshi, Y. (1998). Embedded neural networks: exploiting constraints. *Neural Networks*, **11**, 1551-1569.

32. Shahinpoor, M., Bar-Cohen, Y., Simpson, J.O., and Smith, J. (2000). Ionic Polymer-Metal Composites (IPMC) as biomimetic sensors, actuators & artificial muscles- A review. http://www.unm.edu/~amri/paper.html

33. Simon, H. A. (1969). *The sciences of the artificial (2nd ed.).* Cambridge, MA: MIT Press.

34. Thelen, E. and Smith, L. (1994). *A dynamic systems approach to the development of cognition and action.* Cambridge, Mass.: MIT Press, Bradford Books.

35. Toepfer, C., Wende, M., Baratoff, G., and Neumann, H. (1998). Robot navigation by combining central and peripheral optical flow detection on a space-variant map. *Proc. Fourteenth Int. Conf. on Pattern Recognition.* Los Alamitos, CA: IEEE Computer Society, 1804-1807.

36. Vinkhuyzen, E. (1998). Expert systems in practice. Unpublished PhD Dissertation, University of Zurich.

37. Wingorad, T., and Flores, F. (1986). Understanding computers and cognition. Reading, Mass.: Addison-Wesley.

Scientific Visualization
- Methods and Applications -

Hans Hagen, Achim Ebert, Rolf Hendrik van Lengen, and Gerik Scheuermann

University of Kaiserslautern

Abstract. Scientific Visualization is currently a very active and vital area of research, teaching and development. The success of Scientific Visualization is mainly due to the soundness of the basic premise behind it, that is, the basic idea of using computer-generated pictures to gain information and understanding from data (geometry) and relationships (topology). This is an extremely intiutive and very important concept which is having a profound and wide spread impact on the methodology of science and engineering.
In this survey we are concentrating on three main research areas in Scientific Visualization
- Intelligent Visualization Systems
- Visualization of Vector- and Tensorfields
- Augmented Reality Simulation

1 Introduction

Scientific Visualization is a new approach in the area of simulation. It allows researchers to observe the results of simulations using complex graphical representations. Visualization provides methods for seeing what is normally not visible, e.g. torsion forces inside a body, wind against a wall, heat conduction, flows, plasmas, earthquake mechanisms, molecules, etc.

Since vision dominates our sensory input, strong efforts have been made to bring the power of mathematical abstraction and modelling to our eyes through the mediation of computer graphics. This interplay between various application areas and their specific problem solving visualization techniques is emphasized in this survey.

We start with "MacVis", a system architecture for intelligent component-based visualization. Next is a presentation of our latest results in topological vector and tensor field visualization. Computational Fluid Dynamics is one, but not the only application area. Last but not least, we present a project in augmented reality simulation - a virtual echocardiography system.

2 MacVis — A System Architecture for Intelligent Component-Based Visualization

Nowadays, most visualization systems available on the market are designed for special purpose and therefore lack the flexibility in regards to their visualization

R. Wilhelm (Ed.): Informatics. 10 Years Back. 10 Years Ahead, LNCS 2000, pp. 311–327, 2001.

process. This means they provide either a high rendering quality with limited interaction possibilities, or real-time visualization going along with a reduced rendering quality. In order to satisfy individual user demands and to adapt to changing system loads and different hardware configurations, an appropriate visualization system architecture should comprise an intelligent control unit supervising and tuning all system components during runtime. Up to now the user manually has to adjust the balance between frame rate and rendering quality by modifying the related control parameters or by discovering and (ex)changing the causative system components. In the course of our work MacVis (**M**ulti **A**gent- and **C**omponent-based Visualization System) we provide a solution for these problems by combining multi agent technology and a component-based implementation of a visualization system.

2.1   General System Architecture

Since a huge monolithic visualization system does not sufficiently support the adjustment or replacement of the implementation of a single functionality, the proposed design consists of several modules grouped into three layers according to their functionality (see figure 1). Each module is controlled by a small number of parameters enabling the management of its functional behavior. The kernel covers basic visualization aspects including the management of scene definition, geometry objects, lighting etc. and is responsible for the optimization of the visualization process. Furthermore generic interfaces provide the link to the extension layer, which adds auxiliary functionality to the system. Examples for such extension modules are import/export, geometry generation, visualization methods and general I/O. In order to preserve platform independency all render routines are encapsulated in hardware specific render managers which form the main parts of the Hardware Abstraction Layer (HAL). Therefore, the design of our visualization system architecture follows proved principles of modern software development like a small and flexible kernel, modularity, expandability, as well as application and platform independence.

2.2   Agent-Based Visualization Control

The monitoring and tuning of a visualization application is a complex problem. Due to continually changing conditions and the variety of parameters even experts with their competent knowledge are not able to solve such a problem in general. On the other hand conditions that change dynamically are the ideal premise for the use of multi agent systems. In order to brake down the complex adjustment process into tasks which are easier to solve, our approach makes use of two types of agents (deliberative and reactive agents). A deliberative agent has the ability to handle complex problems, but in general it is not able to process such jobs in real time on his own because of the applied sophisticated calculation methods. Reactive agents on the other hand only perform simpler tasks but they can be easily integrated into dynamic environments. Concerning the architecture of a visualization system, a module or a group of modules always performs one fixed task, this means that terms of regulation (e.g. frame rate and rendering quality) can be described by straightforward static rules. Thus, a reactive agent is always assigned to either a module or a group of modules and it controls the modules' parameters on demand. Since a reactive agent only needs the knowledge in the module specific context it acts similar to a control loop. The supervision of the reactive agents, as well as the analysis of information generated by them, is done by the Performance Agent, which consists of a hierarchy of deliberative agents. Based on the overall knowledge about the involved visualization components and with respect to the user specific demands it automatically responds to changes in the environment (e.g. the system load) by modifying the desired values of the subordinated reactive agents.

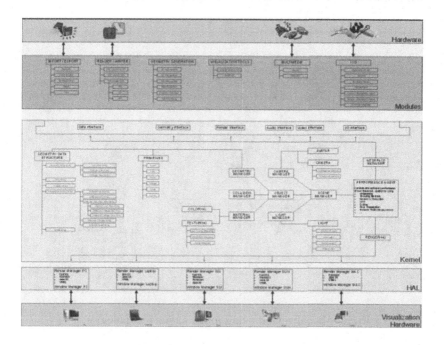

Fig. 1: System architecture.

Figure 2 shows an example of a visualization pipeline controlled by agents. In the data generation process an unstructured point set is imported and triangulated. After generating and assigning texture coordinates to the resulting object the data conversion process creates different, predefined levels of detail for the corresponding object representation. Within the data visualization process the selected representation is rendered by mapping it onto the underlying hardware abstraction layer. To achieve the user defined rendering quality and performance reactive agents are assigned to each component of the pipeline and are supervised by the Performance Agent. Exemplarily we will briefly describe the interplay of the Data Conversion and Data Visualization modules and the Performance Manager in the present case: The reactive agent of the Data Conversion module controls the level of detail component by altering its parameters affecting the level of detail algorithm, the reduction level and the accuracy demand. The output of the Data Conversion module is the effective accuracy level and the number of generated triangles. he reactive agent of the Data Visualization module controls the render component by varying the representation model (wire frame, solid), the shading model, the rendering algorithm, the resolution and the lighting and texturing parameters. The output of the Data Visualization module is the current frame rate or the render time respectively. Both modules receive their permitted parameter ranges from the Performance Agent which in its turn is biased by user demands and the system environment.

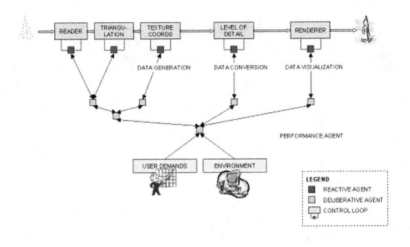

Fig. 2: Visualization using multi agent technologies.

Component-based implementation Component technology offers an ideal platform to achieve the uncoupling of visualization modules and visualization systems. In this context a component is an encapsulated piece of software with a standardized, contractually specified interface giving access to a corresponding functionality (service). The definition of interfaces as well as its administration are regulated by a component system (repository). Therefore a calling process (client) only gets the information about the logical structure of the service according to the interface definition and experiences the behavior through invocation. Consequently the strict separation between implementation and provided functionality supports the development of independent and reusable software components, which leads to the following advantages:

- Dynamic linking: Components can be replaced, added to or deleted from an application at runtime.
- Faster application development: The effort necessary to build / assemble new applications can be reduced when suitable components are available.
- Small costs: If an application can be assembled out of already existing components, reduced expenes arise due to the shorter development times.
- Reliability: Components are permanently extended and improved leading to a higher reliability of the respective applications.
- Flexible system architectures: Easy exchange and customization of components

leads to an improved extendibility and maintainability of applications. In our implementation we decided to use Sun's Java Beans component technology to realize the modules described in section 2.1 With the use of a visual prototyping system new applications can be plugged together at runtime. The control of visualization parameters can be automatically handled by attaching appropriate reactive and deliberative agents to the components. Here the integration of agents directly fits into the concepts of the desired component technology, that is reactive and deliberative agents are software components themselves.

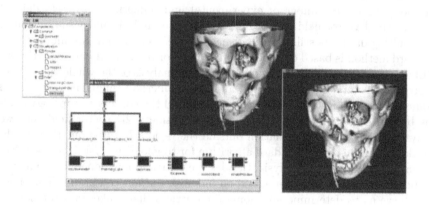

Fig. 3: Snapshot of our visual prototyping system.

Figure 3 shows a snapshot of our visual prototyping system while assembling a special volume data visualization application. The intelligent visualization system response which depends on the users interaction demands and the system environment is illustrated by the two images showing different levels of detail.

3   Topological Vector and Tensor Field Visualization

Our group for the past several years has made mesurable strides in the visualization of vector and tensor fields. We are especially interested in the analysis and presentation of structural information obtained from the data based on physical and mathematical models. Therefore, we extract the topology of these fields and present the results to the user. In the following, we describe three recent approaches to deal with large data sets by simplifying the structure or concentrating on the structure in local regions of interest only.

3.1   Local Vector Field Topology

Fluid mechanics is a major application for vector field visualization. A velocity field contains the answers to many of the important questions asked by both phycisists and engineers. Due to rotation, the velocity can usually not be described by a gradient field, so an analysis of a single scalar field does not capture the whole structure. Since fluid mechanics is an essential part of the aerospace and automotive industries, there is a strong need for better analysis and visualization methods. Topology has been used in fluid mechanics for several years to interpret experiments and deduct theoretical results, see [CPC80], [Dal83], [Lig63]. These ideas provided the foundation for the use of vector field topology for the analysis and visualization by Helman and Hesselink [HH90] as well as Globus et al. [GLL91].

Mathematically, vector fields are geometric representations of differential equations, and the number of experimental and numerical data sets defined by discretized vector field is growing rapidly. The analysis and visualization of the resulting data sets still pose challenges to the visualization community. One standard method is based on topological analysis of vector field data, see [HH90], [GLL91], [SKMR98]. These methods require an analysis of the whole vector field to provide answers on the structure, and certain methods might not contain all required features. [KHL99]. Recently, we localized the concept of topology analysis by concentrating on an arbitrary region inside a 2D vector field that we analyze without using information outside the region. It turns out that a substantial extension of the standard algorithm for topology analysis is necessary to accomplish correct local analysis. Besides the critical points, one has to analyze the boundary of a local region based on *inflow* or *outflow* conditions. This analysis allows us to determine additional separatrices that make, in a topological sense, a separation of the local region into areas of topologically uniform flow possible. The result is shown in Fig. 4.

3.2   Vector Field Topology Simplification

Simulations and measurements provide scientists and engineers with large vector data sets. A major visualization challenge is to extract essential information for interpretation. For turbulent flows, topology-based methods lead to cluttered pictures usually preventing the user from large scale qualitative analysis (see Fig. 5). Since turbulent flows are characterized by a large number of close vortices of different scales, we developed a description with a reduced number of critical points that still contains the topological information of the given data set. This leads to new methods for vector field topology simplification. Our

Fig. 4: Local topology analysis

central idea is to merge close critical points into one, potentially higher order, critical point. This reduces the clutter, but it keeps the topology consistent. The described method starts with a planar piecewise bilinear structured grid. We locate all critical points in an usual zero search over the cells. Then, we partition the grid into convex cell clusters, called *supercells*. In each supercell, the distances between the critical points must be below a prescribed value. We use a typical top-down clustering approach starting with the whole grid as first cluster and successive subdivision until all clusters obey the rule. Now, we know which critical points to merge. Since we want to have a piecewise analytic description of our vector field, we have to modify the intern supercell geometry and/or interpolation. We choose the grid point closest to the center of all critical points in the supercell and set its vector value to zero. Then, we connect all grid points from the supercell boundary to this point. This results in a new mesh that has exactly one critical point in each supercell. Since this critical point is on a vertex in a piecewise linear field, we may produce a higher order critical point of arbitrary complexity. Essentially, we concentrate the preexisting topological flow properties in a single point. In this sense, our grid modification acts as a fusion of all singularities in the supercell.

The analysis of the resulting higher order singularity requires a generalization of the usual critical point analysis, since there is no valid derivative at a grid vertex. The general idea goes back to work by Andronov et al. [AAIM73]. It is based on a partition of the neighborhood of the critical point into sectors of different behavior. The sequence of these sectors defines the topological type of the critical point. The sectors are divided into three types: hyperbolic, parabolic and elliptic. A hyperbolic sector contains only streamlines that pass the critical point without approaching it. The simple case is a saddle point with its four hyperbolic sectors. A parabolic sector consists of streamlines that start/end at the critical point and end somewhere else. Simple sources or sinks have only parabolic sectors. Finally, elliptic sectors consist of streamlines that loop back to the critical point, i. e. that start and end at this point. There are no elliptic sectors in linear vector field, but one may imagine a simple dipole with two elliptic sectors. We present the details on definitions and analysis including calculating the separatrices in later sections. Figures 5-7 show the result of our method with the data set used before.

3.3   Tensor Field Topology Simplification

Tensors are the language of mechanics. Therefore, tensor field visualization is a challenging issue for Scientific Visualization. We need to provide scientists and engineers with techniques that enable both qualitative and quantitative analysis of the tensor data sets resulting from experiments or numerical simulations. A topology-based visualization method of symmetric, second-order tensor fields in two dimensions [DH94] has been designed for that purpose: It focuses on one of the two eigenvector fields corresponding to the minor or major eigenvalues. Like the vector case, the displayed graph consists of so-called degenerate points connected by particular integral curves, the separatrices. This technique proved to be suitable for tensor fields with simple structure because the extracted topology contains few degenerate points and separatrices, leading to a comprehensible structure description. However, for tensor fields with complicated structure (like those encountered in turbulent flows, for instance), topology-based methods lead to cluttered pictures that confuse the interpretation. Our hierarchical method merges close degenerate points into one, which results in a simplified topology and a clarified depiction, though globally maintaining the qualitative properties of the original data. We assume a planar, piecewise bilinear interpolated, symmetric, second-order tensor field over a structured grid. The degenerate points are determined. A clustering strategy is applied on the resulting set of degenerate points. This leads to a grid partition into cell clusters such that the distance between degenerate points in each cluster is below a user-prescribed threshold. After this, we merge the degenerate points lying in each cluster to get the desired scaling effect. Finally, we determine the resulting separatrices.

The merging process and the analysis of the resulting degenerate points are new and detailed in the following. We want to maintain a piecewise analytic description of the tensor field. This is accomplished by a local grid deformation inside each cluster, leaving its boundary unchanged. More precisely, we insert a new vertex with null tensor value at the center of gravity of the previous degenerate points and connect it to all cluster boundary vertices. Therefore, the new tensor field is consistent with the original and contains a single degenerate point in each cluster. Once this has been done, we have to determine the structure of these artificially created degenerate points. Because they lie on a grid vertex, they may be of higher order and arbitrary complexity. Consequently, their analysis requires a partition of their neighborhood in several sectors, generalizing

Fig. 5: original topology

Fig. 6: simplified topology (threshold = 0.2)

Fig. 7: simplified topology (threshold = 0.4)

work of Andronov [AAIM73] to bidirectional vector fields, since eigenvectors do not have an inherent orientation. In contrary to the vector fields in our Visualization 2000 paper, the eigenvector fields are not linear on the cluster boundary edges. Cubic equations must be solved to locate the possible positions of the separatrices. Then we determine which are actual separatrices and integrate them to form the simplified topological graph. We have applied our method below to the rate of strain tensor of the swirling jet simulation used before. In this case, the topology is clarified, the separatrices easier to track while the significant structural features have been preserved as can be seen in figures 8-10.

4   Virtual Echocardiography System

On account of the high diagnostic expressiveness of the images achieved by sophisticated computer technology, examination of the structure and function of the heart and great vessel structures by ultrasound are producing images of better quality. Due to the non-invasive nature of ultrasound and the expansion of the roles of cardiac technicians and radiographers, ultrasound scanning is becoming a fast and readily available modality, which is able to give immediate results at relatively low cost.

Currently, real time scanners are in routine use, which depict a continuos two-dimensional picture of medical structures on a monitor screen. According to the diagnostic question very high frequency sound waves of between 2 to 10 megahertz are generally used for this purpose. They are emitted from a transducer which is placed in contact with the human body, and is moved around to get a general idea of the interesting region. Repetitive arrays of ultrasound beams scan the region in thin slices and are reflected back onto the same transducer. The information obtained from different reflections are recomposed back into a sequence of pictures. Movements such as fetal heart beat can be judged and physiologic measurements can be made to very accurate levels by means of these images. The selected frequency depends on the required image details needed for examination, and always represents a compromise between an excellent image resolution with small penetration depth into the tissue and vice versa.

Although echocardiography plays an important role in clinical diagnostics, there are still some major drawbacks associated with this technique. Due to the clinical day's work the time for monitored and guided examinations is quite limited. Many findings are rare compared to the number of examinations done every year, but may have lethal consequences nevertheless. In consequence, untrained medical personnel is doing every day clinical routine far before they have acquired a thorough experience in the vision process. Therefore, computerized education and training will become particularly important with the increasing role played by echocardiography in the management of patients. In previous years the echocardiography department in each hospital adopted its own style of work and training, and hence the standards and quality of work vary from place to place. In most countries there have been continuous efforts to standardize the education and training requirements for echocardiographers, so that an uniform

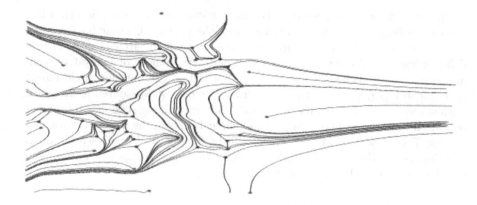

Fig. 8: Original topology: 61 degenerate points

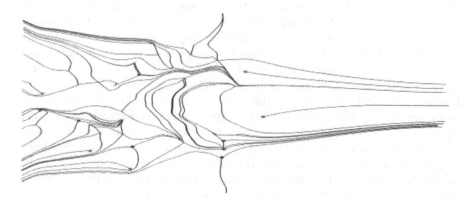

Fig. 9: Simplified topology: threshold=0.4, 31 degenerate points

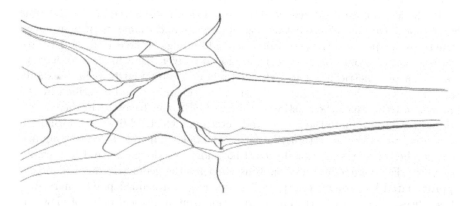

Fig. 10: Simplified topology: threshold=0.8, 15 degenerate points

quality of work can be expected. In Germany a standardized education guideline for echocardiographers can be obtained from the German Cardiac Society.

In this contex the main objective of the ongoing research project Virtual Echocardiography System is the research and development of innovative techniques and solutions for the achievement of a virtual examination environment for echocardiography. Applying the technologies that will be developed medical students and echocardiographers can take part in training sessions and further education to improve their technical and clinical skills in the field of echocardiography. The work done in this project will be focused on three research topics (1.) Parametric Heart Model, (2.) Artificial Ultrasound Image Generation, and (3.) Augmented Reality Environment.

4.1   Parametric Heart Model

As part of research in the field of echocardiography the EchoBefundSystem (EBS) was developed in cooperation with the faculty of Klinische Medizin Mannheim der Universität Heidelberg. EBS is a web based client-server application for standardised documentation on echocardiography results right at the workplace. The software leads the examiner by means of user interface design and stored medical knowledge. The level of detail scales automatically to the ongoing examination. While the examiner is discovering more and more special findings or might even enter a complete medical study the interface offers more and more fields and checkboxes. The structured user interface reflects the organ structure as well as examination methods familiar to the examiner. Automatically calculated fields are speeding up the examination. Judgements, diagnoses, values and ranges are interrelated. The findings entered into the EBS are intended for standardised documentation and reflect general aspects (e.g. patient data), data concerning the actual examination (e.g. screening quality for three different axes), wall motion, descriptions of valves (e.g. degree of calcification), description of artificial valves, description of jets (e.g. approximated diameter), description of left and right atrium, description of left and right chamber.

Realistic simulation of echocardiography examinations requires a dynamic heart model capable of predicting the movement and moments of anatomical structures. To perform the step from medical findings entered into the EBS towards a spatial geometric representation for any given point in time we have to research a parametric heart model. This model is supposed to behave exactly the same way as the real heart does, which was examined and described by the findings in EBS. Since the existing ontology of EBS was driven by medical interests we have to evaluate the results and determine which additional information is required to reduce uncertainty in our heart model. The real heart is examined in a number of representational slices (like short axis, long axis and four chamber view). For volume and flow analysis purposes the geometric shape is merely approximated by geometric objects like spheres with defined points marked in these slices. This is a practical approximation from a medical point of view but may not result in any sensible spatial representation. In addition many findings in the EBS are of a linguistic type, e.g. the wall motion is "reduced", the ejection fraction is "increased" and the shunt is "severe". Some of these parameters may need to be quantified.

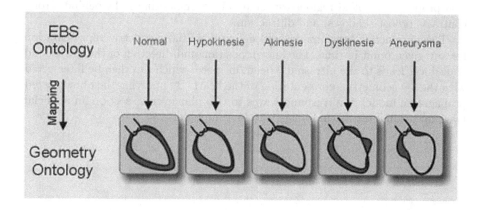

Fig. 11: Ontology mapping

The ontology of EBS is used in examining the heart and determining the heart's appearance. We have to add an ontology of the anatomical structure of a heart, e.g. the heart consists of four chambers. Based on these ontologies and the mapping between them we will research modelling techniques and algorithms for a dynamic parametric heart model which will have a shape, beat, struggle and motion like the original one which we know only from a description (findings in EBS). For this task we have to consider not only abstract medical (EBS findings) and anatomical aspects (components of a heart and their interrelation) but also physiological aspects (how the muscle is constructed, how stimuli are transmitted, the reaction on limited oxygenation) and dynamic ones (inertia, speed, flow, motion).

The parametric heart model will finally define a spatial geometric representation for any given point in time of a complete heart cycle. Variations in the primary findings in the EBS will directly be reflected by an other shape or dynamic behaviour.

4.2   Artificial Ultrasound Image Generation

As part of the augmented reality environment (see section 4.3) a positioning device will be attached to the ultrasound probe, which will continuously report the spatial location (six degrees of freedom) of the transducer to a workstation. Based on these spatial parameters an artificial two-dimensional ultrasound image will be calculated as soon as the transducer gets in contact with the mockup during a training session.

The creation of an artificial ultrasound image requires the development of a physical model, which simulates the propagation of ultrasound waves through human tissue. For a realistic impression several physical effects have to be taken into consideration. The model must be capable to simulate e. g. reflection depending on surface angle, tissue properties and differences in density, the absorption properties of filled regions especially air, overshooting right behind strong contrasts (ghost shadows) and diffraction.

The parametric heart model will define a spatial geometric representation for any given point in time. The known position and direction of the ultrasound transducer leads to the ultrasound beam in space, which can then be intersected with the 3D geometric representation of the heart. By applying the above stated propagation model of ultrasound waves to this planar cross-section an artificial two-dimensional ultrasound image can be computed.

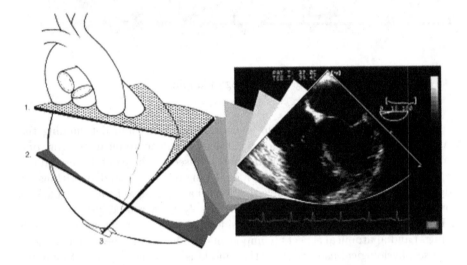

Fig. 12: Artificial ultrasound image generation.

It may be useful to store the output of this simulation process as a pre-calculated volumetric dataset in order to guarantee fast access by the visualization engine during a training session. To accomplish this we have to compute a series of parallel slices through the heart (artificial ultrasound data) for a set of discrete time steps covering a complete heart cycle. During a training session we have to interpolate ultrasound images from this dataset, because the transducer is not always at the same position we used to create the volumetric data set.

4.3 Augmented Reality Environment

As an important part of the training system and for the purpose of validation our modelling algorithms an experimental augmented reality environment facility will be developed, which will provide mechanisms to create a realistic artificial examination atmosphere.

As an initial step we will simulate a simple examination environment with mockup and transducer. A positioning device will be attached to the transducer to get the position and orientation of the simulated ultrasound beam as input for the calculation of an artificial ultrasound image. This scenario represents only a minimal environment to achieve the training of basic skills in echocardiography examination.

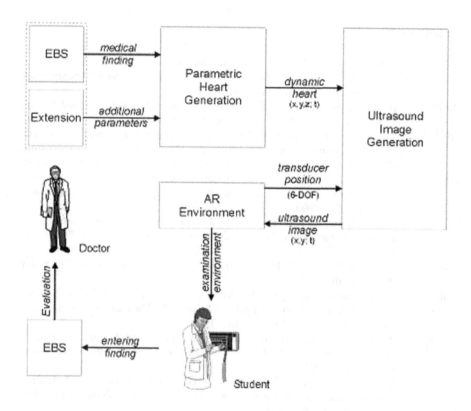

Fig. 13: The overall system design with basic augmented reality environment.

In a second step the examination environment will be extended by a head mounted display, which provides the student with the impression of being immersed in a simulated 3D training environment. The outcome is the visualisation of the beating heart together ith the artificial ultrasound image in combination with the real mockup and transducer. This visual imformation is very important for a novice to learn the correct handling of the transducer.

Registration and positioning of virtual objects in the real environment requires accurate tracking of the user's head and sensing the locations of other objects in the environment. A tracking mechanism registers any head movement to make the required changes of the viewing point in the modeled scene. The registration problem is far from being solved and will be part of our research in this area. For a realistic examination atmosphere sound integration into the augmented reality environment may be supportive. The Virtual Echocardiography System will provide a simple mechanism to generate artificial sounds of the blood flow as usually provided by an ultrasound scanner.

References

[AAIM73]   Andronov A. A., Leontovich E. A., Gordon I. I., and A. G. Maier. *Qualitative Theory of Second-Order Dynamic Systems*. Israel Program for Scientific Translation, Jerusalem, 1973.

[Azu97]   R.T. Azuma. A survey of augmented reality. *Teleoperators and Virtual Environments*, 6(4):355 – 385, August 1997.

[BFR92]   M. Bajura, H. Fuchs, and R.Ohbuchi. Merging virtual reality with the real world: Seeing ultrasound imagery within the patient. In *Proceedings of SIGGRAPH '92*, pages 203 – 210. Computer Graphics 26, 2, July 1992.

[BN95]   M. Bajura and U. Neumann. Dynamic registration correction in video-based augmented reality systems. *IEEE Computer Graphics and Applications*, 5(15), 1995.

[CPC80]   M. S. Chong, A. E. Perry, and B. J. Cantwell. A General Classification of Three-Dimensional Flow Fields. *Physics of Fluids A*, 2(5):765 – 777, 1980.

[CW99]   C. Walsh C and P. Wilde. *Practical Echocardiography*. Oxford University Press, London, 1999.

[Dal83]   U. Dallmann. Topological Structures of Three-Dimensional Flow Separations. Technical Report 221-82 A 07, Deutsche Forschungs- und Versuchsanstalt für Luft- und Raumfahrt, 1983.

[DH94]   T. Delmarcelle and H. Hesselink. The Topology of Symmetric, Second-Order Tensor Fields. In *IEEE Visualization '94*, pages 140 – 147, Tysons Corner, VA, 1994.

[EKG+97]   R. Erbel, G.D. Kneissl, P. Schweizer G.D, H.J. Lambertz, and R. Engberding. Qualitätsleitlinien in der Echokardiographie. *Zeitschrift fü Kardiologie*, 86:387–403, 1997.

[GEW+95]   W.E.L. Grimson, S.J. Ettinger, P.L. White, T. Gleason, and et. al:. Evaluating and validating an automated registration system for enhanced reality visualization in surgery. In *Proceedings of Computer Vision, Virtual Reality, and Robotics in Medicine '95*, pages 3 – 12, April 1995.

[GLL91]   A. Globus, C. Levit, and T. Lasinski. A Tool for Visualizing the Topology of Three-Dimensional Vector Fields. In *IEEE Visualization '91*, pages 33 – 40, San Diego, 1991.

[HH90]   J. L. Helman and L. Hesselink. Surface Representations of Two- and Three-Dimensional Fluid Flow Topology. In G. M. Nielson and B. Shriver, editors, *Visualization in scientific computing*, pages 6–13, Los Alamitos, CA, 1990.

[KDS92]   C. Krishnaswamy, A.J. D'Adamo, and C.M. Sehgal. Three dimensional re-
            construction of intravascular ultrasound images. In P.G. Yock J.M. Tobis,
            editor, *Intravascular Ultrasound Imaging*, 1992.

[KHL99]   D. N. Kenwright, C. Heinze, and C. Levit. Feature Extraction of Sepa-
            ration and Attachment Lines. *IEEE Transactions on Visualization and
            Computer Graphics*, 5(2):135–144, April–June 1999.

[Lig63]   M. J. Lighthill. Attachment and Separation in Three Dimensional Flow.
            In Rosenhead L., editor, *Laminar Boundary Layers II*, pages 72 – 82.
            Oxford University Press, Oxford, 1963.

[RLR$^+$91] K. Rosenfield, D.W. Losordo, K. Ramaswamy, J.O. Pastore, E. Langevin,
            S. Razvi, B.D. Kosowski, and J.M. Isner. Three dimensional reconstruc-
            tion of human coronary and peripheral arteries from images recorded dur-
            ing two-dimensional intravascular ultrasound examination. *Circulation*,
            84:1938 – 1956, 1991.

[RMP$^+$94] J.R. Roedlandt, C. Di Mario, N.G. Pandian, L. Wenguang, L. Keane, C.J.
            Slager, P.J. De Feyter, and P.W. Serrius. Three dimensional reconstruc-
            tion of intracoronary ultrasound images. *Circulation*, 90, 1994.

[SG98]   G. Sakas and M. Grimm. 4d/5d echocardiographic data visualization. In
            *Proceedings of the Third Korea-Germany Joint Workshop on Advanced
            Medical Image Processing*, Seoul, Korea, 13-16, August 1998.

[SKMR98]   G. Scheuermann, H. Krüger, M. Menzel, and A. Rockwood. Visualizing
            Nonlinear Vector Field Topology. *IEEE Transactions on Visualization
            and Computer Graphics*, 4(2):109–116, April–June 1998.

[SLH$^+$96] A. State, M.A. Livingston, G. Hirota, W.F. Garrett, M.C. Whitton,
            H. Fuchs, and E.D. Pisano. Techniques for augmented reality systems: Re-
            alizing ultrasound-guided needle biopsies. In *Proceedings of SIGGRAPH
            '96*, pages 439 – 446, August 1996.

[SM]   O. Schweikard and F. Metzger.   Standardisierte Befunderfassung in
            der Echokardiographie mittels Echobefundsystem.   to be published in
            Zeitschrift für Kardiologie.

[TSH00]   X. Tricoche, G. Scheuermann, and H. Hagen. A topology simplification
            method for 2d vector fields. In *IEEE Visualization 2000*, pages 359 – 366,
            Los Alamitos, 2000.

Computer Vision: Past and Future

Jan-Olof Eklundh and Henrik I. Christensen

Computational Vision and Active Perception
Numerical Analysis and Computing Science
Royal Institute of Technology
SE-100 44 Stockholm, Sweden
{joe,hic}@nada.kth.se

1   Introduction

"What does it mean to see? The plain man's answer (and Aristotle's too) would be to know what is where by looking." These introductory words in the seminal book of David Marr [54] capture the essence of what researchers in computer vision have been trying to make computers do for almost half a century. In this paper we will outline the development of the field, emphasising the last ten years, and the discuss what the challenges in the field are.

We will, in particular, focus the account of the past and the future around the question: Can we make computers see? Of course, any answer to such a question must be partial and subjective. Nevertheless considerable insights can be gained about the challenges that the field faces, by looking at how it has evolved so far. This will be the starting point of the presentation, that will begin with an outline of the development of the field and end with a list of key issues.

2   The First Attempts

Computer vision dates back to the earliest days of computing. In 1951 John von Neumann proposed to analyse micrographs using computers by comparing intensities at adjacent locations in the images. This seems to be the earliest reference in computer vision, or at least on extraction of information from images with computers. Of course, various techniques for signal processing existed at that time, but computer vision had and still has a more far-reaching goal: to develop machines that can "see". An early landmark contribution was the dissertation by Roberts [65]. Roberts derived three-dimensional models of scenes consisting of polyhedral objects. He considered perspective transformations and used the fact that lines and intersection of lines are projective invariants. His program created a line drawing from a picture by differentiation, a simple version of contour detection that seems to have worked well enough for the pictures used. Many of these approaches are still in use in the field.

In parallel to this work there were extensive early efforts in pictorial pattern recognition. Two problems that attracted particular interest were interpretation of printed and hand-written text and classification of chromosomes and cells in microscopic images.

R. Wilhelm (Ed.): Informatics. 10 Years Back. 10 Years Ahead, LNCS 2000, pp. 328–340, 2001.

3   The First Paradigms

The first successes, limited as they were, created a feeling that computers that could "see" were imminent. In fact, this field shared such optimism with many other AI-related areas, such as natural language understanding, common sense reasoning, and expert systems. However, it turned out that neither the approaches, nor the models of the world used, generalized to the extent one hoped for.

The world we live in is not polyhedral and doesn't share the mathematical simplicity of such a world. Polyhedra exist in lattices of planes-lines-points, and lines and points are invariant under perspective viewing. These facts provide precise tools for dealing with such worlds, such as matroid theory and linear programming used by Sugihara [72]. However, although both lines and points are abundant in our visual environment, they don't provide enough information to account for its full structure and appearance. Roberts' idea to proceed via a line-drawing, although appropriate in his case, has in addition turned out to be far more difficult than expected and it's not likely to be a viable approach for general scene analysis.

A more subtle misconception followed from early pattern recognition studies. The work on characters and chromosomes relied on the fact that the underlying categories were well-defined (and finite). When going to recognition of objects of more general types it became clear that the definition of categories, as well as their appearance and similarity in images, was not a straightforward matter. This decreased the interest in applying pattern recognition techniques to computer vision problems for a long time. However, in recent years advances in the field have created a revitalisation of it. We will return to that in a later section.

The realization that the relation between images of the world and the three-dimensional scenes they depict is very complicated led to an emphasis on image formation. Marr [54], Horn [38], Binford [8], Koenderick [42], Rosenfelt [67] and others contributed to a deepened understanding of how various monocular, binocular and motion cues to scene structure could be derived from images. This development was considerably influenced by psychologists like Gibson [31] and Julesz [41], but also used knowledge from optics. Dealing with a world consisting of coherent matter it became natural to put an emphasis on reconstruction of the visible surfaces bounding objects. Marr named this the 2.5-D sketch, and important progress was made on such problems. Vision was considered as an ill-posed inverse problem, which led to mathematically sophisticated approaches, research that still goes on today, now with new applications on visualization as one of the driving forces.

The theme of research along these lines, seemed to be "first reconstruct the world, then understand it". As we will see below there were later researchers opposing this perspective. More about that in a while. However, one observation that can be made is that the highly sophisticated work on how to derive the spatio-temporal structure of the world hardly brought any machines that could "see". The main results, were deep insights and advanced reconstruction algorithms.

4   The Past Ten Years

Research during the 1970-80's undoubtedly furthered our understanding of the problems in computer vision. Many of the trends emerging then are still there, but during the past ten years we have also seen some new areas that have attracted interest. Let us highlight three prominent areas which cover some of the most important work done:

- refined methods for extracting information from images
- pattern recognition revived
- animate vision

These areas are not in any way commensurable, and the first one, on methodology, together with work on new and old applications certainly account for a majority of the research efforts worldwide. In the next few sections we will discuss the ideas behind and some of the most important directions in this research.

4.1   Methods and Techniques

Methods for extracting information from images have become increasingly sophisticated in their use of mathematical and physical models and computational techniques. The field is today so vast, that writing a textbook covering all of it is no longer possible, although good introductory texts exist, for instance Trucco and Verri [74]. Neither is it possible to even briefly capture all areas in which important progress have been made. A subjective selection has therefore led us to focus on three areas that we think has undergone particularly strong development in recent years:

- early visual computations
- multiview geometry
- motion analysis

We will in the ensuing sections consider each of these areas in more detail.

Early Visual Computations The problem of what to compute at the early stages of computer vision, i.e. on the raw image input, has been discussed since Roberts differentiated his images [65, 66]. Marr [53] introduced the primal sketch, a rich but still sparse representation of variations and "events" in the luminance fields of images. This and other work was inspired by the then rapidly increasing understanding of primate vision, especially the uncovering of the role of areas V1 (primary visual cortex) and V2.

During the past 10-15 years the basic principles that these early computations should follow have become well-understood in machine vision. As Koenderink and van Doorn [45] points out, they should be unbiased: they should not be a priori tuned to any specific stimuli or luminance patterns. They should also be sensitive to events, such as rapid luminance changes (contours) and combinations of them (junctions), of different sizes and orientations. Koenderink [43], following Witkin [84], formalized this in his development of linear scale-space (in fact suggested as early as 1959 by Iijima, see [81]). Linear scale-space is formed by an embedding of an image in a set of images formed according to the linear diffusion equation, i.e. in a set of images formed by Gaussian smoothing.

Filtering based on linear diffusion has been analyzed extensively, see e.g. [70], and has moreover been applied to derive three-dimensional scene structure from images [40], and [30], motion [80], and image structure [49]. However, several other approaches to multi-scale image processing have been developed. Perona [62] proposed a non-linear diffusion process, where the degree of diffusion is adapted to the underlying image structure. More general techniques based on non-linear partial differential equations, designed to have various invariances, have also been developed, e.g. see [17]. These models have in addition been applied for describing shapes using deformable models, see e.g. [24]. A key to these approaches is the introduction of level set methods, [68], which has had considerable impact in scientific computing in general.

Yet other methods for early visual processing have been developed based on Gabor filters, which are regarded as good models for early computations in primate vision, see [83]. In fact, Gabor himself proposed this in a paper already 1965 [29]. Recently there has been a considerable interest in methods based on wavelets, see [52] for an overview, while so-called tunable filters, Freeman and Adelson [28], give a flexible way of creating an early computational layer based on more generally selected filter bases. In all, these efforts have provided us with a thorough knowledge about how early visual computations should be performed, and although what should be computed still seems to be a matter of discussion, the field is fairly mature with regard to the lowest levels. The required functionality of a visual front-end is basically well-known, and Burt [11] have in fact implemented such mechanisms in real-time hardware.

Multiview Geometry The shape of objects and the visible structure of the world are essential elements to our visual systems. Hence, geometry plays a key role in any attempt to develop machine vision systems. The geometrical structure of the scene and how it is mapped onto images was discussed by Roberts [65] and in the early and still very readable book by Duda and Hart [19] there are sections on projective geometry and reconstruction of three dimensional scenes from stereoscopic images. Such issues had traditionally been addressed in photogrammetry, but in general by solving the problem of what points in the image pairs corresponded to each other by human intervention, and performing the needed calibration of the cameras manually. Computer vision researchers wanted to automate the three dimensional reconstruction without having full knowledge of where the cameras where, how they were directed, and what their so-called interior parameters were. They also wanted to solve the corresponding problem algorithmically. Our insights into these problems, and in particular in the geometric aspects of them, have deepened considerably over the past ten years.

Longuet-Higgins [50] published a paper showing that a bilinear relation holds for the images of two corresponding points in a stereo pair of images. The observation was simply that the depicted point in the scene and the two optical centers of the cameras form a plane, the epipolar plane, that contains the two image points. The introduction of epipolar geometry into computer vision formed a starting point for extensive work on multiview geometry, especially in the 1990's. The relation was well-known in photogrammetry [71], but that had previously not had any impact in computer vision. Notably, Tsai and Huang [75] independently presented analogous results for the motion case.

Another development on geometry was that of formulating the problems in projective terms and explicitly using geometric invariants. Geometry and invariant theory were well established fields of mathematics and, for instance homogeneous coordinates had been used in both graphics and computer vision, see e.g. [19]. In the 1980's the interest of using more of the wealth of knowledge in classical geometry increased: Naeve and Eklundh [56] pointed out that performing the computations in projective space and choosing bases there, have several advantages beyond what (Cartesian) homogeneous coordinates offer; Nielsen [59], Lamden [47], and Weiss [82] and several others triggered a major effort of using geometric invariants for visual analysis.

One of the first problems attracting interest concerned auto-calibration. Constraints, such as the bilinear epipolar constraints, can be used to solve the auto-calibration equations. Since Faugeras [25] and Hartley [37] addressed the projective case a host of results and several numerical methods have been presented. Hartley and Zisserman [36] give an excellent guide into these problems, as well as the whole field of multiview geometry. It is beyond the scope of this exposé to try to capture this rich field in a few sections. Let us only note that among other topics and approaches that have been studied are multi-linear constraints and their use for reconstruction, using e.g. planarity and parallelity for reconstruction from single views, and using geometric and differential invariants for matching and recognition. Researchers have used both classical and more recent mathematics in this area, which now is based on a solid foundation and which have ample potential applications in visualization and multi-media systems.

Visual Motion Motion is a prerequisite for visual perception: if nothing moved in the scene and if the seeing agent couldn't move there wouldn't be much purpose in seeing. Computer vision has treated problems on visual motion since the 1970's; Nagel [57] mentions that he launched a project on image sequence analysis starting in 1971. Change detection and tracking had been studied long before that, especially in military applications and radar signal processing, see e.g. [48] and [6]. Human perception of motion had of course been studied earlier than that, with roots that go centuries back. The main reason why computer vision researchers considered motion analysis so late were probably of a technical nature: it was difficult to digitize image sequences and it led to computations on very large datasets. These obstacles have gradually lost their importance, and today motion analysis is one of the most active areas in computer vision - just as it should be.

Two problems have dominated the area: to compute optic flow, the distribution of apparent velocities of movement of brightness patterns in an image, and to derive three dimensional structure from image motion. There has been considerable progress on these and other topics and surveying them would go beyond what can be done in a presentation like this. Let us instead highlight a few subtopics and approaches, on which interesting advances have been made during the past ten years.

One important topic concerns parameterized linear, or low-order polynomial models for describing local motion [79]. Such approaches have been shown to apply to rather general cases of scenes and motions, see [27] for an example and numerous pointers to the literature. Another topic is structure from motion [44], [23], and [73]. Commonly, this problem has been addressed by first computing optic flow and then using epipolar or multi linear constraints to determine structure. There is a wealth of results and successful experiments along these lines, but their robustness in real life situations is questionable. Alternative methods that compute motion and structure simultaneously have been suggested to remedy this, see e.g. [10] for an example. However, the same question remains and much more research is needed.

Many of the methods mentioned cast their problems in terms of statistical estimation. Statistical methods have always been important in motion analysis. Recently, particularly interesting work has been done on tracking based on random sampling and propagation of conditional densities, "Condensation", applied to model based tracking. Such models have been studied in statistics, see e.g. [34] and [32]. Although Grenander et al actually consider vision problems, the technique was primarily introduced into the field by Isard and Blake [39] and [9]. Considerable work on these approaches have appeared more recently, e.g. dealing with multiple models and three dimensional models.

A summary of the research on motion analysis could be that an emphasis on geometry and statistics together with use of tools from mathematical analysis have resulted in considerable advances. In applications, time-varying imagery has been used with great success, for instance in automatic driving, see e.g. [18]. However, many problems remain unsolved before we have robust methods good enough for a "seeing" system existing and moving about in a general environment.

4.2 Pattern Recognition Revived

Computer vision and pattern recognition became two distinct disciplines in the 1970's. Model and feature based techniques were used in object recognition and traditional pattern recognition methods for a long time played a minor role although Grenander et al. [33] has laid a firm foundation for the field early. In the past ten years this picture has changed dramatically, seemingly for a number of reasons. One was, of course, that progress had been fairly slow and that researchers therefore looked for new approaches. A rapidly growing interest in face recognition spurred the development of methods using the entire image as input to a recognition mechanism. Face recognition, that had been studied 20 years earlier, became a hot topic due to its importance in applications where identity control was needed. Some solutions were based on filters of various types for creation of representations for a pattern recognition engine [64, 46], while others used normalized versions of the image directly [77]. Such "appearance" based techniques were also tried on more general classes of objects [15] and used image cues such as color and shape [58] and [20]. The interest in memory representations was naturally coupled to learning. Research in learning, especially using artificial neural networks, had developed rapidly in the 1980's. Much of this work was applied to simple patterns, such as hand-written text, and did not scale up easily to real imagery. However, powerful new paradigms for learning appeared, such as those based on radial basis functions (see e.g. [63]), and support vector machines and statistical learning theory [78]. They were shown to be well suited for image pattern recognition. Much of this work on pattern recognition tried to find biologically plausible solutions, since humans indeed can recognize objects, while machines so far had been quite unsuccessful in this respect.

The strong arguments for appearance based recognition methods were not undisputed. Biederman [7] and others argued that there is strong evidence for part and feature based methods in humans, and that the primitives could be both in the image and in 3D. Studies of brain lesions causing visual agnosias, i.e. leaving vision basically unimpaired, but destroying e.g. the capability of recognizing faces (prosopagnosia), seems to indicate that both approaches are prevalent in human vision [22]. Face recognition tends to be based on the entire image, while recognition of other objects uses several mechanisms. It would bring us too far to go deeper into that discussion here, the book by Edelman [21] and [26], give a perspective of the positions taken. Here the point is that the revived interest in pattern recognition approaches, learning, and memory, all areas that have advanced considerably recently, has had a great impact on the development of computer vision in the 1990's. We're still to have systems that can see and recognize things in the real world in any general sense, but new important pieces of knowledge have been added.

4.3   Animate Vision

The view that vision aims "to transform two dimensional data into a description of the three dimensional spatiotemporal world" [69], was challenged by Bajcsy [3], Aloimonos [1], Ballard [5] and others. They argued that vision is better understood in the context of the visual behaviors that the system is engaged in. This led to extensive research that included the embodiment of the visual system in terms of head-eye systems, and how to control the oculomotor behaviors became an important issue [14], [13], [61], and [55]. Problems on how to use observer motion and choosing view point to systematically infer shape, were addressed by e.g [12] and [51]. By integrating monocular, binocular and motion cues it was shown that systems could segment out and stabilize objects in a cluttered, dynamic environment, [4] and [60]. In many ways these efforts showed promise for "seeing" systems functioning in closed loop with reality. However, despite ambitious attempts, such as Crowley and Christensen [16], almost no results were reported on systems capable of more than fixating objects, or deriving shape and motion properties of them. More sophisticated or cognitive behaviors were not achieved, and largely the community turned to other areas towards the end of the decade. Modeling the full system, the "seeing agent", with its drives and purposes, had eluded the researchers. At the same time, the advances in tracking and real-time analysis of dynamic imagery found amble use in emerging applications, such as camera based, surveillance and human-machine interaction, today very hot topics.

5   Challenges of the Future

In the previous sections we have given some snapshots of the state-of-the-art in computer vision. There has undeniably been great progress in the field, not least during the past ten years. However, despite the progress we have still not reached many of the desirable goals. There are today numerous sophisticated methods for extracting visual information, but they seldom work consistently and robustly in the real, dynamically changing world. Recognition of certain classes of objects, such as human faces, has be achieved with success, but little is known of how to form recognizable categories, or performing recognition when figure-ground segmentation is not trivial. What constitutes an object for us, i.e. which objects we become explicitly aware of, depends on several contextual facts, the tasks we are involved in, our current interest and so on, and is not only defined by what's in the environment. This has not been taken into account. Many approaches implicitly assume a task of recognizing all the objects in the scene, but this is an intractable problem, as Tsotsos [76] has shown. Animate vision systems that can react, or, to a very limited degree are active, have been studied, but it is far from obvious that they really "see" anything.

At the same time it is clear that information in terms of imagery today is ubiquitous, in applications such as medicine, industrial inspection, surveillance, and internet and media, as well as in our daily life at work and at home. Hence, techniques for analyzing these enormous amounts of information are urgently needed. In addition, the even greater problem of developing "seeing" machines remains unsolved. Computer vision research is today more relevant than ever. What are then the great challenges in the field for the next decade? Let us suggest three:

1. *Furthering the work on theoretically well-founded methods for extracting information from imagery to develop methods that function* **robustly** *on real world data.*

   The required means for this have already been in use: computational, mathematical, statistical, and physical modeling of the environment and the observers. However, what appears to be needed are improved empirical foundations and implementations that scale up to the real world situations.

2. *Understanding visual recognition and categorization*

   Today there are partial solutions to these problems, often based on the model of "first see, then understand". It is likely that deeper insights and more general results only can be obtained if the processes are regarded in the context of a system that "sees", the next challenge on the list. However, there are also specific aspects of these problems, especially such that concern representations, memory, and learning. In biology, recognition and categorization is all about association. Although, simulated associative processes have been studied extensively, we are far from knowing how they can be implemented to be sufficiently efficient and scalable on existing hardware. We lack "smart visual memories".

3. *Developing systems that can "see"*

   Such systems must include the drives, tasks, and actions of the seeing agent. It involves pure computer vision problems, but also problems about behaviors, learning and memory, embodiment, and the use of non-visual cues. Reconciling top-down and bottom-up influences have been studied for artificial systems with simple perceptual capabilities, e.g. by [2] and [35], but much remains to be done for systems with a rich repertoire of visual behaviors and processes. There are also a number of problems more closely related to computer science: dealing with asynchronous and distributed computations, scheduling and control, and scalable architectures and systems. Biological systems achieve this with completely distributed control, as demonstrated by Zeki [85] in his seminal work on the functional specificity of primate vision. It is likely that artificial vision systems should do so too, to be able to adapt to the environment and learn new capabilities, and display scalability in these respects. Little is known about how to achieve this.

Computer vision raises many grand challenges at the same time as it is becoming increasingly important in a wide range of applications. That promises an exciting development of the field in the coming ten years.

References

[1] J. Aloimonos, I. Weiss, and A. Bandyopadhyay. Active vision. *Intl. Jour. of Computer Vision*, 1(4):333–356, January 1988.

[2] M. A. Arbib. From vision to action via distributed computation. In S.-I. Amari and N. Kasabov, editors, *Brain-like computing and intelligent information systems*, pages 315–347. Springer Verlag, Singapore, 1997.

[3] R. Bajcsy. Active perception vs. passive perception. In *Proc. 3rd Workshop on Computer Vision: Representation and Control*, pages 55–59, Washington, DC., October 1985. IEEE Press.

[4] D. Ballard and A. Ozcandarli. Eye fixation and early vision: kinetic depth. In *Proc. 2nd ICCV*, pages 524–531, Washington, DC., 1988. IEEE Press.

[5] D. H. Ballard. Animate vision. *Artificial Intelligence*, 48(1):57–86, February 1991.

[6] Y. Bar-Shalom and T. Fortmann. *Tracking and Data Association*. Academic Press, New York, NY., 1987.

[7] I. Biederman. Recognition by Components: A theory of human image understanding. *Psychological Review*, 94:115–147, 1987.

[8] T. O. Binford. Inferring surfaces from images. *Artificial Intelligence*, 17:205–244, 1981.

[9] A. Blake and M. Isard. *Active Contours*. Springer Verlag, Berlin, 1998.

[10] T. Brodsky, C. Fermüller, and Y. Aloimonos. Structure from Motion: Beyond the Epipolar Constraint. *Intl. Jour. of Computer Vision*, 37(3):231–258, 2000.

[11] P. Burt. Smart sensing within a pyramid vision machine. *IEEE Proceedings*, 76(8):1006–1015, August 1988.

[12] R. Cipolla and A. Blake. Motion planning using image divergence and deformation. In A. Blake and A. Yuille, editors, *Active Vision*, pages 189–202. MIT Press, Cambridge, MA., 1992.

[13] J. J. Clark and N. Ferrier. Modal control of an attentive vision system. In *Proc. 2nd ICCV*, pages 514–523. IEEE CS Press, December 1988.

[14] D. Coombs and C.M. Brown. Real-time binocular smooth-pursuit. *Intl. Jour of Computer Vision*, 11(2):147–165, October 1993.

[15] T.F. Cootes and C.J. Taylor. A mixture model for representing shape variation. *Image and Vision Computing*, 17(8):567–573, June 1999.

[16] J. L. Crowley and H.I. Christensen. *Vision as Process*. ESPRIT BR Series. Springer Verlag, Heidelberg, December 1995.

[17] R. Deriche and O. Faugeras. Pde's in image processing and computer vision. *(in French)*, 13(6), 1996.

[18] E. Dickmanns. Vehicles capable of dynamic vision: a new breed of technical beings? *Artificial Intelligence*, 103(1–2):49–76, August 1998.

[19] R. O. Duda and P. E. Hart. *Pattern Cclassification and Scene Analysis*. Wiley-Interscience, New York, NY., 1973.

[20] S. Edelman and S. Duvdevani-Bar. A model of visual recognition and categorization. *Proc. of the Royal Society of London*, B-352:1191–1202, 1997.

[21] S. Edelman. *Representation and Recognition in Vision*. MIT Press, Cambridge, MA, 1999.

[22] M.J. Farah. *Visual Agnosia*. MIT Press, Cambridge, MA, 1990.

[23] O. Faugeras. *Three-Dimensional Computer Vision: A Geometric Viewpoint*. MIT Press, Cambridge, MA, 1993.

[24] O.D. Faugeras and R. Keriven. Variational-principles, surface evolution, pdes, level set methods, and the stereo problem. *Image Processing*, 7(3):336–344, March 1998.

[25] O. Faugeras. What can be seen in the three dimensions with an uncalibrated stereo rig? In G. Sandini, editor, *Proc. 2nd ECCV*, volume 588 of *LNCS*, pages 563–578, Berlin, May 1992. Springer Verlag.

[26] J. Fiser, I. Biederman, and E.E. Cooper. To what extent can matching algorithms based on direct outputs of spatial filters account for human object recognition? *Spatial Vision*, 10(3):237–272, 1996.

[27] D. J. Fleet, M. J. Black, Y.Yacoob, and A. D. Jepson. Design and use of linear models for image motion analysis. *Intl. Jour. of Computer Vision*, 36(3):171–193, 2000.

[28] W. T. Freeman and E. H. Adelson. The design and use of steerable filters. *IEEE Trans. on Pattern Analysis and Machine Intelligence*, PAMI-13(9):891–906, September 1991.

[29] D. Gabor. Information theory in electron microscopy. *Laboratory Investigation*, 14:801–807, 1965.

[30] J. Gårding and T. Lindeberg. Direct computation of shape cues using scale-adapted spatial derivative operators. *Intl. Jour. of Computer Vision*, 17(2):163–191, February 1996.

[31] J. Gibson. *The Perception of the Visual World*. Houghton Mifflin, Boston USA, 1950.

[32] N. Gordon, D. Salmond, and A. Smith. A novel approach to nonlinear/non-gaussian bayesian state estimation. *IEE Proc. F*, 140(2):107–113, 1993.

[33] U. Grenander. *A unified approach to pattern analysis*, volume 10. Advanced is Computers, 1970.

[34] U. Grenander, Y. Chow, and D. Keenan. *HANDS – A Pattern Theoretical Study of Biological Shapes*. Springer Verlag, New York, NY, 1991.

[35] S. Grossberg and G.A. Carpenter. *Neural networks for vision and image processing*. MIT Press, Cambridge, MA, 1992.

[36] R. Hartley and A. Zisserman. *Multiple View Geometry in Computer Vision*. Cambridge University Press, Cambridge, UK., 2000.

[37] R. I. Hartley. Estimation of relative camera positions for uncalibrated cameras. In G. Sandini, editor, *Proc. 2nd ECCV*, volume 588 of *LNCS*, pages 579–587, Berlin, May 1992. Springer Verlag.

[38] B. K. P. Horn. Understanding image intensities. *Artificial Intelligence*, 8(2):201–231, 1977.

[39] M. Isard and A. Blake. Contour tracking by stochastic propagation of conditional density. In B. Buxton and R. Cipolla, editors, *ECCV-96*, LNCS, pages I:343–356, Berlin, June 1996. Springer Verlag.

[40] D.G. Jones and J. Malik. Determining three-dimensional shape from orientation and spatial frequency disparities. In *Proc. 2nd ECCV*, LNCS, pages 661–669, Berlin, 1992. Springer Verlag.

[41] B. Julesz. Visual pattern discrimination. *IRE Transaction on Information Theory*, IT-8:84–92, February 1962.

[42] J. J. Koenderick and A. J. van Doorn. Invariant properties of the motion parallax field due to the movement of rigid bodies relative to an observer. *Optica Acta*, 22(9):773–791, 1975.

[43] J. Koenderink. The structure of images. *Biological Cybernetics*, 50:363 – 370, 1984.

[44] J. J. Koenderink and A. J. vanDoorn. Affine structure from motion. *Jour of Optical Society of America*, 8(2):377–385, 1991.

[45] J.J. Koenderink and A.J. van Doorn. Representation of local geometry in the visual system. *Biological Cybernetics*, 55:367–375, 1987.

[46] M. Lades, C.C. Vorbruggen, J. Buhmann, J. Langeand C. von der Malsburg, R.P. Wurtz, and W. Konen. Distortion invariant object recognition in the dynamic link architecture. *IEEE Trans. Computers*, 42(3):300–311, March 1993.

[47] Y. Lamdan, J.T. Swartz, and H.J. Wolfson. Object recognition by affine invariant matching. In *IEEE Conf. on Pattern Recognition and Computer Vision*, pages 335–344, Ann Arbor, MI, June 1988.

[48] R. L. Lillestrand. Techniques for change detection. *IEEE Trans. on Computers*, 21(7):654–659, 1972.

[49] T. Lindeberg. *Scale-Space Theory in Computer Vision*. Kluwer Academic Publishers, Dordrecht, NL, 1994.

[50] H.C. Longuet-Higgins. A computer algorithm for reconstructing a scene from two projections. *Nature*, 293:133–135, September 1981.

[51] C. B. Madsen and H. I. Christensen. A viewpoint planning strategy for determining true angles on polyhedral objects by camera alignment. *IEEE Trans. PAMI*, 19(2):158–163, February 1997.

[52] S. Mallat. *A wavelet tour of signal processing*. Academic Press, New York, NY., 1997.

[53] D. Marr. Early processing of visual information. *Proceedings of the Royal Society of London*, B-275:483–524, 1976.

[54] D. Marr. *Vision*. W.H. Freeman and Company, New York, N.Y., 1980.

[55] D. W. Murray, K.J. Bradshaw, P.F. McLauchlan, I.D. Reid, and P.M. Sharkey. Driving saccade to pursuit using image motion. *Intl. Jour. of Computer Vision*, 16(3):205–228, November 1995.

[56] A. Naeve and J.-O. Eklundh. On projective geometry and the recovery of 3-D structure. In *Proc. 1st ICCV*, pages 128–135, Washington, DC, June 1987. IEEE Press.

[57] H.-H. Nagel. Image sequence evaluation: 30 years and still going strong. In *Proc. 15th ICPR*, pages 148–158, Washington, DC, September 2000. IEEE Press.

[58] S. K. Nayar, H. Murase, and S. A. Nene. Parametric appearance representation. In S.K. Nayar and T. Poggio, editors, *Early Visual Learning*. Oxford University Press, 1996.

[59] L. Nielsen and G. Sparr. Perspective area-invariants. In J.O. Eklundh, editor, *Image Analysis, Proc. SCIA-87*, volume 1, pages 209–216, Stockholm, Sweden, June 1987.

[60] K. Pahlavan, T. Uhlin, and J.-O. Eklundh. Dynamic fixation and active perception. *Intl. Jour. of Computer Vision*, 17(2):113–136, February 1996.

[61] K. Pahlavan, T. Uhlin, and J.O. Eklundh. Integrating primary ocular processes. *Image and Vision Computing*, 10:645–662, December 1992.

[62] P. Perona and J. Malik. Scale space and edge diffusion using anisotropic diffusion. *IEEE Trans. PAMI*, 12(7):629–639, July 1990.

[63] T. Poggio. A theory of how the brain might work. In *Cold Spring Harbor Symposia on Qualitative Biology*, pages 899–910. LV, 1990.

[64] T. Poggio and S. Edelman. A neural network that learns to recognize three dimensional objects. *Nature*, 343:263–266, 1990.

[65] L. G. Roberts. *Machine Perception of 3-D Solids*. PhD thesis, MIT, Cambridge, MA, May 1963.

[66] L. G. Roberts. Machine perception of three-dimensional solids. In J. P. Tippett et al., editor, *Optical and Electrooptical Information Processing*, pages 159–197. MIT Press, Cambridge, MA, 1965.

[67] A. Rosenfeld, R. Hummel, and S. W. Zucker. Scene labeling by relaxation operations. *IEEE Trans. SMC*, 6:420–422, 1976.

[68] J. A. Sethian. *Level Set Methods: Evolving Interfaces in Geometry, Fluid Mechanics, Computer Vision and Materials Science*. Cambridge University Press, 1996.

[69] S. C. Shapiro. Artificial intelligence. In S.C. Shapiro, editor, *Encyclopedia of Artificial Intelligence*, pages 54–57. John Wiley and Sons, Inc., New York, NY., 1992.

[70] J. Sporring, M. Nielsen, L.M.J. Florack, and P. Johansen, editors. *Gaussian Scale-Space Theory*. Kluwer, 1997.

[71] P. Stefanovic. Relative orientation – a new approach. *ITC-Journal*, 3:417–448, 1973.

[72] K. Sugihara. An algebraic approach to shape-from-image problems. *Artificial Intelligence*, 23(1):59–95, 1984.

[73] C. Tomasi and T. Kanade. The factorization method for the recovery of shape and motion from image streams. *Intl. Jour. of Computer Vision*, 9:2:137–154, 1992.

[74] E. Trucco and A. Verri. *Introductory Techniques for 3-D Computer Vision*. Prentice Hall Inc., London, U.K., 1998.

[75] R.Y. Tsai and T.S. Huang. Estimating 3-D Motion Parameters of a Rigid Planar patch I. *IEEE Trans on ASSP.*, 29(12):1147–1152, December 1981.

[76] J. T. Tsotsos. On relative complexity of active vs. passive visual search. *Intl. Jour. of Computer Vision*, 7(2):127–141, 1992.

[77] M. Turk and A. Pentland. Eigenfaces for recognition. *Journal of Cognitive Neuroscience*, 3(1):71–86, 1991.

[78] V. Vapnik. *The nature of statistical learning theory*. Springer Verlag, Berlin, 1995.

[79] A. M. Waxman and K. Wohn. Contour evolution, neighborhood deformation and global image flow: Planar surfaces in motion. *Intl. Jour. of Robotics Research*, 4:95–108, 1985.

[80] J. Weber and J. Malik. Robust computation of optical flow in a multi-scale differential framework. *Intl. Jour. of Computer Vision*, 14(1), 1995.

[81] J. Weickert, S. Ishikawa, and A. Imiya. linear scale-space has first been proposed in japan. *Journal of Mathematical Imaging and Vision*, 10(3):237–252, May 1999.

[82] I. Weiss. Geometric invariants and object recognition. *Intl. Jour. of Computer Vision*, 10(3):207–231, 1993.

[83] H.R. Wilson. Pschophysical evidence for spatial channels. In O. Braddick and A.C. Sleigh, editors, *Physical and Biological Processing of Images*, New York, N.Y., 1983. Springer Verlag.

[84] A. Witkin. Scale-space filtering. In *8th Int. Joint Conf. Artificial Intelligence*, pages 1019–1022, Karlsruhe, 1983.

[85] S. Zeki. *A vision of the brain*. Oxford: Blackwell Scientific, Oxford, UK, 1993.

Computational Biology
at the Beginning of the Post-genomic Era

Thomas Lengauer

Institute for Algorithms and Scientific Computing
GMD - German National Research Center for Information Technology
and Institute of Computer Science
University of Bonn
lengauer@gmd.de

Abstract. The year 2000 will be remembered in history as the year in which the human genome has been sequenced. This marks the end of the pre-genomic era which was characterized by strong world-wide efforts to sequence the human genome and, in fact, ended significantly ahead of schedule. Today, we are at the entry of the probably much longer post-genomic era, which is characterized by the grand quest of making sense of the genomic text. This goal can only be achieved by a concerted effort involving biological experiments and computer analyses. Conquering the computer part is the task of the scientific field of *computational biology* or *bioinformatics*. Here we will describe two facets of computational biology. One is that of a discipline shaped by several grand challenge basic research problems. The other is that of a field driven by a strong demand for immediate answers to pressing practical problems in biotechnology, notably in pharmaceutics and medicine.

1. Introduction

Computational biology and bioinformatics are terms for an interdisciplinary field joining information technology and biology that has skyrocketed in recent years. The field is located at the interface between the two scientific and technological disciplines that can be argued to drive a significant if not the dominating part of contemporary scientific innovation. In the English language, computational biology refers mostly to the scientific part of the field, whereas bioinformatics addresses more the infrastructure part. In other languages (e.g. German) bioinformatics covers both aspects of the field.

The goal of this field is to provide computer-based methods for coping with and interpreting the genomic data that are being uncovered in large volumes within the diverse genome sequencing projects and other new experimental technology in molecular biology. The field presents one of the grand challenges of our times. It has a large basic research aspect, since we cannot claim to be close to understanding biological systems on an organism or even cellular level. At the same time, the field is faced with a strong demand for immediate solutions, because the genomic data that are being uncovered encode many biological insights whose deciphering can be the basis for dramatic scientific and economical success. At the end of the pre-genomic

R. Wilhelm (Ed.): Informatics. 10 Years Back. 10 Years Ahead, LNCS 2000, pp. 341-355, 2001.

era that was characterized by the effort to sequence the human genome we are entering the post-genomic era that concentrates on harvesting the fruits hidden in the genomic text. In contrast to the pre-genomic era which, from the announcement of the quest to sequence the human genome to its completion, has lasted less than 15 years, the post-genomic era can be expected to last much longer, probably extending over several generations.

2. Grand Challenge Problems in Computational Biology

At the basis of the scientific challenge in computational biology there are fundamental problems in computational biology that are independent from applications and very hard to solve. In this section we will mention a number of these problems. We choose to list these problems in order of increasing "distance" from the genetic sequence. We start with problems that deal directly with the sequence and then step progressively towards analyzing issues of phenotype.

Grand Challenge 1: Finding Genes in Genomic Sequences

The genomic blue prints of proteins are provided by genes. Via the genetic code, the gene determines the exact amino acid sequence of the protein chain. The transcription machinery of the cell reads genes and translates them into the appropriate protein chain. In higher organisms, only a minor part of the genome codes for proteins. For man, this fraction lies in the low percentage range (3 to 6 percent).

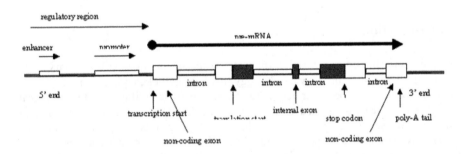

Fig. 1. Structure of a eucaryotic gene (adapted from [2])

The gene is much more than the coding sequence along the genome. There is associated infrastructure to help the transcription machinery to attach to the DNA, in order to read off the coding information, see Figure 1. Furthermore, there are sequence regions that help regulate the transcription, including mechanisms for blocking the transcription. In eucaryotes, genes also have a complex internal structure. They are not contiguous, but parts of the gene, the so-called introns, are eliminated before the translation into the protein. In Figure 1, only the pre-mRNA part is transcribed from the DNA sequence, and only the coding exons, depicted by the gray boxes finally make it into protein. Gene identification is tantamount to elucidating all aspects of the gene structure. The especially taxing part is the location and interpretation of functional signals in the upstream (left-hand) regulatory region of the gene. This is where proteins bind to the DNA in order to regulate gene transcription [1]. Gene identification algorithms use typical sequence analysis methods, including string comparison and alignment, for instance based on dynamic programming, and statistical methods such as hidden Markov models [2].

Grand Challenge 2: Protein Folding and Protein Structure Prediction

The famed protein folding problem asks, how the amino-acid sequence of a protein adopts its native three-dimensional structure under natural conditions (e.g. in aqueous solution, with neutral pH at room temperature). People develop Molecular Dynamics methods to solve this very difficult problem [3]. IBMs highly advertized Blue Gene Project aims at building a supercomputer that is supposed to provide the resources for solving this problem. Very recent developments raise hope that the problem may not be as difficult as has been thought previously [4].

Protein folding has to be distinguished from protein structure prediction. In the latter problem, we are not interested in the folding process but just in the final structure attained. Stated as such, the problem is also called the ab initio protein structure prediction problem, because no additional information is accessible to aid in the task. People prefer Monte Carlo methods to solve this problem [5]. This is because the folding process takes too much time to be effectively simulated by today's Molecular dynamics methods. So far only short helical protein sequences can be folded successfully.

There is a substantially easier version of the protein structure prediction problem that is much further along its way to solution. This version is based on the observation that the many millions of protein sequences that life has come up with so far fold into a remarkably small set of basic protein structures, only a few thousand. Assume that we know one representative protein for each structure. Then it seems reasonable to ask the question as follows: Given a protein sequence A, does protein A fold into a structure of type 1 or type 2, etc. After a few thousand queries, we are done. Interestingly enough, each query can be answered with increasing reliability on a PC in a few minutes or so. This method is covered by the terms protein threading - for finding the structural backbone of the protein - and homology-based modeling - for filling in the atomic details. It is the workhorse of today's protein structure predictions [6,7]. At GMD, we have contributed effective software to this field [8,9]. The method is limited only by the fact, that it cannot invent a protein structure that has never been seen before. And, as of now, we know only an estimated 20 to 30% of the several thousand presumed protein structures. For more details on protein structure prediction, see [10,11].

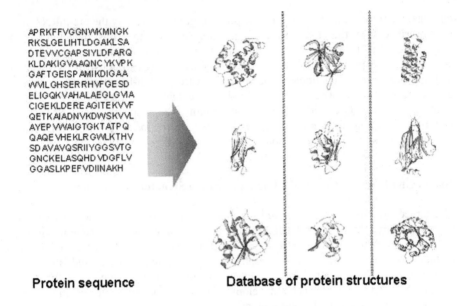

APRKFFVGGNWKMNGK
RKSLGELIHTLDGAKLSA
DTEVVCGAPSIYLDFARQ
KLDAKIGVAAQNCYKVPK
GAFTGEISPAMIKDIGAA
WVLGHSERRHVFGESD
ELIGQKVAHALAEGLGVIA
CIGEKLDEREAGITEKVVF
QETKAIADNVKDWSKVVL
AYEPWWAIGTGKTATPQ
QAQEVHEKLRGWLKTHV
SDAVAVQSRIIYGGSVTG
GNCKELASQHDVDGFLV
GGASLKPEFVDIINAKH

Protein sequence   **Database of protein structures**

Fig. 2. Homology-based Protein Structure Prediction

Now that, in principle, we can access all genes in a genome, we can also start a genome-wide structure prediction effort. This is the object of several Structural Genomics projects world-wide [12]. All of them combine experimental methods for resolving new protein structures (by X-ray or NMR techniques) with homology-based modeling to find related protein structures. However, several classes of protein structures - such as proteins that are located inside the cell membrane - are extremely hard to resolve.

In the presence of Structural Genomics efforts, it will be interesting to see, whether ab initio protein structure prediction will play a significant role in elucidating protein structure space.

Grand Challenge 3: Estimating the Free Energy of Biomolecules and Their Complexes

Part of why the protein structure prediction problem is so hard is that estimating the free energy of a protein conformation accurately is impossible, so far. However, molecules adopt the conformation of lowest free energy. Thus Nature solves a complex minimization problem in a very high-dimensional space. Each atom has three coordinates, thus the dimension of the space is three times the number of atoms, which is in the many thousands for a protein. Covalent bonds reduce this number somewhat, but not enough to make a difference computationally. In addition, up to millions of surrounding water molecules contribute to the energy balance. The scalar energy function that forms a landscape above this space has innumerably many local minima at approximately the same low energy. We are looking for the global minimum among them. This multiminima problem is at the heart of the difficulty of protein folding [13,14].

In this paragraph, we address an even more fundamental issue, however. Even computing a single point on the free energy landscape is impossible. The reason is that free energy is a thermodynamic average involving enthalpic (force) contributions as well as entropic (disorder) contributions. Computing free energies would actually necessitate performing statistics on large molecular ensembles. This exceeds any envisionable computing power. However, the picture may not be as bleak, if we are just interested in energy differences [15,16]. This problem is important not only for protein folding but also for molecular docking: One criterion for distinguishing good drugs from bad drugs is that good drugs bind tightly to their target protein, resulting in a low free energy of the molecular complex as compared to the dissociated molecules (see Section 3 below). Ranking drug molecules accurately according to this measure is a critical step in a computer-based approach to drug design [17,18].

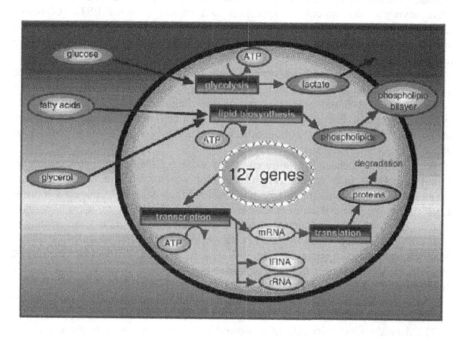

Fig. 3. Schema of a model for simulating a (very simple) bacterial cell (taken from [20])

Grand Challenge 4: Simulating a Cell

In the last paragraph we have stepped up from discussing molecular structures to discussing molecular interaction. Inside a cell, life's processes are motorized by complex networks of such interactions involving many thousands different proteins and metabolites. Even understanding only the connectivity of such a network, e.g. the topology of signal transduction pathways, on a cell-wide scale is beyond us, today. Ultimately we want to understand its kinetics, i.e. what effects up-regulating or down-regulating an enzyme would have on the equilibrium reached by the cell. Mathematical methods for analyzing these interdependencies touch the difficult field of dynamic systems [19] and are restricted to very small networks, currently. In addition, we are lacking important experimental data that are needed as input to the respective algorithms. The goal of simulating a cell has been formulated, and a few groups are working on it [20] (see Figure 3), but we are very far from a solution.

3. Computational Biology in Applied Biology and Medicine

Besides the more "timeless" scientific Grand Challenge problems, there is a significant part of computational biology that is driven by new experimental data provided through the dramatic progress in molecular biology techniques. The past few years have provided so-called expression data on the basis of ESTs (expressed sequence tags) and DNA microarrays (DNA chips). These data go far beyond just uncovering genomic sequences. Essentially, we obtain a cell-wide census of certain molecular species.

There are two levels on which we can envision such a census. The first is covered by the term genomics. Here we tally all messenger RNA (mRNA) in the cell. mRNA is the result of the initial gene transcription and the intermediate on the way to the synthesized protein. Presumably lots of mRNA of a certain protein inside a cell also means that the cell is producing lots of this protein. At least this is the hypothesis on which mRNA expression studies are based.

We can expect thousands of different expressed genes inside a complex eucaryotic cell. Using DNA microarrays, for instance, for which there are several different technologies, we can obtain a differential profile of the total mRNA population inside a cell in two specific cell states. This means that, for each gene, we learn how much more or less mRNA there is in cell state 1 than in cell state 2. It is most interesting to compare different cell states of the same tissue, e.g. normal temperature/heat shock, healthy/sick, neutral pH/acidic etc. With a series of differential expression experiments one can even follow trajectories of expression levels, e.g. as a disease develops.

Expression data are a rich source of fundamental biological insight. Harvesting the signals buried in these data is burdened by three major complications:

1. The data are very noisy. Up to a twofold increase or decrease in the expression level is within the noise margin. This makes it very difficult to interpret expression data.

2. We do not know much about most of the genes. Beyond the gene sequence that is coded by the mRNA, we would like to know the structure, function, and cellular localization of the encoded protein, its binding partners and its role in metabolic or regulatory pathways. Most of this information is inaccessible by experiment. Thus it has to be hypothesized with bioinformatics methods. This is why bioinformatics is a key ingredient in the interpretation of expression data [21,22].

3. mRNA is not proteins. There are critical translation steps on the way from mRNA to the mature protein. These steps involve regulation events which are poorly understood as of yet and may prevent mRNA to be translated to a protein or the protein to survive inside the cell. Also, proteins are modified after their synthesis, e.g. by adding sugar or phosphate groups, and these modifications greatly influence protein function.

It is the problems pertaining to point 3 above that motivate to perform the census not on the mRNA level (genomics) but with the synthesized and matured proteins (proteomics). The resulting experimental technologies are more complicated and not as highly developed as genomics [23]. But with mounting progress on the experimental front, proteomics can be expected to dominate a significant part of computational biology within a few years.

The rapidity with which the experimental procedures develop and the demand to find quick answers to mining the incurring data puts Computational biology under great pressure. We need appropriate statistical tools to correlate homogeneous and inhomogeneous data. In addition to expression data which are at the center of many analyses, there are other sources of knowledge that it would be foolish not to tap:

1. Traditionally sequence comparisons have been the major source of function predictions. If two protein sequences have a large similarity then we can wage to infer the function of one sequence from that of the other. While this technology is not failsafe, it can be very powerful, if exercised with caution [24].

2. The comparison of completely sequenced genomes of different organisms can lead to important insights. For instance asking which proteins occur in a genome of a toxic bacterium but not in that of a benign bacterium helps us to find proteins that play a role in the development of the toxic effect [25]. By the same token, proteins that are fused into a single chain in one organism and separated into different chains in another organism are interesting candidates for sharing common functions or being interaction partners [26].

3. The knowledge of metabolic or regulatory pathways involved in the disease can help reduce the signal-to-noise ratio in expression data. We have a similar situation as in protein folding. Telling if a protein adopts a certain shape or not is easier than finding that shape. By the same token, here, telling whether a protein belongs on a path can be easier than finding that path [21].

4. Finally lots of biological information is contained in the scientific literature that is available online, e.g. via PubMed, the online literature database at the National Institutes of Health in Bethesda, Maryland [27]. Computational biology is taking on the challenge of mining that literature, e.g., in order to find functional relationships between genes [28].

For efficient mining of gene expression data we eventually have to combine all of this information in the quest to come up with new biological insight. The purposes of this endeavor are manifold. Here we will concentrate on a pharmaceutical application.

Molecular Therapy of Diseases

The development of a new drug as a cure for a disease is performed in two basic steps. The first is the identification of a key molecule, usually a protein, the so-called target protein, whose biochemical function is causative of or at least intimately involved in the disease. The second step is the search for or development of a drug that moderates - often blocks - the function of the target protein.

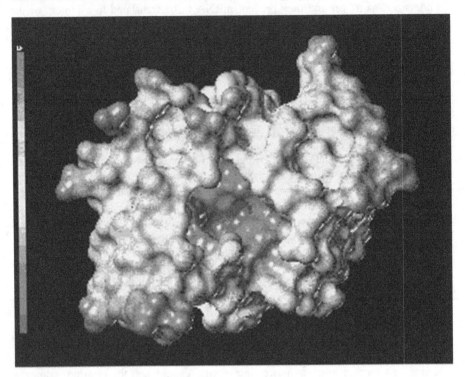

Fig. 4. The protein dihydrofolate reductase (DHFR)

Figure 4 shows the three-dimensional shape of the protein dihydrofolate reductase (DHFR) which catalyzes a reaction that is important in the cell division cycle. DHFR has a prominent binding pocket in its center that is specifically designed to bind to the substrate molecule dihydrofolate and induce a small modification of this molecule. This activity of DHFR can be blocked by administering the drug molecule methotrexate (MTX) (Figure 5). MTX binds tightly to DHFR and prevents the protein from exercising its catalytic function. MTX is a commonly administered drug in cancer treatment, where our goal is to break the (uncontrolled) cell division cycle. This example shows both the benefits and the problems of current drug design. Using MTX, we can in fact break the cell division cycle and stop tumor growth. However, DHFR is actually the wrong target molecule. It is expressed not only inside the tumor but in all dividing cells, thus a treatment with MTX not only affects the tumor but all dividing cells in the body. This leads to severe side effects such as losing one's hair and intestinal lining. What we need is a more appropriate target protein - one that is specifically expressed inside the tumor and whose inhibition does not cause side effects in other tissues.

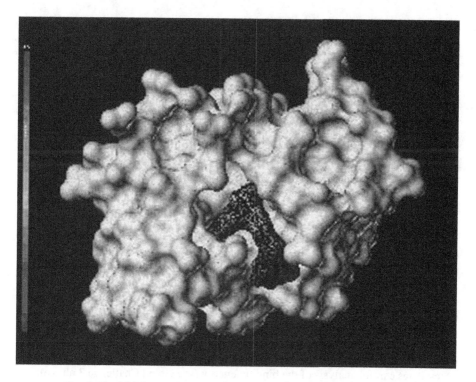

Fig. 5. The inhibitor methotrexate (MTX) bound to dihydrofolate reductase

There are presumably at least several thousand suitable drug targets among the perhaps 50 000 different proteins in our body. Less than 500 proteins are targeted by all drugs on the market today. This shows the potential of innovation in this field. It is only by the new expression measurements that we can attempt to globally search for suitable drug targets. The whole experimental and computer-based machinery described above can be employed for this purpose. Pharmaceutical industry is currently placing large bets on this approach - and this again drives much of the bioinformatics research in this area. Recent findings support the hope that this approach is very promising [29]. At GMD we are currently developing software for target protein finding in the context of a couple of concrete human diseases.

Searching for New Drugs

Once we have identified the target protein we have to search for a drug that binds tightly to that protein. This search also has been systematized greatly with the advent of very efficient methods for synthesizing new compounds (combinatorial chemistry) and testing their binding properties to the protein target (high-throughput screening). Combinatorial libraries provide a carefully selected set of molecular building blocks - usually dozens or hundreds - together with a small set of chemical reactions that link the modules. In this way, a combinatorial library can theoretically provide a diversity of up to billions of molecules from a small set of reactants. Up to millions of these molecules can be synthesized daily in a robotized process and submitted to chemical test in a high-throughput screening procedure. In our context, the objective of the test is to find out which compounds bind tightly to a given target protein.

Here we have a similar situation as in the search for target proteins. We have to inspect compounds among a very large set of molecular candidates, in order to select those that we want to inspect further. Again, computer help is necessary for preselection of molecular candidates and interpretation of experimental data.

In the computer, finding out whether a drug binds tightly to the target protein can best be done if the protein structure is available. If the spatial shape of the site of the protein to which the drug is supposed to bind is known, then we can apply docking methods to select suitable lead compounds which have the potential of being refined to drugs. The speed of a docking method determines whether the method can be employed for screening compound databases in the search for drug leads. At GMD, we developed the docking method FlexX that takes a minute per instance and can be used to screen up to thousands of compounds on a PC or a hundredthousand drugs on a suitable parallel computer [30]. Docking methods that take the better part of an hour cannot suitably be employed for such large scale screening purposes.

In order to screen really large drug databases with several hundred thousand compounds or more we need docking methods that can handle single protein/drug pairs within seconds or less [31]. The high conformational flexibility of small molecules as well as the subtle structural changes in the protein binding pocket upon docking (induced fit) are major complications in docking. Furthermore, docking necessitates careful analysis of the binding energy (see Grand Challenge 3 above).

Perspectives of Computational Biology in Medical and Pharmaceutical Applications

With the advent of expression measurements, computational biology has gained a major push towards application. We can expect this push to drive much of the field for coming years. The high demand for innovation in medicinal chemistry and molecular medicine will generate new problems for computational biology in short succession. These problems will be tied to emerging experimental methods. Two major directions will be:

1. Proteomics: We alluded to this field in above previously. The prominent experimental technologies exhibiting cellular protein populations are 2D gels and mass spectrometry [23]. Part of the involved computational problem is the image analysis of the gels and the interpretation of the mass spectra in order to identify the chains of the occurring proteins. There is a comparatively far developed software scene for these problems. In the end, these data also give us clues as to the post-translational modification of proteins. Correlating these modifications with protein function is a field that computational biology has yet to invade, leave alone conquer.

2. Analyzing genetic variations: Genomic differences between human individuals largely amount to single letter changes (Single Nucleotide Polymorphisms, SNPs), about in every 1000 letters in the genome. Some of these differences are inside coding regions, sometimes even leading to varying protein chains. Most of them

however, are in non-coding regions and affect more subtle and less understood regulatory processes. These differences are the key for varying predisposition to diseases and different effectivity of drugs [32]. Genetic differences are uncovered by traditional sequencing techniques and emerging techniques for genome-wide scans. Analyzing these differences requires joining the fields of molecular biology, genetics, epidemiology and pharmacy. The pharmaceutical side of this area is commonly called pharmacogenomics.

4. Methodical Demands on Computational Biology

Of course, nature is much too complex to be modeled to any sufficiently accurate detail. And we have little time to spend on each molecular candidate. Thus we mostly do not even attempt to model things in great physical detail, instead we use techniques from statistics and machine learning to infer "signals" in the data and separate them from "noise". Just as people interpret facial expressions of their dialog partners not by a thorough physiological analysis that reasons backwards from the shape of the muscles to the neurological state of the brain but learn on (usually vast amounts of) data how to tell whether somebody is happy or sad, attentive or bored, so do computational biology models query hopefully large sets of data to infer the signals. Here signal is a very general notion that can mean just about anything of biological interest - from a sequence alignment exhibiting the evolutionary relationship of the two proteins involved over a predicted 2D or 3D structure of a protein to the structure of a complex of two molecules binding to each other. On the sequence level, the splice sites in complex eucaryotic genes, the location and makeup of regulatory regions or the design of signal peptides giving away the final location of the protein in the cells are examples of interesting signals.

Methods that are used to learn from biological data have classically included neural nets and genetic algorithms. Hidden-Markov models [33,34] are a very popular method of generating models for biological signals of all kinds. Recently support vector machines have been applied very successfully to solving classification problems in computational biology [35,36].

As the methods of analysis are inexact so are the results. The analyses yield predictions that cannot be trusted, in general. This is quite different from the usual situation in theoretical computer science, where you are either required to compute the optimum solution or, at least, optimum means something and so does the distance of the computed solution to the optimum, in case that you do not hit the optimum. Not so here. Cost functions in computational biology usually miss the goal. Notions such as evolutionary distance or free energy are much too complex to be reflected adequately by easy-to-compute cost functions. Thus, computational biology is dominated by the search for suitable cost functions. Those cost functions can be trained, just as the models in toto. At GMD, we have developed a training procedure based on linear programming to improve the predictive power of our protein structure prediction methods [37], and employed support vector machines to find initiation sites for the translation of genes into proteins [36]. Another possibility is to leave the mystical parameters in the cost function variable and study the effect of changing them on the outcome. A method for doing this in the area of sequence alignment is presented in [38].

Whether a method or a cost function is good or bad cannot be proved but has to be validated against biologically interpreted data that are taken as a gold standard for purposes of the validation. Several respective data sets have evolved in different bioinformatics domains. Examples are the SCOP [39] and CATH [40] structural protein classifications for validating methods for protein structure prediction and analysis. These sets are not only taken to validate the different methods but also to compare them community-wide.

Validating methods and cost functions on known biological data has a serious drawback. One is not prepared to answer the question whether the method uses the knowledge of the intended outcome, either on purpose or inadvertently. Therefore, the ultimate test of any computational biology methods is a blind prediction, one that convincingly makes a prediction without previous knowledge of the outcome. To stage a blind prediction experiment involves a certifying authority that vouches for the fact that the knowledge to be predicted was not known to the predictor. The biannual CASP (Critical Assessment of Structure Prediction Methods [10]) experiment series that was started in 1994 performs this task for protein structure prediction methods. The CASP team provides a world-wide clearing house for protein sequences whose structures are in the process of being resolved, e.g. by crystallographers. The group that resolves the structure communicates the protein sequence to the CASP team that puts it on the web up for prediction. Sufficiently long before the crystallographers resolve the structure, the prediction contest closes on that sequence. After the structure is resolved it is compared with the predictions. CASP has been a tremendous help in gaining acknowledgement for the scientific discipline of protein structure prediction.

5. Summary

Computational biology is an highly significant and very demanding branch of applied computer science. This article could only touch upon a few research topics in this complex field. computational biology is a young field. The biological systems under study are not very well understood yet. Models are rough, data are voluminous but often noisy. This limits the accuracy of computational biology predictions. However, the analyses improve quickly, due to improvements on the algorithmic and statistical side and to the accessibility to more and better data. Nevertheless, computational biology can be expected to be a major challenge for some time to come.

Pharmaceutical industry was the first branch of the economy to strongly engage in the new technology combining high-throughput experimentation with bioinformatics analysis. Medicine is following closely. Medical applications step beyond trying to find new drugs on the basis of genomic data. The aim here is to develop more effective diagnostic techniques and to optimize therapies. The first steps to engage computational biology in this quest have already been taken.

While driven by the biological and medical demand, computational biology will also exert a strong impact onto information technology. Since, due to their complexity, we are not able to simulate biological processes on the basis of first principles, we resort to statistical learning and data mining techniques, methods that are at the heart of modern information technology. The mysterious encoding that Nature has afforded for biological signals as well as the enormous data volume present large challenges and are continuing to have large impact on the processes of information technology themselves.

One important point that we want to stress in the end is this. The impact of computational biology research critically depends on an accurate understanding of the biological process under investigation. It is essential to ask the right questions, and often modeling takes priority over optimization. Therefore, we need people that understand and love both computer science and biology to bring the field forward. Fortunately, it seems that a growing number of people discover their interest in both disciplines that make up computational biology.

6. Acknowledgements

I am grateful to Joannis Apostolakis and Joachim Selbig for helpful remarks on the draft of this manuscript.

7. References

1   T. Werner, Analyzing Regulatory Regions in Genomes, in Bioinformatics - From Genomes to Drugs (T. Lengauer, ed.), Wiley-VCH, Heidelberg, to appear.
2   V. Solovyev, Structure, Properties and Computer Identification of Eucaryotic Genes, in Bioinformatics - From Genomes to Drugs (T. Lengauer, ed.), Wiley-VCH, Heidelberg, to appear.
3   S. He, H. A. Scheraga, Brownian Dynamics Simulations of Protein Folding. J. Chem. Phys. 108 (1998) 287-300.
4   D. Baker, A Surprising Simplicity to Protein Folding, Nature 405 (2000) 39-42.
5   J. Kostrowicki, H. A. Scheraga, Application of the Diffusion Equation Method for Global Optimization of Oligopeptides, J. Phys. Chem. 96 (1992) 7442--7449.
6   R. L. Dunbrack, Jr., Homology Modeling in Biology and Medicine, in Bioinformatics - From Genomes to Drugs (T. Lengauer, ed.), Wiley-VCH, Heidelberg, to appear.
7   R. M. Zimmer, Protein Structure Prediction and Applications in Structural Genomics, Protein Function Assignment and Drug Target Finding, in Bioinformatics - From Genomes to Drugs (T. Lengauer, ed.), Wiley-VCH, Heidelberg, to appear.
8   R. M. Zimmer, R. Thiele, Fast Protein Fold Recognition and Accurate Sequence-Structure Alignment, Proceedings of German Conference on Bioinformatics (GCB'96), R. Hofestädt, T. Lengauer, M. Löffler, D. Schomburg, eds., Springer Lecture Notes in Computer Science No. 1278 (1997) 137-148.
9   R. Thiele, R. M. Zimmer, T. Lengauer, Protein Threading by Recursive Dynamic Programming. J. Mol. Biol. 290, 3 (1999) 757-779
10 Proteins: Structure, Function and Genetics, Suppl: Third Meeting on the Critical Assessment of Techniques for Protein Structure Prediction (1999). http://PredictionCenter.llnl.gov/casp3/Casp3.html
11 T. Lengauer, R. Zimmer, Structure Prediction Methods for Drug Design, Briefings in Bioinformatics 1,3 (2000)

12 S. Anderson , Structural genomics: keystone for a Human Proteome Project. Nat Struct Biol. 6,1 (1999)11-12

13 I. Andricioaei, J. E. Straub, Finding the Needle in the Haystack: Algorithms for Conformal Optimization, Computers in Physics 10, 5 (1996) 449.

14 L. Piela, J. Kostrowicki, H. A. Scheraga, The Multiple--Minima Problem in the Conformational Analysis of Molecules. Deformation of the Potential Energy Hypersurface by the Diffusion Equation Method, J. Phys. Chem. 93 (1989) 3339--3346.

15 P. Kollman, Free Energy Calculations: Applications to Chemical and Biochemical Phenomena, Chemical Reviews 93 (1993) 2395-2417.

16 M. K. Gilson et al., The Statistical-Thermodynmic Basis for Computation of Binding Affinities: A Critical review, Biophysical Journal 72 (1997) 1047-1069.

17 J. D. Hirst, Predicting ligand binding energies, Current Opinion in Drug Discovery and Development 1 (1998) 28-33.

18 M. Rarey, M. Stahl, G. Klebe, Screening of Drug Databases, in Bioinformatics - From Genomes to Drugs (T. Lengauer, ed.), Wiley-VCH, Heidelberg, to appear.

19 E. O. Voit, Computational Analysis of Biochemical Systems, Cambridge University Press (2000)

20 M. Tomita et al., E-CELL: Software Environment for Whole-Cell Simulation, Bioinformatics 15, 1 (1999) 72-84.

21 A. Zien, R. Küffner, R. Zimmer., T. Lengauer, Analysis of Gene Expression Data With Pathway Scores, Proceedings of the Eighth International Conference on Intelligent Systems for Molecular Biology (ISMB2000), AAAI Press (2000) 407-417.

22 S. Fuhrman, S. Liang, X. Wen, R. Somogyi, Target Finding in Genomes and Proteomes, in Bioinformatics - From Genomes to Drugs (T. Lengauer, ed.), Wiley-VCH, Heidelberg, to appear.

23 P.-A. Binz et al., Proteome Analysis, in Bioinformatics - From Genomes to Drugs (T. Lengauer, ed.), Wiley-VCH, Heidelberg, to appear.

24 P., Bork, E.V. Koonin, Predicting Function from Protein Sequences: Where are the Bottlenecks? Nature Genet. 18 (1998) 313-318.

25 M. A. Huynen, Y. Diaz-Lazcoz and P. Bork, Differential Genome Display, Trends in Genetics 13 (1997) 389-390.

26 E. M. Marcotte et al., Detecting Protein Function and Protein-Protein Interactions from Genome Sequences, Science 285, 5428 (1999)751-753.

27 http://www.ncbi.nlm.nih.gov/PubMed/

28 H. Shatkay et al., Genes, Themes and Microarrays, Proceedings of the Eighth International Conference on Intelligent Systems for Molecular Biology (ISMB2000), AAAI Press (2000) 317-328.

29 E. A. Clark et al., Genomic Analysis of Metastasis Reveals an Essential Role for RhoC, Nature 406 (2000)532-535.

30 B. Kramer, G. Metz, M. Rarey, T. Lengauer, Ligand Docking and Screening with FlexX, Medical Chemistry Research 9, 7/8 (1999) 463-478.

31 M. Rarey, J. S. Dixon, Feature Trees: A New Molecular Similarity Measure Based on Tree Matching, J Comput Aided Mol Des. 12, 5 (1998) 471-490.

32 M. J. Rieder, D. A. Nickerson, Analysis of Sequence Variations, in Bioinformatics - From Genomes to Drugs (T. Lengauer, ed.), Wiley-VCH, Heidelberg, to appear.

33 A. Krogh, M. Brown, I. S. Mian, K. Sjölander, D. Haussler, Hidden Markov Models in Computational Biology: Application to Protein Modeling, J. Mol. Biol. 235 (1994) 1501--1531.

34 S. R. Eddy, Profile Hidden Markov Models, Bioinformatics 14,9 (1998) 755-763.

35 T. Jaakola, M. Diekhans, D. Haussler, Using the Fisher Kernel Method to Detect Remote Protein Homologies, Proceedings of the Seventh International Conference on Intelligent Systems for Molecular Biology (ISMB'99), AAAI Press (1999) 149-158.

36 A. Zien et al., Engineering Support Vector Machines Kernels that Recognize Translation Initiation Sites, Bioinformatics (2000) to appear.

37 A. Zien, R. Zimmer, T. Lengauer, A Simple Iterative Approach to Parameter Optimization, Proceedings of the Fourth Annual Conference on Research in Computational Molecular Biology (RECOMB'00), ACM Press (2000) 318-327.

38 R. Zimmer, T. Lengauer, Fast and Numerically Stable Parametric Alignment of Biosequences. Proceedings of the First Annual Conference on Research in Computational Molecular Biology (RECOMB'97) (1997) 344-353.

39 http://scop.mrc-lmb.cam.ac.uk/scop/

40 http://www.biochem.ucl.ac.uk/bsm/cath/

Computer Science in Physics

A. Peter Young

Physics Department
University of California
Santa CruzYCA FERwk
peter@bartok.ucsc.edu
http://bartok.ucsc.edu/peter

Abstract. This talk describes how techniques developed by Computer Scientists have helped our understanding of certain problems in statisti4 cal physics which involve randomness and "frustration"8 Examples will be given from two problems that have been widely studied: the "spin glass" and the "random field model"8

1 Introduction

An important part of the area of physics known as "statistical physics" is the study of phase transitions, at which the system converts from one state to another. Most interest has centered on "second order" or "continuous" transitions, in which the property which distinguishes the two phases vanishes continuously as the transition is approached. The disappearance of the magnetization of a ferromagnet, such as iron, as the temperature is increased is generally continuous. At the other type of transition, known as "first order" or "discontinuous", there is a jump in the properties of the system as the transition is crossed, and also a latent heat. An everyday example of a first order transition is the freezing of water.

We shall focus on magnetic transitions in this talk because (i) they can be represented by simple models amenable to numerical study, and (ii) there are many experimental systems which are describable by these models. One of the major advances in the field has been the realization that behavior in the vicinity of the transition (called the "critical point") is "universal" [1]. This means that "critical behavior" does not depend on the microscopic details of the system but only on much more basic features such its dimensionality and symmetry. Consequently one can use relatively simple models, which can be readily simulated, to make precise comparisons with experiment. That said, it should be emphasized that universality is much better justified for clean systems than for the systems with disorder which we shall be considering in this talk. One goal of applying sophisticated algorithms from computer science to these problems will be to see if universality also holds for disordered systems.

The simplest model which describes a magnetic transition, known as the Ising model, has a variable at each site on a regular lattice which can point either "up" or "down". This represents the orientation of the magnetic moment of an atom,

R. Wilhelm (Ed.): Informatics. 10 Years Back. 10 Years Ahead, LNCS 2000, pp. 356–368, 2001.

and is simplified to only allow two possible orientations. We shall follow standard notation in calling these variables "spins", labeled S_i where i denotes a lattice site. It is convenient to denote the up spin state by $S_i = 1$ and the down spin state by $S_i = -1$.

Neighboring sites on the lattice interact with each other. If the interaction favors parallel alignment of the spins, it is called "ferromagnetic", while an interaction favoring anti-parallel alignment is called "anti-ferromagnetic". The energy (confusingly called the "Hamiltonian" in the physics literature) can therefore be written as

$$E = - \sum_{\langle i,j \rangle} J_{ij} S_i S_j, \tag{1}$$

where the sum is over all nearest neighbor pairs of the lattice (counted once) and the interactions are labeled J_{ij}. If all the J_{ij} are positive then the state of lowest energy (ground state) has all spins parallel (either all $+1$ or all -1) and is called a ferromagnet. As the temperature is increased, the net alignment of the spins, the magnetization, decreases and vanishes at a critical temperature T_c, where thermal noise, which tends to randomize the spins, overcomes the interactions, which tend to make them order.

The situation with all interactions negative is simple if the sites of the lattice can be divided into two sublattices, A and B, such that all the neighbors of A are in B and vice-versa. Such lattices are said to be "bi-partite", and are the only type that we shall consider here. A square grid is an example of a bipartite lattice. The ground state for a bipartite lattice with negative interactions has all spins $+1$ on sublattice A and all spins -1 on sublattice B, or vice-versa. Such a state is called an antiferromagnet. Again the ordering decreases to zero at a critical temperature.

The problems of interest to us have two more ingredients. The first is *disorder*. The interactions are not all equal but are chosen in some random way. The simplest model for disorder is to pick each interaction from a probability distribution, independently of all the others. The second ingredient is *"frustration"* or competition between the interactions. For the model in Eq. (1) this can be incorporated by allowing the *sign* as well as the magnitude of the interaction to be random.

That this leads to frustration can be seen in the "toy" example in Fig. 1. This shows just four sites round a square with one anti-ferromagnetic (negative) interaction and three ferromagnetic (positive) interactions. If the spins along the bottom row and top left corner are oriented in directions which minimize the energy (as shown) the spin at the top right is "frustrated" since it receives conflicting instructions from its two neighbors. It wants to be parallel to both of them which is impossible. It is easy to see that there is frustration if there is an odd number of negative interactions round the square, which is then called a "frustrated square".

If we extend this toy example of four sites to a large lattice, choosing the sign (and possibly the magnitude) of the interactions at random, determining the ground state is non-trivial, which is not the case if all interactions have the

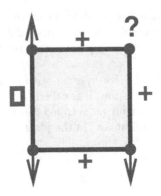

Fig. 1. A simple example illustration frustration as discussed in the text.

same sign. This type of problem, which has been extensively studied, is called a "spin glass" [2,3]. There are many experiments on magnetic systems with these features of disorder and frustration but it would take us too far afield to discuss them here. Spin glasses are also considered as prototypes for other systems with frustration and disorder which have many features in common. Examples are neural networks, protein folding models, elastic manifolds in random media, and the "vortex glass" transition in superconductors in a magnetic field. These are discussed in the articles in Ref. [2]

Determination of the ground state in systems with disorder and frustration is an optimization problem, in which the "cost function" that has to be minimized is the energy. As we shall see, algorithms from computer science enable us to calculate the ground state of spin glasses for surprisingly large lattice sizes, at least in certain cases. An excellent introduction to optimization algorithms as applied to problems in physics is the review by Rieger [4].

Spin glasses and other problems with disorder and frustration are hard because the energy varies in a complicated manner as one moves through configuration space. There are local minima of the energy, which we will call "valleys" in the "energy landscape", separated by "barriers" (i.e. saddle points). Different local minima can have similar energies but have very different configurations of the spins. At a finite temperature the systems should spend time in different valleys with relative proportions given by the appropriate Boltzmann factors [5]. Only one of the local minima will be the global minimum (ground state). This can be hard to find if there are many minima and/or the global minimum has a small "basin of attraction". However, it is generally quite easy to find a minimum with energy close to the ground state energy, for example by the method of "simulated annealing" [6].

The precise value of the ground state energy will depend on the particular choice of the random interactions (remember they were picked from a distribution). In physics we usually look at "intensive" quantities (those which do not depend on size of the system, N, as $N \to \infty$) such as the ground state energy *per spin*. Many intensive quantities are "self-averaging" which means that its value does not depend on the realization of disorder for $N \to \infty$. However, there *are* sample-to-sample fluctuations, generally of order $1/\sqrt{N}$, for finite-sized systems, so we need to average results over many realizations of disorder. This makes the problem even more computationally challenging than if we just had to solve for one sample, but fortunately averaging over samples is clearly "trivially paralleliz- able", so we can easily take advantage of the large-scale parallel machines that are widely available at present, or just run the code on a "farm" of independent workstations.

In this talk I will also discuss another widely studied problem with frustration and disorder, known as the random field model. A magnetic field will prefer a spin to align in one direction rather than the other, and so can be represented in the expression for the energy by terms linear in the spins. Eq. (1) is therefore modified to

$$E = -\sum_{\langle i,j \rangle} J_{ij} S_i S_j - \sum_i h_i S_i, \tag{2}$$

where we have allowed for a different field h_i on each site. The random field model is obtained if one chooses the h_i at random with zero average value, and has the J_{ij} unfrustrated (so we could set them all to equal unity). Again there are experimental systems which have been widely studied but which space does not allow me to discuss. For more information see Ref. [7] and the articles in Ref. [2]. In Eq. (2) frustration comes from competition between the interactions on the one hand, which prefer the spins to be parallel, and the random fields on the other, which prefer the spins to follow the local field direction.

The traditional physics approach to studying problems with frustration and disorder is the Monte Carlo simulation, i.e. a random sampling of the states according to the Boltzmann distribution [5]. However, at low temperatures the system gets trapped in one of the valleys for a long "time" and is only very rarely able to escape over a barrier in the energy landscape to another valley. The probability for escape is exponentially small in the ratio of the barrier height to the temperature. As a result, equilibrium simulations can only be done on very small systems at low temperatures. Some speed up can be obtained from recently developed Monte Carlo algorithms such as parallel tempering [8,9] (also known as "exchange Monte Carlo") but the range of sizes that can be studied is still quite limited.

In this talk I will discuss an alternative approach which uses sophisticated optimization algorithms from Computer Science [4] to find the exact ground state. The idea will be to "beat the small size limit" of Monte Carlo methods. The advantages of the computer science approach are:

1. It is exact. There are no statistical errors or problems of equilibration.
2. One can study large sizes.

However, there are also some disadvantages. These are:

1. Only the ground state is determined, so one is restricted to zero temperature properties.
2. Only for some models are there efficient algorithms.

In the rest of this talk I will discuss what has been learned from applying optimization algorithms to the spin glass and random field problems, and also describe some prospects for the future.

2   The Random Field Model

In this section I will discuss how optimization algorithms have enhanced our understanding of the random field model. The energy is given by Eq. (2) with the sites on a regular lattice, which we take to be a square grid in two-dimensions, a simple cubic grid in three-dimensions, and similarly in higher dimensions. The interactions J_{ij} are all set to unity and the random fields are chosen from a symmetric distribution with mean and variance given by

$$[h_i] = 0, \qquad [h_i^2] = h_R^2, \tag{3}$$

where the rectangular brackets $[\cdots]$ denote an average over the disorder, so h_R is the strength of the random field.

In the absence of random fields it is known that there is a non-zero magnetization $\langle S_i \rangle$ at low temperatures and we say that there is "long range order". This long range order vanishes continuously at critical temperature. When the random fields are turned on one could ask whether even a small random field prevents the formation of long range order at *any* temperature or whether a critical field strength is needed to destroy long range order at low temperature. A famous argument due to Imry and Ma [10] states that for dimension two and lower, the random field always "wins" in the sense that long range order is destroyed by an arbitrarily weak random field, with the system "breaking up" into domains of parallel spins. The domain size diverges as $h_R \to 0$ so one recovers long range order for h_R strictly zero. However, in dimension, d, greater than two an arbitrarily small random field does not cause the system to break up into domains on long length scales and long range order is preserved up to a critical field strength.

For $d > 2$, the phase diagram is that sketched in Fig. 2. For $h_R = 0$ the ferromagnetic phase disappears at $T = T_c$ due to thermal fluctuations, while at $T = 0$ the ferromagnetic phase disappears at a critical value of the random field, h_c, due to the disordering effects of the random field. This will be important later.

What aspects of the random field problem are physicists interested in? It turns out that many quantities vary with a power law in the vicinity of the critical point. Denoting by δ the deviation from the phase boundary in Fig. 2, the magnetization varies, for δ small, like

$$\langle S_i \rangle \sim |\delta|^\beta, \tag{4}$$

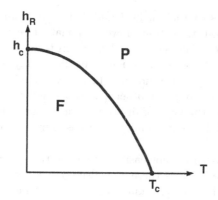

Fig. 2. The phase diagram of the random field model in dimension greater than two. "P" denotes the paramagnetic phase with no long range ferromagnetic order, while "F" denotes the ferromagnetic phase.

where β is known as a "critical exponent". Other quantities of interest are the specific heat, C, and the magnetic susceptibility, χ, which vary as

$$\langle C \rangle \sim \delta^{-\alpha},$$
$$\langle \chi \rangle \sim \delta^{-\gamma}. \tag{5}$$

Critical exponents such as α, β and γ are of interest because they are universal [1], only depending on broad features of the problem such as the dimensionality of the lattice and whether or not there is a random field. They are not expected to depend on the strength of the random field, as long as it is non-zero, or the distribution used for the random fields, as long as it is symmetric.

Physicists would like to the understand universal critical behavior, such as the values of the critical exponents. Since the phase boundary is crossed at zero temperature by varying h_R one *can* investigate the behavior near the phase boundary using optimization (i.e. $T = 0$) algorithms. Fortunately, determining the ground state energy is equivalent to a Max-Flow problem [4] which can be solved in polynomial time. This was first realized by Barahona and Anglès d'Auriac et al. [11] and subsequently used by Ogielski [12], Sourlas and collaborators [13], and others.

Here I will just discuss briefly some of the results found in Ref. [13], which investigated the random field model in $d = 3$. In their optimized implementation of the Max-Flow algorithm, they studied L^3 lattices up to $L = 90$, and found empirically that the CPU time varied as L^4. This is remarkably efficient, being not much more than the time (L^3) needed to scan once through the lattice. Ref. [13] provides strong evidence that the transition is actually discontinuous, corresponding to an exponent $\beta = 0$. This had been suspected earlier from finite-T Monte Carlo simulations [14] on sizes up to $L = 16$ but the results of Ref. [13] are more convincing because they are on much larger systems. Normally a first order transition leads to a latent heat and rather weak fluctuation effects compared with a continuous transition. However, no latent heat is seen in the random field problem and, in other respects, there seem to be large fluctuation effects characteristic of a continuous transition. This dichotomy is not understood.

Several different types of random field distribution were used in Ref. [13]. While they all gave rise to $\beta = 0$, other quantities, also expected to be universal, seemed to depend on the type of disorder, casting some doubt on the hypothesis that universality holds for random systems. This important question needs further work.

The $T = 0$ approach cannot easily determine the specific heat exponent α, which is unfortunate because there is a discrepancy between the experimental value [15] which is close to zero and results from Monte Carlo simulations, e.g. Ref. [14], which give $\alpha \simeq -0.5$.

3   The Spin Glass

The energy of the spin glass problem is given by Eq. (1) where the J_{ij} are taken from a symmetric distribution with mean and variance given by

$$[J_{ij}] = 0, \qquad [J_{ij}^2] = 1. \tag{6}$$

One often takes a Gaussian distribution, though another popular choice is is the bimodal distribution, also the called $\pm J$ distribution, in which the interactions have values $+1$ and -1 with equal probability. The latter distribution has the special feature that there are *many* ground states (we say that the ground state is "degenerate"). In fact the number of ground states is exponentially large in the number of spins N giving rise to a finite ground state entropy.

Two principal questions have been asked about spin glasses:

1. Is there a phase transition at finite temperature T_c?
2. What is the nature of the spin glass state below T_c?

For the first question, Monte Carlo simulations and early (unsophisticated) ground state calculations have shown;

- In $d = 2$ the transition is only at $T = 0$.
- In $d = 3$ (and higher) the transition is at finite temperature.

The conclusion for $d = 2$ is very strong and so is the situation in $d = 4, 5, \cdots$ etc. The case of $d = 3$ has been the most difficult to resolve and earlier work was not very conclusive, but the most recent simulations [16] seem rather convincing.

Concerning the second question, we have already noted that, because of the complicated energy landscape, there are large clusters of (carefully chosen) spins which can be flipped with rather low energy cost. Is it possible to quantify this remark? Two principal scenarios have been proposed which differ, mainly, as to the energy of these large-scale excitations. These scenarios are:

– The "droplet model" of Fisher and Huse [17]. In this phenomenological picture a few very plausible assumptions are made. The lowest energy to create an excitation of linear size L is assumed to vary as

$$\Delta E \sim L^\theta, \tag{7}$$

where θ (> 0) is an exponent. θ can not be negative if $T_c > 0$ otherwise there would be large scale excitations which cost vanishingly small energy and the system would break up into domains at any finite temperature. We shall see below that this is what happens in $d = 2$. Note that for a ferromagnet there is a positive energy cost for each interaction on the wall of the excitation and, since the wall area goes like L^{d-1}, one has $\theta = d - 1$ in that case. However, for a spin glass it turns out that $\theta < d - 1$ (in fact it is also true that $\theta < (d-1)/2$). Hence, there is a near cancellation between the effects of the bonds which were "unsatisfied" before the excitation is flipped and then become "satisfied" (which lower the excitation energy), and the the effects of the satisfied bonds which become unsatisfied (which increase the excitation energy).

– The "replica symmetry breaking" (RSB) picture of Parisi [18]. The Parisi theory is the (presumably) exact solution of an artificial model with infinite-range interactions. The assumption is then made that qualitatively similar behavior also occurs for more realistic models with short range interactions. An important ingredient of the RSB picture is that there are excitations of order the size of the system whose energy does *not* grow with the size of the system i.e.

$$\Delta E \sim \text{const.} \tag{8}$$

This is in contrast to the prediction of the droplet theory in Eq. (7). The cancellation between the effects of the satisfied and unsatisfied bonds on the boundary of the excitation is then even more complete than in the droplet model.

To discuss what has been learned from optimization algorithms it is necessary to distinguish $d = 2$ from higher dimensions. We first consider $d = 2$.

We have already noted that a square is frustrated if an odd number of its bonds are negative and the converse, that the square is unfrustrated (i.e. each bond can be satisfied) if there are an even number of negative bonds, is also true. Changing the sign of the bonds in such a way that the frustration remains unchanged has no effect on the ground state energy because it can be compensated for by changing the sign of appropriate spins. Hence, for the $\pm J$ distribution, the ground state energy is determined entirely by the location of the frustrated squares. For a distribution in which the magnitude of the bonds is not constant we also need to keep track of the magnitude of the bonds (though not the sign) plus the location of the frustrated squares.

Let us therefore indicate the frustrated squares on the lattice by drawing a cross in their center, as shown in Fig. 3. We indicate the unsatisfied bonds by drawing dashed lines at right angles across them. Clearly the lines must begin

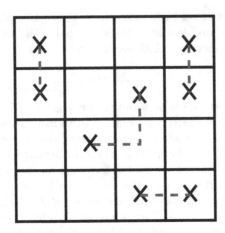

Fig. 3. A two dimensional spin glass in which the frustrated squares are denoted by crosses. The ground state energy is obtained from the minimum length of the strings connecting the frustrated squares. For a distribution of interactions where the magnitude as well as the sign varies there is a weight to each string segment equal to the magnitude of the bond which it crosses.

and end on frustrated squares and so form "strings" connecting the crosses. The ground state energy is increased relative to that of the unfrustrated system by the energy of the bonds crossed by the strings. For a $\pm J$ distribution the ground state energy is therefore determined by minimizing the length of the strings. For a distribution of interactions where the magnitude as well as the sign varies one has to minimize the total "weight" of the string, where the weight of a string segment is equal to the magnitude of the bond which it crosses.

This problem is equivalent to a Minimum Weight Perfect Matching Problem [4] as first realized by Barahona et al. [19] which can be solved in polynomial time, i.e. it belongs to the category "P" of optimization problems. To be more precise it is a polynomial algorithm provided the lattice is a "planar graph", i.e. it can be drawn on a piece of paper with no lines crossing. Unfortunately this rules out periodic boundary conditions which are often imposed to eliminate surface effects which arise from the spins on the surface having a different number of neighbors from the spins in the bulk. With periodic boundary conditions the problem belongs to the class "NP". However, an efficient "Branch and Cut" algorithm [4] enables quite large sizes to be studied [20].

In three dimensions or higher calculating the ground state of spin glass is NP for all boundary conditions. Most work has used "heuristic" algorithms, which are not guaranteed to give the exact ground states, but which, when used carefully, do seem to give the true ground state in most instances. The most effective such approach seems to be the "genetic algorithm" developed for spin glasses by Pal [21] and subsequently used by Palassini and me [22,23] and Marinari and Parisi [24].

Let us now discuss what has been learned about spin glasses from optimization techniques, starting with $d = 2$.

First we note that the restriction to $T = 0$ is more serious than for the random field problem because we cannot go through the critical point. We can, however, learn about low energy excitations by computing the ground state, then perturbing the system in some way, and finally recomputing the ground state. As an example let us start with periodic boundary conditions and then change to anti-periodic boundary conditions in one direction, which simply corresponds to changing the sign of the bonds across one boundary. This induces a domain wall across the system, as shown in Fig. 4, such that all the spins on one side of the wall are flipped.

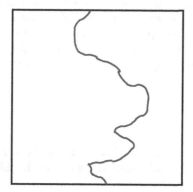

Fig. 4. A domain wall crossing a two-dimensional lattice. Its energy will be of order L^θ, where is L is the size of the lattice in each dimension, and it will have a fractal dimension d_s.

The wall will have an energy, which could have either sign, and its characteristic scale varies with the size of the system in each direction, L, as in Eq. (7). Starting with the pioneering work of Bray and Moore [25], and followed by later studies [26,27] for larger sizes (up to about 30^2) using the Branch and Cut method, it has been found that θ is negative in $d = 2$ with a value of around -0.28. The negative value means that the system will break up into large domains at any finite temperature, so there is no spin glass state except at $T = 0$. These studies also show that the wall is a fractal with fractal dimension d_s about 1.28, greater than 1 so it is not a smooth curve, but also less than 2 so the wall is not "space filling".

Recently Middleton [28] has used the Matching algorithm to determine ground states of two-dimensional spin glasses with free boundaries for very large sizes, up to 512^2, using a different approach to generate excitations from which θ and d_s can be determined. His results agree well with the other work.

The case of $d = 3$ is more interesting that that of $d = 2$ not only because this is the physical dimension but also because there is a finite temperature spin glass state. There is general agreement that $\theta \simeq 0.20$ in $d = 3$, starting with the first studies of Bray and Moore [25] which could only consider sizes up to 4^3, and followed by later work [22,29] which could go up to about 10^3 using heuristic optimization algorithms. The positive value indicates that the spin glass state should be stable at low but finite temperatures. Ref. [22] also find that $d_s \simeq 2.68$.

Subsequently, two papers [30,23] have argued that a different value of θ, consistent with zero, is obtained from excitations in which the boundary conditions are not changed but a carefully chosen set of spins is flipped, for example by thermal noise. This suggests that the spin glass is actually quite close to the RSB picture. However, the sizes are still quite small, up to around 10^3, and the assertion that there are two values (at least) for θ depending the type of excitation being considered is quite messy, so this claim needs further study.

Given the considerable interest in the spin glass in three-dimensions, it is unfortunate that there are no polynomial algorithms for finding the ground state. It is to be hoped that, in the future, algorithms will be developed which both give exact ground states and can treat larger sizes than the present heuristic algorithms.

4   Conclusions

This discussion of the role of optimization algorithms in statistical physics has been very brief. For further information the reader should consult the references. Ref. [4] is a good place to start.

The main conclusions of this talk are:

1. Algorithms from computer science have "broken the size barrier" for some problems in statistical physics, e.g.
   (a) The random field model
   (b) The spin glass in two-dimensions
2. The application of algorithms from computer science to physics problems works best as a collaboration between computer scientists and physicist, e.g. Ref. [26].
3. For the future I expect there will be developments in the following areas:
   (a) More models will be solved.
   (b) More efficient algorithms will be developed for NP problems such as the spin glass in three-dimensions. So far, with the genetic algorithm, we can study up to of order 10^3 spins. Surely we do better than this.
   (c) Spin glasses will be used to investigate the statistics of "hardness". For example, given an algorithm for the exact ground state of a three-dimensional spin glass such as branch-and-cut, one can study the *distribution* of CPU times required to solve the problem for different realizations of disorder. It would be interesting to see how the *average* CPU

time varies with system size and do the same for the *typical* (e.g. median) CPU time. If the distribution of CPU times is very broad, the average may be dominated by a few rare samples which are extremely "hard" and vary with size in a different way from the typical CPU time. This distinction has been made recently in statistical physics in the study of some *quantum* systems undergoing phase transitions at zero temperature [31] but, to my knowledge, does not seem to have been investigated systematically in studies of hardness of NP problems.

Acknowledgments:
I would like to thank Heiko Rieger for educating me about the algorithms mentioned in this talk and many other topics. Much of my own work in this field has been with Matteo Palassini and I would like to thank him for a stimulating collaboration. I am especially grateful to the organizer, Reinhard Wilhelm, for inviting me to speak at the 10th Anniversary Dagstuhl conference, which introduced me to large areas of computer science about which I knew nothing before. My research is supported by the NSF under grant DMR-9713977.

References

1. Universality became well established after the development of renormalization group theory by K. Wilson. A good reference is J. Cardy, *Scaling and Renormalization in Statistical Physics*, (Cambridge University Press, Cambridge, 1996).
2. *Spin Glasses and Random Fields*, A. P. Young Ed., (World Scientific, Singapore, 1998)
3. K. Binder and A. P. Young, *Spin Glasses: Experimental Facts, Theoretical Concepts and Open Questions*, Rev. Mod. Phys. **58**, 801 (1986).
4. A good review of the application of optimization methods to problems in statistical physics is H. Rieger, *Frustrated Systems: Ground State Properties via Combinatorial Optimization*, in *Advances in Computer Simulations*, Lecture Notes in Physics, **501**, J. Kertész and I. Kondor Eds., (Springer-Verlag, Heidelberg, 1998). This is also available on the cond-mat archive as cond-mat/9705010. The URL for cond-mat is http://xxx.lanl.gov/archive/cond-mat.
5. According to statistical mechanics, a system in thermal equilibrium has a probability proportional to $\exp(-E_l/k_B T)$ of being in a state l with energy E_l, where T is the temperature, and k_B is Boltzmann's constant (usually set to unity in model calculations). This exponential is known as a "Boltzmann factor".
6. S. Kirkpatrick, C. D. Gelatt and M. P. Vecchi, *Optimization by Simulated Annealing*, Science **220** 671 (1983).
7. D. P. Belanger and A. P. Young, *The Random Field Ising model*, J. Magn. and Magn. Mat. **100**, 272 (1991).
8. K. Hukushima and K. Nemoto, *Exchange Monte Carlo Method and Application to Spin Glass Simulations*, J. Phys. Soc. Japan **65**, 1604 (1996).
9. H. G. Katzgraber, M. Palassini and A. P. Young, *Spin Glasses at Low Temperatures*, cond-mat/0007113.
10. Y. Imry and S. K. Ma, Phys. Rev. Lett. **35**, 1399 (1975).
11. F. Barahona, J. Phys. A. **18**, L673 (1985); J.-C. Anglès d'Auriac, M. Preissman and R. Rammal, J. de Physique Lett. **46**, L173 (1985).

12. A. T. Ogielski, Phys. Rev. Lett. **57**, 1251 (1986).
13. N. Sourlas, *Universality in Random Systems: The Case of the 3-d Random Field Ising model* cond-mat/9810231; J.-C. Anglès d'Auriac and N. Sourlas, *The 3-d Random Field Ising Model at Zero Temperature*, Europhysics Lett. **39**, 473 (1997).
14. H. Rieger and A. P. Young, *Critical Exponents of the Three Dimensional Random Field Ising Model*, J. Phys. A, **26**, 5279 (1993); H. Rieger, *Critical Behavior of the 3d Random Field Ising Model: Two-Exponent Scaling or First Order Phase Transition?*, Phys. Rev. B **52**, 6659 (1995).
15. D. P. Belanger, A. R. King and V. Jaccarino, Phys. Rev. B **31**, 4538 (1985).
16. H. G. Ballesteros, A. Cruz, L.A. Fernandez, V. Martin-Mayor, J. Pech, J. J. Ruiz-Lorenzo, A. Tarancon, P. Tellez, C.L. Ullod, and C. Ungil, *Critical Behavior of the Three-Dimensional Ising Spin Glass*, cond-mat/0006211.
17. D. S. Fisher and D. A. Huse, J. Phys. A. **20** L997 (1987); D. A. Huse and D. S. Fisher, J. Phys. A. **20** L1005 (1987); D. S. Fisher and D. A. Huse, Phys. Rev. B **38** 386 (1988).
18. G. Parisi, Phys. Rev. Lett. **43**, 1754 (1979); J. Phys. A **13**, 1101, 1887, L115 (1980; Phys. Rev. Lett. **50**, 1946 (1983).
19. F. Barahona, J. Phys. A **15**, 3241 (1982); F. Barahona, R. Maynard, R. Rammal and J. P. Uhry, J. Phys. A **15**, 673 (1982).
20. The group of Prof. M. Jünger, at the University of Cologne, has generously made available to the public a server which calculates exact ground states of the Ising spin glass in two dimensions with periodic boundary conditions using a Branch and Cut algorithm. Information about this service can be obtained at http://www.informatik.uni-koeln.de/ls_juenger/projects/sgs.html.
21. K. F. Pal, *The Ground State Energy of the Edwards-Anderson Ising Spin Glass with a Hybrid Genetic Algorithm*, Physica A **223**, 283 (1996); *The Ground State of the Cubic Spin Glass with Short-Range Interactions of Gaussian Distribution*, **233**, 60 (1996).
22. M. Palassini and A. P. Young, *Triviality of the Ground State Structure in Ising Spin Glasses*, Phys. Rev. Lett. **83**, 5126 (1999);
23. M. Palassini and A. P. Young, *Nature of the Spin Glass State*, Phys. Rev. Lett. **85**, 3017 (2000);
24. E. Marinari and G. Parisi, *On the Effects of a Bulk Perturbation on the Ground State of 3D Ising Spin Glasses*, cond-mat/0007493; E. Marinari and G. Parisi, *On the Effects of Changing the Boundary Conditions on the Ground State of Ising Spin Glasses*, cond-mat/0005047;
25. A. J. Bray and M. A. Moore, J. Phys. C **17**, L463 (1984).
26. H. Rieger, L. Santen, U. Blasum, M. Diehl, and M. Jünger, *The Critical Exponents of the Two-Dimensional Ising Spin Glass Revisited: Exact Ground State Calculations and Monte Carlo Simulations*, J. Phys. A **29**, 3939 (1996).
27. M. Palassini and A. P. Young, *Trivial Ground State Structure in the Two-Dimensional Ising Spin Glass*, Phys. Rev. B. **60**, R9919 (1999).
28. A. A. Middleton, *Numerical Investigation of the Thermodynamic Limit for Ground States in Models with Quenched Disorder*, Phys. Rev. Lett. **83**, 1672 (1999); *Energetics and geometry of excitations in random systems*, cond-mat/0007375.
29. A. K. Hartmann, *Scaling of Stiffness Energy for 3d ±J Ising Spin Glasses*, Phys. Rev. E **59**, 84 (1999).
30. F. Krzakala and O. C. Martin, *Spin and Link Overlaps in Three-Dimensional Spin Glasses*, Phys. Rev. Lett, **85**, 3013 (2000).
31. D. S. Fisher, Phys. Rev. B **51**, 6411 (1995).

Author Index

Lecture Notes in Computer Science

For information about Vols. 1–1914
please contact your bookseller or Springer-Verlag

Vol. 1945: W. Grieskamp, T. Santen, B. Stoddart (Eds.), Integrated Formal Methods. Proceedings, 2000. X, 441 pages. 2000.

Vol. 1946: P. Palanque, F. Paternò (Eds.), Interactive Systems. Proceedings, 2000. X, 251 pages. 2001.

Vol. 1948: T. Tan, Y. Shi, W. Gao (Eds.), Advances in Multimodal Interfaces – ICMI 2000. Proceedings, 2000. XVI, 678 pages. 2000.

Vol. 1949: R. Connor, A. Mendelzon (Eds.), Research Issues in Structured and Semistructured Database Programming. Proceedings, 1999. XII, 325 pages. 2000.

Vol. 1950: D. van Melkebeek, Randomness and Completeness in Computational Complexity. XV, 196 pages. 2000.

Vol. 1951: F. van der Linden (Ed.), Software Architectures for Product Families. Proceedings, 2000. VIII, 255 pages. 2000.

Vol. 1952: M.C. Monard, J. Simão Sichman (Eds.), Advances in Artificial Intelligence. Proceedings, 2000. XV, 498 pages. 2000. (Subseries LNAI).

Vol. 1953: G. Borgefors, I. Nyström, G. Sanniti di Baja (Eds.), Discrete Geometry for Computer Imagery. Proceedings, 2000. XI, 544 pages. 2000.

Vol. 1954: W.A. Hunt, Jr., S.D. Johnson (Eds.), Formal Methods in Computer-Aided Design. Proceedings, 2000. XI, 539 pages. 2000.

Vol. 1955: M. Parigot, A. Voronkov (Eds.), Logic for Programming and Automated Reasoning. Proceedings, 2000. XIII, 487 pages. 2000. (Subseries LNAI).

Vol. 1956: T. Coquand, P. Dybjer, B. Nordström, J. Smith (Eds.), Types for Proofs and Programs. Proceedings, 1999. VII, 195 pages. 2000.

Vol. 1957: P. Ciancarini, M. Wooldridge (Eds.), Agent-Oriented Software Engineering. Proceedings, 2000. X, 323 pages. 2001.

Vol. 1960: A. Ambler, S.B. Calo, G. Kar (Eds.), Services Management in Intelligent Networks. Proceedings, 2000. X, 259 pages. 2000.

Vol. 1961: J. He, M. Sato (Eds.), Advances in Computing Science – ASIAN 2000. Proceedings, 2000. X, 299 pages. 2000.

Vol. 1963: V. Hlaváč, K.G. Jeffery, J. Wiedermann (Eds.), SOFSEM 2000: Theory and Practice of Informatics. Proceedings, 2000. XI, 460 pages. 2000.

Vol. 1964: J. Malenfant, S. Moisan, A. Moreira (Eds.), Object-Oriented Technology. Proceedings, 2000. XI, 309 pages. 2000.

Vol. 1965: Ç. K. Koç, C. Paar (Eds.), Cryptographic Hardware and Embedded Systems – CHES 2000. Proceedings, 2000. XI, 355 pages. 2000.

Vol. 1966: S. Bhalla (Ed.), Databases in Networked Information Systems. Proceedings, 2000. VIII, 247 pages. 2000.

Vol. 1967: S. Arikawa, S. Morishita (Eds.), Discovery Science. Proceedings, 2000. XII, 332 pages. 2000. (Subseries LNAI).

Vol. 1968: H. Arimura, S. Jain, A. Sharma (Eds.), Algorithmic Learning Theory. Proceedings, 2000. XI, 335 pages. 2000. (Subseries LNAI).

Vol. 1969: D.T. Lee, S.-H. Teng (Eds.), Algorithms and Computation. Proceedings, 2000. XIV, 578 pages. 2000.

Vol. 1970: M. Valero, V.K. Prasanna, S. Vajapeyam (Eds.), High Performance Computing – HiPC 2000. Proceedings, 2000. XVIII, 568 pages. 2000.

Vol. 1971: R. Buyya, M. Baker (Eds.), Grid Computing – GRID 2000. Proceedings, 2000. XIV, 229 pages. 2000.

Vol. 1972: A. Omicini, R. Tolksdorf, F. Zambonelli (Eds.), Engineering Societies in the Agents World. Proceedings, 2000. IX, 143 pages. 2000. (Subseries LNAI).

Vol. 1973: J. Van den Bussche, V. Vianu (Eds.), Database Theory – ICDT 2001. Proceedings, 2001. X, 451 pages. 2001.

Vol. 1974: S. Kapoor, S. Prasad (Eds.), FST TCS 2000: Foundations of Software Technology and Theoretical Computer Science. Proceedings, 2000. XIII, 532 pages. 2000.

Vol. 1975: J. Pieprzyk, E. Okamoto, J. Seberry (Eds.), Information Security. Proceedings, 2000. X, 323 pages. 2000.

Vol. 1976: T. Okamoto (Ed.), Advances in Cryptology – ASIACRYPT 2000. Proceedings, 2000. XII, 630 pages. 2000.

Vol. 1977: B. Roy, E. Okamoto (Eds.), Progress in Cryptology – INDOCRYPT 2000. Proceedings, 2000. X, 295 pages. 2000.

Vol. 1979: S. Moss, P. Davidsson (Eds.), Multi-Agent-Based Simulation. Proceedings, 2000. VIII, 267 pages. 2001. (Subseries LNAI).

Vol. 1983: K.S. Leung, L.-W. Chan, H. Meng (Eds.), Intelligent Data Engineering and Automated Learning – IDEAL 2000. Proceedings, 2000. XVI, 573 pages. 2000.

Vol. 1984: J. Marks (Ed.), Graph Drawing. Proceedings, 2001. XII, 419 pages. 2001.

Vol. 1987: K.-L. Tan, M.J. Franklin, J. C.-S. Lui (Eds.), Mobile Data Management. Proceedings, 2001. XIII, 289 pages. 2001.

Vol. 1989: M. Ajmone Marsan, A. Bianco (Eds.), Quality of Service in Multiservice IP Networks. Proceedings, 2001. XII, 440 pages. 2001.

Vol. 1991: F. Dignum, C. Sierra (Eds.), Agent Mediated Electronic Commerce. VIII, 241 pages. 2001. (Subseries LNAI).

Vol. 1992: K. Kim (Ed.), Public Key Cryptography. Proceedings, 2001. XI, 423 pages. 2001.

Vol. 1995: M. Sloman, J. Lobo, E.C. Lupu (Eds.), Policies for Distributed Systems and Networks. Proceedings, 2001. X, 263 pages. 2001.

Vol. 1998: R. Klette, S. Peleg, G. Sommer (Eds.), Robot Vision. Proceedings, 2001. IX, 285 pages. 2001.

Vol. 2000: R. Wilhelm (Ed.), Informatics: 10 Years Back, 10 Years Ahead. IX, 369 pages. 2001.

Vol. 2004: A. Gelbukh (Ed.), Computational Linguistics and Intelligent Text Processing. Proceedings, 2001. XII, 528 pages. 2001.

Vol. 2010: A. Ferreira, H. Reichel (Eds.), STACS 2001. Proceedings, 2001. XV, 576 pages. 2001.